Bound by Our Constitution

PRINCETON STUDIES IN AMERICAN POLITICS:
HISTORICAL, INTERNATIONAL, AND
COMPARATIVE PERSPECTIVES

SERIES EDITORS

IRA KATZNELSON, MARTIN SHEFTER, THEDA SKOCPOL

Bound by Our Constitution

WOMEN, WORKERS,

AND THE MINIMUM WAGE

• *VIVIEN HART* •

PRINCETON UNIVERSITY PRESS

PRINCETON, NEW JERSEY

Library of Congress Cataloging-in-Publication Data

Hart, Vivien.
Bound by our Constitution: women, workers, and the minimum wage / Vivien Hart.
p.   cm.
Includes index.
ISBN 0-691-03480-X (acid-free paper)
1. Wages—Minimum wage—Law and legislation—United States—History.
2. Sex discrimination in employment—Law and legislation—United States—History.
3. Wages—Women—Law and legislation—United States—History.
4. Women—Employment—United States—History.
5. Wages—Minimum wage—Law and legislation—Great Britain—History.
6. Sex discrimination in employment—Law and legislation—Great Britain—History.
7. Wages—Women—Law and legislation—Great Britain—History.
8. Women—Employment—Great Britain—History.   I. Title.
K1781.H37   1994
344′.0121—dc20
[342.4121]   94-1052

This book has been composed in Bitstream Caledonia

Princeton University Press books are printed on acid-free paper and meet the guidelines
for permanence and durability of the Committee on Production Guidelines for Book
Longevity of the Council on Library Resources

Printed in the United States of America

1   3   5   7   9   10   8   6   4   2

• *TO SAMUEL H. BEER* •

AND IN MEMORY OF MARCUS CUNLIFFE

• *CONTENTS* •

MENTION THE SUBJECT of this book, the minimum wage, and Americans often respond with anecdote, remembering their first job as a teenager, student, or unskilled worker and accurately recalling their hourly rate of pay years later. Mention the minimum wage in Britain and the common response is a blank look or a question: "Do we have one?"

The concept of a minimum wage—a statutory basic rate of pay, a bottom line for waged work, set not by market forces or individual negotiation but by law— is familiar to Americans, many of whom also know that the present minimum wage dates from the New Deal and the Fair Labor Standards Act of 1938. Less well known is that this legislation was preceded by state minimum wage laws for women workers, pioneered by Massachusetts in 1912 and inspired by a British model.

From 1909 until 1993 Britain *did* have a minimum wage policy, albeit something of a well-kept secret. The British Trade Boards Act, passed in 1909 to protect the wages of low-paid workers, may have had even less effect in Britain than in America, where its example initiated a dynamic policy history. For most of this century minimum wage policy has been a live issue in American politics. In Britain it affected only a handful of occupations, changed only at the margins of coverage, and finally disappeared, to widespread indifference, in the Trade Union Reform and Employment Rights Act of 1993.

Britain was the model; British and American policies began at the same time and in markedly similar circumstances. Although economists differ on the impact of the policy on jobs and profits, all agree that in both countries the monetary value of the minimum wage has always been low and the numbers who have benefited small. But if quantitative comparisons point to similar results of minimum wage policy in each nation, a historical perspective on how each nation developed its own policy reveals strikingly different trajectories.

Britain's path might be portrayed as an insignificant, but completed, circle. The reach of the law, never intended to benefit more than a few low-paid workers, fluctuated, dwindled, and ended. American legislation has had a more dramatic zigzag track, each new direction characterized by a new principle of coverage and a momentum absent in Britain. The first phase of state laws for women, between 1912 and 1923, was abruptly ended by decision of the Supreme Court, after which any principle of entitlement was in doubt, and neither gendered nor general legislation succeeded. In 1938, the federal Fair Labor Standards Act introduced the quasi-universal, ostensibly gender-neutral, terminology of employees and interstate commerce, a promise of inclusiveness gradually pushed toward fulfillment.

Why did these two nations, from their shared beginning, determine the scope of their policy so differently? Why did Americans conduct a continuing public dialogue about who should benefit, while the British tinkered at the margins and did so outside the public eye? Why did the development of minimum wage policy in America generate open debate about state responsibilities to women in the work force, while in Britain the same question was addressed only obliquely or evaded altogether? The argument of this book is that one factor above all has steered the crucial decision—who should benefit from minimum wage policy—down a different path in America from that in Britain: the United States Constitution.

This is a book about constitutional politics as much as one about the minimum wage. The narrative tale reveals other influences on the policy. Institutional, demographic, and cultural factors, political opportunities, and specific forms of political organization had much to do with why a minimum wage was legislated at all. It is safe to assume that the existence of a written constitution in the United States also had some effect on politics and public policy. This study asks not whether but *what* and *how* that difference was worked out in day-to-day political activity. When it came to the form the policy should take, to the question of whose circumstances the policy should address, constitutional issues dominated the American debate and separated it from its origin in Britain, a nation with no equivalent written guarantees of fair procedure or equitable outcome.

This book is also one about women, work, and the state. On this fundamental question of who should benefit, constitutional politics framed the process of classification in America and at first narrowed the focus to gender. The problem of the working poor, in Britain and America, was complex. Gender was an important factor, but not the only one that trapped individuals in desperate and powerless working lives. The identity of the woman worker, however, was a troubling one wherever cultural values contrasted the domestic role of women with the breadwinning responsibilities of men. American minimum wage policy, framed to meet formal constitutional principles, addressed this disturbing dual identity directly, if with difficulty. The British skirted around the same dilemma.

A familiar argument, sketched here in chapter 1, is that Britain, without a written constitution, has had an admirable flexibility to match social policy to social problem. In this instance, British minimum wage policy left decisions about who should benefit to the unreflective interaction of powerful interests. The Labour party, trade unions, and employers can be blamed for the feebleness of minimum wage policy over the years, precisely because no other consideration than self-interest challenged their habitual indifference to female and nonunionized workers. No reasoned position on the standing of women workers in relation to men and the state, or comparison of the equity of one principle of coverage with another, was required. A debate about just these issues reached early closure in Britain, at the moment that the policy became a serious item on the political agenda. This early debate, which took place among women, the change of direction within parliamentary politics, and the finality of the economic analysis embodied in the Trade Boards Act are the subjects of chapters 2 and 3 of this book.

In Britain's parliamentary system, business, labor, partisan, and administrative interests pursued their own preferences in a direct and unrestrained way that was the envy of their American counterparts. Bostonian Elizabeth Glendower Evans was one of many minimum wagers (a collective noun conveniently coined by one of their number) to emphasize the comparison, with her observation during the first American campaign that in no other nation was the cause "bound by our constitutional limitations."[1] As the campaign opened at the turn of the century, Evans's phrase was rich with meaning for the situation of women workers. Bound by their physical constitution as the bearers of children (the frequent excuse for different and unequal treatment in the workplace), bounded by the ways in which the broader social meaning of gender was constituted, American women workers were bound yet again by the constraints on policy imposed by the Constitution. A struggle to redefine the civil, economic, and social status of women, and to match the language of constitutional interpretation to the circumstances of women's lives, is central to the American policy history.

American campaigners saw constitutional interpretation as an obstacle to overcome but also as a political resource to contest and control. The prize was authority and legitimacy in defining the functions of the state and the public standing of the exploited workers whose situation inspired the minimum wage campaign. In chapters 4 through 8, the formative phases of minimum wage policy, from its introduction to America in the first decade of the century to its transformation in the Fair Labor Standards Act, evidence the contribution of constitutional politics. A set of discourses engaged the claims of women and men, crusaders and lawyers, outsiders and vested interests on whether policy was to be made in the language of gender or of labor, of public health or of economic health, profit, property, or contract. Such is the history of minimum wage policy that this is a case study on gender and work. The lessons from these engagements are for any policymaker choosing between a universal strategy or a targeted one and for any social group seeking equity in social policy.

In the final chapter of this book, the issues are brought up-to-date. Legislatures, courts, and women still seek to reconcile the conflicting claims of their social and physical constitutions and the Constitution. Minimum wage campaigns have illuminated rather than solved the problems of economic inequities meshed with hierarchies of gender or race. Formal principles of fairness and equity still sit uneasily with complex structural facts. What, then, does constitutionalism contribute toward making policies that fit the problems? The British history provides a touchstone. Britain's membership in the European Union has created a new constitutional politics. Treaty obligations and binding directives impose formal standards for equal treatment in statute law. In the 1990s, British minimum wagers are finally learning the ways of constitutionalism, and undertaking an appeal to the European courts against the abolition of the minimum wage, on grounds of gender discrimination.

The conclusion that emerges at the end of this comparative history of the making of public policy, challenging conventional wisdoms about the constitutional differences between Britain and America and about the merits of a politics of rights, is that, when all the disadvantages have been faced, having a written constitution matters. A formal, constitutional right is better than no right at all. Americans who fear that the individualism embedded in their Constitution may preempt the possibility of a communal social politics may find this unduly optimistic, the grass looking greener on the other side of the fence from within Britain's tradition of unwritten political rules. American constitutionalism has indeed often been viewed from the distance of Britain, usually with a good deal of skepticism about its restrictive role and its gift of power to lawyers. But demands for the devolution of power within the United Kingdom, the experience of a form of dual sovereignty within Europe, and mounting public concern about the strength of the state and the absence of guaranteed rights and limitations have affected the discussion. British readers may find evidence here favoring both sides of current debates on a British Bill of Rights and on the value of the written precepts accompanying membership in the European Union. At the end of a story that began in Britain, the flow of influence may have reversed as the long experience of American constitutionalism acquires a more than theoretical interest for Britain.

In an often abstract debate about the premises of gender equality and workplace justice, rights, and needs, this account of the integration of a discourse of principle with the practice of politics may also stand as a corrective. It reminds us that egalitarian proposals must be firmly rooted in an understanding of the complexity and ambiguity of social structure and social process. Both nations continue to confront the kinds of poverty encountered by the first minimum wagers and to do so with ambivalence about how public policy should respond, whether in terms targeted to gender or race, or to poverty, by universal policies, or by reform of the economic and social processes within which personal and social attributes become structured inequalities. Neither nation has found a language or principle for policy to match the complexity of social problems. Conceptual refinement, however necessary and pleasing, has practical implications and human consequences. Minimum wagers trod a narrow path between the attractions of theoretical perfection and the urgent need for practical solutions. Their dilemma, and ours, in choosing between the best policy or the best they could get, was never better stated than by New York activist Pauline Newman, reminding yet another preliminary inquiry in 1915 that, while the theoretical debates roll on, "in the meantime the girls are absolutely starved."[2]

I HAVE RECEIVED much scholarly, financial, and practical help over the years that this book has been in the making. The formal awards, and the old and new friendships I have depended upon, are all greatly appreciated. But the views expressed are, of course, my responsibility alone and not necessarily those of any of these institutions or individuals.

The book has been written both despite and because of my teaching at two institutions whose faculty and students have taken time and been generous with ideas and comments in return. The University of Sussex nurtures inter-disciplinary work; a succession of deans of the School of English and American Studies, John Whitley, John Rosselli, Colin Brooks, and Bob Benewick, have granted leave and travel funds at various moments since 1981. From 1982 to 1984, a visiting post teaching American government at Smith College brought new comparative perspectives, proximity to archives, funding to interview Clara Beyer, and research assistance from Susan Pollack and Tamar Raphael. At Smith, Martha Ackelsberg, Dorothy Green, Philip Green, Mary McFeely, and members of the Mellon Project on Women and Social Change gave much help.

Two periods of uninterrupted research and writing have been invaluable. An American Studies fellowship from the American Council of Learned Societies and a guest scholarship at the Brookings Institution in Washington, D.C., started the research rolling in 1981; I am grateful to Martha Derthick and other members of the Brookings Governmental Studies Program. A fellowship at the Woodrow Wilson International Center for Scholars, also in Washington, D.C., in 1988, brought the work closer to completion, aided by Michael J. Lacey and the Division of United States Studies and especially by comments from James B. Gilbert and James T. Patterson. Most generous of the generous resources provided by the Wilson Center was the assistance of Toni Horst, an outstanding researcher whose work has made the book more complete and more accurate. Finally, many loose ends were tied up on a return visit to the Wilson Center as a guest scholar in 1993, aided by Amy Meselson.

My access to archives has also been funded by a historical research award from the Twenty-Seven Foundation, a social science grant from the Nuffield Foundation, and a travel award from the U.S./U.K. Fulbright Commission. And my use of those archives has depended greatly on the expertise and advice of archivists and librarians, especially at the Schlesinger Library, the Franklin D. Roosevelt Library, the AFL-CIO and the Massachusetts and New York State Departments of Labor, and, in London, at the Public Record Office, the Trades Union Congress, and the British Library of Economic and Political Science at the London School of Economics. I am grateful to the Harvard Law School library both for advice from Erica Chadbourn and for permission to quote from the papers of H. LaRue Brown. David Wigdor, at the Manuscript Division of the Library of Congress, gave good advice and much encouragement.

Some of the ideas in chapters 7 and 8 first appeared in essays in the *Journal of Policy History* 1 (1989): 319–43 (I am grateful for permission to quote some passages); *American Studies: Essays in Honour of Marcus Cunliffe*, edited by Brian Holden Reid and John White (London: Macmillan, 1991); and *Writing a National Identity: Political, Economic and Cultural Perspectives on the Written Constitution*, which I edited with Shannon C. Stimson, Fulbright Papers no. 11 (Manchester: Manchester University Press, 1993). I appreciate these opportunities to test my argument.

Some personal contributions call for special thanks. Clara Mortenson Beyer established the District of Columbia Minimum Wage Board in 1918 and later was associate director of the Division of Labor Standards in the Labor Department. She brought minimum wage history alive when we first talked in 1984; she remained generous with recollections and papers, and her continuing commitment to fighting for decency and justice in the labor market, until her death at the age of ninety-eight in 1990, was an inspiration. A successor as executive secretary of the D.C. Wages and Hours Board, Richard R. Seideman, generously granted access to the board's records and insights on its recent work.

In many conversations and conference sessions, more people have listened and commented than I can mention individually. For formative discussion, I am particularly grateful to participants at the Berkshire Conference on the History of Women at Smith College in 1984 and Douglass College in 1990; the Organization of American Historians, Reno, 1988; the Social Science History Association, Minneapolis, 1990; the Fulbright Colloquium, University of Sussex, 1991; and the Commonwealth Fund Conference, University College, London, 1993. One of the most enlivening and enlightening aspects of this project has been collaboration in research, writing, and debate with Eileen Boris, historian of home work; Phyllis Palmer, historian of domestic workers and the state; and Kathryn Kish Sklar, biographer of Florence Kelley. Their historians' eyes on my research, our exchanges of ideas and archives, and their comments on my drafts have clarified and extended my analysis here, have been fun, and will, I am sure, continue in future projects. I owe thanks for particular advice and sources, or for critical readings and other encouragement, to Paul Betz, Anne Benewick, Bob Benewick, Charles Brooks, Richard Crockatt, Stephen Fender, Meg Forgan, Steve Fraser, Cynthia Harrison, Alan Hart, Barbara Melosh, Constance Ashton Myers, Elisabeth I. Perry, Mary Lyndon Shanley, Shannon Stimson, Paul Weissman, Cheryl B. Welch, and Eileen Yeo; for computer advice to Tim Kennedy; to several publishers' readers for constructive comments; and to Josephine Woll, a peerless volunteer-editor, for sparing time from her own scholarship to improve my text.

This book has been written not from one side of the Atlantic or another but from being at home on both shores. That this has been possible is due to the invariable welcome from Sarah Bartlett and John and Emilia Petrarca, Gina King, and Phyllis Palmer and Marcus Cunliffe.

My great debt to two exemplars of Anglo-American life and scholarship is acknowledged by the dedication of this book. Sam Beer and the late Marcus Cunliffe have been wise advisers and generous friends. That Marcus Cunliffe is not here for the publication party is a sadness.

September 1993

Bound by Our Constitution

Constitutional Politics

THE DIFFERENCE between British parliamentary sovereignty and American constitutional government has long intrigued commentators on both sides of the Atlantic. In the late nineteenth century, a distinguished Anglo-American group of scholars and friends produced a set of classic studies of the politics of these two nations, whose wisdom has in many respects become the convention. The effect of their respective national frameworks of institutions and powers on social policy was predicted by such experts as James Bryce, erstwhile British ambassador to Washington; Abbott Lawrence Lowell, anglophile and Harvard president; and A. V. Dicey, Oxford professor lecturing at Harvard. Their conclusions shaped the work of scholars following in their footsteps, as well as being familiar and influential in the turn-of-the-century intellectual circles shared by academics and social reformers, minimum wagers included. Like Elizabeth Glendower Evans commenting from the thick of a political campaign, Bryce, Lowell, and Dicey from their desks contrasted the unrestricted scope of parliamentary policymaking with the limitations imposed on American legislatures by constitutional precepts.[1]

The constitutional difference was a given fact for these writers. In contrast to the American written Constitution and Bill of Rights, British political institutions and practices were (and are) organized by a considerable, but uncodified, accumulation of understandings, common law precedents, crown prerogatives, and statute laws. These have to do with the institutions and procedures of the state, and its powers, upon which no limits are imposed and against which no rights are invulnerable. Visiting Americans are still often surprised to find that regular parliamentary elections are guaranteed only by act of the same Parliament or that the ancient right not to be held without charge could be suspended for suspected terrorists by legislation passed almost overnight after a bomb explosion in Birmingham.

What this Anglo-American difference meant for good governance was the most interesting issue for Bryce, Dicey, and Lowell. Reflecting on British government, in lectures first given in 1898, Dicey noted the "omnipotence of Parliament," which in the abstract, he thought, might well "command the acquiescent admiration of the commentator." But, like all these scholars, he not only was interested in theory but was a close observer of the practical implications. Parliamentary sovereignty, "turned into a reality, and directed by bold reformers towards the removal of all actual or apparent abuses," might well alarm, he continued, and was, in short, "an instrument well adapted for the establishment of democratic despotism."[2] Dicey's friend, Lord Bryce, detected the opposite problem in the American system, in which popular sovereignty was combined with a written constitution expressly designed to contain "democratic despotism." The fact was that the Constitution was "not only a fundamental law, but an unchangeable law, unchangeable, that is to say, by the national legislature, and changeable even by the people only through a slow and difficult process." Bryce was puzzled by the implication: "How can a country whose very name suggests to us movement and progress be governed by a system and under an instrument which remains the same from year to year and from century to century?"[3]

The classic distinction, Bryce summarized, was that "in some countries the rules or laws which make up the Constitution can be made and changed by the ordinary legislature just like any other laws, while in other countries such rules are placed above and out of the reach of the legislature, having been enacted and being changeable only by some superior authority."[4] The consequences for policy, according to these seminal analyses, were that an unrestrained freedom of form and content was permitted British legislation, in contrast to the limits and external discipline imposed on policymaking within the American system. A potential for adaptability characterized Britain; a propensity to fixity the United States. The stagnation of British minimum wage policy and the periodic paradigmatic leaps and bounds taken by the policy in the United States confound these expectations.

Abbott Lawrence Lowell placed Britain at the flexible extreme of a scale represented at the opposite end, rigidity, by the United States. In Britain, "no laws are ear-marked as constitutional,—all laws can be changed by Parliament." Britain was, Lowell added, mysteriously scrupulous about observing unwritten constitutional conventions. But these conventions, as others have noted, had to do with proper procedure rather than the substance of legislation.[5] What Britain got, in the absence of substantive constraints on policy, was a free rein for pragmatism. The 1909 Trade Boards Act was an ad hoc response to the economic process and social conditions of sweating. Despite decades of debate about the nature of sweating, a solution could in the end be devised without regard to precedent or necessary consistency with other laws. The textual silences of the act are among its most telling features. Lacking any definition of the status of women workers, who constituted some two-thirds of sweated labor, failing to lay down a standard for the value of the minimum wage, the act evaded major contemporary debates about gender and economic justice and delegated the most crucial decisions.

The American Constitution serves a double function. First, it establishes institutions and processes of government, whose structures, development, and political formations influence public policy. The evolution of federalism and of the roles of courts, parties, and administrative agencies within a constitutional framework of separated powers all affected the introduction and development of social policies like the minimum wage. The structures of the British state, though operating by unwritten constitutional rules, similarly fostered particular kinds of opportunities and of expertise that affected policy. Parliamentary government, centralism, civil service expertise, and vested interest created a powerful executive, checked and balanced only by powerful social interests.

Second, the American Constitution specifies what government may do in pursuit of its definition of the public interest, and, within its guarantees of rights, prescribes a set of relationships among the state, the society, and the individual. It is this dimension of constitutionalism that has most sharply differentiated the discourse surrounding American minimum wage policy from the British debate and, in turn, the policy outcomes. The individual rights to liberty and due process promised by the Fifth and Fourteenth Amendments, and the constitutional responsibility of the state to preserve the public welfare and of Congress to regulate commerce have framed minimum wage legislation. In recent decades, claims of equal rights to the benefits of social policy have been spurs to the drive to achieve comprehensive coverage.[6] Constitutional terms are embedded in the formulas of minimum wage policy. Yet they have never foreclosed debate. Quite the opposite, the ambiguities and silences of the constitutional text have ensured that even the most authoritative utterances from the Supreme Court will be taken as a challenge, not as a closure. All along the line, constitutional conflict, requiring that choice or compromise be justified, has given momentum to American policy and forced issues of equality and discrimination, fairness, and procedural clarity and delegation into the open. This debate has been without parallel in Britain.

Democratic despotism of the sort Dicey feared was precisely the reason for a constitutional system imposing, as Lowell contrasted America with Britain, "a law of superior obligation which controls legally the acts of the legislature."[7] American minimum wagers had to find authority for involving the state in wage setting and to account for the reasonableness of their purpose and procedure. Reasonableness, a guarantee against arbitrary treatment, also prohibited delegation of responsibility on the scale possible in Britain. As a result of these necessities, the first laws were constrained into a form—for women only—that failed to fit the social problem of sweating and were defended in terms that skated, knowingly, over very thin logical ice in emphasizing the gender difference of the woman worker. On the face of it, constitutional constraints obstructed social purpose and did so even more obviously in 1923, when the Supreme Court ruled wage regulation and gendered legislation out altogether.

The British comparison, however, gives a different slant on minimum wage history in America. Dicey saw British parliamentary sovereignty as a grant of license. Bryce predicted that the subordination of legislation to the American Constitution would encourage immobility and conservatism. But minimum wage policy in Britain was static, cautious, and skewed in favor of the powerful. In the United States, the Constitution blocked and constrained, but in the long run also stimulated change and development. Bryce himself pointed out how this apparent contradiction might be resolved. The inflexibility of the American Constitution, subject to the slow processes of amendment and interpretation, was mitigated by what he called "Usage." "Usage" was the finessing of legislation "on matters which are within [the Constitution's] general scope, but have not been dealt with by its words, by the creation of machinery which it has not provided for the attainment of objects it contemplates, or, to vary the metaphor, by ploughing or planting ground which though included within the boundaries of the Constitution, was left waste and untilled by those who drew up the original instrument."[8] Creative thinking about policy and constitutional law, in dialogue with the text of the Constitution and its judicial interpretation, and in the predicament of matching formal precepts with the complex structures of the labor market and workplace relations, provided a momentum lacking in Britain to American minimum wage policy.

LAW AND POLITICS

The phases of the American minimum wage debate can be signposted by a sequence of Supreme Court decisions: in 1908, *Muller v. Oregon* opened new possibilities for labor legislation for women; in 1923, *Adkins v. Children's Hospital of Washington, D.C.* disastrously rejected the strategy both of legislating for women and of the statutory setting of wages at all; in 1937, *West Coast Hotel Co. v. Parrish* overturned *Adkins*, reinstated gendered minimum wage legislation, and went further, hinting that even gender-neutral wage laws might now be approved.[9] Demarcation by landmark judgments draws attention to the familiar influence of Constitution and courts on American policy, through direct "judicial policymaking" in case law and judicial review. Policymakers attend to the precedents, and policies are retrospectively tested in the courts; in both processes policies are seen to be characteristically reactive or subordinate to the formal framework of constitutional law.[10]

Blocking out minimum wage history by such landmarks of judicial review is convenient but carries the wrong message—that the courts made the running. The law both constrained minimum wagers and was a political resource to take hold of and use. The possibility that, under some circumstances, reformers might anticipate and shape the development of law contrasts with a view that sees mainly the oppressive and resistant relationship of law to social policy. Minimum wage history exemplifies policymaking as a process of interaction rather than reaction or subordination to the law. The characteristics of legal process and the patterns of legal bias do have the capacity to constrain and distort the intentions of policymakers. But their effects are complex, and the question of who controls them and who benefits has more than one answer.

Legal process, the way in which legal decisions are reached, has its own logic. This may change the definition of policy issues and privilege or foreclose options that might remain open in the different forum of public or legislative debate. Anthropologist Clifford Geertz identified the defining feature of legal process as "the skeletonization of fact so as to narrow moral issues to the point where determinate rules can be employed to decide them."[11] "Constitutionalizing" policy may reconceive the original problem as well as the policy outcome, as it did in this case from a problem of economic process to one of women's need, and later from the welfare of women to the welfare of the economy. Constitutional parameters may also narrow the vision of policymakers to the precedents, may formalize relationships with the state that might otherwise be left private, and, as Bryce proposed, may not only skeletonize but rigidify decisions in sharp and firm distinctions, unconditional and unresponsive to social change.[12] Furthermore, legal advisers are not always as wise as Assistant Attorney General Robert H. Jackson, whose exposition of a solution to the constitutional difficulties of minimum wage policy in 1937 came with the reminder that "a technique for surmounting certain constitutional obstacles . . . does not profess to determine the *desirability* of any of the provisions."[13]

Legal bias may, of course, derive directly from the personal prejudices of lawyers. It may also be that biases are inherent in the legal process, that issues come to be framed and reasoned selectively in ways that by their very nature express particular, and interested, perspectives. Scholars have uncovered bias at work in the relationship of the law to both organized labor and women. Labor historians and legal theorists have contrasted "the spirit of the law and the ethos of trade unionism," the one individualistic, the other cooperative. The adjudication of labor rights, they claim, has characteristically favored the law's individualistic spirit, denying or reconstructing even legislation specifically framed to recognize cooperation and communality.[14] Likewise, some feminist scholars have found a male bias in both the process and the substance of legal decision making. Their argument is not unlike the labor critique of individualism, but with a yet more fundamental claim of an (almost) inevitable difference between the sexes. The individualism of the law, they suggest, derives from the "paradigmatically male experience of the inevitability of the separation of the self from the rest of the species." Such a law is incapable of recognizing a female "potential for material connection with the other" and consequently imposes upon women's lives an inappropriate and hostile rule of law.[15]

These complex debates easily shade over into the simpler proposition that law is either inherently conservative in substance or normally is under the ideological control of inherently conservative social groups. Law becomes only the agent of power, capitalist or male, in a world of domination and subordination. Organized labor or women become the subjects of its oppression. There is no doubt that historically law has served the purposes of dominant classes and their interest in the preservation of a society from which they (and the lawyers) primarily benefit. One need not accept wholesale the accusation that law is part of the ideology of the ruling class, however, to see that its pervasive influence in American society will lead to competition to control its substance as a mechanism of political power. Or that, like all political competitions, this will be one in which vested interests devoted to the status quo from which they benefit will be at an advantage. But minimum wage history does not support a theory of impenetrable legal conservatism nor one of an impervious antilabor, antiwoman bias. Bias indeed existed. But so did a contest over control of legal and political power in which vested interests were not the guaranteed winners.

Two major prizes were at stake during the development of minimum wage policy—first, getting such a policy authorized under the Constitution at all; and second, determining in what precise terms legislation might be written. Or, as lawyer Ben Cohen once phrased his advice on the minimum wage, "The important thing is to get the camel's head under the constitutional tent and when that has been done it is time to begin to curry and groom the camel."[16] Given the pressing problems of procedural restraint and professional bias that can bedevil policymaking when constitutional guidelines and constitutional lawyers are involved, it might be asked why entry into the sphere of constitutional politics should be a prize at all. The comparison for Americans was not with the unthinkable freedom of British parliamentary sovereignty. It was between common law made by judges and statute law made by legislators within a constitutional framework.[17]

The Constitution not only established governmental responsibilities in some areas, it excluded government from others, deliberately placing some aspects of everyday life beyond interference by the state. For much of the nineteenth century, both family and work roles were examples where judge-made common law set rules of relationships and arbitrated disputes. Judges were, of course, part of the structure of the state. But the point was that these relationships were constitutionally set within the sphere of individual liberty, and with this sphere legislatures could not meddle. The frustration this circumstance created in reformers eager, as they saw it, to use public policy to ameliorate social ills, not to meddle with privacy, was great. Judge-made law grew piecemeal as cases came up, and looked constantly backward to the great body of precedents laid down in the Anglo-American common law tradition. Statute law would be made by legislators who could be responsive to the electorate, could choose their own timing, and could innovate to meet new social conditions. The shift of initiative from precedent and tradition to even a limited democratic purpose and accountability seemed a prize worth winning.

Bringing minimum wage policy under the constitutional tent was part of this struggle for the right to legislate to regulate the economy and make some basic welfare provision. Under contemporary interpretations of the Constitution, the kinds of labor laws and welfare measures introduced in Europe at the turn of the century fell victim in the United States to judicial respect for individual constitutional rights. The social circumstances of late nineteenth-century industrial and urban society, however, were a challenge to a constitutional status quo that had, as historian Jennifer Nedelsky observed, been framed in eighteenth-century America with "the urgent sense that property rights had to be protected from democratic legislatures."[18] So long as property rights were taken to include one's own labor, the whole paraphernalia of negotiation between employers and employees was regulated by common law, not by statute law. There was, Karen Orren has argued, more than a whiff of feudalism in this survival of a preconstitutional status of "relations between employers and employees [as] . . . the domain of the courts, subject to a regimen of common law that was inaccessible to the electorate."[19] The legal struggle to change constitutional interpretation and enable purposive public policy to be made in the democratic forum of the legislature was crucial for control of economic relationships. Employers and labor organizations alike sought to rewrite the constitutional rules.[20]

Women had fought their own battle during the nineteenth century, to bring gender and domestic relations under statute law. They started from a point of greater difficulty than did labor, since the political standing held by men and, for married women, the legal standing too, did not apply to them. In a striking example, for much of the century, in many states of the union, the labor of married women and its rewards belonged in law to their husbands. Women's status as citizens was still unresolved at the time of the minimum wage campaign, as the long-running campaign for the right to vote reminded minimum wagers. Women's recognition as workers, socially and legally, was meanwhile becoming more pressing, as more women spent longer in the labor force.[21]

In minimum wage policy, economic and gender concerns converged. To institute a policy resembling the British Trade Boards Act would require redefinition of the general limits of state intervention in the market, especially to allow the regulation of the heretofore untouchable wage mechanism. The "currying and grooming" of the details would decide for whom, by what branch of government, and on what terms and procedures. At this point, the question of whether the low-paid or woman worker was to be the recipient of this statutory protection would be central. On all these matters, minimum wagers did not just wait for the courts. Legislatures, according to Felix Frankfurter, the constitutional lawyer who was an adviser and strategist for the American minimum wage movement throughout its formative years, should decide on the "wisdom" of policy. Legislative decisions would, Frankfurter thought quite rightly, remain subject to judicial review for their "reasonableness."[22] Minimum wagers attempted to anticipate and even set the terms on which cases would come for judicial review, and to legitimate a new definition of reasonableness.[23]

The phases of American minimum wage policy marked off by major court cases can equally be represented by the content of the constitutional debates at each stage. These debates, about the relationship between state, economy, and women and men, were attempts to preempt the courts as the fundamental decision-makers. In the first phase, from around 1908, the issue was the expansion of the police power of the state (to protect the health, welfare, morals, and safety of society). Minimum wagers sought to redefine the police power to allow wage regulation at least for women. In the second phase, when policy was in a hiatus from 1923 to 1937, minimum wagers cast around widely for loopholes, and especially for new ways of using the concept of due process to guarantee "fair" wages. In their more desperate moments, they even talked of constitutional amendments to remove the whole issue from judicial oversight. Finally, from 1937, minimum wagers set out to change the terrain of the constitutional battle, devising an alternative that shifted the policy from state to federal government and finding a new authority in the Commerce Clause of the Constitution.

Each of these stages was a dialogue rather than a response—a dialogue whose content, even when on the face of it about technical legal doctrine, was also about work and gender. In the first years, minimum wagers had to justify to themselves the change from the "low-paid workers" of the British Act to the "women" of their own statutes. In the second phase, they had to defend a gender distinction that they had come to believe was constitutionally unavoidable, against the passionate rejection of such a distinction by the newly active equal rights wing of feminism and also by the courts. Finally, the federal Commerce Clause rationale of legislation for employees might seem to have brought equality. Instead, the effect of the Fair Labor Standards Act was to demonstrate how ostensibly universal rights, imposed upon biased labor market structures, create new discriminations. "Employees" were mostly men, and women again had to turn to a Constitution whose requirements had first privileged then overlooked their circumstances, using rights arguments over a thirty-year period to bring most female occupations into the scope of the law.

In constitutional politics, as the case of the minimum wage well illustrates, legal and political struggle are integrated into a single process. Contested interpretations of fundamental law become part of the competition of political interests, while that competition itself is significantly structured by legal precepts. Political campaigners necessarily work closely with lawyers; lawyers are activated by the political purpose of the cause that calls upon their constitutional skills. But, as the case of the minimum wage also illustrates, law and politics, lawyers and campaigners still retain a distinctive identity within the framework of constitutional politics. When, as in this case, the lawyers are mostly men and the political leaders often women, collaboration is doubly threatened by the tensions between professional expertise and political motivation, male and female perspectives on problem, strategy, and solution.

Law, Policy, and Society

Minimum wage policy addressed the problem of the working poor. Minimum wagers sought to make informed policy choices and to overwhelm opposition by bombardment with justificatory facts. To that end, they investigated, accumulated data, and analyzed in vast detail the circumstances of workers who were in employment, toiling for all the hours God gave them but still failing to make a subsistence wage. Yet in neither Britain nor America did the coverage achieved by minimum wage law ever entirely match the need. This well-intentioned policy missed its target sometimes in obeisance to political power, and sometimes from a judgment that a partial policy was better than no policy at all. Sometimes the failure was less deliberate, if not inadvertent, originating in the covert biases of constitutional and colloquial language and the failure of formal, skeletonized, legal imperatives to match the complexity of the structure of the labor market or the social expectations of women's dual role in family and economy.

Powerful economic interests, including agricultural employers in the United States and labor unions in both nations, won exemptions and restrictions on the scope of legislation. These deliberate exclusions of functional categories might also effect a different kind of discrimination—American farm workers were predominantly black, whereas organized industrial workers were everywhere white and male. In constructing the British Trade Boards Act, legislators defined the problem as sweated labor and identified the class involved by an economic characteristic, low pay, accepting that this better matched the problem than did the alternative of classification by gender. But the British failure to specify rules for inclusion allowed prejudice to creep into the coverage of the law—its use, for example, to price women out of occupations regarded as unfeminine. Americans likewise addressed the problem of sweated labor in their first round of minimum wage laws, but they wrote gendered legislation. Neither a different sweated work force nor different attitudes toward women workers determined this choice. Gender was the only basis for which constitutional approval seemed certain.

With this decision, and in their acceptance that the legislative responsibility for welfare or labor problems lay with the states, not with federal government, American minimum wagers knowingly excluded workers who by any objective definition were sweated. Most reliable estimates concluded that some one-third of sweated labor was male. The decision to isolate, and "protect," the two-thirds who were female has been controversial. Advocates of the minimum wage deliberately chose a gendered rationale. They did so out of their sense of constitutional necessity and with a justification that intended female difference, not female inferiority. When they emphasized women's maternal role, many minimum wagers were following their hearts. Their heads told them that the maternal ideal of mothers at home was problematic for twentieth-century working women and that it was, nonetheless, the most secure constitutional defense of their policy.[24]

As to the difference between state and federal legislation, minimum wagers knew that some states, principally in the South, would never legislate and, indeed, would stand to benefit as low-wage economies if more liberal states imposed statutory rates. The hidden agenda here was race. The political map drawn by state lines overlaid a racial map in which the African-American population was largely concentrated in reactionary southern states and, a small middle class excepted, concentrated in the unskilled, low-wage sector of the economy. If the Constitution required state-by-state labor legislation, the effect was to ensure that most black workers would be beyond its reach.

Race and gender bias materialized in new forms in the Fair Labor Standards Act. Ostensibly this legislation was neutral as to the sex and race of workers. Discrimination against women was specifically disbarred, and the fact that this was federal legislation should have overridden the problem of geographically specific labor markets. Yet, advisedly, exclusions that discriminated were written in. The problem was constitutional geography. The space mapped by the legal definition of interstate commerce did not fit with the structural map of sweated labor. The lowest-paid workers—who were also predominantly women and African-Americans—were disproportionately found in those small local production and service industries that never entered into interstate commerce. Minimum wagers were not normally motivated by racism or sexism. But their well-meaning concern about poverty and inequality did not focus sharply enough on these difficult issues.[25] This fight came later, when the mobilization of African-Americans and women themselves behind demands for rights shone a spotlight on previous discriminations.

Finally, in addition to the biases introduced by power, prejudice, and in America the requirements of the Constitution, legislation might fail to fit the problem because statutory language did not, or could not, accurately articulate the social circumstances involved. The incorporation of constitutional terminology into political debate did not create this problem and often helped bring it into the open as lawyers and campaigners debated the principles on which their policy might be based. The Fair Labor Standards Act may stand again as exemplar of this problem. *Employees* was no more neutral a term than *interstate commerce*, since it could be construed to exclude subcontracting (black) farm workers and (female) home workers. Yet more fundamental, the concept of "work" itself was limiting, as the entry into the debate of the question of (female and largely black) domestic "help" demonstrated.

In both Britain and America, the development of minimum wage policy has been primarily the development of a policy for women workers. Much of the theoretical debate about gender equality fostered by the American policy discourse can be transposed to discussions about racial and ethnic equality. That it rarely was thus transposed within minimum wage campaigns—and that as a result racial and ethnic discrimination, some preexistent in the economy, some introduced by minimum wage policy itself—was all too easily ignored means that race and ethnicity appear here as subtexts to a narrative of gender. But just as minimum wagers could have drawn a broader social lesson from their wrestlings with the disjunctions of constitutional axioms, discriminatory social structures, and policy prescriptions, so too may the readers of this book.

This goes for Britain, too, although there the absence of issues of racial and ethnic discrimination from the story is primarily due to the near-absence of racial and ethnic groups from the labor force until after the Second World War. There is a general lesson to be drawn even here. When ethnic groups have clustered in the kinds of occupations and in the deprived circumstances characteristic of the sweated industries—whether Jewish immigrant garment workers of the late nineteenth century or their Asian counterparts of recent years—they, like British women workers, have been disproportionately *included* in designated minimum wage industries. The designation of coverage has focused on economic conditions, not ethnicity. But the piecemeal application of that principle to single industries has meant that neither all underpaid women nor all underpaid ethnic workers have been included, introducing a kind of functional or occupational discrimination in the benefits of policy.

Both British and American minimum wagers, while failing to eliminate either sex or race discrimination, went somewhat further in addressing the problems of women than they did of racial minorities. Neither prejudice nor ignorance fully explains their omissions and failures. The problem in all these exclusions from the formulations of minimum wage law was that something—

political power, bias, constitutional precept, language—intervened to distort the fit of policy with the structural conditions. Equality of form, in Deborah Rhode's phrase, by no means ensured equality in fact.[26] The labor market itself consisted of deeply embedded structures of discrimination in which employment and rewards were sometimes distributed according to labor value or to qualifications but often according to prejudices about what kind of work and what social groups carried what prestige and status. Groups that held prestige, status, and privilege in the labor market could be expected to fight to maintain their position. But irony or disappointment were more in order when the constitutionalizing of policy had the effect of reinforcing old discriminations or creating new ones, in contravention of egalitarian constitutional values.

Evolving and legislating a minimum wage policy required fundamental choices. Within particular political constraints, both British and American minimum wagers had to decide how to define the social problem, who to cover, and by what means. In America they had also, because of the Constitution, to explain precisely why. In both countries substantial compromises were involved, but these differed, particularly because in America women workers and their protagonists were doubly "bound by [their] constitutional limitations," labeled with biological finality as "the weaker sex" or the "mothers of the race" and legally classified as "different." In addition, with or without a constitution, in neither country did minimum wagers ever resolve the problem of writing legislation congruent with a labor market structured and discriminating by sex, race, ethnicity, age, and cultural assumptions about what counted as "work," and who did it. In both countries, a similar political contest revolved around the language of the statutes. The concept of a "statutory reality," a pragmatic compromise lying somewhere between an imagined ideal and the economic facts, was described by Robert H. Jackson, counsel for the minimum wage in 1937: "Bringing principles down to statutory reality is a tough-minded process. It means making decisions—practical decisions on the balance of advantage and disadvantage—in the face of legal ambiguity, economic variation, and the human limitations of administration. It often means choosing the lesser evil—and making the choice work."[27] The imaginative concept of a "statutory reality" may smack of lawyerly evasion of responsibility. Or it may come closer to the realities of policymaking than do accounts with a more purely idealist or materialist bent. The chapters that follow, with these considerations in mind, investigate key decisions so far as possible as their makers understood them and evaluate the choices made, the constraints upon and the autonomy of those involved in the formulation of minimum wage policy in Britain and the United States.

TWO

No Sweat

WORK AND WOMEN, BRITAIN, 1895–1905

MINIMUM WAGE POLICY in Britain became law in the Trade Boards Act of 1909. Officials of the Board of Trade, the national government department responsible, could apply the act to any industry, provided they were "satisfied that the rate of wages prevailing in any branch of the trade is exceptionally low, as compared with that in other employments, and that the other circumstances of the trade are such as to render the application of this Act to the trade expedient."[1] These "other circumstances" were limited by a promise to Parliament, to "exceptional cases where two fundamental conditions are absent . . . the mobility of labour in its true sense and effective organisation," in other words, to trades where low pay, a work force trapped by its circumstances, and no unions existed.[2]

The act specified procedures for setting up a Trade Board (a locally or industrially based commission) for each designated industry. Representatives of employers and workers, nominated or elected, would be joined by members appointed by the department, who must be less than half the board. Women were "eligible as members of Trade Boards as well as men," and home workers must be directly represented if they formed a "considerable proportion" of the trade. For trades "in which women are largely employed," one board member must be a woman. A professional secretary to each board, and staff appointed centrally, would investigate conditions and enforce decisions, backed by legal powers and criminal sanctions. This elaborate structure was designed to produce orders setting "minimum rates of wages for timework for their trades" and, if necessary, also for piecework, "to apply either universally, or to any special process, or to any special class of worker, or to any special area." The act listed circumstances justifying special rates and appeals and created procedures for implementing the rates.

Dealing with every last point of procedure, the Trade Boards Act was mysteriously silent on major points of substance. The gender-neutral term *low-paid workers* left to boards to decide whether this meant low-paid *women* workers. No criteria for setting a monetary value for a minimum wage were specified. Boards were thus delegated great scope for initiative, but they did not have the last word. Another elaborate procedure referred all decisions back up the administrative chain and ultimately to Parliament for ratification. In fact, no decision was ever final. Individual orders and whole boards could be rescinded or abolished if their circumstances changed.

This Trade Boards Act was regarded, in 1909, at one and the same time as a radical innovation and a carefully limited compromise, "a revolution" *and* a remedy "only intended to apply to a very limited extent."[3] Indeed the fight for a statutory wage opened up fundamental issues with wide ramifications. The responsibility of the state for the regulation of the economy, the right of public intervention in private business, the blurring of gender roles and family values as women left their homes to work in industry and as industry farmed out manufacturing tasks to family members in their homes, the causes of poverty, the domestic economy of poor families, and the reciprocal rights and responsibilities of state and citizens—all these factors impinged on this policy debate. Participants of all persuasions, however inconsistent and incomplete their analyses, struggled with difficult issues and did so in times of economic, social, and political change. Their discourse, defining the identities of and relationships between women and workers, families and homes, and all these and the state was framed by the growth and problems of industrial and urban environments, the formation of a Labour Party and the concomitant unpredictability of three-party politics, the gradual displacement of laissez-faire ideology by collectivism, and the expansion of the state through an array of new social policies.

The contest over minimum wage policy was a minor part of a period of innovation in social thought and policy. With hindsight, the contemporary introduction of unemployment insurance, pensions, and other policies by the Liberal government between 1906 and 1912 marks the origin of the modern British welfare state.[4] Minimum wage policy was distinctive in spanning what are often treated as two separate strands of social policy— redistributive, providing pensions, benefits, or welfare to the unemployed; and regulatory, restricting the free market, for example, to protect the health and safety of workers. The history of each type of policy is loaded with assumptions about gender roles in family, economy, and state. Much redistributive policy assumed an ideal family, with a working male breadwinner and a dependent, female wife and mother. From their status as workers, men accrued, or earned by contributory payments, entitlements to unemployment insurance or pensions. In the absence of an earning male, women's dependency was transferred to the state, by the payment, for example, of widows' pensions. The assumption of different roles for men and women was reinforced by policies for the support of mothers, in maternal and infant health programs. Despite national differences in the emphasis and form of legislation, redistributive welfare policies everywhere institutionalized gender difference.[5] Regulatory policies carried the same message. The history of labor law for women was the history of "protective labor legislation," laws to restrict the terms and conditions of women's work, with the "protective" label again pointing to the dependency of women. Legislation might regulate the grossest health hazards for male workers, but labor law for men above all meant industrial relations law, the setting of a framework of procedures to enable male workers and unions to protect themselves.[6]

Minimum wage policy sought to regulate the market through its wage mechanism, in order to redistribute to those at work yet still in poverty rather than to those whose poverty was a consequence of unemployment. The idea of a minimum wage arose during the 1890s, as a response to mounting public concern about so-called sweated industries. Ambiguities entrenched in public perceptions of sweating were carried over into the debate about a minimum wage. When minimum wagers confronted the conditions of the sweated industries, they confronted a world in which women might be breadwinners, men might be dependents, and breadwinners of either sex could work night and day and fail to make a subsistence living. Gendered assumptions, prejudices, and possibilities were usually at the center of the debate, but they intersected with questions of class. Those who argued for a minimum wage often did so with a heartfelt preference for the idealized family of the family wage and gendered welfare state. But whereas policies for mothers, for widows, or for emergencies faced by male workers fit comfortably with an idealized separation of gender roles, a policy for workers who were at the same time children, mothers, widows, fathers, women, and men created mental confusion.

In a political system without constitutional guidelines for the framing of social policy, the formulation of a minimum wage law could latch on to one social fact or another, follow normative preferences for sex or class definitions, or be driven one way or the other by the power of vested interests. The options, like the players, were multiple. As the debate unfolded, the attributes of participants did not always align predictably with views on the policy, making for some unlikely alliances and antagonisms.

SWEATING: FACT AND MYTH

The minimum wage was adopted by the Women's Trade Union League in 1897 as a solution to the intractable social problems of sweating. Sweating—the production of goods by piecework processes subcontracted out to unskilled workers—was characterized by intense price competition and the appalling pay and circumstances of its work force. The public image of sweating mixed fact and myth to create many of the definitional problems that plagued the minimum wage campaign and to stimulate a potent political mixture of alarmist self-interest with humanitarianism, embracing both the menace of household goods produced in unhygienic conditions and the welfare of the workers, a combination of domestic and industrial concerns.

Sweating was first associated with the garment trades. In 1849, Charles Kingsley berated consumers for complicity in purchasing "Cheap Clothes and Nasty" and warned that "diseases numberless" were thus spread.[7] Consumers campaigned for production in licensed premises and for labels on goods made in approved conditions. Workers organized, defining the problem as entrapment and poverty, the solution as truck acts and union rates. But, after several decades of such efforts, it appeared that, without the imposition of some "radical remedy," sweating "and its kindred woes will continue to thrive with the horrible rapidity and vigour of a poisonous creeper in a South American forest."[8]

By the 1890s, sweating was widespread. Manufacturers capitalized on an oversupply of unskilled labor to meet the demands of a mass market for ready-made products. Production was disaggregated into multiple simple operations and piecework, and more tasks were farmed out in more industries to more people, often women, sometimes immigrants, working in small shops and their own homes. The kinds of people involved and the scattered workplaces made regulation and organization difficult. Reflecting these changes, the public image of sweating also changed. A handbill issued by the National Anti-Sweating League (NASL) at the height of the campaign to end sweated labor summarized the public view of sweating, circa 1906. The definition had been pared down to wage rates:

"*What is Sweating?* Sweating is acute under-payment."

But the consequences of this basic fact ramified: "It entails overwork, under-feeding, bad housing conditions, and a poverty and debasement that lie at the root of many other social evils." Sweating was associated with gender: "A 'sweated' woman worker will probably earn an average wage of 1d. an hour." The victim was not to blame, since "she will work as many hours as she can endure." Sweating threatened children: "wretched parents" were forced to employ their offspring, "often mere babies." It was "the typical condition of a great many [industries]," and its products, bought by members of all social classes, could not be distinguished by any particular criterion of social usefulness or moral worth, including as they did everything from Bibles to umbrellas. Furthermore, sweating was increasing, and its apparent cheapness was no bargain, entailing as it did the ruin of the workers. The remedy, "such legislation as will secure to each sweated worker a wage upon which at any rate life can be maintained," followed from the initial definition.[9]

NASL's headlines were well documented. Government and private investigations using the new techniques of the social survey gave substance to the propaganda.[10] Jenny Morris used census data on twenty-seven sweated trades to verify contemporary studies and confirm that sweating was not just on the margins of industry: "In total, these trades accounted for 1,754,369 workers in 1891, 24% of the industrial workforce."[11] Women workers predominated, performing industrial work in homes and factories. The 1891 census found 647,930 women employed in sweated trades, a little over a third of the total (37 percent). Excluding building and dock labor, however, 60 percent were female. Within each sweated trade, "in the areas and in the type of work where very low wages were common, there was a higher proportion of women workers." In shirt, dress, paper box and lace making, and the production of fancy goods, women were virtually the entire work force.[12] Children worked too, many off the record, as a government committee admitted when it took a published figure of 150,000 full-time child workers and simply doubled it "to make up for its defects."[13] And sweating was associated with immigrant labor, although nativism was a declining theme in the antisweating campaign, perhaps because immigrants were a tiny percentage of the population, and largely confined to tailoring and boot and cabinet making among sweated industries. Although many immigrants were sweated, little sweated labor was immigrant.[14]

An influential report by the House of Lords in 1890 identified sweating by "1. a rate of wages inadequate to the necessities of the worker or disproportionate to the work done; 2. excessive hours of labour; 3. an unsanitary state of the houses in which the work is carried on."[15] These criteria were not easily measured. Wage rates were most difficult to pin down. Mary Macarthur, of the Women's Trade Union League, warned the parliamentary Select Committee on Homework, a committee of M.P.'s whose hearings in 1907 and 1908 constitute the most complete record of views on minimum wage policy: "We have no really reliable means of recording what the statistics of wages really are."[16] She herself sailed past this problem: "She mentioned 7s. as the average woman's wage, . . . rather to the alarm of some of her colleagues with a higher respect for statistics. They knew the figure, however accurate it might be, could not be substantiated, and feared lest it should be challenged. She herself admitted privately that she did not know where or how she had got it, but it was a good figure and probably near the truth!"[17] Rates multiplied with the subdivision of tasks, varied locally, and changed, usually for the worse, continuously. Many sweated trades were seasonal. In many, workers provided materials—cotton and glue for carding hooks and eyes, or thread for sewing—and suffered punitive deductions for damage, so that the real wage was invariably less than the going rate. The average weekly wages in seventy-six home work occupations in 1908 ranged from 18s 4d for voile skirtmaking, down to 2s 3d for binding hair nets (annotated "Provides silk for sewing. 2s. 3d. to 2s. 6d. per gross. Cannot do a gross in a week.").[18]

This was a sex-segregated labor market in which "generally women do not do the same work as men, but follow certain branches of trade which both men and women admit is peculiarly women's work." Pay differentials bore no relation to skill or intelligence. Like the gendering of jobs, the gendering of labor value meant that "a woman worker receives less just because she is a woman." Generally, "a woman gets one-third to one half the wages of a man."[19] The House of Lords defined sweated wages as inadequate for subsistence. For women, this involved a loaded judgment on whether they worked to support themselves or to contribute, as wives or daughters, to the family income. Many women workers were in fact supporting families, whether as single parents or as partners of unemployed or disabled men. Yet most model budgets were constructed in terms of family income. A typical estimate suggested a weekly wage of 25s for a man with a wife and three children, and 14s to 16s for a woman's necessary contribution to a similar family.[20]

Average wage statistics meant little without comparison with industrial wages and hours. Engineering fitters and turners in 1906 received a weekly average of 36s to 39s; printers 35s to 39s; the average in footwear manufacturing was 25s to 30s.[21] As for hours, the NASL handbill reported accurately that a "'sweated' woman . . . will work as many hours as she can endure," and some women in one study simply recorded "all day" as their average working day. The "high-paid" voile skirt-makers averaged ten to thirteen hours a day, and twenty-five trades recorded averages of thirteen to sixteen hours.[22] Women workers carried the double burden of household duties, reporting that "we do them afterward." "Mrs. F.," a shirtmaker, told M.P.'s that she worked fifteen or sixteen hours a day, plus household duties. To the question: "How do you manage to live?" she replied: "We do not live."[23] Engineers averaged forty-eight to fifty-four hours, printers fifty to fifty-two, and footwear workers fifty-four—eight to nine hours' daily work in a six-day week.[24]

The Lords' definition also mentioned the sanitary state of the houses where work was undertaken. Sweating was sometimes considered synonymous with home work, and the distinction between work done at home or in workshops later became the focus of an argument about legislation to license premises or control wages. The Select Committee concentrated on home workers but acknowledged that "it has been shown that very low rates of remuneration are by no means confined to them, but are not infrequently the lot of factory workers also in trades in which Home Work is prevalent." James A. Schmiechen's "reasonable guess" was that "as many as half of the workers in the London clothing trades were out-workers—either in their own homes or in the homes of others."[25] Few had a separate work room. Most workers worked in kitchens, sitting rooms, bedrooms, or the multipurpose space where they and their families also cooked, lived, and slept.[26] There was a clear gender difference in the incidence of home work, according to Jenny Morris's analysis of census data. Ninety percent of men were defined as employees, normally in factories and shops; 74 percent of women were home workers.[27]

The typical sweated worker, then, was a woman who, married or single, supported other family members—aged parents, disabled husband, children. Whatever her product, the actual task performed was mindless, repetitive, and often damaging to her health, and the finished product rarely an object of pride. For this work, she earned seven to ten shillings for upward of sixty hours' work each week—about one-third of average manufacturing wages, earned over longer-than-average hours, and sandwiched in with domestic duties. She worked at home, probably in her kitchen, or in a small neighborhood sweat-shop, and always in unhealthy conditions.

Yet for all this, sweated industries were rarely profitable industries. Mary Macarthur's "experience [was] that the small, badly equipped employer who pays the worst wages makes the smallest profit."[28] The self-perpetuating nature of sweating lay in the constant undercutting by employers in order to survive. Sidney and Beatrice Webb called this the "Higgling of the Market": "This competitive pressure pushes [the employer], in sheer self-defence, to take as much advantage of his work-people as the most grasping and short-sighted of his rivals."[29] In this market, wages might also be disproportionately low in relation to the effort of the worker but disproportionately high in relation to the production costs of new technology. The sweater was more likely to reduce his labor costs yet again than to invest in new methods.

These were the bare facts. The language of the campaign was often more emotional. The politically effective association of sweating with unwholesomeness and disease added passion to economic pragmatism. The Trade Boards Bill itself was introduced to the Commons with a fine medical metaphor: "The application of this measure is very limited. It is intended to be applied exclusively to exceptionally unhealthy patches of the body politic where the development has been arrested in spite of the growth of the rest of the organism. It is to the morbid and diseased places—to the industrial diphtheritic spots that we should apply the antitoxin of trade Boards."[30] Opponents thought it would only "apply poultices to sores which have their causes deep-seated in a vitiated and poisoned system."[31] The disease metaphor went beyond the transmission of smallpox and typhoid in garments made in sweatshops, to social health and moral purity, to sin and morbidity. In the eyes of NASL the system was an evil, a sham, an indulgence and a source of ruin. "Ruin" encoded a concern with the purity of mothers and homes that ranged from the literal ("domestic uncleanliness, as it is sometimes called—where the beds are not properly made, and that sort of thing") to darker hints ("the worker, in the case of women, finds money in a way that is far more common than many people think").[32] The campaign thus started in a pattern of dualities: emotion and hard fact, health and hygiene threats to consumer and worker alike, fears of both economic anarchy and economic exploitation.

WORK AND THE STATE

Nineteenth-century factory laws, generously provided with loopholes, had failed to deal with the problem of sweating and been indecisive about protecting men as well as women and children. In 1907, Malcolm Delevingne, principal clerk in the Industrial Department of the Home Office, the department with authority over labor conditions, summarized the facts. Existing laws were few and ill-enforced, limited in their coverage of sweated workers and worthless for home workers. The Factory Act of 1901 applied to the sweatshop in rented premises, to "domestic factories" where the "employer" worked at home and employed his own family, and to "workshops" in domestic premises but employing outsiders. The act excluded the home worker working alone or "jointly with others" at home and regulated only sanitation, overcrowding, and temperature. Sanitary conditions were different from "unhealthy" conditions, the latter coming under legislation for public health and a separate inspectorate. Wage rates must be publicly posted, but only in industries designated by the Home Office (which did include some classic sweated trades such as chain making). The Truck Acts were supposed to guarantee payment in cash—

but only where a personal contract existed, a technicality that excluded those receiving work from middlemen. Delevingne was reluctant to admit it, but the facts spoke for themselves: sweating was untouched by law wherever work was done outside regular factory premises.[33]

A contemporary study of factory laws argued that this failure lay in the unsystematic development of legislation. Regulatory laws had accumulated in a random fashion as particular abuses caught the public eye, and there were always unregulated areas for the unscrupulous to exploit.[34] But the failure was more than one of haphazard pragmatism. The inherent flaw of all these acts was that they failed women, the greater number of sweated workers, by failing to come to terms with the gendered structure of the economy or to match the gendered assumptions of language and culture. The sweater evaded regulation by moving production just outside the bounds of the definition of "a factory," with the effect that the "range of Factory Legislation has, in fact, . . . become co-extensive with the conditions of *industrial employment*."[35] Sweating formed a kind of subindustrial sector, operating in legally defined domestic workplaces, shops, and homes, and the domestic sphere was exempt from factory legislation. Even what was regarded as industrial employment in a factory had as much to do with culture as with conditions. Thus "in steam laundries there is a quantity of machinery used without any safeguards." But laundries were exempt from the Factory Acts until 1907, because "it is a more or less domestic industry."[36] Sweated production counted neither as "industrial" nor as "employment," whenever the industry smacked too much of domestic, that is to say, women's, work.

Britain had long accepted different treatment for women. The Mines Act of 1842, banning women from underground work, allowed the contingency of gender to override the market mechanism. The 1844 Factory Act set a twelve-hour day for women. By the end of the century some legislation on dangerous trades and sanitary conditions applied directly to men. Hutchins and Harrison acknowledged that since the 1830s the principle of protecting all workers against some features of the free market economy had been accepted by educated opinion, and fought for by the labor movement "behind the women's petticoats." But they called "these apparently unimportant provisions which at first sight read only like a trifling extension of regulations already enacted" a "remarkable departure" from the laws of the free market.[37] Opposition to equality between the sexes had sharpened during the 1870s, following demands from some women that sex discrimination in factory laws cease. But, by 1900, "cause being shown," the principle had been accepted that "the protection of the law can be extended to men as well as to women and children."[38] The issue in Britain was not the survival of a pure free market but the pragmatic acceptance of specific cases for regulation on assorted grounds, including age, sex, and danger.

The regulation of wages was of a different order from health and safety laws. It was logical, once wages became defined as the basic feature of sweating, that wage legislation should be proposed. But, it was noted in 1907, "the law has never yet intervened, directly and of set purpose, to raise wages."[39] So the Liberal government announced its innovation dramatically: "This is the first occasion . . . in which any Government has proposed machinery, first for deciding, and secondly for enforcing, a legal rate of wages. To that extent the proposal is new—to that extent the proposal is a revolution."[40]

The prospect that the minimum wage opened the door for state intervention in all wage bargaining, though denied by the government, pleased supporters of the arbitration of wage disputes and advocates of Beatrice and Sidney Webb's plan for a National Minimum (a guaranteed comprehensive set of standards). The Fabians thought that the minimum wage would conquer an outdated taboo: "There appears to be a superstition held by economists and politicians, even by those who have no prejudice against State regulation in itself, that the cash relation between employer and employed is so sacred that to interfere with it by law is to commit the unpardonable economic and political sin."[41] But the policy alarmed their normal allies, the trade unions, and their predictable opponents, the adherents of an unrestrained free market. A defense of the status quo came from both left and right.

Unions and employers had agreed spheres of influence: "There is in theory a divorce . . . between the manner of dealing with the conditions of work and that of dealing with its remuneration. The questions are treated as separate and requiring different leverage to force up their position . . . by English theory the industrial laws which regulate the conditions of work do not touch wages, and the work of improving wages is relegated to the action of the Trade Unions."[42] The attraction for trade unions of this recognition of a single, clear, and crucial function as their sphere was evident. The reasoning of conservative forces fearful of minimum wage legislation was spelled out in 1909 in the *Quarterly Review*. The modern British economy was ruled by the principle of exchange in a free market; the essential transaction in this market was the exchange by individuals of labor for wages; economic efficiency and social well-being depended upon "the rise and fall of wages in the open market." Acts regulating hours and conditions were tolerable because they had arisen piecemeal and functionally, to patch up "dislocations of industry, the result of inevitable change; and those dislocations may engender explosive force to the danger of society at large"; also because they were marginal to the market: "The object of Factory Acts has not hitherto been to destroy or supersede the market, but to regulate certain conditions that, as a rule, do not enter into the bargain at all." The distinction may seem specious, since regulations inevitably added to costs, but to the writer the minimum wage threatened the compromise between freedom and regulation: "The present proposal, on the other hand, has the appearance of an attempt to supersede the market altogether as being an injurious and inequitable tribunal." A minimum wage was uncalled for: "Natural economic causes are eliminating gradually the less favourable occupations. This natural method is more humane and considerate to the class for whom we are concerned; and, further, the only guide which we possess for the better redistribution of labour is dependent on the indications of the open market."[43]

Sidney and Beatrice Webb's plan for a National Minimum also relied on the market, in which competition ideally stimulated new heights of efficiency, new technology, and cheaper products. But they identified sweated trades as a pathological form of competition, deserving of public intervention. "Under the competitive pressure described in our chapter on 'The Higgling of the Market' some of the unregulated trades become, in fact, parasitic," they wrote.[44] The link between economics and politics was this concept of social parasitism. Employers became sweaters when they were "able to take such advantage of the necessities of their workpeople as to hire them for wages actually insufficient to provide enough food, clothing, and shelter to maintain them in average health; if they are able to work them for hours so long as to deprive them of adequate rest and recreation; or if they can subject them to conditions so dangerous or insanitary as positively to shorten their lives, that trade is clearly obtaining a supply of labor-force which it does not pay for."[45] In such circumstances, someone, charities, poor relief, or "parents, husbands, or lovers" paid the balance. Or the worker was being worn out: "In thus deteriorating the physique, intelligence and character of their operative, they are drawing on the capital stock of the nation."[46]

The Webbs' was a chilly argument about National Efficiency. George Shann was more humane, when he explained the human costs of "the non-living wage." Shann concluded that "in our collective capacity as certain social groups, and as municipalities and the State, we have in various ways to bear the costs of the poverty which exists in our midst" and that "the employer who obtains labour for which he does not pay in his wages bill is a parasite on the present and the future of the nation."[47] Where a public or national interest in wages existed, so did a reason to regulate. In 1908, the Commons Select Committee on Home Work gave official blessing to the principle of wage legislation:

> It is quite as legitimate to establish by legislation a minimum standard of remuneration as it is to establish such a standard of sanitation, cleanliness, ventilation, air space, and hours of work. . . . It is doubtful whether there is any more important condition of individual and general well-being than the possibility of obtaining an income sufficient to enable those who earn it to secure, at any rate, the necessaries of life. If a trade will not yield such an income to average industrious workers engaged in it, it is a parasite industry, and it is contrary to the general well-being that it should continue.[48]

The unlikely coalition of left and right had to be reassured that sweating was a limited, pathological sector of the economy. Opponents "may say that [the Trade Boards Act] is the thin end of the wedge. It is not a wedge at all. Our remedy is only intended to apply to a very limited extent. It is a remedy which has reference to low wages, and does not deal with the question whether State action can, or ought, to control wages."[49] It was also a remedy defined with reference to a pathology of economic process, not with reference to gender. But it was taken up and pushed onto the public agenda by reformers, mainly women, whose greatest experience was with the problems of women and families. Part of the difficulty of reconciling an economic analysis with a sense of a gendered problem lay in the varying success of these women reformers in coming to terms with women's changing role in industrial society.

THE WOMEN'S CAMPAIGN

The Trade Boards Act, textually neutral on gender, might appear to be a step forward for equal rights. It has also been cited as an example of a "paternalist" British welfare state, in which "male bureaucrats and party leaders designed policies 'for the good' of male wage-workers and their dependents."[50] The formulation of minimum wage policy in Britain is incomprehensible apart from its gendered origins, but its inspiration was not paternalistic. J. R. Hay at least placed women first when he described the Trade Boards Act as "the result of pressure from women's organisations; individual politicians, including Ramsay MacDonald and Sir Charles Dilke . . . and a public campaign mounted by the *Daily Mail*."[51] The Women's Trade Union League, National Federation of Women Workers, Women's Labour League, Women's Industrial Council, National Council of Women, National Union of Women Workers, were indeed prime actors in the campaign, though by no means always in agreement.

Individual politicians and newspaper proprietors became involved around 1906, when the cause became a public crusade. Women, disenfranchised and excluded from Parliament, had to be spoken for within political institutions by sympathetic men who, like Margaret and Ramsay MacDonald, Lady Dilke, her niece Gertrude Tuckwell, and Sir Charles Dilke, might be family partnerships. Men did not necessarily control the debate. "I waited to consult Miss Tuckwell, regarded by me as the real author of the Bill," Sir Charles Dilke wrote to Home Secretary Gladstone in 1908.[52] The *Daily News* (not the *Daily Mail*), owned by Liberal businessman George Cadbury, was vital to the eventual success of the campaign. However, one account has the paper persuaded into action by Mary Macarthur, the secretary of the Women's Trade Union League (WTUL). Although the editor worked closely with the campaign, there is little evidence that he ran it.[53] The initiative, for a decade before 1906, rested with the women's organizations.

The Women's Trade Union League first sponsored the minimum wage proposal, in the mid-1890s. Its timing was good. Wages had been identified as the key to the problem of sweating. Dilke had chaired an Industrial Remuneration Conference in 1885, where, he recalled, "the minimum wage made its first bow to a mixed audience in London."[54] The Webbs were developing their theory of a National Minimum of industrial standards, including wages, for nonunionized workers.[55] The failure of Factory Acts to regulate sweating was known, but alternatives such as the licensing of tenement premises were controversial.[56]

And a minimum wage policy was tried for the first time in 1896, in Victoria, Australia, by provincial premier Arthur Deakin. "Australia has tried experiments for us, and we have the advantage of being able to note their success or failure before we imitate or vary them at home," Dilke remarked.[57] Dilke's friendship with Alfred Deakin provided the introduction: "In 1887, Mr. Deakin was over here, and the subject was in his mind, and he and I had conversations with regard to it; and, although his proposals were not formulated in Victoria till a good deal later, and although my Bill was not drawn here till much later, I think we had already discussed the lines on which both the Victorian Bill and my Bill were drawn."[58] But Dilke was mainly an intermediary for his wife and niece, as a postscript to a letter from Deakin confirms: "Regards to Lady Dilke and Miss Tuckwell for whom I am getting an article on Wages Boards."[59]

The WTUL targeted sweating because "almost all trades in which women are employed are based on sweating principles," and launched a campaign for organization and legislation. Organization was their first and continuing goal: "By combination alone can we ensure a just remuneration for women's labour or hope to touch the insanitary conditions which sow the seeds of disease and death in the children of our labouring mothers."[60] Shortly, the WTUL discovered a symbiotic role for the state: "We believe in legislative interference, but since we find it is never roused so steadily as in answer to the demands of a strong organisation, we urge on our readers their need for legislative interference as being one further argument in favour of their radical need for efficient trades organisation."[61] "Our readers" were the estimated three thousand members of the WTUL, plus forty-five thousand in affiliated organizations.[62] The WTUL, founded in 1874 by Emma Paterson to organize women and fight for their employment on equal terms with men, combined with difficulty a membership of middle-class women (and some men) with women workers, and the functions of union, pressure group, and (its original name) provident society. It consistently fostered women's unions. But its campaign of the 1870s against gendered Factory Acts was abandoned in the 1880s, when the league accepted protective laws for women, fought for women inspectors to enforce them, and sought new measures to help women workers. This change of attitude was encouraged by a change of regime in 1886, when Lady Emilia Dilke became WTUL president following Paterson's death. Lady Dilke led the league until the year before her own death in 1904.[63]

Until the advent of the National Anti-Sweating League in 1906 gave them a partner, the league's leadership was the minimum wage leadership. Lady Dilke was succeeded as president by her niece, league secretary Gertrude Tuckwell. The WTUL was reinvigorated, and the minimum wage acquired its most effective campaigner when Mary Macarthur became secretary in 1903.[64] The league was also well connected through marriages and friendships with the two political parties sympathetic to labor legislation, Liberals and Labour. The league was refused affiliation with the Trades Union Congress because it was not itself a union, but it held its annual meeting under the same roof and hosted events for TUC members at their national congress.[65] From 1906, its offshoot, the

National Federation of Women Workers (NFWW), was affiliated and was able to preach the virtues of the policy within the organized labor movement.[66]

In 1895, the WTUL was pressing for licensing out-work to control sweating and was skeptical about wages boards. A year later, however, it was "inclined to wonder whether . . . it would not be possible for the State to further some such arrangement where organisation is weak."[67] In 1898, Sir Charles Dilke sponsored the first bill for the league and submitted it annually to Parliament from 1898 until 1906, with support from the same handful of M.P.'s. His Wages Board Bill was never debated. Opposition mobilized around a rival Home Work Regulation Bill, introduced from 1902 onward for the Women's Industrial Council (WIC) but making no more progress than Dilke's bill. At this stage, the significant campaign was not in Parliament but among women reformers. Lifeless as legislative proposals, the Wages Board and Home Work Regulation Bills represented a lively debate outside Parliament about the best way to attack sweating. They focused the competing proposals of the WTUL and the second major women's organization involved, the WIC.

The Wages Board Bill of the WTUL, modeled directly on Deakin's Victorian precedent, "proposes to give power to the Secretary of State—on the representation of employer or employed that such action is desirable—to appoint Wages Boards in sweated trades to settle the minimum rate of wages; the Boards to consist of an equal number of employers and employed."[68] This was the logical corollary to an analysis of low wages as the key to sweating: "Sweating brings us naturally to Wages Boards," and Wages Boards were "the best weapon against sweating yet invented."[69] The bill differed from the eventual Trade Boards Act in giving the initiative to employers and employed, in the absence of public representatives, in the lack of a tight definition of sweated industries. Like the Trade Boards Act, this original WTUL version made no reference to gender and no specification of a value for the statutory minimum wage.

The Home Work Regulation Bill was more in the spirit of existing factory laws, indeed designed to plug holes of concern to both WIC and WTUL. The WIC hoped to raise standards, especially sanitary standards, within the sweated industries by requiring workers in home workshops and homes to obtain a license for their premises.[70] Margaret MacDonald and her husband, Ramsay (one of the first Labour M.P.'s and a future prime minister), had been committed to licensing home workers' premises since their discovery of American tenement licensing laws during a visit in 1897. Ramsay noted in his diary that in New York State the "Tenement House law seemed to be working well," and, in Massachusetts, that "homework was done in clean houses."[71] Margaret MacDonald recalled that "my husband and I were convinced by the very simple testimony of our noses; tenements which were licensed were clean and sweet, though poor; across the same street we would come upon a block which it was unpleasant to go near, but in that block we found no industries carried on, for the inspectors would grant no license."[72] She thought that a licensing bill would simplify implementation by putting the onus on workers to obtain licenses and would foster social stability because "the licenses discourage casual Homeworkers . . . [and] the license is an encouragement to Homeworkers to shift less frequently from premises for which they have secured a license, and to land-lords who want rent paid regularly to keep their premises in good order."[73]

Margaret MacDonald's forum was the WIC, founded in 1894 to replace the short-lived Women's Trade Union Association. Clementina Black, a middle-class socialist and former secretary of the WTUL, led the WTUA, organizing female trades in the East End of London. Contemplating the difficulty of or-ganizing this sector of the economy, WTUA and WTUL took different direc-tions. The league remained a cross-class group, developing a plan for women's unions, *and* pressure for access to men's unions, *and* legislation. The associa-tion capitalized on its middle-class skills, reorganizing as the WIC "to organize special and systematic inquiry into the conditions of working women, to pro-vide accurate information concerning those interests, and to promote such ac-tions as may seem conducive to their improvement."[74] The WIC produced a stream of studies of women's work, becoming, Ellen Mappen notes, an impor-tant clearinghouse for information, a connection for women reformers, and "a common meeting ground in London for those who were also active in or sup-porters of other groups, ranging from women's organizations such as the Na-tional Union of Women Workers, the Women's Labour League, the Women's Liberal Federation and the Women's Co-operative Guild to the Fabian Society, the Independent Labour Party and the Labour Party."[75] The council con-demned sweating but divided over strategy. Margaret MacDonald led opposi-tion to the minimum wage. Yet one of MacDonald's closest friends was Mary Macarthur of the WTUL. Macarthur's office at the NFWW/WTUL, it was said, might "claim to share with the MacDonald's home . . . the title of the idea-factory of the Labour Party. Mrs. MacDonald regularly contributed to the *Woman Worker* a couple of columns on the doings of the Women's Labour League, of which she was president and Mary Middleton secretary; and she and Mary Macarthur sparred, more or less seriously, over the Minimum Wage, the one subject on which they definitely and openly differed."[76]

There was no reason in principle why a minimum wage bill and a licensing bill should not have been brought in together. Clementina Black, representing the WIC before the Select Committee on Home Work in 1907, was asked if there was anything "in any licensing system which would in the least conflict with the operation of a Wages Board?" "Not at all," she replied; the two were "perfectly compatible."[77] Dilke, too, recalled that he had supported "licensing of workplaces in '95 before the Standing Committee on the Factory Act of that year: and I am still a heretic as I should like licensing in addition to Wages Boards."[78] The WTUL had also favored some form of regulation of premises, with responsibility on the shoulders of employers and landlords rather than workers.[79] But after 1896, perhaps influenced by an article they ran on the problems of inspection in Illinois, they turned to the minimum wage as a more efficient, more appropriate, and more comprehensive remedy for sweating.[80]

MacDonald, however, held tenaciously to her licensing bill, even when her inquiries were rewarded with the information that the New York licensing law "had effected nothing."[81] Right up to 1909, she attempted to maintain gendered legislation and public health measures as the solution to sweating, defending them, in increasing isolation, against the WTUL analysis of low wages and industrial work. She did admit that the WIC bill "is not expected to do more than obviate some of the evils attendant upon home work." Her hope was that "by setting a standard in any one particular . . . one indirectly raises the minimum standard all round."[82] She came to feel so passionately about the minimum wage that, as James Mallon once observed, it was the one issue on which she could lose her temper.[83] Her opposition split at least two women's organizations to which she belonged, the National Council of Women and WIC.

Clementina Black, who belonged to both NASL and WIC, was a prominent supporter of the minimum wage and the author of a book arguing for its application to sweated industries.[84] When Black proposed that WIC endorse a minimum wage for home and factory workers, MacDonald was furious. MacDonald had placed herself on one end of the range of opinion: she stood for no Wages Boards at all; Black's group within WIC and the WTUL for Wages Boards for all sweated workers. "What fun it would be if we all converted each other on Jan. 20th, it seems so silly to start from much the same standpoint and to go in exactly opposite directions, but I suppose it would be dull and unprogressive if we didn't do that kind of thing," MacDonald concluded early in 1908.[85] There was no such unlikely "fun." WIC and WTUL shared only the ultimate goal of ending sweating. The focus of the council on the workplace rather than the wage, the impression sometimes given of "blaming the victim," and the intention to tidy up the home and to "protect the public against the dissemination of disease and dirt" contrasted with the WTUL's focus on broader structural causes and a solution that addressed the wage-earner and not the homemaker.[86] The two groups had been far apart in 1902 when their two bills were on the parliamentary agenda. In 1909, a short report in the *Times* noted Black's resolution at the annual business meeting "that the Women's Industrial Council earnestly begs the government in the case of the establishment of wages boards not to limit the scope of these boards to homeworkers." MacDonald proposed an amendment: "That in view of the failure of the supporters of wages boards to present workable proposals . . . the council take no official action in the matter." The council escaped with a compromise that left WIC itself out of the debate and MacDonald to fight on alone: "After discussion, it was resolved to alter the amendment so as to read:—'That the council take no present official action with regard to the statutory establishment of wages boards.'"[87]

But by this time the WIC split was inconsequential. Legislation was certain to pass. Since 1906, the action had moved elsewhere, under the male leadership of the National Anti-Sweating League, in close association with the WTUL. But, though neither the WTUL's Wages Board Bill nor the WIC's Home Work Regulation Bill became law, the years had not been wasted. Women had brought the policy into serious contention, and in the process brought definitions of both gender and class identities to a new complexity, more appropriate to women's lives in industrial Britain.

Women's Voices

The dispute over whether home workers (virtually a gendered category), or sweated labor (a class category), should benefit was the crux of the division between women in the first years of the minimum wage campaign. The technical use of the term *home* to mean a form of workplace embodied a gendered discourse. Home workers might in theory be men, women, or children. The concept of home work contained, to many people's minds, an internal contradiction, an unacceptable conflation of domesticity and industrialism. When home work was the issue, the terminology of domesticity, of cleanliness and healthiness, and a mother's responsibility to her family, most directly challenged the terminology of class and of the exploitation of workers. Homes were women's domain, the ideal home defined in contrast to the world of work, as domesticity rather than industry, as harmony rather than competition, its relationships affectionate or dutiful rather than monetary, located in the private, not the public, sphere. Home work was, in short, an impropriety, disturbing all these gendered assumptions.[88]

The women's debate about minimum wage policy opened up these alternatives of gender and class. It took place primarily among leaders of their organizations. When, occasionally, the women who actually worked at home and in the sweatshops joined in, they, quoted by their leaders or brought before committees, were torn between desire for improvement and fear of losing the home work upon which they depended.[89] These leaders were political activists, not feminist theorists, and their underlying beliefs about gender and work were rarely made explicit. But their political language and policy choices also articulated the beliefs that both motivated and divided them. The voices of Lady Dilke and Gertrude Tuckwell, Mary Macarthur, and Margaret MacDonald are on the record. They were friends and fellow workers, prominent in the collectivist causes that united the radical wing of the Liberal party with Labour. Their differences arose over how to respond to women's presence in the industrial work force, in contravention of the middle-class Victorian ideal of domesticity that most of them held dear. Socialist contemporaries Mary Macarthur and Margaret MacDonald represented the clearest alternatives. Macarthur sought legislation for a class of workers, arguing that although women might be the prime victims of sweating, gender was not the fundamental characteristic of sweated labor. For MacDonald, the problem was one of women and homes. Midway between these two extremes, trying to balance class and gender perspectives, were leading minimum wagers like Lady Dilke, Gertrude Tuckwell, and Clementina Black.

Emilia Dilke has left the most explicit statement of principle on women and work. Dilke was no equal rights feminist. She dismissed the equal rights campaigners of the 1870s as a "shrieking sisterhood" whose "absurd suggestion of equality between the sexes" had only fostered a dogmatic rejection of "the just claims of women." But in a preface to a study of women's work by Amy Bulley and Margaret Whitley, she argued that women did have just claims to equal rights at work, "for consideration in respect of their labour and wages, their education, the protection of their earnings and property, the removal of such trade and professional restrictions as are of an artificial character, and the opening out to them of wider means of obtaining a livelihood."[90] They also had different claims "in the case of mothers at least," for whom "there are many occupations for which they are wholly unfit, but in which men may engage with impunity," she argued, citing work with white lead. This was the pragmatic solution of a woman who was both idealistic and realistic about women's place, who rejected simple dichotomies between male and female spheres, acknowledged difference between the sexes but also their common experience. At bottom, Lady Dilke believed, the ideal was "the restoration of as many as possible to their post of honour as queens of the hearth." But she also understood "the necessity of recognising, legally and socially, that development in the relations of women to the state and society which has been brought about by the pressure of altered circumstances."

Gendered legislation, Dilke believed, was appropriate where childbearing and marital roles were involved: "There is no danger to society in the recognition of equal human rights for both sexes, if we are also ready to recognise the divergence of their capabilities, for the relations of men and women to each other, their functions in the family and the state, must ultimately be determined—however ill it may please the more ardent female reformer—by the operation of natural laws." Thus, "certain restrictions on the labour of children and child-bearing women may be required by the interests of that society of which they are a part"; but "further than this it seems scarcely wise to go in our demand for anything like legislative interference in respect to this matter of 'unfitness.'" Beyond this point, the sexes should find common cause: "The cardinal points of the leaders of labour—the shortening of hours, the abolition of overtime, the regulation of wages, the limitation of the number of apprentices in the overcrowded trades—these are matters of chief importance to all workers, matters in which the interests of all, whether they be men or women, precisely coincide."

Dilke was therefore able simultaneously to acknowledge women's equality in their claim to voting rights, their difference in a conditional claim to protective legislation, and the irrelevance of gender where the class interest of all workers was involved.[91] American minimum wagers became caught in the contradiction between their demands for equality of suffrage and for the inequality implied by protective legislation. Suffrage in Britain meant either support for equal suffrage—that is, for admitting middle-class women to the existing property-based franchise—or adult suffrage, the abolition of both gender and class distinctions. Women like Dilke did not advocate suffrage for the middle class and protection for working women. A conditional relationship of biological difference to social structure allowed different claims for rights to vote and rights at work.

Emilia Dilke was the daughter of an East India Company officer, widow of the master of an Oxford College, an art historian of some standing, and had married Liberal Sir Charles Dilke in 1885. These were hardly the expected qualifications for a trade union leader but very much the middle-class background associated with moralistic crusades to turn working-class women into housewives on the middle-class model. Dilke and her niece Gertrude Tuckwell were uncomfortable when the protection of the maternal role that they idealized clashed with the needs of a class whose rights they recognized. But they were not just uncomprehending middle-class women. If their maternalism led them to advocate special legislation for mothers—Tuckwell was a strong supporter of free medical care for mothers and children, and of widows' pensions—their class analysis led them to conclude that the dirt and chaos of the lives of sweated workers were the product of hardship, not of inadequate character. As fellow minimum wager Clementina Black concluded, "The class which we sometimes call degenerate is, as a class, merely starved."[92]

Tuckwell's principle was to take care of the wages, and the rest would take care of itself. Asked by the chairman of the Select Committee on Homework about sanitation and "domestic cleanliness," she replied: "I am afraid I do not attach very much importance to that. It is not fundamental as the question of the rate of wage is. People do not like to be dirty."[93] The minimum wage may have been seen as a measure of control of industrial instability by some businessmen. The WTUL women who initiated the campaign had a different agenda. They blamed economic structures, explained dirt and disease as the consequence of life on starvation wages, applied the analysis to home and factory, and promulgated a solution that would provide sweated workers with the wherewithal to live without imposing rules on how to live.

The views of Mary Macarthur suggest that a different class, generation, and the rise of collectivist-socialist ideas represented a new stage in the definition of women's politics. Her claim for equal rights for women in the labor force compared women's rights and men's rights within and between classes, rather than women's rights and mother's roles. Macarthur was a generation younger than Dilke, Tuckwell, and Black. She was born in Glasgow in 1880, had a high school education before going to work for her father, a draper and a Conservative, and became involved in the Shop Assistants' Union and thereafter in the Independent Labour Party. There she made the friends who took her into London politics—Margaret Bondfield of the union, her future husband, Will Anderson, of the ILP, and, at the annual conference of the ILP in 1903, James J. Mallon, who was chairman of the Conference Hospitality Committee and "later to become one of her closest friends."[94] Bondfield introduced her to Gertrude Tuckwell, who was then searching for a new secretary to revitalize the WTUL.

Macarthur came from a formative youth as a worker and from two organizations that involved women and men on unusually equal terms. Women in the Shop Assistants' Union were "strongly opposed to sex distinctions" and were enrolled in the same branches as men.[95] The ILP, "more than any other party, was sympathetic to the aspirations of feminism," supported equal suffrage, and accepted "men and women as members on an equal basis, and unlike other political parties did not relegate women to support organizations."[96] Macarthur expressed the possibility of both sex equality and socialism. Her biographer recalled: "She worked for women, but her vision was not bounded by them any more than it was bounded by industry. Trade unionism was their salvation, but it was an idea that transcended sex."[97] When she campaigned for the abolition of sex discrimination, it was in tandem with the abolition of class distinctions. Thus, for example, her position on suffrage: "If, in the later stages of the Women's Suffrage agitation she seemed to undervalue the vote, it was because the working women who most needed its protection were left out in the cold under the Limited Bill, as were large numbers of working men. She was, on the other hand, an ardent supporter of adult suffrage."[98]

Macarthur did not use Dilke's language of "queens of the hearth," though her gift to readers of the first issue of the *Woman Worker*, the journal she edited for the NFWW, was a print of a famous American poster of "Sacred Motherhood." With a dollar sign in place of the capital S, the drawing implied, through its portrayal of a nursing mother rocking both her baby and the treadle of her sewing machine, the destruction of the maternal ideal by the conditions of sweated labor.[99] She understood the plight of women carrying the double burden of work and home responsibilities. She located the problem of organizing women in their circumstances, not their sex: "There is no inherent sex incapacity to recognise the necessity for corporate action. The probability of marriage is not the insurmountable obstacle we are often led to believe it is." The fact that women were typically transient workers made organization harder: "The lack of permanence, however, from other causes affects men in the same way. First, the low standard of living may be stated to be at once the cause and consequence of women's lack of organization. This sounds paradoxical, but it is nevertheless true that, while women are badly paid because of their unorganized condition, they may be unorganized mainly because they are badly paid."[100] To reach women who made lace at home, could not easily attend meetings even if they thought of doing so, were intensely suspicious of outsiders, and "did not open the door readily when someone knocked, who might be 'The Rent,'" Macarthur "held forth on a chair at the street corner." J. J. Mallon called these "queer, unreported assemblies," at which at first a few women would stand in the street "while others would open their windows so as to listen to what took place." Since Macarthur was a great stump-speaker ("Keep on, miss, it's better than t'seaside," was a Lancashire comment) she gathered crowds.[101]

Macarthur led opposition to limiting a minimum wage law either to women or to home workers. These were arbitrary distinctions, she believed, in a situation in which class was the defining characteristic. A rumor that "it is proposed that the [Trade Boards] Act should apply to women only" inflamed her. "This, it will be seen, not only excludes men, but also withholds the benefits to be conferred by the proposed legislation from children and young persons."[102] A more serious threat of restriction to home workers was equally unacceptable. Macarthur used her position as editor of the *Woman Worker* to argue that "the plight of the sweated factory worker is as bad as that of her sister who toils in the home." Where the work was done was irrelevant, "We quite recognise that the experiment must be made gradually, but . . . whilst we will accept, as a beginning, a Wages Board, even if it be limited to one trade, we do demand that in that one trade no arbitrary distinctions should be made between people doing the same work under different circumstances."[103] Speaking to the Select Committee on Home Work, Macarthur was more concerned with demolishing the rationale for legislating for home work alone than with the possibility of a law for women alone. She made clear that the presence of women workers in a trade was not a sufficient criterion for identifying sweating: "It depends upon one's definition of sweated conditions; there are trades where women are not employed where the conditions are far from satisfactory, but certainly there are no trades where the level is anything like so low."[104] But she spoke of sweated workers as women, while equating their problem regardless of workplace: "I wish to make clear . . . that the low rates of wages are not confined to the homeworkers, and that the question of organisation is equally difficult with the similar class of labour in the factory . . . It is very difficult to form a permanent organisation amongst lowly paid women workers, either in the factory or the home."[105] She was, perhaps, equivocating on one arbitrary distinction, that of sex, in order to block another, that of workplace, because she knew that the committee would shortly hear from Margaret MacDonald, whose licensing proposal for home work was quite explicitly a proposal not for women only but for women working in the home only.

Margaret MacDonald, from a middle-class London family, a devoutly Christian young woman whose faith transmuted to socialism, joined the WIC in 1895, married J. Ramsay MacDonald in 1896, and maintained a hectic life of social investigation and political activism in the midst of raising a family, until her death at the age of forty-one in 1911.[106] MacDonald shared with Macarthur and Black the long-term goal of a socialist society. She once evaded a question about the principle of Wages Boards with the answer that "I am in favour of Socialism, which is quite a different thing."[107] MacDonald argued that Wages Boards for factory as well as home workers would drive home workers out of business, because the increased efficiency of mechanized factories could support higher wages. The WTUL could accept this as a lesser evil. But MacDonald's defense of home work in conjunction with opposition to the minimum wage derived from her underlying beliefs on gender—on the woman's role in home and family—not from her socialism.

The issue between MacDonald and the WTUL was the best way to fulfill the necessity for women to perform both family labor and wage labor. On the one hand, home work allowed women to be workers and carers simultaneously; on the other hand, it laid them open to exploitation. On the one hand, work at home might give the woman rather than the foreman some control over when and how the work was done. On the other, the conditions of factory work were easier to organize and regulate so as to win the self-respect of better wages. Indeed the WTUL expected a side benefit of Wages Boards to be the empowerment of women, contrasting "a continuation of fierce competition of which hapless girl workers are the victims, women's unions weak and impermanent, striking sometimes in sudden wrath and at last may be ending in failure and despair. With Wages Boards a new hope colours the prospect. Behind the little union will be the force and presence of statutory power supporting the organisation so that it knits and thrives and comes at last unto a great strength of its own."[108]

Margaret MacDonald's defense of home work in licensed premises reflected her belief that home workers could not help themselves and that the state must be convinced to intervene. This was "the whole problem of why there are slum people, why the people do not come out of the slums straight away. They get into such a state, I think, that they have not got the initiative themselves."[109] Blaming a loss of character in the home workers was a far cry from the class basis of Tuckwell's assertion that initiative was dulled by low wages. MacDonald was questioned by Labour M.P. Arthur Henderson. He first asked whether she had "formed any opinion as to whether the evils of the home work system are greater from the sanitary or the economic standpoints?" She equivocated: both were bad, the two factors inseparable. When Henderson persisted, she admitted: "On the whole, the low wages." The exchanges that followed, questions from Henderson, answers from MacDonald, are revealing of her priorities. Henderson pushed MacDonald to the admission that her licensing bill "would improve the sanitation, and, in an indirect way, the whole industrial status; but I quite concede it would not touch some of the worst evils."

Part of the cost of raising the standard of premises to meet the terms of a license, MacDonald believed, would fall on the landlord, who would otherwise lose his tenants. Some effort would also be required of the tenants, but "as for domestic cleanliness, it really does not take very much longer to be clean than to be dirty when you once start at it." She dismissed the idea that cleanliness cost money or that home workers might lack the time for housework. It was a matter of character:

> —I think, from one's own case, one gets into a slovenly way, and one sticks there.
> Surely you are not to compare your own case with these slum workers?
> —I do not think there is so very much difference.

Henderson was skeptical that time meant the same to MacDonald as to "these poor people." MacDonald replied with a tale of her experience "in a home worker's place only yesterday." Preserving the worker's anonymity, she said that the task "was a thing you might not at all particularly like at this season of the year [August] to know was being done in a dirty place, and her beds were not made, and everything was dirty and untidy, and the floor was unswept. If she had got into the way of making her beds in the morning and cleaning up her floor, and so on, it would not have taken her much longer every day. I think if an Inspector coming could have given her that little extra inducement to make her do these things, it would not have taken any appreciable amount of time off her work."[110] As a woman who once defined socialism as "the State of homes," she found her ideal of the home offended against by the conditions of sweated labor therein.[111] MacDonald's real agenda was the creation of ideal homes, and of ideal women's lives within them, even if this required an inspector calling to check that the beds were made.

The crux of MacDonald's gender philosophy, according to her husband, was that she "was interested in woman as a citizen, but infinitely more so in woman as a woman, the embodiment of the qualities and instincts of maternity—not as a thing of sex but as a specialised aspect of humanity."[112] Her complex if muddled views gave priority to gender difference and an ideal of domesticity encapsulated in such comments as "'To work for the economic independence of women is to work for the purity of family life'; and again 'I am interested in housing because I am interested in homing. I want houses for souls as well as for bodies.'"[113] MacDonald affirmed the ideal of the male breadwinner but recognized need in his absence. She condemned the feckless male who exploited his wife but she would provide incentives where the need was genuine. Her moralistic streak showed in a comment on the casual home worker: "I think there are a good many cases . . . where it would not be so very necessary to the house; . . . where it encourages the man not to work, and to let his wife work." But she also told the Select Committee that "a great deal of this misery is due to the unemployment or casual employment amongst the men, that a great many of those workers who are the worst paid, should not be taking work for wages at all, that if their husbands were earning wages they would not be, and, of course, anything you can do to meet that unemployment amongst men would help very directly to cut off a great deal of this wretched competition amongst the home workers." And that "I feel very strongly about the point of widows, and women with sick husbands, or other sick relations," for whom state programs should be initiated.[114]

MacDonald's plan for "complete supervision and oversight of all home workers and out workers" and "a sufficient force of Factory Inspectors to carry it out" patronized the workers, intruded on their privacy, and imposed standards for the conduct of their lives.[115] She alone of these labor-oriented women came to policymaking from the Charity Organisation Society with its emphasis on the voluntary sector, individualistic social work methods, moral purpose, and insistence on "the restorative power of character."[116] By contrast, a structural analysis fitted the beliefs, socialist in the broad sense, "rather a sentiment than a doctrine," of radical Liberals like Dilke and Tuckwell and those doctrinally socialist such as Clementina Black and Mary Macarthur.[117] Partisan loyalties did not explain the division. MacDonald was a socialist woman for whom the priority of the maternal role and the sanctity of the home were paramount. Beatrice Webb was a socialist woman who accepted the existing pay differentials between men and women and argued that they should be reproduced in a statutory minimum wage structure. Socialist Clementina Black and the Liberals of the WTUL were women who firmly endorsed the principle of equal pay: "The relation between the minimum wage of men and women seems to us to admit of no doubt whatever. It must be that of equality."[118]

Age played a role. Dilke's generation, as was said of their American counterparts, "battled economic and social injustice quite self-consciously as women reformers" and developed "a female symbolic system that expressed women's attitudes toward family change and justified new roles for women outside the family."[119] They were "social feminists" in the sense of holding a position that "derives from women's specificity an argument for wider public action on the part of women," discriminating between the specificity of biological difference and that of socially constructed roles.[120] MacDonald, thirty years younger than Dilke, fell outside a generational pattern, instead showing the strength of religious and moralistic influences in sustaining both domestic values and socialism. Macarthur, ten years younger again, reached political maturity within socialism.

The views of the home workers themselves are hard to retrieve and perhaps always were impossible to know. When the Select Committee met delegations of workers assembled by Mary Macarthur and by Miss Vynne of the National Home Workers' League, they heard a sad story of deference, ignorance, confusion, and fear. Macarthur's group appeared anonymously, fearing victimization. None had any idea how their wages related to the selling price of their products, nor could they guess at their employers' profits. They generally supported a minimum wage and agreed that knowledge was the key to negotiating better deals for themselves. Vynne spoke of her group's dislike of any intervention: "As a practical fact they always find that any legislation, any agitation, any worrying about home-work makes the masters stop giving it out." This went for inspections too, as home workers were "a less danger to the public than anyone else." Vynne's delegation defended home work as a necessity to keep their families together: "I think it would be awful cruel to interfere with us, because it means poverty for a good few of us if we are not able to earn something to help the husband."[121]

Vynne's delegation discriminated between the sanitary inspector, whom they would tolerate, and the factory inspector, whom for reasons not explained they particularly disliked. Macarthur's group qualified their endorsement of the minimum wage proposal with the caution that it not "crush out" less efficient needy workers. They lacked information to disentangle alarmist rumors from plausible anticipation of the effects of legislation. Leo Chiozza-Money, a radical Liberal member of the committee and a good friend of the Dilkes, suspected that Miss Vynne's delegation had been brainwashed. He asked, "Has anybody told you that Wages Boards would take away home-work altogether. Is that what you understand?" One of the home workers explained: "It is like this, you see some are quick and some are medium and some slow. I understand that they would take the medium and those that are slow they would not have anything to do with at the factories and it would stop their working altogether." Miss Vynne's assistant rebutted the brainwashing charge. "When we have put the Wages Board before them—perhaps not exactly as you do, for we think you have a one-sided way," she declared, "invariably when we have simply explained what it would be and have not pointed out anything, they have expressed an opinion."[122] Wages Boards promised no intrusion into the home, no rules on how to live, and a framework within which to learn the skills of organization and representation. They constituted a self-respecting solution promising empowerment—but only for those women who were confident that they would be survivors in the new regime. The more fearful the home worker, the more defensive against intervention of any kind. A promise of empowerment was an irrelevance to those who had little and saw only the promise of losing even that.

By focusing on the regulation of the workplace and on homes rather than factories, MacDonald shifted the debate toward reform of the victims rather than of the economic system, toward gender issues rather than class issues. In her hands, the meaning of "home" as workplace connoted "home" as a gendered ideal. In pursuit of her ideal, she was as single-minded for the abolition of sweating in the name of domesticity as Macarthur was single-minded for the abolition of sweating in the name of the exploitation of a class. In between fell the group of women represented by Dilke, Tuckwell, and Black, who tried to reconcile their agreement with MacDonald on an ideal gender role and their agreement with Macarthur that problem and solution originated in the economy and not in gender. For them, as Black represented to the Select Committee, the presence of married women in the work force and the cultural expectations of married women's domesticity were facts to be established and dealt with without moral judgment. Black expected that "if the Wages Boards were to fix a reasonable minimum wage for a man, in nine cases out of ten his wife would not work either at home or outside, at any rate while the children were young."[123] But she did not accept "that the position and attitude of an unmarried woman is always different from that of a married woman . . . in all these women's labour questions." On the contrary, she did not think "that it is inherent, because when there are trades in which a woman is expected to go on working all her life she is generally paid more; she is not different then."[124]

The gendered structure of the economy infused analysis of sweating, and thence the minimum wage, with considerations of gender. The responses of all but Margaret MacDonald combined, without inconsistency, elements of what have been labeled maternalist, paternalist, equality, and difference theories. Such dichotomies are, perhaps, more useful as tools for disentangling elements of both ideology and practice than as adequate descriptions of the reality of women struggling with the difficult transition in women's ideas about women. The WTUL represented the possibilities of a new social feminism in its assertion that women had roles and rights in both domestic and labor worlds and in its vision of the minimum wage as a strategy for empowerment. MacDonald demonstrated the problems women faced, both in making the transition themselves to a wholehearted acceptance of new roles and in implementing their ideas in a situation in which culture as well as structure inhibited change. Despite her socialist convictions, MacDonald could not equate the demands of women as workers with those of their maternal role, let alone give the worker priority. So, in the last years of the minimum wage campaign, it was MacDonald—not, as one might expect, male organizations like trade unions—who was foremost in opposition against a measure that did just that.

This women's debate had flourished for a decade before the issue was taken up seriously in "high politics" in 1906. Male leaders might well have taken for granted its being a gender issue. Yet the seeds of a gender-neutral Trade Boards Act had also been sown, by the insistence of women that it was not *only* a question of gender. If the curious compromise of the Trade Boards Act, a gender-neutral law commonly understood to be for the benefit of women, was merely a continuation of earlier confusions, it might also be taken as evidence of women's control not only of the agenda but of the final outcome of public policy. But even as the women's debate intensified, the campaign acquired a new momentum and direction and began to move into parliamentary committees and departmental territories, where women were outsiders.

Low-Paid Workers

THE TRADE BOARDS ACT, BRITAIN, 1906–1909

IN 1906, the minimum wage ceased to be the parochial concern of a small circle of female, Liberal, and Labour reformers and became a national issue. The dramatic general election of January 1906 replaced a Conservative government with a Liberal one, gave the Liberals a huge majority (400 seats to the Conservatives' 157), and brought a sizable block of thirty Labour M.P.'s into office. Minimum wagers had an unprecedented opportunity. They could hope to place their bill on the programs of both a new and sympathetic Liberal government and a new and sympathetic Labour party. But in February 1906, when Dilke introduced his regular Wages Board Bill, the only sign of gathering momentum was that his usual four co-sponsors doubled to eight.[1] In July, the new Liberal government prevaricated. The Labour party made the first move later in the year, placing the minimum wage "fourth in the list of the reforms for which they as a party were to ballot and work."[2]

Meanwhile, minimum wagers were embarking on a dazzlingly successful propaganda campaign, using publicity and lobbying techniques in a model of modern political methods. Women were much involved. Nine women on an executive committee of thirty-three included Clementina Black, Mary Macarthur, Margaret MacDonald, and Gertrude Tuckwell. Public relations was political activity in which women could be equal participants, operating where no male traditions hampered them, pioneering new techniques of communication and publicity as well as continuing traditional volunteer work. The new phase was launched in May 1906, by a Sweated Industries Exhibition at the Queens Hall in London. Forty-five workers, mostly women, plied their trades in the hall, making trousers, match boxes, grummets, sacks, beaded ornaments. Their wages and circumstances were detailed in the catalog. There was a daily program of afternoon lectures, plus illustrations "by means of an Oxy-Hydrogen Lantern" in the evenings. The organizers "rigorously excluded sweated industries other than home industries, not because the promoters failed to realise the suffering these entail, but because they rightly considered that to attempt too much in an initial effort was to risk the success of the work they believed it was in their power to accomplish provided their whole strength could be concentrated upon it." The work they had in mind, by this account, was not to abolish home work but to regulate it and ensure that "it shall be done under conditions which guarantee the public no less than the worker from disease."[3] The exhibition became a national event, with some thirty thousand visitors and a sale of twenty thousand copies of the catalog.[4]

The exhibition catalog gave credit for the event to "the proprietors of the *Daily News.*" George Cadbury, Birmingham cocoa manufacturer, owned the *Daily News*; its editor, Alfred Gardiner, took the chair of the executive committee for the occasion.[5] Mary Macarthur's biographer was convinced that Cadbury was merely the agent of the WTUL and of Macarthur, who was "stirred to the soul by a strike in which she had been called in only to find herself hopeless to do anything because of the all-round disorganization of the industry." Macarthur turned to the press, in the form of the *Daily News*, for help, "broke in upon Mr. A. G. Gardiner . . . and, white-faced, with burning eyes, poured forth her story and appealed for his help. He listened, greatly moved; when, however, he began to suggest some difficulties . . . she disarmed and alarmed him by bursting into tears. Perhaps this moved him more than argument; anyhow, he soon after had a highly practical plan. He determined to put the weight and publicity of the *Daily News* behind an Exhibition of Sweated Industries."[6] WTUL minutes record considerable discussion on the question of its own participation, and sparring with the radical Labour group, the Social Democratic Federation, over who should sponsor and control an exhibition. When the SDF withdrew in favor of the *Daily News*, the WTUL settled their own role and agreed that "the League be represented by Miss Tuckwell & Miss Macarthur on the Sweated Industries Exhibition Committee."[7]

A new level of feuding had opened up, as organizations competing for national power and ideological supremacy joined the women's debate. From 1906 onward, the minimum wage campaign was no longer primarily within and between women's organizations. Now it was within and between women's organizations, political parties, pressure groups, unions, businessmen and their organizations, and the legislative and executive arms of the state. The final Trade Boards Act was an elaborate bureaucratic construction, empty of direction on issues of both gender and value. Was this outcome, so lacking in the human content of the initial women's debate because male organization, leadership, and state had superceded that of females? Or were bureaucratic priorities triumphant as the state took over from reform movements and parties?

PRESSURE POLITICS: THE NATIONAL ANTI-SWEATING LEAGUE CAMPAIGN

The breadth of the coalition formed in 1906 is surprising, given the air of discord at several major public events. George Cadbury, for example, supported the minimum wage, although he was a vice president of the Women's Industrial Council and although Mudie-Smith's introduction to the exhibition, focusing on home work, dirt, and disease, smacked of Margaret MacDonald's case for the regulation of premises. MacDonald herself spoke on American legislation at the exhibition, and Ramsay MacDonald on the Home Work Regulation Bill. He later disdained the whole exercise as trivial, even while crediting his wife for its substance.[8] The SDF tried again to take control of the popular cause of sweating, at a NASL conference later that year.[9] But it was the pragmatists in the Labour movement, the Fabians, and the established trade unions, not the ideological wing, who determined Labour policy on the minimum wage and who could easily ally with radical Liberals like Dilke.

The enthusiasm generated by the Exhibition led to the founding of the National Anti-Sweating League. "The exhibition had been held with a constructive intention. At its close there was a large demand for a practical policy, which it fell to the Committee of the exhibition to endeavour to formulate." Unions, consumers' leagues, the licensing of home work or its abolition were all considered.[10] The strength of NASL lay in its single-mindedness. All its efforts were addressed to a single social problem, sweating, and to a single solution, the minimum wage. James J. Mallon, a socialist and well-connected settlement worker, was engaged as full-time secretary. Within a year, NASL had raised funds for an office, built up a considerable list of subscribers (George Cadbury, one of more than six hundred founding members, paid the largest single sub of £20), opened several provincial branches, and been endorsed by "(among others) the Women's Trade Union League, the Women's Co-operative Guild, the Women's Liberal Federation, the Women's National Liberal Association, the Co-operative Congress, the Christian Social Union, the Wesleyan Conference, and by almost all the large Trade Unions and Trades Councils in the country." NASL had also arranged a three-day conference on the minimum wage and distributed fifteen thousand copies of its proceedings, hosted visiting speakers, started its own publications program, "and about 50,000 leaflets have been distributed, newspaper correspondence has been maintained, and a mass of inquiries answered through the post."[11]

NASL became a conduit for pressure on the male establishment and political institutions. Women's access had been behind the scenes, through WTUL receptions at TUC meetings or personal connections. A letter to Gertrude Tuckwell from Dorothy Gladstone, wife of the home secretary, showed the limitations of women's networks. Mrs. Gladstone had had to wait for an appropriate moment but thereafter wrote that "I have now talked over your letter with Mr. Gladstone." He thought that a minimum wage bill would wait its turn for government time for at least another year. Women were fully engaged in political causes yet were structurally confined to the margins, excluded from the formal roles of voter and politician, and barred by social proprieties and male power from the networks through which important decisions were made. Dorothy Gladstone could inquire of her husband. Beyond that, she wrote, "Our work— yours and mine, must be to educate public opinion so as to give the necessary impetus to the Bill, so that it shall not be pushed aside to make room for other questions with more noise behind them!"[12] A tribute to Dilke, at a dinner celebrating passage of the Trade Boards Act, illuminated the real loci of power: "Sir Charles has played a great part publicly. In finding out, however, what has been going on behind the scenes, I am led to know that, great as has been the public part, there is a greater part Sir Charles has played in the region which the newspapers do not penetrate—the region where important decisions are hatched and matured, and differences made up, before appearances are made in public."[13]

Nevertheless, NASL did not supplant the WTUL. From 1906, the two organizations worked together. They had premises in the same building; and Mallon and Macarthur investigated and campaigned together, the WTUL reported: "As usual, a good deal of time has been devoted by the President and Secretary of the [WTUL] to helping in the work of the Anti-Sweating League"; and a year later: "During the Committee stage of the [Trade Boards] Bill the Secretary of the Women's Trade Union League and the Secretary of the Anti-Sweating League attended all meetings."[14] NASL also acknowledged the relationship: "Acting, as usually, in concert with the Women's Trade Union League and the National Federation of Women Workers, the League has held a succession of meetings in Nottingham."[15] Macarthur helped organize NASL's first major event, the Conference on a Minimum Wage, in October 1906, and was instrumental in saving it from factional disintegration.

The 1906 conference was a landmark, confirming a broad alliance of political and industrial organizations under NASL leadership. Public office–holders, necessarily men, were now brought into the campaign, including "the Right Hon. the Lord Mayor (Sir Walter Vaughan Morgan, Bart.)" and "Earl Beauchamp, Professor Stephen Bauer, Mr. Stephen Walsh, M.P., Mr. Askwith, K.C. . . . , Mr. A. G. Gardiner (editor of the *Daily News*), Mr. W. Pember Reeves (High Commissioner for New Zealand)."[16] This leadership pattern was repeated most notably in the delegation that met the Prime Minister in 1908, to press for a minimum wage. "It was introduced," Macarthur wrote, "by the Archbishop of Canterbury, and included many other Bishops, leading Nonconformist divines, noble lords, and prominent politicians, as well as a few common garden folk like blunt George Barnes [a Labour M.P.] and myself."[17]

The 341 delegates to the conference also demonstrated how the campaign had escalated and changed. NASL planned "a National Conference of Labour representatives" and invited the "Labour Party, TUCs (English, Scottish and Irish), General Federation of Trade Unions, ILP, SDF, Fabian Society, Co-operative Societies, Trade Unions, Trades Councils, Women's Co-operative Guild, Women's Industrial Council, Scottish Council of Women's Trades."[18] All but the Irish were present on the day. Union delegates came from many of the trades on the periphery of the sweated industries, such as hosiery, tailoring, and trimming makers, and also from the great industrial "New" unions that had grown in recent decades—dockers, iron and steel workers, postmen, miners. An unusual coalition of men's and women's political, industrial, and reform organizations formed behind the proposition, moved by TUC and Labour delegate Pete Curran, "that this Conference welcomes the formation of the National Anti-Sweating League, heartily endorses the policy of securing by legislative action a minimum wage in the sweated industries, and pledges itself to forward that policy by every means in its power."[19]

The conference program had a different emphasis from the earlier concerns of women. Twelve of fourteen platform speeches were delivered by men. Dilke reviewed the campaign for the renamed Sweated Industries Bill, Sidney Webb presented a long summary of his views on the economics of sweating, and three old friends from Australia and New Zealand spoke of their practical experience of minimum wage laws. The effect on the national economy loomed large, in papers by Liberals Leo Chiozza Money on national income and J. A. Hobson on employment. A significant new contribution was the paper on the arbitration of wage disputes under state authority by the experienced arbitration lawyer George Askwith. Representatives of trade unions spoke at length on sweated labor and the minimum wage. Which way the trade union movement—and with it its political arm, the Labour party—would go on the issue was crucial.

The delicacy of this moment can be deduced from Tuckwell's presentation on "Sweating in Relation to Trade Unions," in which she politely asked "the indulgence" of "a body composed in preponderating numbers of Trade Unionists." She argued that they could not separate the problem of sweating, even of home work, as a woman's problem: "It is not possible to treat this question of sweated home-work as one of women's labour only. There are many men's trades which in some branches can be carried on at home." Nor was it possible "to confine instances of starvation wages to the home." The problem was one of class, of the "less skilled ranks of factory and workshop life" as well as the home workers "at the bottom of the industrial ladder." The question was how unions, whose strength lay with male, more skilled, and higher-paid workers, would respond. They might ignore the problem, for example, or adopt policies to stamp out predominantly female occupations. Fear of competition from lower-paid women and the ideology that woman's place was in the home predisposed them to view women workers as a threat. They might also resist a statutory minimum wage as an encroachment on the central function of unions, the bargaining of wages. So Tuckwell carefully demonstrated that "the competition of the sweated branches of trades with those which are organised, and demand a standard rate, is disastrous. . . . The direct effect of this competition in affected trades is the most obvious, but it must not be forgotten that its effect on the whole trade of the country is, though less obvious, quite as serious." The problem was, she suggested, a "mischievous want of organisation." Although, she assured her audience, she would never attempt to "trench on the province of the great Trade Unions," the plight of sweated labor "appears to be an instance in which our intervention as citizens rather than as Trade Unionists is necessary. . . . To suggest that where it is impossible to form a combination to regulate wages in a trade, the State should be called on to give us machinery by which the wages of that trade can be regulated is, I think, to ask for that which must be an essential help, not a hindrance, to Trade Unionism."[20]

Tuckwell's answer came the next morning from George Barnes, a Glasgow Labour M.P., TUC delegate to this conference, and past leader of the Amalgamated Society of Engineers. Barnes summarized labor's ambivalence toward sweated labor and the proposed minimum wage. He recognized the threat of sweating to his members, using the conservative language of organized labor and skilled workers: "The condition of that class [sweated labor] constitutes a menace if not a positive danger to society." But he acknowledged that some unions "have been able to lift themselves out of the industrial mire, but those in the lowest ranks are left to the tender mercies of competition and to stew in their own juice. These latter form a residuum as men without hope and incapable of effort." Clearly referring to Tuckwell, "a speaker of yesterday," Barnes granted "that it is just that class which requires help," through no fault of their own, for "we are all in some degree the creatures of our own surroundings." He proposed two forms of help:

> The first is the extension and encouragement of collectivist activity on democratic lines; the second is the closer association of the State and voluntary organizations, such as Trade Unions and co-operative societies. . . . The aid of the State should be brought in to supplement voluntary effort . . . voluntary associations of workmen have done something to establish minimum conditions, and I think a Wages Board might very well be set up to ratify those conditions.[21]

Barnes had summarized the official position of organized labor. The unions would lead. The state would impose organization only where none emerged voluntarily. The movement did not oppose the minimum wage. The TUC formally endorsed it, and Labour members of Parliament mostly voted for it. But they did little more.

The involvement of the British labor movement in parliamentary politics made for common cause with women reformers, who had long supplemented union organizing with legislative campaigns. The industrial "New" unions of Britain, more like the CIO of the 1930s in America, had since the 1880s attempted to organize unskilled workers. Often, they had acknowledged the fact of women employees in their trades, on the one hand excluding women from some, usually highly paid, processes, yet on the other hand granting membership on terms varying from special low subscriptions, to separate sections, to full and equal standing.[22] They were in agreement with the WTUL on both the difficulty and the necessity of bringing women into unions. There were grounds for the unions to be sympathetic to a proposal that might supplement their own activities and, by raising wages, either drive female competitors from the labor market or put their costs on a par with union rates.

The caution of the labor movement was understandable, for its relationship with the state had never been happy. In particular, a crippling court judgment against the Amalgamated Society of Railway Servants in the Taff Vale case of 1901, making unions subject to injunctions and liable for damages for strikes, was fresh in their minds. In the Trade Disputes Act of 1906, labor had won a full but controversial restitution of legal immunity from actions for tort. It was hardly likely that, in the very same year, they would wax enthusiastic over a new encroachment by the state into their central function of wage bargaining. Ramsay MacDonald played on their fear, holding up Australia as a warning.

Despite a more sympathetic judiciary in the colonies, minimum wage laws there had brought about "the spread of a most objectionable confusion between judicial, industrial and legislative functions." Unions registered and accepted state supervision in order to participate in statutory wage setting. Likewise in Britain: "Trade Unions would require to allow themselves to become legal entities and would have to abandon the position from which they fought for the Trade Disputes Bill of 1906."[23]

It was, however, the radical, ideological wing of the socialist movement, rather than the unions, who agreed with Ramsay MacDonald's conclusion that the minimum wage campaign was a diversion: "What is the wise line of advance to secure a redistribution of wealth? There is but one, and it is a readjustment of economic relationships." MacDonald's position was that the "Labour Party should not tinker with nominal wages, it should not dally with sweating . . . it should not be diverted from going to the root of things and from its attempts to eliminate the useless parasitic classes."[24] In 1906, SDF members turned up in numbers at the NASL conference. They bid to outflank NASL by proposing a radical amendment: "That this Conference recognises that sweating is inevitable in the capitalist system, and can only be abolished when all the means and sources of wealth are socially owned, and a system of production for use is substituted for that of production of profit." Their spokesman, Harry Quelch, proposed a package of measures including the minimum wage but also the banning of out-work, the eight-hour day, raising the school-leaving age, and state provision for the unemployed.[25]

With the conference platform graced by yet more dignitaries for its final day, including Lord Dunraven who had chaired the House of Lords investigation of sweating in 1890, and with A. G. Gardiner, Cadbury's Liberal editor, waiting to acknowledge the vote of thanks to the committee, it was hardly likely that a motion proposing the overthrow of the capitalist system would meet with unanimous proposal. Mary Macarthur saved the conference with a successful demand for unity behind the NASL resolution and a reminder that the strength of single-issue politics is its ability to close off the complexities and inevitable disagreements of more comprehensive policymaking:

> We Socialists . . . have had an opportunity of voicing our views, . . . but the point is—are we going to render useless all the labour and thought and time that has been expended on arranging the Conference in order to deal with this one phase of the social problem? . . . she hoped she was as consistent a Socialist as Mr. Quelch or any man or women in that hall, but she appealed to the Conference for the cause which they all held so dear to pass the resolution unanimously.[26]

According to another, more dramatic account, Macarthur urged her audience "to remember why they were there. In countless miserable garrets, in the dense slums of London all about them, women and their famished children were toiling day and night, with aching fingers, burning eyes and breaking hearts. The Guildhall with its ornate ornamentation disappeared, silence fell upon the floor; the struggle of contending factions was forgotten; they saw the woman and her child." As a result, "the victory was won. The Trade Union movement was committed to the principle of a Minimum Wage."[27]

"The effect of the conference," NASL reported, "was to give to the minimum wage proposal the large support that was necessary to transform it into practical politics."[28] Unions, the Labour party, and major reform groups were now committed. The campaign moved into Parliament, where the transition from diffuse public sentiment against sweating to mobilized organizational support for the minimum wage transformed the possibilities: "In February, 1908, we talked of the Sweating Bill. Two years before, [Dilke] said, it could command so little support that, having obtained for it the first private members' night, he withdrew it. Now it was accepted with enthusiasm, and the second reading passed without a division—the change, he added, entirely due to the Women's Trade Union League."[29]

PARLIAMENTARY POLITICS AND THE SELECT COMMITTEE ON HOME WORK

From late 1906, the issue was not whether but when the government would commit itself to legislation, and what form it would approve—for women, for home workers, for workers. Supporters of the home work proposition appeared to win the first battle, over the terms of yet another parliamentary inquiry into sweating, but they lost the war. The Select Committee (an ad hoc committee of M.P.'s, appointed by the government), which sat in 1907 and 1908, was confined by its terms of office to investigating home work but was loaded with supporters of the minimum wage.

In the summer of 1906, Liberal Prime Minister Sir Henry Campbell-Bannerman refused a royal commission on sweating, even when urged to admit that "the greatest pressure came from wages as well as from sanitation, that the law could not interfere with that matter," and that, therefore, the government must take action.[30] Asked to devote government time to Dilke's bill, Campbell-Bannerman declined summarily, although privately NASL obtained a more encouraging response.[31] NASL therefore developed a dual strategy. Dilke's original bill was kept on the agenda, with only marginal amendments and a new name, the Sweated Industries Bill.[32] Meanwhile, NASL monitored developments within government and lobbied assiduously.

Home Secretary Gladstone's decision in 1906 to send Ernest Aves, a Home Office civil servant, to examine the workings of wages boards in Australia and New Zealand was more than likely a delaying tactic. The model of the "great sociological and legislative laboratories of the Antipodes" was already well known and had become politicized and somewhat of a liability to minimum wagers, although they continued to cite Australasia's achievements.[33] By 1908, when Aves reported, skepticism was widespread. Margaret MacDonald had seen for herself. "My own experience in an investigation . . . on the spot in Australia and New Zealand two years ago, is largely responsible for my opposition to the proposed adaptation of similar legislation to 'remove' sweating here," she claimed.[34] Critics were pleased to point out that Australian legislation had been used to regulate unions and reported evasion by Chinese firms as proof of the impossibility of enforcement and the dangers of foreign competition. Critics also sensibly kept in mind the structural differences of the Australian economy, arguing that even with easier enforcement in a smaller work force and smaller cities, even given the shortage of female labor that characterized Australia, the law had failed to end sweating.[35]

Aves proved cautious and bureaucratic. His personal dislike of the idea kept slipping out as he attempted to report the facts both fairly and unfavorably. An Australian evaluation, he reported, was "a very strange mixture" of the "favourable and unfavourable. At the first blush it seems almost entirely unfavourable, . . . but if one reads it more carefully, there is a good deal that means approval in it." He admitted that wages boards appeared to have raised wages, that sweating in the clothing trades had largely disappeared, and that public opinion favored the legislation. But he found unique Australian circumstances to account for these successes, and when he did express a view it was that "my own feeling is that there are so many other grave complexities, and I do not even know, in connection with certain trades, whether it would be economically possible . . . and the legal superstructure that it seems to me would have to follow any attempt at present to fix a legal wage seems to me so formidable that I am driven back from the acceptance of the view that it is possible to fix a legal rate."[36]

Aves's report had a mixed reception. Margaret MacDonald seized on it, writing angrily to Clementina Black as they fought over endorsement by the WIC: "We all agreed to let the Council wait for Mr. Aves's Report. Well! Are you willing now to recommend it to mould its opinions upon the Report? If so it will decide that there is 'serious danger of giving to the community a fresh and harmful lesson in administrative helplessness . . . and thus constituting a fresh injury to the community.'"[37] The home secretary was forewarned of Aves's ambivalent report: "I believe it will be favourable, but that he considers the application of the Australian scheme *in toto* to England would not be practicable." He turned this to his advantage by recommending to the Cabinet that the time had come to decide for themselves what they wanted.[38]

The Home Office may have been inefficient and resistant to new ideas, and the home secretary, Herbert Gladstone, indecisive.[39] But Gladstone had taken a second significant step toward eventual legislation. In a "gratifying announcement" to the first annual meeting of NASL, Sir Charles Dilke reported that "the Government had consented to appoint a Select Committee to consider and report upon the question of sweating in trades in which there was home work, and the creation of wages boards as suggested in the Bill of the League."[40] Dilke glossed over the full remit of the Select Committee, "to consider and Report upon the conditions of Labour in Trades in which HOME WORK is prevalent and the proposals, including those for the establishment of WAGES BOARDS and the licensing of Work Places, which have been made for the remedying of existing abuses."[41] NASL had waged a considerable campaign over the commissioning of the Select Committee by Gladstone, in a contest for control between supporters of home work and licensing, trade regulation and the minimum wage.

A. G. Gardiner, chairman of the NASL Executive Committee as well as Cadbury's editor, wrote blatantly asking that the committee be rigged. "As Mrs. Gladstone, whose interest in the subject is greatly appreciated by us, knows," he opened, in a bid for her husband's attention, "the League is unanimous in the view that concentration on the single question of the minimum wage is the most hopeful and practicable cause." He was anxious not to "blur the immediate issue and to dissipate our force." Therefore, "we all hope that the reference will be as definite & restricted as possible, that it shall be assumed that the evil has been abundantly revealed & that the only question for consideration is that of possible remedies & that the Committee shall be strong in sympathy and capacity rather than numbers."[42] Dilke discussed both terms of reference and membership in more detail, with Arthur Henderson, the Labour co-sponsor of Dilke's bill, and Gladstone. Henderson wanted to cut the reference to licensing, and Dilke concurred: "The Committee of the Anti-Sweating League are strongly opposed to licensing workplaces, & the Inspectors of the Home Office are so fiercely against it that I have hardly dared open my mouth on the subject for many years." A diplomatic solution might be that licensing should "not be excluded but only not suggested." Dilke forwarded, but did not support, Henderson's other proposals, that the committee should consider Wages Boards "for the feeble and more specially sweated industries" along with "the application and administration of existing laws" more effectively than at the present to trades without wages boards. There were negotiations, also, on the size of the committee, with Gladstone hoping to air all views in a large committee prior to drafting legislation, Dilke and Henderson preferring a small and purposive group.[43]

In the end, the committee had twenty-one members and a remit to study wages boards *and* licensing, in home work industries. Liberal Sir Thomas Whittaker took the chair, and Dilke's nominees Henderson, Masterman, and Money, plus several more committed supporters of the minimum wage, were on the roster. Ramsay MacDonald was neither on the committee nor on record as trying to influence its formation, but Gladstone's insistence on giving the licensing proposal equal standing with wages boards left the issue open.

The Select Committee on Home Work did not take its name too literally but "considered such matters connected with labour in factories and workshops, in trades in which Home Work is prevalent, as seemed to be connected with and bear upon the purpose of our inquiry."[44] The committee sat during the summer of 1907 and in 1908, with expert witnesses from the civil service, business, nonindustrial unions, and reform groups. The serious and detailed discussion ranged across the nature of sweating, current law and its enforcement, and possible new measures. The majority of witnesses did favor some form of minimum wage, but it seems unlikely that the witness list was fixed. Rather, both public and expert opinions were becoming concentrated in support of the minimum wage.

The home secretary advised the Cabinet in February 1908, after the first round of hearings, that "two remedies have been proposed for the great and admitted evil of sweating: (1) A system of licensing . . . This plan, which is backed by Mr. Ramsay MacDonald, has few supporters, and for present purposes may be put aside; (2) the establishment of Wages Boards . . ." The political situation, as Gladstone assessed it, was that minimum wage legislation would be welcomed by most employers and would meet little opposition in Parliament, carrying the majority of Liberals ("I don't know who will vote against it, excepting, perhaps, Mr. Harold Cox"), Labour ("which has placed this question next in importance to the grant of Old Age Pensions and the question of the unemployed") and even a "large section of Conservatives."[45] With the text of their own Sweated Industries bill under review by the committee, at the request of the Cabinet, NASL had progressed.[46] They turned their attention to what might appear in the report of the Select Committee, due that summer.

In July 1908, the Select Committee recommended that "there should be legislation with regard to the rates of payment made to Home Workers," that such legislation should at first be "tentative and experimental," and that "Wages Boards should be established in selected trades to fix minimum time and piece rates of payment for Home Workers in those trades."[47] The report was a victory for minimum wagers: it defined sweating solely by low wages, "to mean that work is paid for at a rate which . . . yields to [the workers] an income which is quite insufficient"; it declared that the proposal for Wages Boards "goes to the root of the matter"; and it confirmed that wage regulation was an entirely legitimate function of government. As to how wage regulation might be implemented, "Your Committee attach special importance to the experience and opinion of Mr. Askwith, who for many years has, from time to time, rendered most valuable service by acting as Arbitrator and Conciliator in trade disputes of various kinds." The report also removed the irritant of the MacDonalds' licensing proposal, declaring it both undesirable and impracticable. The only question between Margaret MacDonald and Mary Macarthur now was whether Wages Boards would work, a practical concern that Macarthur, at least, was ready to have settled by experience.[48]

The report made no direct distinction of sex. Shortly before its publication, Macarthur heard that the recommendation for minimum wage legislation would apply to women only: "Rumour has been busy . . . and if the lying jade speaks truly for once, limitations of a most serious character have been suggested . . . it is proposed that the Act should apply to women only. This, it will be seen, not only excludes men, but also withholds the benefits to be conferred by the proposed legislation from children and young persons."[49] Rumor had not lied about Chairman Whittaker's intention to suggest that "the experiment should be limited to women home workers, as their case is the most difficult and urgent, and they are individually and collectively the least able to help themselves, and consequently most need the assistance of legislation." But it was only a suggestion: "The general opinion of the Committee, however, was that it was undesirable to make any distinction as regards the sex of workers."[50]

Understanding a problem as one for women does not necessarily lead to legislating in sex-specific terms. The committee's failure to carry through Whittaker's plan may have reflected a conceptual confusion between women and workers in the minds of many of those involved. A surprised interjection by Conservative Arthur Fell illustrates the common assumption. An assistant inspector of factories was speaking when Fell interrupted, "I notice we were both led into the error of calling the worker he; . . . I think you are the first witness who has really described them as men; we have always been talking of women and children?" The witness spoke of London, where "most of the outworkers are men. Taking them generally, as I say, in all these smaller light trades they would be women."[51] Whittaker himself assumed that a minimum wage law, however written, would effectively apply to women: "As a matter of fact, the overwhelming majority of the home workers whose earnings and conditions of labour are such as to be brought within the scope of the operations of the proposed Wages Boards are women. The number of men home workers whose rates of payment would be expected to be determined by these boards are extremely few."[52]

Confusion was multiplied by the committee's official concern with home work, which led it to ignore Tuckwell's insistence that "it is very difficult to give you evidence about home work without touching upon factory work, because the same class of workers are employed in factories and in workshops, and are also doing home work; of course, work is very often done at home after they have done their work at a factory."[53] Gender was hidden in the language but assured in the practice when Whittaker reported that it "was decided to recommend the limitation of [Wages Boards] to home workers." He believed that, for the most part, "the case of home workers is a special and distinct one, and should be considered and dealt with separately."[54] Home workers, he explained, needed the work, but were not competitive with factory workers. In a joint board their interests would often be opposed. Putting his finger on the problem of organization without mentioning gender, he had found home workers "so helpless, and entirely without organisation. It will not be so easy to get them to meet or act together, or to secure the election or selection by them of suitable representatives for the boards. The factory hands work together, have much more leisure, and are far more capable of organisation and united action."[55]

The minimum wage was recommended in gender-neutral terms but embedded in a traditional view of gender roles and of the family. The wife and mother was assumed to be a worker only under unfortunate circumstances or in a supplementary role to the husband. The report categorized home workers: the employer with a workshop and employees in his (sic) home; the employer in his

(again) own home, employing "his own family"; and "persons who do not employ any other person, but who undertake work for others, and do it in their
own homes." Identifying the third group as the problem, they classified these
"persons" with telling detail:

> 1. Single women, widows, wives deserted by or separated from their husbands,
> and wives whose husbands are ill or unable to work. . . .
> 2. Wives who obtain work when their husbands are out of employment. . . .
> 3. Wives and daughters of men in regular employment, who wish to increase
> the family income.[56]

Yet, while identifying women by their family status, the committee gave no
consideration to the current issue of the family wage—payment to male workers of a rate calculated as sufficient to maintain a family. Nor did members of
the committee evidence any desire to push women out of the work force, except where they were "old or crippled, or in feeble health."[57] For all its conventional assumptions, the minimum wage was radical in assuming the fact of
women working, for whatever reasons, and in attempting to guarantee their
adequate remuneration for that work.[58]

Despite a contemporary upsurge of interest and concern in the standards of
motherhood, there was little talk about protecting the "mothers of the race."[59]
Nor was the tone denigratory. It was not that women did not possess the ability
to work or to organize on their own behalf. It was simply, according to Whittaker, that in the case of the women home workers "we have the problem in its
most aggravated form."[60] The committee report attributed "small earnings" to
"Women home workers, because they are very poor and helpless, and work
separately, are unorganised, and cannot act together to promote common interests and secure better and uniform rates of payment. They have to bear more
than their share of the consequences of uncertainty and irregularity in the
trades in which they are engaged; and they are powerless to resist the tendency
to reduce rates, which is caused by the keen competition of employers to un-
dersell each other."[61]

Macarthur, however, was right to sound the alarm over the arbitrary and
inseparable distinctions of gender and workplace. She was furious at the "farci-
cal" limitation to home work: "If a legal minimum wage is to be fixed for home
workers only, the results will certainly not be such as to justify the experiment,
and, personally, I would rather see the Bill defeated than passed into law in a
form so mutilated as to be almost unrecognisable by the original promoters, and
worse than useless to the great body of workers it was designed to benefit."[62]
Perhaps responding to her outrage, supporters on the committee managed to
insert two potentially significant small clauses. Money added the statement that
"while our evidence has been chiefly concerned with Home Workers, it has
been shown that very low rates of remuneration are by no means confined to
them, but are not infrequently the lot of factory workers also in the trades in
which Home Work is prevalent."[63] His Liberal colleague, G. P. Gooch, added
a single sentence to the recommendations on Wages Boards: "If these Wages

Boards were found to be successful they might be extended to other workers in the trades in which Home Work is prevalent."[64]

Margaret MacDonald was left almost isolated in her opposition to the minimum wage. She did her best to undermine the Select Committee's conclusion, spreading inside information that it had been hopelessly divided, carrying its recommendations by only two votes. She wrote indignantly to Clementina Black that "my husband thinks it more logical to apply the bill to homeworkers only if you have it at all; and the Home Work Committee themselves, I believe, look upon their decision as a compromise. (on Mr. Gooch's authority I say that.)"[65] But the committee's report conveyed no doubt but that the problem of sweating was one of the economy, not of sanitary conditions or the moral standards of home life. There was a significant shift within their economic analysis, however, from concern for an exploitative pathology in the market to an emphasis on a loss of efficiency in the economy. The poor needed home work, but home work represented a cost to the nation. The committee was consequently willing to contemplate the reduction of home work, which would result from the higher costs of minimum wages. Their rationale was the familiar one of parasitism: "If a trade will not yield such an income to average industrious workers engaged in it, it is a parasite industry, and it is contrary to the general well-being that it should continue. Experience, however, teaches that the usual result of legislation of the nature referred to is not to kill the industry, but to reform it."[66]

Such comments, and the observation that the committee had "been impressed by the testimony [it had] received to the effect that most, if not indeed all, employers would be glad to have fixed a minimum rate of payment and conditions below which neither they nor their competitors should be allowed to go," suggest a different motivation from that of the WTUL. These were the arguments of people who saw stability—industrial, social, or political—as the primary victim of sweating.[67] Organizations such as the Chambers of Commerce, and individual businessmen such as George and Edward Cadbury, did support both unions and legislation in the interests of industrial stability and hence in their own interest. In this view, they were at one with Fabian socialists such as Beatrice Webb, who quoted the "enlightened capitalist" approvingly: "More recently Mr. Edward Cadbury, a large employer of labour, advocated Trade Unionism for women and girls. 'If good discipline is to be maintained,' he writes, 'There must be justice without favouritism, a high moral tone, a sense of self-respect, and *esprit de corps* among the workers.'"[68] Clearly also such businessmen preferred not to see married women working. They would benefit if employment was concentrated in their factories. But they also adhered to the ideal of women's domestic and maternal role. So Edward Cadbury and his associate George Shann supported a living wage, by which they meant that "a man must receive sufficient to enable him to keep himself in a state of efficiency and at the same time to rear a family to a standard equal to his own. This means that a man's wife has to receive payment indirectly through her husband for her domestic work, including child-bearing and the rearing of children."[69] They also felt less compunction than many reformers, at the prospect of minimum wage legislation pricing home workers out of the market, for, as Shann testified to the Select Committee, "the evil of the present system, especially in regard to the children, is so great that the benefit of the greatest number would come in."[70]

But control, of society and of women, was not their only motivation. Self-interest, Quaker humanitarian traditions and the dominant social constructions of women and the family coincided, allowing families like the Cadburys to justify their support of the antisweating movement without contradiction. And the situation in which the cycle of undercutting by sweating employers did both menace their own businesses and create an exploited and helpless class of workers, many of whom were women carrying the double burden of work and home responsibilities, left them with little option but to invite criticism, whether by ignoring the problem or by intervening. But in allying with Cadburys, Liberals, and other agents of the existing order, socialists like Macarthur and MacDonald were recognizing the dilemma of many radical movements, of choosing between the attainable and the ideal. There were many shadings of position among the minimum wagers, from the women whose theory of structural helplessness made the minimum wage a step toward self-organization and self-respect for sweated labor, to these welfare capitalists. As became apparent in the final stages of the drafting of legislation, there was also more than one opinion within the institutions of the state.

ADMINISTRATIVE POLITICS AND THE TRADE BOARDS BILL

The Select Committee report in July 1908 coincided with the opening of the final stage of the minimum wage campaign. The goal of industrial stability now loomed larger, and home work and gender faded into the background. NASL and the WTUL had kept the issue in the public eye, with a large demonstration in January 1908, public meetings up and down the country, exhibits in circulation, and the Sweated Industries Bill still on the agenda. In February, Gladstone had submitted his memorandum to the Cabinet, concluding that "under these circumstances, the Government will have to consider the course it will take."[71] Political changes now brought the minimum wage within sight of the statute book. Campbell-Bannerman, conservative on social reform, resigned as prime minister in April and was succeeded by H. H. Asquith. Asquith appointed Winston Churchill, an ambitious radical Liberal, to the Cabinet position of president of the Board of Trade, a department with its own ambitions to rise from minor to major rank.[72]

Responsibility for industry was divided among Home Office, Board of Trade, and city and county councils centrally supervised by the Local Government Board. Up to 1908, sweating had been the province of the Home Office, who administered the Factory Acts, and women's wages and deductions had been monitored by the Home Office Woman Inspectorate.[73] The minimum wage was associated with these responsibilities and first fell into the hands of the department that inspected premises, not the department (the Board of Trade) that oversaw industrial relations and operated the legal machinery of conciliation and arbitration. The Board of Trade already had considerable experience of wages and wage bargaining because of its responsibility for administration of the Conciliation Act of 1895, and had also developed a far more sophisticated statistical base than had the old-fashioned Home Office.[74] By mid-1908, civil servants had initiated discussions about the appropriate institutional home for legislation. In August, the influential permanent secretary to the Board of Trade, Hubert Llewellyn Smith, wrote to Churchill that he was working on "such problems as Bankruptcy amendment, casual labour, and the sweated trades. The last named question will give some trouble next year after the report of the Select Committee on Home-Workers. The question will arise: if there is to be legislation on what lines should it proceed, and should it be in charge of the Home Office or Board of Trade? The latter question will be partly determined by the answer to the former."[75]

The transfer of responsibility to the Board of Trade had been signaled by discussions between Home Secretary Gladstone and George Askwith back in July.[76] Askwith, the much-respected witness to the Select Committee, was an assistant secretary in the Board of Trade and had been employed by that department for some years as their representative in arbitration proceedings. Transferring minimum wage policy to the Board of Trade removed it from a department accustomed to administering laws relating to hours and conditions, particularly of women workers, to one accustomed to monitoring the wages and industrial relations of organized industries. According to Roger Davidson, its expertise "as a data-bank for late-Victorian government," was as important a source of the new primacy of the Board of Trade in labor policy as was the ambition of Churchill.[77] In the case of the minimum wage, the two impulses worked together. Churchill had announced an interest in social reform, arguing that an alliance between Liberals, Radicals, and Labour made possible the implementation of a Minimum Standard "below which competition cannot be allowed, but above which it may be continued healthy and free, to vivify and fertilise the world." His proposals noted that Parliament had approved "the institution of Wages Boards in certain notoriously 'sweated' industries, and this principle may be found capable of almost indefinite extension in those industries which employ parasitically underpaid labour."[78]

The heavyweight deputation from NASL, led by the archbishop of Canterbury, visited the prime minister in December 1908 to urge "immediate legislation to insure the fixing of a legal minimum wage for sweated workers." Asquith stonewalled, as Macarthur reported: "Mr. Asquith's reply was of the kind which is known as 'sympathetic.' Out of a conglomeration—verbally perfect—of 'ifs' and 'mights,' 'buts,' 'nevertheless,' and 'howevers' one extracted the information that the Premier personally was on our side, but there was no trace of any pledge of immediate, or indeed of any, action."[79] In fact, by the eighteenth of the month, Gladstone was handing over the brief to Churchill, with some friendly advice. First, Churchill should make full use of Askwith, with his "rare combination of enthusiasm and practical knowledge." Second, "the creation of public opinion has been largely due to the anti-sweating League, headed by G. Cadbury and Gardiner of the D.N. [*Daily News*]. I venture to hope you will take them into council for all they are worth. The sec^y is a little man of energy who knows the ropes of the public movement & it will be worth your while to see him." Third, "on the other side is Ramsay MacDonald whose opposition to the minimum wage has long ago reached the personal stage. But he stands alone among his fellows."[80] When Asquith reported his program for 1909 to the king in January, a "Sweated Industries Bill which will provide much-needed machinery for the regulation of unorganised trades" was included.[81]

By that time, Churchill, Llewellyn Smith, and George Askwith had almost finished drafting the Trade Boards Bill. Premier Asquith appointed his brother-in-law, H. J. Tennant, as Churchill's junior minister. Tennant's assets included his familiarity with labor questions (assisted by his association with the WTUL), his wife May (formerly Lady Dilke's secretary, a factory inspector in the Home Office, and "far the most *capable* of the women who have given their brains and lives to industrial reform"), and not least his wealth: his "business training & connections, would [make him] *persona grata* (or *gratiori* than some others) to the City & to Capital."[82]

The team wasted no time. At the end of December, Churchill expected to be "working in London continuously from 5th Jany onwards, & hope to have definite proposals before Cabinets begin." By 12 January, he was writing to Asquith that, after a "vy fruitful week here" he was ready to bring the bill to Cabinet.[83]

The bill drafted in January became the Trade Boards Act in October, with little change and little opposition. But although the drafters took note of Dilke's Sweated Industries Bill, the change of name indicated a change of perspective, in its definition of the problem, the source of initiative, the structure of the Boards, the implications for women, and the calculation of the minimum wage. Most changes can be attributed to the outlook and interests of the Board of Trade.[84]

The Trade Boards Act did not define sweating. The machinery would be set in motion when the department was satisfied that an industry met the criteria of low wages and an unorganized and immobile work force. This was no more restrictive than the Sweated Industries Bill, but the conditions were expressed more precisely and were primarily conditional on the documentation of wage levels. The Sweated Industries Bill was casual by comparison, as if everyone understood the dimensions of the problem of industries with "men, women and children overworked, underpaid, underfed, living in unhealthy and often degrading surroundings."[85] In the government bill, the Board of Trade gained control of the scope of the policy and ensured that implementation would be dependent on criteria and statistics that they alone could provide.

The centralizing tendency of the Trade Boards Act even made some supporters uneasy.[86] The process worked from the bottom up in Dilke's bill. Employers and employees could request a Wages Board: "Any six matchbox makers or button carders or other sweated workers may ask the Home Secretary to make inquiry into the conditions of their trade, and to set up a wages board should inquiry suggest that a board is desirable."[87] The act reversed the initiative, placing it in the hands of the Board of Trade. The Wages Boards of the Sweated Industries Bill were to be composed of employers, workers, and a neutral chairperson. Churchill emphasized the innovation made by the Trade Boards Act: "The mainspring consists in the 3 paid permanent members, common to all the Boards in any trade . . . who are to grip, guide & coordinate the operations of local Wages boards. . . . You will see running through this organism the same idea wh the Germans call 'Paritätisch'—joint and equal representn of masters & men plus the skilled permanent impartial element."[88] There was a considerable difference between the presence of the state in the chair and the presence of state appointees with equal weight in the discussions. The government, like NASL, envisaged regional subboards, and the public members were to ensure against regional competition and undercutting. But Churchill also spoke repeatedly of their role as the disinterested coordinators of policy, the liaison with those equally "expert impartial officials" from the Board of Trade who would service the boards.[89]

Two points that the government bill did *not* mention were significant. First, the Trade Boards Bill referred to women or home work only to ensure that women and home workers would be represented on appropriate boards. In this, it followed the Sweated Industries Bill and the strong feelings of those such as Mary Macarthur that a gender-neutral law would help equalize women's status in the work force: "The boards would tend also by their determinations to fix a general minimum standard of payment for women. Thus, the term sweating would be given sharper meaning, and fair wages clauses in the contracts of public bodies would begin to apply to women as well as to men."[90] On the face of it, the gender-blindness of the Trade Boards Bill was a victory for NASL and a public recognition of equal rights in the work force.

But the language of debate always conveyed confusion over whether the government bill, like the NASL bill, was gendered in all but name. Liberal Alfred Lyttelton supported the government bill because he understood it to be for women: "The condition of some poor women and girls in this trade is infinitely behind that of slaves. When we reflect that these people have no political power, I think their condition makes a most cogent appeal to the chivalrous instincts of the House, and . . . is a menace to the essential well-being of the State."[91] Unionist M.P. Ebenezer Parkes, on the other hand, thought the government bill would be a measure against women, because it seemed to him "directed more particularly against home work, not against factory work."[92] Churchill rigorously confined himself to class: "It is a serious national evil that any class of His Majesty's subjects should receive less than a living wage in return for their utmost exertions."[93]

In theory, by basing the bill on statistical determinations of "low-paid workers," the issue of gender was neutralized. In practice, the gendered structure of the distribution of jobs and their valuation in wage scales, resulting in the segregation of women in the lowest-paid occupations, should have meant that the law would be applied to women. But the specification of industries to be covered was never free of politics and prejudice. NASL had envisioned that the first trades covered by its bill would be tailoring (46 percent female), dressmaking (99 percent), and shirtmaking (96 percent).[94] The Board of Trade first proposed tailoring, lace making, blouse- and shirtmaking, box making, and brush making.[95] The act scheduled tailoring, paper boxes (90 percent female), lace (62 percent), and chain making (between 30 and 40 percent). The apparent rise in the proportion of men to be covered might mean that male workers had seen the advantage of the legislation, or that the overall figures for these occupations disguised gender differentials in pay within them so that women would be the principal beneficiaries; or even that revised statistics found the lowest pay after all in mixed occupations. In fact, around two-thirds of the workers covered by the act since 1909 have been women, an outcome that seems above all to have been a combination of pragmatism and political interest, in which gender concerns have continued to play a part.

The inclusion of chain making illustrates how gendered perceptions could override technical criteria, for, as Conservative Sir Frederick Banbury was glad to point out, the House had been told that "there was a trade union at Cradley."[96] Despite this, the chain-makers won a minimum wage, an outcome ensured by the offense caused by the nature of the women chain-makers' work. They were engaged, as a House of Lords report had said, in "work often unsuitable to their sex."[97] The "domestic" tasks of sewing and many other of the light, dexterous tasks performed by working women offended not because of the nature of the work itself, but only because of the sweatshop conditions in which it was done. But the tone changed from straightforward description to moral outrage when investigators came to chain making: "As one looks in the shop lit up with the glare of the fire and hot irons and sees the women bare-armed, bare-chested, perspiring and working with feverish eagerness, . . . the shock to the sensibilities of the visitor is almost overpowering."[98] Faced with intense pressure from Macarthur and her allies, Parliament had no wish to be seen not to act on such an inflammatory issue.

A second omission from the act left a second major decision open to the play of political interests. The law contained no formula for the value of the minimum wage. This was a bill "for the establishment of Trade Boards." Parliament authorized boards; the boards sought a rate appropriate for their industry. In practice, Trade Boards started by checking prevailing wages in related industries, but this was not a requirement, and, after four years of practice, the experienced R. H. Tawney could still ask: "On what principles are minimum rates to be fixed? Should they be 'the highest that the trade will bear'? Or should they be based on some rough idea as to what constitutes a living wage? Should there be a flat rate for all the workers in an industry? Or should the minimum fixed vary from one district to another?" The best answer he could give himself was that it was "obvious that questions such as these cannot be answered with confidence till after the lapse of a much longer period than has yet intervened."[99]

NASL had intended each wages board to "turn to the consideration of the problems of the trade with which it is dealing, and . . . fix such wages of time or piece as seem to it possible or desirable, having regard to the whole circumstances of the case," and had allowed that rates might "vary in accordance with the variation of cost of living." At the start of the campaign, in the 1890s, the minimum wage was by definition related to the living wage. The Webbs' argument that state intervention was justifiable only in parasitic industries paying less than subsistence rates required that the minimum wage be a living wage. If the trade was unable to pay a living wage, then it had no right to exist.[100] The Sweated Industries Bill attempted to reconcile the wish of NASL to "secure to each sweated worker a wage upon which at any rate life can be maintained," and the business pressure to stabilize the sweated trades without destroying them.[101] The government sidestepped this conflict, delegating power to the boards to do as they thought fit. This "flexibility" was a strength, according to Churchill, listing the merits of his draft to the Cabinet: "Great flexibility of procedure, treatment which varies with the complexity of each special case, a wide discretion entrusted to Boards of persons interested in the fortunes of each trade and each district, and the guidance, at every stage, of expert impartial officials, are the necessary features of the administrative machinery proposed."[102]

The Trade Boards Act

When the Board of Trade bill had its second reading in the House of Commons on 28 April 1909, there was little opposition. NASL had built an effective cross-party coalition behind the principle of a minimum wage. Government revisions and further assurances during the debate made the measure yet harder to oppose. Churchill wrote a note to his wife from his seat in the Commons: "The Trade Boards Bill has been beautifully received & will be passed without a division. . . . All opposition has faded away."[103] The residual anxieties of surviving opponents were mostly halfhearted and easily set at rest.

With his promise of strictly limited use of the act, Tennant reassured doubters among trade unionists more than those free marketeers who saw the bill as a license to invade the entire economy. He calmed fears of cheap imports among members seeking tariff reform, and Dilke intervened to reassure Irish members that their wage differentials could be maintained.[104] Tennant exuded confidence that local interests would be safeguarded by the sub-boards and that it was proper to give the Board of Trade, "the authority responsible to Parliament," such considerable powers. He and Churchill were accommodatingly ready to negotiate details in committee, being sure "an arrangement can be arrived at between the hon. Gentlemen below the Gangway and ourselves which we practically came to yesterday, by which we may arrive at a working agreement."[105]

Such last-minute negotiations worried NASL: "The text of the Government measure was for some time not available. When it appeared, its provisions for inspection and enforcement were considered to be unsatisfactory, and this opinion was not entirely removed by the reassuring speech in which Mr. Churchill introduced it to the House of Commons."[106] The cumbersome mechanisms compromised between NASL's preference for authority with the boards, the Board of Trade's desire to "grip, guide and coordinate," and opponents' insistence that crucial decisions be made in Parliament. The end result was that the Trade Boards fixed wages, allowing a statutory three months for objections. The Board of Trade, after a further six months, was enabled to make the rates obligatory. But Parliament would have the final say on the inclusion of new trades. NASL could only hope that the success of the first boards would "be of so unequivocal a character as to ensure that Parliament will ultimately accept a more flexible method of extension."[107] Gertrude Tuckwell kept watch on the final stages of legislation, mindful of the warning of one parliamentarian that the House of Lords might yet make difficulties and that if they did, "there is great danger that Govt will weaken."[108] Such fears proved groundless, and the act received the Royal Assent on 20 October.

Minimum wagers did not disband after their twenty-year fight. NASL honored Dilke and celebrated with a banquet, then turned its attention "from propaganda and investigation to the more definite and difficult task of assisting the operations of an Act of Parliament."[109] Macarthur and Mallon became board members. Had they achieved what the minimum wage campaign set out to do in the 1890s? Minimum wagers had won the principle of state intervention in wage setting, no small victory. "I feel proud to tell you," Macarthur acknowledged to American colleagues, "that we have got so far ahead and are actually interfering with the sacred matter of wages."[110] They had achieved official recognition that workers, not just women and children, were, through no fault of their own, so placed as to be helpless in the face of economic forces and ruthless employers. Indeed, they won a remarkable degree of unanimity about their measure by criminalizing employers, first in public opinion and then in law. "We called this bill the sweated industries bill, and the title turned out to be good tactics, because none of the manufacturers dared to come into the open to oppose it. They did not wish to be dubbed 'sweaters,'" Macarthur claimed.[111] The minimum wage campaign had fought for a class, against a class enemy.

A formulation in terms of class rather than gender meant the expansion of factory legislation without dependence on easy arguments about the "weaker sex" or patriotic arguments about motherhood. The minimum wage debate was a small advance for the equal rights of women at work in its recognition of women as workers, and the apparent acceptance that although women might be at work because of their family role, they should not be paid on the basis of their family role. It was to be a minimum wage law for workers, not a family wage law for mothers and fathers; a law addressed to malfunctions of the economy, not to the moral economy of the family.

If the minimum wage debate was an advance for the understanding of women's place in the economy, however, and the language of the law an achievement in not making distinctions on grounds of sex, it was also an object lesson in the problems of imposing such nominally neutral terms on an economy that was far from neutral in structure. The intended coverage depended on equality of condition, not sex. Whether this would in practice be a law for women workers was left to subsequent battles over the inclusion and exclusion of industries. Just as important, although it did not require family or prevailing wages—that is, unequal wages for women—neither did it explicitly instruct on the principle of equal pay for women. By leaving the fixing of wage scales to the Trade Boards and permitting their application "universally to the trade, or so as to apply to any special process in the work of the trade or to any special class of workers in the trade," the way was left open for the replication of existing sexist patterns of wage differentials.[112]

The Trade Boards Act, in the minds of many, was women's legislation, framed with conventional understandings of women's role in mind. Its terms, though ostensibly neutral with respect to gender, did not specify what was meant or intended by gender equality in an unequally structured and segregated economy. The experience of selecting industries for inclusion suggests that it is not enough, for the purpose of advancing equality between the sexes, to pass legislation that ignores, or maintains neutrality toward, existing inequalities. To break both the gendered structure of the labor market and the cultural preconceptions of women's work, a positive statement of equality rather than a nonprescriptive neutrality was needed. The Trade Boards Act allowed the status quo to be continued. It imposed requirements that narrowed inequalities at the bottom of the economic hierarchy but did nothing to abolish that hierarchy or to delineate an alternative.

There was nothing except administrative detail in the Trade Boards Act that was not talked about in the 1890s. Yet there were major changes in emphasis during the campaign. For a decade, the campaign was led by women's organizations, debated principally between women, and focused most sharply on the plight of women workers. Because women lacked direct access to political institutions, a coalition with men was essential if the cause was ever to be more than an interesting idea. The foundation of NASL in 1906 created this coalition, an unassailable alliance of industrial and political organizations. The compromises that followed, from causes including the perspective of businessmen like Cadbury, the transition from female to predominantly male leadership between 1906 and 1909, and the role of the Board of Trade were thought necessary for passage of a law. Had the original women's organizations been able to control it to the end, the standard of a living wage would surely have been more prominent, and the act stronger and more specific about who would benefit, and to what extent. The democratic potential would have been clearer and the bureaucratic grip less tight. Women's victories in the circumstances of national politics and administrative co-optation were real but negative—the prevention of the arbitrary and harmful distinctions that might have limited the law to women or to home workers alone.

The Trade Boards Act was a comprehensive compromise: wages were regulated but with such caution that the minimum wage in Britain remained a paper tiger; the law managed to be primarily a law for women without ever saying so; the relationship of minimum wage to family wage, living wage, market wage, and equal pay was dodged by the simple device of not defining the minimum wage at all. If business, unions, the state, the pressure groups, and women and men all could live with the legislation after 1909, the radical ideas involved in its formulation had surely been equivocated and rendered anodyne.

POSTSCRIPT: TRADE BOARDS AFTER 1909

From New Year's Day 1910, when the Trade Boards Act of 1909 came into force, until passage of the Wages Act of 1986, little changed in British minimum wage policy. Trade Boards were renamed Wages Councils (in 1945), and their numbers fluctuated. But the essential principle remained inclusion by government decision. Four boards were established in 1910 and a further five in 1913, covering half a million workers. Not one minimum wage had become legally enforceable under the complex procedure of the act by the outbreak of war in 1914. The war experience of economic management, in which labor played a major part, stimulated what Dorothy Sells described as "a new conception of democracy," a combination of the old idea of a National Minimum standard of living and the new idea of a corporatist structure of "industrial democracy."[113] Trade Boards provided a model of joint decision making by business, labor, and the state, with legislation already on the books. Momentarily it appeared that the Trade Boards Act might indeed be the precursor of dramatic change in the management of the British economy. Trade Boards would be transformed from an "ambulance" for victims of the economy to a juggernaut bringing radical change in the structure of industrial relations.[114]

The reaction bore witness to the limits of the victory won by minimum wagers in 1909. An ambulance would be tolerated by business; a juggernaut would not. The 1909 act threatened no established institutions; it only removed the destabilizing influence and widespread embarrassment of sweating, providing a measure of control at the margins. No wider application was tolerable to business interests. Unions welcomed temporary cooperation in wartime. In the postwar economic downturn and the return to normal adversarial industrial relations, organized labor manifested its old ambivalence toward the state, even as it lost power in a declining economy. Implementation reverted to the caution of 1909, with only three new boards established in 1921 and then none for a decade. The introduction of new boards followed political or economic, rather than statistical, guidelines—six between 1933 and 1939 to protect depressed industries, four each in 1947 and 1948 as, once again, corporatist wartime practice exemplified a comprehensive and guaranteed structure of labor relations. Wages Councils remained a little-known and broad-meshed safety net through the 1970s.

Until 1986, minimum wage rates varied between industries, maintained the complex formulas of time and piece rates, and recognized differentials in skill and process within industries. Such differentials often effectively discriminated between men and women and could do so legally until the Equal Pay and Sex

Discrimination Acts of 1970 and 1975 required equal wages for broadly similar work. The number of workers covered remained close to 10 percent of the work force, and the proportion of women remained close to two-thirds of the total. Only in the eighties, with a Conservative government determined upon abolition, and a new European politics, did a new era of minimum wage politics open.[115]

But in 1909, the future seemed to promise much. Despite the compromise and evasion of fundamental issues, the act was lauded as a triumph by British delegates to American labor conventions. Macarthur told the National Women's Trade Union League that "I don't think England quite realizes what it has done. It is simply a revolution. It means revolution in our industrial conditions."[116] Labour M.P. J. R. Clynes proudly reported to the American Federation of Labor that "we have begun quite a new legislative principle I hope to see extended the world over—the principle of fixing by law a human level of wages and conditions, below which no master's power can drive a human being. We have recently passed what is known as a Wages Boards Bill."[117] Modest compromise or revolution for Britain, the British boast did not fall on deaf ears. For the British minimum wage had recently been taken as a model for a new American attack on sweating, in what started as a simple transfer of an idea from one polity to the other and resulted in a long and different history across the Atlantic.

A Sex Problem

THE POLITICS OF DIFFERENCE, U.S.A., 1907–1921

IN THE UNITED STATES as in Britain, at the turn of the century sweating was widespread and alarming. American reformers responded to similar perceptions of similarly dire conditions, importing the solution of minimum wage policy during 1907–8 from Britain. Portents of a transformation in American hands from negotiating machinery for low-paid workers to a living wage for women were visible in 1908, when James Mallon of NASL shared a platform in Geneva with Florence Kelley of the National Consumers' League (NCL). Kelley became the leader of the American campaign and regularly sought advice from Mallon and NASL. At this first encounter, though, she was skeptical of Mallon and his scheme for a statutory minimum wage. Mallon cannot have endeared himself with a paper on "Ineffective Remedies"—which, though not targeted personally at Kelley, hit directly at her work. He ruled out both Consumers' Leagues themselves and the American legislation for licensing home work premises with which she had been involved for years. Kelley, in turn, was dismissive: Mallon's work was a second-best, for only in countries where the abolition of home work was a lost cause was it, no doubt, desirable to pursue the regulation of wages and Wages Boards.[1]

Kelley spoke of home work, Mallon of sweated workers, a conceptual choice that in Britain had represented the difference between a moralistic and gendered deprecation of the prevalence of women in sweated industries as against a class-oriented deprecation of an economic process of sweating that exploited both women and men. Kelley's first reaction, in terms of home work, might seem to signal an American predisposition to legislate for women. But Emilie Hutchinson, a student of women's wages, pointed to the logical flaw: "Resting as [minimum wage laws] do on the principle of establishing a living wage as the point in the wage scale below which rates may not fall, there is no logical reason for fixing it only for women. If the principle is sound for women's wages, it is also sound for men's. However this may be, in the United States the minimum-wage movement has been connected with the question of wages not primarily as a labor problem but as a sex problem."[2]

A history of women's labor laws, written by minimum wager Clara Mortenson Beyer for the Women's Bureau in 1929, located the "impetus to wage legislation" in a combination of news of the British act and the near-simultaneous publication of a series of major investigations of women's work by the federal Bureau of Labor, the Pittsburgh survey, and individual social scientists.[3] American laws did resemble the British Trade Boards Act, in their bold intention to regulate the wage relationship, their modest restriction of regulation to a defined and limited subgroup of workers, the mechanism of inquiries and wages boards, and legal sanctions to back the statutory wage. But American laws applied to women and children only. Unlike the freedom of British trade boards to reach consensus on wage rates, American boards were constrained by a cost-of-living formula.

The British economic formulation was imported into an American debate focused, by leaders like Kelley, on home work and gender. This was not, however, the *cause* of the American limitation of legislation to women. Both the prominence of the discourse of home work and the gendering of the minimum wage were products of circumstances disposing American reformers toward gender rather than class solutions to problems such as sweating. This chapter describes formative episodes in the political campaign in the United States from around 1907 to 1921. A network of reform organizations compensated for the fragmenting effect of federalism, creating a national campaign not dissimilar to Britain's. In the following chapter, I examine the legal framework that clinched the decision to respond to low wages in the sweated industries as a "sex problem."

ORIGINS: SWEATING IN THE UNITED STATES

The American minimum wage campaign was motivated by public concern about sweating, and the history of sweating in the United States had many parallels with Britain.[4] The explosive growth of American cities in the late nineteenth century consolidated the mass market, the physical conditions, and the growing work force upon which sweating thrived.[5] By the turn of the century, sweating occurred in the same industries as in Britain. It aroused disgust and dismay, fueled by the early association of sweating with the garment trades and the threat to consumers from diseased clothes. In 1897, Bliss's authoritative *Encyclopedia of Social Reform* associated sweating with "almost all branches of the clothing trade."[6] A decade later, sweating was widespread. The federal Bureau of Labor Statistics, reporting on women's work in 1907–9, listed low-paying industries from canning, cans, cigars, clocks, confectionery, core making, corsets, and crackers through woolen and worsted goods.[7]

Evidence collected for the New York State Factory Investigating Commission (FIC) in 1914 revealed a labor market structured, as in Britain, by sex and age. A survey of "over 104,000 employees" in 570 establishments determined that "in the main they were young men and girls. Three fifths for whom I have returns were females. The proportion varies in different trades, from 59 per cent. in the stores to 77 per cent. in the shirt making industry." In 1910, the census reported 25.2 percent of women in the labor force. They were disproportionately concentrated in the sweated trades.[8] Children formed a small but calculable proportion of the work force, in line again with the census estimate of 3.17 percent: "In the next place, as to their age, we found that over 60 per cent. were adults, about one-third between 16 and 20, and 4 per cent. were children, that is under the age of 16."[9]

The ethnic and racial composition of the work force differed from Britain. Many sweated workers were recent immigrants: "As to the nativity of the persons. We found that about 30 per cent. of all were foreigners." The ethnic and gender division of labor varied between industries, cities, and regions, although the underlying economic process remained the same.[10] Race, another major structural feature of the labor market, was barely an issue as yet. Most African-American men and women resided in the southern states and were employed principally in agriculture, the women also in domestic work. Their occupations met the objective definition of sweating as poor wages and conditions of work, but cultural and political definitions of industry excluded farm and domestic workers: sweating was consistently associated with urban white production and retail workers. For those black workers who were employed in northern low-paid industries, work in homes and small workshops could be an opportunity in the face of discrimination rather than a strategy of desperation.[11]

Americans, unlike the British, included retail store workers in their campaigns. Massachusetts and New York surveyed employment in department stores in anticipation of legislation, and in California the "first conferences were with the retail dry goods people."[12] Sales staff hardly fitted the classic image of the sweated industries, yet objectively they shared the low pay and long hours of the stereotypically ragged garment worker. The presence of active Consumers' Leagues, born out of middle-class women shoppers' consciences, almost guaranteed their inclusion.[13] In addition, there was no workers' organization remotely equivalent to the British National Union of Shop Assistants, spoken for in Parliament by Dilke, recruiting women like Mary Macarthur into labor politics. The American Retail Clerks Association, founded in 1890, based in a few cities mainly in the midwest, ambivalent on women's issues, and favoring voluntary schemes akin to those of Consumers' Leagues (until their first major strike in 1913) was hardly a presence.[14]

Estimates of wage rates were as problematic as in Britain. Howard Woolston, director of the FIC survey, quoted figures that assumed a full week's work and no deductions. Weekly pay ranged from five to fifteen dollars a week, with almost half the sample clustered "from five to ten dollars." But averages concealed wide variations between occupations and sexes: "For example, in the stores, one-half of all the male employees are quoted at rates less than fourteen dollars per week. One-half of all the females in the stores throughout the State are quoted at rates of less than seven and one-half dollars a week." Women reached the top rates for their sex, and thereby lost hope of betterment, some five to ten years earlier than men. And, as Mary Van Kleeck found in a study of the millinery trade in Manhattan, even skilled workers faced irregular, seasonal employment, so that "only 110, or 2.8 per cent., of 3983 women employed sometime in the course of that year were on the same payroll in the same shop for fifty-two weeks."[15]

The commission learned from the budgets of unskilled women that the thousands who earned "only $5, $6 and $7 a week" could have no more than "a cramped, subnormal way of life, a mere existing, not a real living."[16] Evidence from factory and shop workers, "establishments," and "payrolls," tended to underrepresent the older, married woman, more often working at home, usually for even less pay and longer hours. The number of documented sweated workers was swollen by thousands of home workers, whose lives were known only through anecdotal and propagandist reports, from journalists and reformers. Cynthia Daniels's estimate is that in 1910 up to 250,000 women may have been home workers in New York City alone. Their "wages differed dramatically between those working at home and those in the factory. On the average, women in the garment industry earned $6.00 per week, while homeworkers could earn only $3.60."[17] In 1910, the average weekly wage for manufacturing workers was $14.71 for a fifty-six-hour week, and for unionized manufacturing workers just over twenty dollars for a fifty-hour week.[18]

As the FIC learned, wages bore little relation to labor value: "Those that are unable to get employment at the prevailing rate of wages will go about offering their services for less, and they will displace other employees, who, in turn, will offer their labor for less, and displace still others, until it will get down to the point where we are now, the point where in a great many cases the wage that is paid is just a little above the starvation line, if it is there." Thus, "when the opponents of minimum wage legislation maintain that the establishment of a minimum wage will compel the State to pay a living wage regardless of what the employee may actually earn, regardless of what may be the value of what the employee produces, the answer is that the present conditions tend to establish a starvation wage regardless of the fact that the employee may actually earn a great deal more."[19]

The sorry condition of the sweated industries was reported in similar terms on both sides of the Atlantic. The data presented by the many inquiries was often inexact and sometimes biased, but it revealed such an overwhelming record of exploitation and suffering, and the studies so consistently validated each other, that, as in Britain, an influential sector of the public was convinced that here was a social problem demanding action.

The Massachusetts Campaign

The era of American legislation that opened with the Massachusetts law in 1912 was paralyzed by 1921 by political resistance and court challenges and was terminated with the rejection of the District of Columbia law by the Supreme Court in the *Adkins* case in 1923. Fifteen states, the District of Columbia, and Puerto Rico passed laws in this period.[20] These had the following in common: they excluded men; they required some form of wages board with worker and employer participation; they (almost all) identified recipients and set wages by a living wage standard; were mandatory, with legal penalties attached—except for Massachusetts, which attracted Kelley's scorn by providing only the sanction of publicity in local newspapers. "Massachusetts marches conservatively at the head of the line of experimenting states," she tartly observed.[21] State alliances generally comprised configurations of the same set of elements, as Clara Beyer noted: "Organized labor; factory inspectors and other officials charged with the enforcement of labor laws; bureaus of labor statistics; special legislative committees or commissions for the study of labor conditions; governors; pioneering employers; social, civic, philanthropic, and church groups; factual studies of conditions to be remedied by law; and, finally, the spirit of the time."[22] Beyer might have added academics, lawyers, and politicians to complete the typical coalition.

The Massachusetts campaign, a reasonably representative case, was part of a developing national network, and its methods and arguments were widely quoted and copied.[23] Massachusetts had pioneered other labor legislation, with an enforceable ten-hour day for women in 1874, strengthened to become a fifty-four-hour law in 1911, and a system of regulating industrial home work in tenements dating from 1891.[24] Even in this sympathetic environment, the regulation of wages was not proposed until 1908. Then leadership came from Beyer's "social, civic and philanthropic" category, from the interlocking memberships of women such as Mary Morton Kehew, Elizabeth Glendower Evans, and Wellesley professor Emily Greene Balch in the Women's Educational and Industrial Union (WEIU), the Women's Trade Union League (WTUL), and a network of interested organizations and experts, including, reluctantly at first, the state branch of the Consumers' League.[25]

WEIU President Kehew (also the first president of the National WTUL) initiated research into the conditions of working women in the Commonwealth. The WEIU annual report for 1908 reported an investigation of the expenditures of single women in Boston: "The purpose of this study is to help toward the establishment of a minimum wage for women, which shall be a living wage, by contributing reliable, vivid and readable information on the purchasing power of wages commonly received by women."[26] The WEIU was well connected with the men in power in state and city, was an effective lobbying organization, and, Sarah Deutsch reports, a "training ground for future female politicians . . . who would then become part of the appointive political structure."[27] WEIU researchers—Susan Kingsbury of Wellesley, for example—were also part of a national, reform-oriented, research network, women who "joined an appreciation for empirical details to a moral vision of social change."[28] Kingsbury compiled a manual of labor law for the WEIU and served on a commission on woman's work for the American Association for Labor Legislation (AALL) with leading minimum wagers.[29] Policy innovations traveled via such personal connections. The well-to-do reformer summered in Europe, spending some of her vacation in social investigation. Delegates attended international congresses. Academics read and exchanged analyses, discussing and recording ideas to be available if and when the appropriate moment arrived.[30]

Consumers' League of Massachusetts (CLM) president Mrs. Thomas Sherwin encountered the minimum wage in 1908, when she interviewed "the Anti-Sweat Shop League in London."[31] At first the CLM maintained its tradition of voluntary action: "[The league] contemplates no attempt at influencing legislation, but it has long been considering the advisability and practicability of requiring that its label shall carry with it the assurance that the worker by whom the labeled garment is made receives at least the minimum wage necessary for tolerable human existence."[32] A year later, the CLM echoed Margaret MacDonald: "[England and Germany] believe that sufficiently paid work may safely be done in tenements: that, given money enough, cleanliness, proper care of disease and consideration for younger children will follow. We think they do not allow sufficiently for ignorance, carelessness and greed and that our method of inspection and license is safer."[33] But momentum was building elsewhere. In 1909, Elizabeth Glendower Evans was in England. "I must confess," she recalled, "to being a somewhat tardy convert to minimum wage legislation. For a good while I could not see much in the proposition."[34] Evans may have been influenced by her British friend Ramsay MacDonald. "My original difficulty," she said, "was of expecting too much in the way of immediate results. I suppose I was looking for a panacea." But by 1911, she was a believer: "I do so much want to make good," she told the NWTUL convention as it applauded her appointment to a state commission, but "you must all be patient if we don't seem to bring the heaven down onto the earth possibly very soon."[35] Likewise, by 1910, Florence Kelley had set doubt aside and committed the NCL to the policy.

The Women's Trade Union League emerged as a leader. The NWTUL made the minimum wage a legislative demand in 1909.[36] In the spring of 1910, the Boston WTUL "called a conference of unionists and social workers to consider bringing in a minimum wage board bill. After much conferring, and upon the urgent advice of Mr. Brandeis, the League decided to postpone legislative work for another year but to have a tentative bill drawn for establishing trade boards and to appoint a committee to work upon this measure for the ensuing year."[37] In December, the Boston WTUL and WEIU voted to form a committee "which might bring into cooperation, to the end of minimum-wage legislation, the forces of organized labor, the consumers' league, and other groups who would naturally be interested." By February 1911, "the committee had grown to include, besides the Women's Trade Union League, the Consumers' League, the child labor committee (of Massachusetts), the Women's Educational and Industrial Union, the Central Labor Union of Boston, and the Massachusetts Branch of the American Association for Labor Legislation."[38] In March, the Boston WTUL was reported to be "the moving force behind the bill which has just been introduced into the Massachusetts legislature."[39] Campaign adviser and Harvard political economist Arthur Holcombe was secretary of the state AALL and a link to the academic community, enabling Evans cheerfully to note "for the benefit of those who think the minimum wage proposition fantastic and contrary to what is conceived as 'economic law' . . . that our Massachusetts bill was endorsed by pretty much the whole economic department of Harvard College."[40] The players had assembled in the short space of three years. Boston lawyer Louis Brandeis, who had persuaded a delay in 1910, now introduced H. LaRue Brown, who "was retained by the Women's Trade Union League of

Boston to head a legislative effort" designed to win an investigatory commission.[41] In May 1911, the legislature agreed to a commission to "study the matter of wages of women and minors" and report on the advisability of setting up Wage Boards.[42]

Legislators may have intended no more than a symbolic gesture, but they reckoned without Mrs. Evans. "Single-handed she instantly raised additional money, recruited a trained force and turned over her house as office space." The trained force was led by Molly Dewson, who became secretary to the commission and subsequently aide to Kelley, researcher for legal counsel Felix Frankfurter, a leader of the New York State campaign in the twenties, and later facilitator of appointments and policies to the Roosevelt administration. Dewson remembered how Evans "reserved to herself her library and bedroom. We swarmed like locusts over every available inch, resigning the dining room table only long enough for her cook, the President of the Union of Domestic Servants, to serve everyone luncheon."[43] In January 1912, the Commission recommended a bill.[44] A period of intense lobbying followed, led by LaRue Brown. When the bill passed in June at the first attempt, Evans wrote Brown a delighted letter "to both thank and congratulate you on your phenomenal accomplishment this winter. It seems too good to be true that the bill is law, and that the work is not all to be done over again next winter."[45]

The Massachusetts triumph was enabled by an unusually wide coalition and a helpful conjunction of circumstances. Support from organized labor was crucial, and unusual. The commission bill was introduced on the petition of John Golden, president of the United Textile Workers, and endorsed (although their practical contribution was "purely nominal") by both the state branch of the AFL and the Boston Central Labor Union.[46] Beyer noted that labor laws "originating with socially minded groups could not have been passed without the support of the organized workers. The labor movement is writ large in the history of labor legislation for women in Massachusetts." The dominance of textile workers in the state economy and their "political strength out of proportion to their numbers" was coupled with a general sympathy for legal protection derived, Beyer believed, from the example of British textile workers and the hope that laws for women would open the way to laws for all.[47] In 1911, Golden addressed the NWTUL: "Outside of being perhaps a little proud of myself to be upon the Minimum Wage Board, I ought to feel doubly proud to have such a splendid fighter along with me as Mrs. Evans. (Applause.) And having worked in harness before on some of these great economic questions, with Mrs. Evans, I think that as the horsemen say, we will hitch up pretty good."[48]

The working relationship with organized labor may explain why the Consumers' League held back. During the 1890s, the CLM awarded a label to garments produced under approved conditions. They clashed repeatedly with the Union Label League, which concentrated on hour and wage criteria for approval. "To work with unions is to antagonize much of present membership, to ignore them is to antagonize working people," a CLM minute for 1901 noted.[49] When Mary Kenney O'Sullivan, secretary of the Union Label League, became a founder of the NWTUL, the mutual suspicion may have carried over. Although the CLM endorsed a "fair wage" in the 1890s, it regularly questioned its wisdom and in 1906 was still resisting a proposed wage standard for the NCL label.[50]

The CLM was eventually converted. Employers and industrialists were not, but they were outflanked by the campaign and by external events that told against them. At legislative hearings, "the opposition was represented by counsel for the Arkwright Club [the textile manufacturers], counsel for the cotton manufacturers of Fall River, the president of the manufacturers' association, a representative of the candy manufacturers' association, and others."[51] There were exceptions among proprietors. Edward Filene, the Boston department store owner, was one of a small number of progressive employers who supported the minimum wage from conscience over low wages and because it would prevent undercutting by unscrupulous competitors.[52] Filene resembled the welfare capitalists of Britain, and indeed the British example was used to flatter employers into support: "From the beginning in England the movement was welcomed and advanced by the better class of English business men and it is significant in Massachusetts among those business men who have taken the trouble to find out or to understand what this movement means, it also meets with support."[53]

The strength of opposition caused Evans to predict in 1911 that "it is going to be a very difficult undertaking and it may be a slow one."[54] A year later, she surmised that opponents had been disarmed by the prospect that employers sitting on the wages boards could "hold the whiphandle" and threaten to take their business elsewhere: "It has never been very strenuously opposed by employers. Many of them, indeed, have favored the plan. That to me is a little alarming; for if there is nothing against the plan, can there be anything for it?"[55] Massachusetts employers underestimated minimum wagers and the law itself. They assumed that a commission would satisfy public demand, then founder for lack of money. When the statutory minimum wage came into force in 1913, employers discovered that "the law had more strength than ordinarily was credited to it and opposition to it grew."[56] They complained that "ninety-nine per cent of employers first learn of this new burden when the Minimum Wage Inspector appears in the factory office."[57] Their most effective resistance came later, by foot-dragging and in the courts.

To Evans's plaudits, Brown replied modestly: "I think we were very fortunate that conditions permitted us to put through in one year legislation which might, perhaps, be expected to require a long time and a gradual moulding of public opinions to achieve success."[58] One such condition, they agreed, was the IWW-led strike of textile workers in Lawrence, protesting implementation of the fifty-four hours law for women and children with a proportionate reduction of wages for the shorter working week. In ten weeks, from January 1912, the Lawrence strike divided the Massachusetts labor movement, divided women reformers especially over the role of the local WTUL and its cooperation with the IWW, and brought about much-publicized incidents like the evacuation of strikers' children, the calling in of the militia by the mayor, and violent clashes. The strikers won a 10 percent wage increase and a guarantee of overtime payments.[59]

Evans was quoted as saying that the bill "was passed through the Legislature because its members were terrorized by the Lawrence strike."[60] Minimum wagers certainly drew lessons from the strike. Brown wrote that it was "a fact of some significance to students of industrial problems that the Lawrence difficulty was settled very speedily after the parties were brought face to face and that the action of our Legislature had a commendable part in that result."[61] The effect was not just one of terror, however: the public was educated by revelations of conditions in Lawrence. In any event, the strike was only one of several circumstances: the strong reform alliance, the support of labor, and the political uncertainty of a year in which the Progressive Party unsettled two-party politics within the state.[62] A crucial concession, making the law nonmandatory and delaying implementation for a year, was made at the last moment. It was, Louis Brandeis advised, "wiser to accept a bill with recommendatory powers than to fail to secure legislation this year."[63]

It appeared to be taken for granted that the minimum wage would be for women and children. LaRue Brown's propaganda claimed the gendered basis as an advantage and reassurance:

For Women and Children

And only for them. For the worst paid of the weakest and least organizable class in industry. For those whose wages are fixed by tradition, by custom and by other considerations peculiar to themselves.[64]

Kelley thought the limitation parochial: "This restriction . . . was in accordance with the Massachusetts tradition of making laws especially in the interest of the health and welfare of women."[65] The policy had indeed been sponsored by organizations whose raison d'être had been to improve women's working conditions. But there remained an awkwardness in arguments for a gendered law. The state commission's ten-point summary started from a maternalist position, emphasising the social benefits of protecting the health and efficiency of young women; it hedged over sweating, arguing that a minimum wage would "tend to prevent exploitation of helpless women, and, *so far as they are concerned*, to do away with sweating"; it quickly slipped into economic arguments about enhancing efficiency, diminishing parasitism, and bringing about industrial peace.[66] Evans herself considered gendered legislation a second-best. Compared with Australian legislation for men and women and for all trades, "its influence must be less momentous here. But even so, it could not fail to be considerable."[67]

Passage of the law, however weakened, would in itself be momentous. As in Britain, language hid a sense of revolution behind a mask of conservatism. The ability to present the policy as a cautious step while actually regarding it as radical called for a certain skill, appreciated by Mary Morton Kehew when she congratulated LaRue Brown on his "masterly gymnastics, by which you managed to keep your head in the clouds, in your proposed role of a 'dreamer,' and also to keep your feet solidly on the ground."[68] Louis Brandeis, an advocate of compromise, reflected that "at all events, the passage of any minimum wage bill in Massachusetts will prove a great encouragement in other states."[69]

So it seemed, when in 1913 eight more states followed with minimum wage laws.

THE NATIONAL COALITION

For all the variation from state to state in socioeconomic and political circumstances, national organizations spread experience and resources so effectively that a national campaign comparable with that in Britain did exist.[70] Kelley explained in 1912 that the issue "was first actively taken up by the Women's Trade Union League. It seems likely to be carried to success in the near future chiefly by the efforts of a public commission and the Consumers' League constituency, the Women's Trade Union League being shaken to its foundations by inner dissension."[71]

Margaret Dreier Robins, NWTUL president from 1907 to 1922, thought it "natural that [the league] should be among the first to understand the need of such legislation."[72] Intending to win industrial rights with union strength, the league worked with laundry workers, hatmakers, and then a whole range of sweated garment trades. These were large-scale employers of women in factories, workshops, and homes, engaged in a historical transition in methods, work force, and organization and experimenting with industrial unionism and arbitration.[73] The NWTUL soon acknowledged the uphill struggle to organize women workers. Although the "enduring remedy" would be "larger liberty to enter new vocations, to acquire training, to be freed from customary limitations shutting [women] into a small number of ill-paid employments"; a realistic "immediate remedy" must be "legislated control intended to prevent their exploitation in their weakness."[74] The 1909 convention accepted an eleven-point agenda for legislation, including "a legal minimum wage in sweated trades."[75] Local leagues pressed for commissions, and by 1911 Robins was sure that the "time is ripe" for a minimum wage bill to be introduced in a progressive state—as indeed one was, unsuccessfully, in Wisconsin.[76] The 1911 convention cheered Evans's appointment to the Massachusetts inquiry and heard Emily Greene Balch warn of the dangers of achieving "cheap abundance" by cutting the "Wages Bill" and John Golden supporting minimum wage laws for women.

Within two years, divisions, both intellectual and personal, were distracting the NWTUL. "A living wage" was a long-standing goal of the NWTUL, inscribed upon its insignia.[77] Compared with the family wage, which assumed female dependency and a priority to "guard the home," the concept of a living wage contained contradictory possibilities. On the one hand, it might be a safety net for women who lacked a male provider. On the other, it might recognize women—and men—as workers in their own right. Either way, as Alice Kessler-Harris has described, the concept was "imbued with gendered expectations," more often defining women as dependents than as workers but always differentiating the female worker from the male.[78] Robins, in her 1913 presidential address, made a strong plea for a minimum wage for women, notable for its structural analysis of women's abilities and rights as workers, but concluding with a burst of maternalist exhortation: "The question of the wage is not whether a girl can or cannot hold her own in the face of suffering and poverty and temptation; but whether any able-bodied, intelligent young woman is to put all the years of her girlhood and womanhood, all the possibilities of the joy of her motherhood, in jeopardy."[79] Divisions within the NWTUL were exacerbated by the tension between motherhood and family roles and women's fulfillment as workers.

Members of the NWTUL were familiar with British legislation and had even considered sponsoring Mary Macarthur for a six-month visit to the States.[80] The Australo-British model had its local exponent in Alice Henry, an Australian journalist who visited the U.S. in 1906 and stayed. From 1907 to 1915 she was local secretary of the Chicago-based NWTUL, and the league's national editor. Henry was a feminist and social reformer in Australia during Alfred Deakin's minimum wage experiment. She interviewed Beatrice Webb in Melbourne in 1898 and, in preparation, read the collected works of the Webbs; the concept of parasitic industries was familiar to her.[81] Henry's biographer, Diane Kirkby, shows that her ideology combined a socialist sense of class with a feminist sense of women's individual and equal rights. A structural analysis of women's inequality allowed her to fight both for special treatment to remedy women's particular disadvantages and for suffrage as an equal right. Her belief was that the minimum wage for women would be, as in Australia, a step toward a minimum wage for all.[82]

Robins's presidential plea for industrial equality for women as workers could have been written by Alice Henry. They worked from the same Chicago offices and must have debated the case for the minimum wage. But by 1913 a rift between Henry and Robins was imminent, the proximate cause being the editorial and financial policy of Life and Labor, the league's journal, edited by Henry and paid for by Robins. Their philosophical differences bore particularly upon the rationale for a gendered minimum wage. Kirkby compares Alice Henry's "secular liberalism and moderate socialism" with Robins's "more romanticized view of a woman's place and a more sentimental crusading attitude towards the correction of industrial wrongs."[83] Robins's premise was that "the task of the League was to secure protection for women workers, through their unions, so that female nature could have the benefit and nurturing influence for which it was intrinsically intended."[84]

Robins, the independently wealthy daughter of a businessman, came to the NWTUL from charitable and philanthropic work, retaining some of the moralistic outlook characteristic of such a background. Henry, daughter of a hard-up accountant, came from years of earning her own living as well as from the greater class-consciousness of Australian society. Henry, straddling the class divide, exemplified the tensions within the NWTUL. She, the socialist employee, may have had less in common with Robins, her middle-class counterpart but also her employer, than with working-class members, at least some of whom would represent a working-class feminism that combined "gender rights and class solidarity."[85] And although the national organization had an eloquent leader in Robins, she inspired resentment along with inspiration—especially since much of the money that kept the NWTUL alive was her own.

Added to the internal problems of the NWTUL was the permanently difficult relationship with the AFL, with which the NWTUL was affiliated but from which it received maximum disapproval and minimum financial and practical help. Involvement in garment trade strikes had brought friendly cooperation with the new Amalgamated Clothing Workers of America headed by Sidney Hillman, whose attitudes smacked of the industrial unionism that the craft unions of the AFL rejected (or feared). The Massachusetts WTUL kept even more dangerous company, cooperating with the radical IWW in the Lawrence strike, to the point that they were ordered by the AFL to withdraw. And the AFL had a more general complaint about the NWTUL, whose hybrid organization— comprising both working women and middle-class "allies"—flouted union conventions as well as fostering dissension.

For all these reasons, when it committed itself to the minimum wage, the National Consumers' League was in better shape to lead the campaign. The function of middle-class women in the class alliance of the NWTUL was to help organize working women to save themselves. The NCL applied conventional middle-class behavior to improving the conditions of working women, in the belief that "conditions could only be changed through enlisting the sympathy and interest of the shopping public." The first Consumers' League was formed in New York City in 1891, and in 1898 several local federations amalgamated into the National Consumers' League, headquartered in New York City.[86]

Many middle-class women—Kelley and Mary Morton Kehew, for example—were members of both NWTUL and NCL. By 1910, political action and labor cooperation were acceptable to most league members. Middle-class women's organizations of the presuffrage years often entered politics by way of voluntary social action. The New York CL began with boycotts of late shopping hours at Christmastime and campaigns for labels on approved goods. Purchasing was a political act but one that could be implemented undeclared; on the one hand, the "White List" of approved retailers "*shall* be made public," on the other, the names of CL members "*shall not*."[87] Maud Nathan, a founder and later NYCL president, described the moral self-improvement anticipated from this privately enacted pressure: "We tried to raise the standard of ethics in money-spending as well as in money-making."[88] To move from the respectably female use of their household budgets in philanthropic consumption to operation as a fully modern pressure group, mobilizing information, drafting statutes and legal briefs, lobbying, was a major step, hastened by the appointment, in

1899, of Florence Kelley as general secretary of the National League. Her varied past in socialism, in residence at Hull House, in campaigns for tenement laws, and in employment by the state of Illinois as a factory inspector, had taken her well beyond the "ethics of money-spending."[89]

The New York League constitution declared that "the interest of the community demands that all workers should receive, not the lowest wages, but fair living wages" and that "this duty is especially incumbent upon consumers in relation to the products of woman's work, since there is no limit beyond which the wages of women may not be pressed down, unless artificially maintained at a living rate by combinations, either of the workers themselves or of consumers."[90] From realizing that a reputable product was one not only sold but made reputably, it was a short step to realizing the futility of voluntary regulation of a vast market. "The Consumers' League," the NCL declared in 1910, "has been forced to the advocacy of minimum wage boards by the stern teachings of experience." The decision to seek "new and more effective ways of compelling payment of a living wage," was an admission that twenty years of voluntary effort had barely skimmed the surface of the problem. As recently as 1907, the NCL had thought it not "expedient to adopt a minimum wage requirement for the whole country at the present time," meaning then a "wage standard for factories granted the use of a label."[91]

Kelley returned from Geneva in 1908 opposed to a statutory rate. But Maud Nathan, who was also in Geneva, liked the British idea: "It was in 1908 that we had our first International Conference of Consumers' Leagues . . . and there I heard the report read by Mr. James J. Mallon . . . and his report was so very interesting . . . that I procured all the pamphlets that I could from him and brought them to the United States and gave them to the Consumers' League of which I was first vice-president and the National Consumers' League formed a national committee to look into the question."[92] Nathan proposed to the NCL Council in 1909 that "minimum wage boards might be established in this country."[93] Before long, Kelley became the dynamo of the campaign for legislation, activating league branches and her own well-established network. The NCL sponsored research, drafted legal briefs, and circulated information; it raised money and staffed state campaigns; and it maintained morale and supplied inspiration. From around 1910 until 1923, Kelley wrote, traveled, exhorted, and badgered for the cause.

In 1909, an NCL minimum wage committee was established, though at first it operated with no great sense of urgency.[94] By 1911, however, the Special Committee was active, with Harvard professor Holcombe in charge. A draft bill circulated for criticism, Holcombe reported, was "based upon the British Trades Board [sic] Act"—"based upon" rather than replicating, for the committee regarded its prime task as "agreement upon a legislative program adapted to the peculiar American conditions." Holcombe felt no need to explain, the peculiarity of gendered legislation being apparently taken for granted. A rare exception, the "wholly new plan" devised in Wisconsin, was so novel that Holcombe appended the full text of the bill, which criminalized "oppressive employment" without reference to sex.[95] Within a year, political action had taken over from discussion. NCL committee members, it was reported, "have been leaders in their several parts of the country in the propaganda for effective laws to protect the wages of working women and girls in American industries."[96] The NCL devised a composite standard law. This offered a declaration of purpose, "providing for the comfort, health, safety and general welfare" of women employees in industries where a substantial number were paid "wages which are not adequate to their maintenance"; designed a board to investigate and to make and enforce rules; guaranteed the representation and protection of workers against victimization; and provided for legal sanctions against violators.[97]

Kelley was in her element. The overlapping memberships, friendships, and family relationships of Kelley and her colleagues placed the NCL at the heart of a network of expertise, contacts, and political access—never better described than in words ascribed to Kelley in the infamous "Spider Web" chart of the 1920s, to the effect that she and her associates "have more interlocking Directorates than business has."[98] Business opponents at the time described the network in the same pejorative terms applied today to defenders of the welfare state: "Men and women whose livelihood is largely derived from service in this or that 'social welfare' organization, theorists on sociology, an occasional college professor, and, finally, a large proportion of well-to-do women whose sympathetic tendencies far outweigh their analytical grasp of the laws underlying the business and economic relations of mankind"; in brief, "an *hysterical crusading element.*"[99]

At any rate, Kelley had ready access to the settlement movement, the conference platforms of the National Conference of Charities and Corrections and its journal, the *Survey*, the compilations of the AALL, the expertise of university departments (through the NCL Special Committee alone of Columbia, Harvard, and Wisconsin).[100] Kelley had helped the National Child Labor Committee pioneer new techniques of political pressure, and the NCLC reciprocated. Many reform organizations, including the NCL, occupied the Charities Building on East 22d Street, leading a passing friend who looked in on a typical gathering of the tenants to ask quizzically, "What's this bunch call itself today?" (It happened to be the founding meeting of the AALL, addressed by John Commons of Wisconsin.)[101] The NCL, Kathryn Kish Sklar has pointed out, also differed from many of its partners in its efforts to build a reform community rather than simply to institutionalize a specialized pressure group. The NCL had branches spanning the Union, contributing essential local mobilization and visibility to the minimum wage cause.[102]

Personal connections brought access to institutions, expertise, and committed volunteers. Josephine Goldmark, in the New York CL, was related by marriage to Louis Brandeis; Kelley's teenage daughter lived for two years with the Brandeises' old friend Elizabeth Glendower Evans. By such informal routes, Evans brought Dewson into the minimum wage campaign, Kelley recruited Brandeis as counsel for the NCL's major cases (and Goldmark provided the data for his briefs), Brandeis recommended LaRue Brown and later Felix Frankfurter to succeed him as legal adviser, Frankfurter introduced Clara Beyer to the District of Columbia Board, and Beyer brought Brandeis's daughter in as her assistant.[103] The interlocking directorates and their potential influence find no better example than the AALL Committee on Woman's Work. Its ten members included Kelley, Goldmark, Brandeis, Robins, Susan Kingsbury of the Boston WEIU, and Mary Van Kleeck. P. Tecumseh Sherman, New York commissioner of labor; Ernst Freund, Chicago law professor; Anne Morgan, daughter of Pierpont Morgan, founder of the Colony Club, member of the National Civic Federation, and volunteer factory inspector; and John Mitchell of the United Mine Workers of America made up the roster. Within six months, the committee had recommended to the AALL Council the "organization of wage-boards to establish a minimum wage in certain industries."[104]

The odd man out on a committee otherwise composed of familiar types of progressive reformer was John Mitchell, president of the mine workers until 1908. In his support for the minimum wage, Mitchell was also out of line with organized labor. Organized labor was the conspicuous absentee from the national coalition for this proposal to reform the labor market.[105] Middle-class women were reluctant to work with the unions, even "to do useful things which [they] promptly [do] when asked by the Consumers' League," but primary responsibility lay with the unions themselves.[106] Their interest in controlling collective bargaining and maintaining the strength of their predominantly craft-based members, their male fears and prejudices about women workers, and their different analyses of gender and of the state hampered, if they did not preclude, cooperation.

The AFL claimed to speak for labor. Certainly its role was crucial: it represented the most powerful workers; it had some access to employers through collective bargaining procedures and in joint talking shops like the National Civic Federation (NCF); and it had a relationship with the NWTUL. But labor was united neither in structure nor in ideas. Union membership was a minority even of the industrial work force, AFL access to federal and state institutions patchy, its relationship with the courts adversarial. In addition, its claim of standing to speak for all of labor was hotly contested from within by State Federations and city affiliates; on behalf of unskilled workers by new organizations such as the Amalgamated Clothing Workers; on behalf of women by both the NWTUL and groups like the NCL; on ideological and strategical grounds by the socialists and IWW. The AFL was the dominant labor organization, but its dominance was shaky. The vehemence with which it contested the minimum wage proposal, and its reluctant compromise on gendered laws, came from insecurity as well as strength.[107]

With some justice, Kelley personalized the friction of the minimum wage campaign with labor as "the stupid folly of that aged Dodo," AFL president Samuel Gompers. Gompers was a prominent public figure, spokesperson for and to labor, member of commissions, vice president of the NCF, and unbending opponent of minimum wages. As Kelley summarized, Gompers had "never had any intelligent perception of the need of organizing women . . . [or] serious interest in their wages and welfare."[108] She reported a revealing question and answer at a Congressional hearing on the minimum wage: "Sam, if this law is good for the girls why isn't it good for the boys?" "Well . . . this protection has to be given to the girls, it's good for the girls. But it's better for the boys to fight for what they get through their unions. They value it more and it makes them strengthen their unions."[109] Unfortunately for the minimum wage campaign, Gompers's dictums carried weight and were crucial in holding the AFL back from commitment.

Gompers's own views, Kelley accused, changed little over forty years. He believed in the right of workers to a living wage but absolutely not in "a governmental enactment of a 'living wage' for wage earners in private employ."[110] His "living wage" was the family wage: "In our time, and at least in our country . . . rich and fertile as any in the world . . . the wife as a wage-earner is a disadvantage economically considered, and socially is unnecessary."[111] The "disadvantage economically considered" that working women created for working men loomed large in consideration of women who did and must work. Frequent references in AFL statements deplored women's failure to organize. "They have failed to realize that they are responsible members of the industrial organization," an official report accused.[112] Yet the AFL ignored prejudice against women in unions and disapproved of the NWTUL, again out of fear that women would be competitors, driving down wages and driving out the men. All too many male industrial workers rejected legislative control of working conditions, believed that women's place was in the home, feared their competition in the workplace, and would not tolerate a male-female or a female cross-class alliance.

With mounting evidence of working women's poverty, and faced with pressure from the NWTUL, from some of the AFL's own affiliates, and from public opinion, Gompers and the AFL modified their absolute hostility. At the 1912 convention, a New York State delegate proposed that "this convention place itself on record for a statute establishing a minimum wage for women."[113] As so often before, the first move was to set up a committee, whose report, the following year, moved a long way from Gompers's outright rejection. First it boldly claimed credit: "The movement for a minimum wage for women and minors has gained considerable headway . . . That this growth of sentiment among the people is due to the activities of the organized wage-earners there can be no doubt." Next, it noted overseas examples and drew a clear boundary to its own concession: "In America these laws relate exclusively to women workers and to minors. If it were proposed in this country to vest authority in any tribunal to fix by law wages for men, Labor would protest by every means in its power." Third, it gave a reason for conceding special treatment for women: "The organization of women workers constitutes a separate and more difficult problem. Women do not organize as readily or as stably as men. They are, therefore, more easily exploited. They certainly are in a greater measure than are men entitled to the concern of society." And finally, it recommended essentially nothing—that for the "information of the labor movement the Executive Council be instructed to watch developments."[114]

The 1913 resolution left the AFL formally neutral on the minimum wage for women. At subsequent conventions, attacks on the idea of minimum wages exempted women's legislation.[115] Gompers himself, however, maintained his opposition, using the columns of the *American Federationist* to editorialize on the evils of statutory wage fixing. In 1914, for example, the March issue contained a long editorial by Gompers, "Working Women, Organize!" May brought his account of a visit to Puerto Rico, where he attempted to divert the local federation from a minimum wage campaign. In June he wrote on labor and the courts, pronouncing that the price of the minimum wage was "too dear for any free people to afford. Freedom of contract is the one narrow distinction between the free worker and the unfree." July confirmed his shift from defending the dependence of women to defending their personal freedom and self-development, a ruse to leave them to sink or swim alone. And so on.[116]

The high point was 1913, when laws passed in eight states. Thereafter only a handful of nonindustrial states legislated, while opposition gathered strength. In industrial states, notably Ohio and New York, legislation failed. Where laws were on the books, some states dragged their feet on implementation; others were paralyzed by legal challenges. In Massachusetts, for example, a test case brought in 1915 took three years to fail. In the interim, "if any wage-board member cared to raise the question of constitutionality the commission was unable to force the work to go forward."[117]

The opposition of the AFL in itself gave ammunition to employers. In addition, labor worked with employers, using the National Civic Federation as a hostile policy institute.[118] NCF secretary Gertrude Beeks's influence and biases showed in her management of an NCF minimum wage committee. She reported to its chair, businessman Andrew J. Porter, that she had included proponents of the policy in the final report only in deference to a single member's "desire that it appear impartial."[119] Invited to advise the research program of the New York Factory Investigating Commission, Beeks advised its abandonment, on the grounds that any conclusion "that such legislation would be practically or economically advantageous would be necessarily barren."[120] Conveniently, the NCF reversed the argument when it suited them. Percy Straus of Macy's wrote approvingly to Beeks of the committee report: "I think it admirable as a means of creating doubts in the minds of reformers as to the adviseability [sic] of reforming before sufficient facts have been accumulated as to the possible results of hasty legislation." Or, as member Charles Morgan Wood's endorsement ran, "Minimum wage is a good thing, but so is aeroplaning. It would be dangerous, however, to try either without first learning how."[121]

NCF members and supporters were a cross-section of employer opposition. Beeks corresponded with retailers and with Emmanuel W. Bloomingdale, counsel for the New York Retail Dry Goods Association.[122] The NCF conference on "Problems in Minimum Wage Legislation" in 1915 featured minimum wager Katherine Philips Edson, of the California Commission on Industrial Welfare, alongside opponents A. Parker Nevin of the National Association of Manufacturers and Hugh Frayne of the AFL (Gompers being invited personally by Ralph Easley, NCF president, with the revealing suggestion that he might be "willing to say something on one side, or both sides" of the question).[123]

A pamphlet put out by the Merchants and Manufacturers of Massachusetts in 1916 summarized "the *inherent disabilities underlying the whole law*" in the business view: employers were required to carry the whole burden of reforming society, yet employers were workers too, and to weaken one weakened all; the law raised the cost of living, nullifying its intended benefit, and produced unemployment; rates based on "the pet theorem of the Minimum Wage advocates," the "irreducible" minimum for an "independent worker," made nonsense of the family economy; labor was divided and its *"more serious-minded thinkers"* feared the policy, while interstate competition (quoting the NCF), made federal legislation, if any, essential. Finally, they argued that the unsettled constitutional status of the minimum wage was reason enough for rejecting the policy.[124] The best hope of business interests lay in proving that industrial relations were individual relations, a private matter. In the words of Rome G. Brown, a Minnesota lawyer who represented minimum wage opponents, "The need of a 'living' is an *individual* need . . . Even if we admit the ethical and economic viewpoint, that each individual has a 'generic' right to receive the full cost of living . . . it does not follow that another individual is or can be obligated to supply that need, simply because there is the relation between the two of employer and employee."[125] The mobilization of political opposition coincided with a faltering campaign. The failure to win legislation in the key state of New York showed how political circumstances had turned against minimum wagers.

NEW YORK: A FAILED CAMPAIGN

Henry Prinz, a Poughkeepsie worker and delegate from the New York State Federation of Labor, fractured the AFL's official opposition to the minimum wage with his resolution that the 1912 convention support the policy. New York was home to leading minimum wagers as well as to concentrations of sweated industries. In 1915, the State Factory Investigating Commission conducted the most comprehensive consideration of the minimum wage. This state's failure to legislate illuminates the political reasons for the downturn in the fortunes of the minimum wage campaign.

In 1900, there were fifty thousand tenement houses in Manhattan. In 1901, sixty thousand registered home workers were the tip of the iceberg of unlicensed workers. The state had a history of regulation by means of licensing workers and premises, approving designs for tenement houses, and imposing rudimentary safety provisions for workshops. The failures of such well-meant laws were brutally brought home to the city on 25 March 1911, when the top-floor premises of the Triangle Shirtwaist Company burned out and 146 workers, mostly young women, died. That shocking event set the frame for the New

York campaign. The first response was the establishment of the Factory Investigating Commission—which, ironically, by prioritizing safety laws, delayed the introduction of minimum wage legislation in New York until it had become politically impossible.[126] The FIC was authorized in 1911. Its final report, on minimum wage legislation, was delivered in 1915. The Commission was dominated by Democrats, chaired by Robert F. Wagner, with Al Smith as vice chairman, and NYWTUL president Mary Dreier and Samuel Gompers as two of seven commissioners. Within three years, the State Department of Labor had been overhauled and more than thirty new labor laws passed.[127]

Health and safety issues were most directly raised by the Triangle fire, but minimum wagers saw a chance to establish a wider conception of state responsibility. Late in 1912, Belle Israels, chair of a committee on women's work of the NYCL, called a conference of reform organizations to meet Elizabeth Glendower Evans and "to consider the feasibility of Minimum Wage Legislation in behalf of underpaid women workers." She had circulated a questionnaire seeking support and a commitment to "take an active part . . . and send representatives to Albany for hearings, etc."[128] By March 1913, the legislature had extended the life and remit of the FIC, "to inquire into the wages of labor in all industries . . . and into the advisability of fixing minimum rates of wages."[129] A massive research program, advised by a committee of businessmen and reformers, was initiated. AALL secretary John Andrews was busy recommending staff, advising on substance, and deputing his wife and assistant, Irene Osgood Andrews, to compile a report on minimum wage legislation, which appeared as a massive appendix to the third (1914) FIC report.[130]

The AFL played its expected part. Gompers used the FIC platform to expound his familiar views against the minimum wage but, perhaps to conform with the policy of his 1913 convention, did not in the end dissent from the FIC recommendation of legislation, for women, without legal sanction. State federation leader Hugh Frayne represented the AFL, declaring flatly that "organized labor of the State of New York is not asking for this law." Frayne, a hostile witness, attacked the right of delegates of the Brooklyn Central Labor Union to speak for their membership, claimed in turn to speak for all workers, whether organized or not, somewhat misrepresented the tacit acceptance of the 1913 resolution when he said the AFL had taken no action on the topic, and wound up by quoting one of Gompers's *Federationist* articles as if it were AFL policy.[131]

Although Elizabeth Payne suggests that the NYWTUL voted against involvement in the campaign "to pacify the Federation," the more complicated reality was a microcosm of divisions that plagued the entire national campaign, within and between sexes, classes, and organizations concerned with labor problems.[132] Personality clashes added to divisions of class and ethnicity over the priorities of organizing, legislating, or fighting for suffrage.[133] The pivotal year was 1910, when the NYWTUL's concentration on organizing was broken. Pressure from members brought league support for a revitalized suffrage movement. Shock at a Newark factory fire launched a Legislative Committee.[134] In

1912, tensions between factions and goals became open. Attorney Bertha Rembaugh, chair of the Legislative Committee, attended an AALL meeting to draw up an action program for the "united organizations," including a proposal for a commission on Minimum Wages Boards. Why not women's suffrage, Leonora O'Reilly queried when Rembaugh reported back, while another member suggested asking the AALL why their clerical workers were not unionized.[135] Class and ethnicity did not explain who took what position. Ally Mary Dreier was as much a suffragist as worker Leonora O'Reilly, and O'Reilly and Rose Schneiderman were worker-supporters of legislation. But resolving differences was all the more difficult because of the diverse backgrounds and interests of the members.

Bertha Rembaugh continued to represent the league with the AALL and NCL. Meanwhile, a shift in state politics boded ill for labor legislation, with Republicans taking control of the state assembly in 1913 and the governor's office in November 1914. The Democrats, although divided, had provided the majority for labor legislation since 1911.[136] The NYWTUL, however, was forced off the fence by difficulties close to home. How should they respond to the invitation from the Brooklyn Central Labor Union to a debate on the minimum wage? Should they testify to the FIC? They had members like Dreier, who strongly advocated minimum wage legislation; like Schneiderman, who supported it but thought suffrage more urgent; and like Helen Marot, who passionately opposed legislation as a threat to organization. They needed to maintain relations with the national WTUL, which strongly supported the policy, with divided male labor organizations (the AFL cool to the policy, Gompers against it, a State Federation evidently divided, and a local CLU strongly supportive) and with their co-workers in many causes now running the FIC.

In these circumstances, the NYWTUL came off the fence only to walk away from the issue. At the executive board on 24 November, unusually, the minimum wage was carried to a recorded vote. Helen Marot (anti) and Mary Dreier (pro) joined to propose a full discussion, with Dreier asking that "she be recorded as not criticizing any one member or group of members in her discussion of the question." When the ten members present were, on a unanimous motion, "polled as to their position on the minimum wage question," the result was "4 for and 6 against." They had little choice but to take the matter to the next league meeting. By thirteen votes to twelve, the NYWTUL supported a recommendation that "the League considers this an innopportune [sic] time for the League to agitate for Minimum Wage Boards and therefore inexpedient to fix its position on this question." As a result, the FIC heard only individual testimony from WTUL members. The diplomatic solution to the invitation from Brooklyn was to send four representatives, "to take up the two sides of the question. Miss Dreier and Miss Schneiderman for Minimum Wage and Miss Marot and Miss Hogan against." In January, Marot reported that the CLU had endorsed a minimum wage for women: "Both Miss Hogan and Miss Marot had spoken against the subject and had lost the day. There was no delegate from the winning side present."[137]

Single-issue political organizations or those with homogeneous constituencies could separate themselves from the kind of conflict over priorities that paralyzed the NYWTUL. The National American Woman Suffrage Association did not feel impelled to take a position on labor issues. Dye quotes NAWSA, in the midst of the New York garment strikes of 1909, declaring that it "neither stands for labor organization nor against it."[138] But in the reverse situation, the WTUL, representing women workers, did feel impelled to take a stand on suffrage. The WTUL represented both a sex and a class, unlike other organizations involved in the minimum wage campaign. The internal divisions of the NYWTUL replicated in one organization the problem of the whole campaign, that of what interest was to be represented—workers, women workers, women, or public interest in an efficient economy or a humane society.

The campaign was thus extremely vulnerable to its own internal uncertainties. It was also vulnerable to failing alliances and to the turn of events in state politics. Irwin Yellowitz found three ingredients for successful reform in New York: cooperation between organized labor and reformers, strong public opinion, and effective cooperation within the reform movement. In the case of the minimum wage campaign, the first was absent, the second was doubtful, and the third, the cooperation of reformers, was present, the WTUL excepted.[139] As for state politics, in New York the political environment was a hindrance. By 1914, recession was biting the economy, and Republicans controlled the administration. In 1915, reformers became preoccupied with the Democrat-instigated, now Republican-controlled constitutional convention; and women with the November suffrage referendum. Opponents were by now energized and organized. It was not a propitious time for new minimum wage legislation. New York had to wait until 1933 to become the leader in a new round of state legislation.

GENDER AS POLITICAL STRATEGY

Local circumstances, economic and political, go far to explain why minimum wage legislation passed in some states and not in others between 1912 and 1923. In particular, Florence Kelley was right to point to the crucial role of labor in tipping the balance toward success or failure. In Massachusetts, where the Textile Workers carried exceptional political clout, labor was supportive or silent. In New York, where both men's and women's labor organizations were deeply divided, Gompers used his own local prominence in FIC and NCF forums to ensure that labor was antagonistic or silent.

Emilie Hutchinson's question, posed in the opening section of this chapter, was not *why* legislation passed but why legislation *for women* passed. On this issue, the political narratives of this chapter are less than conclusive. The AFL would support nothing else, and its grudging tolerance for gendered legislation was clear encouragement to minimum wagers to go forward with this "half loaf." But the AFL endorsement came only late in 1913, after nine states had passed laws for women. The opposition of business interests was general and pragmatic, to any intervention in their affairs and to any regulation that would disadvantage them. Gender issues were not their priority.

In Britain, labor and business had acquiesced to variations on the theme of controlling the anarchic fringe of the market for the greater good of those who upheld mainstream order. By comparison, American opponents seem barely to have considered arguments about the educative function of boards for the nonunionized or the harm inflicted by the downward spiral of price wars and sweating. The community interest in outlawing industrial parasitism did not have the same resonance in the United States. American minimum wagers had to deal with one fact that existed only on the philosophical margins in the British debate. In contest with each other, American labor and business were both using as weapons individualist doctrines and their legal manifestation in the principle of freedom of contract. Community—implying state—intervention challenged the turf and the ideologies of these vested interests. Insofar as those turfs and ideologies were particularly male preserves, a gendered law might provide not just the easiest but the only possible way forward.

The advantage of a gendered strategy was of using women's actual, cultural, and legal standing of inequality and dependence to counter both pragmatic and principled objections. In dealing with American opponents, this was the key point. After the political campaigns and the first wave of legislation described in this chapter, when businessmen mounted a rearguard action and moved the contest to the courts, the gender rationale came into its own. The gender strategy might therefore have been astute foresight on the part of minimum wagers or luck in the light of subsequent events.

Alternatively, it has been suggested, gendered legislation may have been a reflection of the social vision and values of minimum wagers themselves. The women who led the minimum wage campaign belonged to a wider reform network. Organizations with a defined mission like the NCL and NWTUL overlapped and cooperated with others, like the General Federation of Women's Clubs, with a broad remit and nationwide membership. Together, they campaigned on a range of social issues to do with the homes, health, and work of women, children, and families. At the turn of the twentieth century, women's private status as mothers, potential if not actual, became a claim to public motherhood, to political standing in the absence (but not in lieu) of full citizenship, a definition of a sphere of political responsibility and a demand to expand the functions of the state. This "maternalist" translation of women's accepted domestic and community role into a public and political movement of size and consequence has been labeled "the domestication of politics." The powerful and effective mobilization of women under the banner of "a political concept that accepts the principle of gender difference, specifically, women's identity as mothers" has been credited as the origin of a welfare state for women.[140] Is this the explanation of the gendering of minimum wage policy?

Minimum wagers did not consider only gendered legislation. In Wisconsin, any "maternalist" origin was much diluted. A bill unsuccessfully introduced in 1911 pronounced: "All employment property is hereby declared to be affected with a public interest to the extent that every employer shall pay to every employee in each oppressive employment [i.e., "an occupation in which employees are unable to earn a living wage"] at least a living wage."[141] A second attempt in 1913 followed the suggestion of the governor, that "in the beginning there should be experimentation in a limited field, dealing with the wages of women employees in the 'most oppressive occupations.'"[142] A gendered law on the NCL pattern was passed.

In Ohio, a proposal that "laws may be passed . . . establishing a minimum wage" for "women, children and persons engaged in hazardous employment" had labor support and was accepted by the Constitutional Convention in 1912 and endorsed by referendum.[143] The Ohio Minimum Wage League, with an all-male committee, ran a legislative campaign, and its vice president sent the AALL a powerful defense of the goal of a "*universal* Minimum Wage": "In our view the accident of sex cannot rightfully be set up as a barrier to the endeavor to rid ourselves of the maladjustments resulting from unrestricted competition for wages. Unaided, women make bad bargains. But none the less do men. Women are exploited. But so are men. Why should the line be drawn because women are not men? Unscrupulous employers take advantage of women's economic necessities. Do they suddenly assume the garb of justice, honesty, and fair dealing when hiring men?"[144] But the league could not carry the legislature. In the next session, "legislation was postponed until a study of *women's* wages could be made," evidently again in response to a cautious Governor Cox, who recommended study and procrastination "except to provide for obviously unjust conditions affecting the wages of women and children."[145] It was not until the early 1920s that women's organizations, led by the Ohio CL, took up the cause and campaigned—too late—for a law for women.[146]

In Wisconsin and Ohio, laws framed under male leadership were formulated for men and women, and failed. "Maternalist" America, where social policies "were championed by elite and middle-class women," and American women "were helped as mothers, or as working women who deserved special protection because they were potential mothers," has been contrasted with "paternalist" Britain, where policies for male wage workers and their dependents were allegedly introduced by the male leadership of agencies and parties.[147] In fact, women were prominent in the British campaign, and men were involved in America. In neither country could the organizational decisions on the formulation of the policy be reliably predicted by the sex of the membership. Typically, women leaders of the American campaign differed from their British counterparts in education and marital status, and operated within different social institutions, in Consumers' Leagues that had failed of establishment in Britain, and in different partisan and governmental institutions. But any simple paternal/maternal contrast quickly breaks down in face of the more complex divisions within the political campaign.

British women like Dilke and Tuckwell were maternalists in their views on women and the family. But they were not automatically and literally maternalist on every policy they adopted. When they insisted on gender-neutral minimum wage legislation, they did so on grounds of the primacy of economic cause and circumstance rather than maternal function. They regarded the different impacts of sweating on women and men because of family circumstances as symptoms, not as causes. Equally, it makes no sense to talk of the American minimum wage as a maternalist policy unless this becomes an all-embracing term for any policy by or for women. Women in the minimum wage campaign were necessarily not talking about just mothers but about working mothers— and specifically about the work component of the working mother's dual identity. For women, then and now, work and motherhood were not alternatives, nor could they be so in policy. British women's discourse, not their patterns of mobilization or of political opportunities alone, explained why, and with what difficulty, they prioritized work in the formulation of minimum wage policy. In the next chapter, I turn to American minimum wagers' discourse in search of a more conclusive explanation of why "a sex problem" rather than "a labor problem" became their priority.

Police Power

THE WELFARE OF WOMEN, U.S.A., 1907–1921

MINIMUM WAGERS faced a dilemma. Women's wages were widely understood, and widely regretted, as a necessary contribution to the family economy: "Many men are receiving low wages and the investigation shows that many men cannot properly support themselves nor support a family on what they receive." But this male responsibility apparently could not be reached by the law: "In America, where the constitutionality of wage legislation is still undecided, even when it affects only women, . . . legislation for men has been generally declared unconstitutional and has thus far received little public support." Therefore, "it has been deemed wiser to deal with this problem solely as it relates to women and minors."[1]

There were many political reasons why *even* laws restricted to women succeeded or failed. But the constraint of the Constitution was the most usual explanation of minimum wagers themselves for the prior decision to make sex the basis of coverage. Sooner or later, almost everyone blamed necessity in the face of constitutional force majeure. Yet they did make a choice, in full knowledge of their departure from the British model.[2] Defensively, Americans admitted the logic of including men, acknowledged the merits of British and Australasian prototypes, or merely regretted their own sense of duress. "In England and Australia, . . . the well-being of men as well as women is held to be vital to the state," Elizabeth Glendower Evans remarked. "Most American states have omitted the regulation of men's employment from the power of the controlling authorities, as very properly regretted by you," J. B. Andrews of the AALL wrote to a British colleague.[3] They could have preferred outright a maternalist policy, family wages, or mothers' pensions to support more women at home, or have rejected compromise and fought for comprehensive coverage. To the extent that the courts were indeed the barrier, they could—as sympathetic Columbia economist Henry Seager advised the NCL—have waited for a change in "the American judicial mind" or sought loopholes in the present judicial reasoning, or experimented with some new legal strategy.[4] But, in line with the strategy, credited to Kelley, of the "half-loaf girl: take what you can get now and try for more later," they chose the more accessible goal of legislation for women.[5]

The constitutional definition of the powers and functions of the state, the biases and opportunities embedded in constitutional concepts and precedents, and the minimum wagers' attempts to construct a watertight legal rationale are the subjects of this chapter. The issue was whether and how minimum wage laws could be brought within the constitutional definition of the police power of the state. Both sides of the equation—policy and law—might be open to change. But the problem raised a series of contradictions for minimum wagers: between their critique of the market economy and sweating, and constitutional interpretations that blocked economic intervention; between their recognition of social changes that were rendering traditional sex roles and family structures unattainable, and the maternalist inclinations of many in the campaign; between their adoption of a British policy innovation that applied to workers, going against both the maternalist view and the constitutional openings. American courts were unlikely to accept economic reasoning but might uphold legislation to help women, particularly, on past precedents, if those women were portrayed as mothers. Here was an open door to frame the policy in maternalist terms. The protection of mothers became the capstone of their edifice. But because minimum wagers also knew that their ideal motherhood was not an option for most working women, and that to act from simple maternalism would belie the facts of sweating and women's work, they were reluctant and conflicted maternalists.

Though the idea of policing nowadays implies regulation and control, the constitutional doctrine of the police power contained potential authority for a democratic politics of community care, for policies to mitigate the harsh conditions of the new industrialism and urbanization, and for the responsibilities and modes of action that women were developing and claiming as their own. It was not coincidental that the range of the police power expanded in the late nineteenth and early twentieth centuries. Reformers, especially women, exploited its possibilities, classically, in Bryce's metaphor, plowing and tilling the unused ground of constitutional law. In a period of personal, social, and legal change, a generation struggled to frame a new understanding of gender and a new political strategy adequate to the problems of an industrial society. The public discourse, involving women and men, about how to reconcile the minimum wage to the police power, is a text of empowerment as well as of compromise.

THE POLICE POWER

The inherent police power of the states was seen by minimum wagers as the most promising constitutional basis for their legislation. Ernst Freund's magisterial text on the police power, published in 1904, found the concept both indispensable and elusive, "without authoritative or generally accepted definition." It was, Freund proposed, loosely, "the power of promoting the public welfare by restraining and regulating the use of liberty and property."[6] Judicial definitions were little more precise. Even a landmark judgment in 1905 identified only "certain powers, existing in the sovereignty of each State in the Union, somewhat vaguely termed police powers, the exact description and limitation of which have not been attempted by the courts." The Supreme Court was not yet prepared to define any "more specific limitation" of its territory. The police power was a concept ripe for development and open to contestation, at the moment when the problems of an urban and industrial world more and more roused concern about just those matters the police power embraced—the "safety, health, morals, and general welfare of the public."[7]

The exercise of the police power ranked one constitutional precept above another; as Freund emphasized, "certain rights yield to the police power, while it respects and accommodates itself to others."[8] Rights could be curtailed only in a manner (procedurally) and, in a recent development, also for a purpose (substantively) conforming to the terms of due process of law. Minimum wage legislation would place the public welfare above the rights of the citizens to their liberty and property in the market. Upon whatever analysis they based their defense of the measure, the problem for minimum wagers remained the same. The circumstances in which courts accepted that a "police" law regulating labor relations or the conditions of work met due process requirements were few, narrowly limited, and gendered.

By 1909, the constitutional status of protective labor legislation was still unresolved. The police power lay with states, and its definition emerged from the decisions of many state courts in addition to the federal Supreme Court. An early New York precedent had voided legislation that banned, for health reasons, the production of cigars in tenement buildings. That court accepted the argument that "the State cannot under the pretence of prescribing a police regulation, encroach upon the just rights of the citizen, secured to him by the Constitution."[9] The "just right" of freedom of contract—that is, the presumptive individual right (of employers and employees alike) to come to their own agreements about the terms and conditions of employment—was set above the potential social benefits of legislation. The ruling that it "cannot be perceived how the cigarmaker is to be improved in his health or his morals" and that it was "plain that this is not a health law, and that it has no relation whatever to public health" also distinguished between protection of the health of the individual worker and of the public.[10] Subsequent judicial decisions wavered between the conflicting demands of freedom and health. In 1897, for example, the Supreme Court subscribed to freedom of contract as a constitutional right; and in 1898 it raised the hopes of labor reformers by allowing Utah miners an eight-hour day, on grounds of the imminent danger of underground mine work.[11]

By the time the minimum wage campaign sought a constitutional base, the *Lochner* decision rejecting an hours law for bakers appeared to have settled for freedom, making the free market itself a substantive constitutional value.[12] After *Lochner*, protection of the individual worker's health apparently had only an outside chance of competing with that worker's right to freedom of contract. But labor reformers were left some strategic openings. *Lochner* dismissed the public health defense of bakers' hours of work: "It does not affect any other portion of the public than those who are engaged in that occupation." By implication, a law striking at physical conditions that delivered infected products to the general public—the classic charge against the sweated garment trades— might stand a better chance. And indeed, Elizabeth Baker noted, after the early cigarmakers case, "[l]ater laws in New York State have attacked the problem indirectly as regulative measures with the explicit purpose of protecting consumers."[13] The prime mode of attack on sweating in states like Massachusetts and New York became the licensing of hygienic premises—that is to say clean homes—as sites of production. As in Britain, monitoring homes rather than regulating business diverted attention toward health and from the economy, toward the woman's place at home rather than in the industrial workplace.[14]

Courts were reluctant to make the leap from giving police power authority to sanitary laws, whose public health function was obvious, to hours laws, where the connection was less direct. The step from hours laws to wages laws promised to be harder. "Wages," Father John A. Ryan observed, "have until quite recently been regarded as something too sacred to be touched by the profane hand of the legislator."[15] Due process requirements encouraged this supposition. The relationship between wages and health and welfare, "while perhaps none the less real than the relation between these and the hours of labor and sanitary conditions, is more difficult to establish and less immediate," economist Harry A. Millis warned.[16] Freund had dismissed the idea of statutory wage regulation in a single paragraph, as a power never claimed by any American state, certain to be resisted by the courts, and, in any case, barely worth discussion "in the absence of legislation raising it." The problem would be, he thought, that "considerations of health and safety which complicate the question of hours of labor do not enter into the question of rates. The regulation would be purely of an economic character."[17] The assumption that health problems *might* be addressed by the police power, while economic problems could not, was crucial to the presentation of the minimum wage.

The constitutional formulation that suggested *how* a minimum wage might be justified also implied *who* might be its subjects, and introduced a bias. The precedents lent authority to a gendered definition of work and workers, elevating assorted values, assumptions, and prejudices to the status of law. For example, Freund thought that health measures *might* be permitted to differentiate between the sexes, while economic measures would not: "If we look upon limitation of hours of labor as a measure of economic and social advancement, and if that principle of limitation [of hours] be conceded as legitimate, the discrimination between men and women can no longer be based upon considerations of physical strength [i.e., health], but must be justified by specific economic and social conditions of employment as affected by difference of sex." Then, if limiting hours of work "is merely a measure of social advancement, a separate rule for women for all purposes hardly represents a reasonable classification, for in the effort to make a living men and women have a right to the greatest possible equality before the law."[18]

But Freund underestimated how the courts had differentiated the freedom of contract of men and of women. The reality was not only that health measures were more easily upheld than economic measures. All types of exemption from freedom of contract were more easily upheld for women than for men.

The *Lochner* ruling declared that laws limiting the hours "in which grown and intelligent men may labor to earn their living" were "mere meddlesome interferences," implying that grown and intelligent men might form a distinct class in the eyes of the law.[19] The issue of class legislation was a subplot of the contest over the meaning of due process. The equal protection of the laws was generally held to be met, provided that the classification of who was affected by a law had a reasonable relationship to the purpose of the law. In *Lochner*, where the legislature had seen bakers, the court saw "grown and intelligent men." In numerous labor law cases, the courts either ruled directly on, or riddled their judgments with assumptions about, gender roles and work.[20] In the cigarmakers' case, for example, "his" (the presumed male cigarmaker's) right to freedom of contract took precedence, protecting him from a "health" law "forcing him from his home" to "earn a livelihood for himself and family," allowing him the freedom to "do his work where he can have the supervision of his family and their help."[21] The New York court lent its support to relations of paternalism, dependency, and support, in its portrayal of family and home (as well as permitting unhygienic and unregulated work to continue in tenement homes). Similar assumptions pervaded freedom of contract cases, including those like *Lochner*, which ostensibly had nothing whatever to do with sex discrimination. The doctrine of freedom of contract was derived from the Fourteenth Amendment ban on deprivation of the rights to life, liberty, and property without due process of law. This interpretation, historian Nancy Erickson points out, "was clearly sex-based at its inception."[22]

The Fourteenth Amendment precedents contemplated by the minimum wage campaign in 1909, from the *Slaughter-House Cases* in 1873 through to *Lochner*, reinforced discrimination, limiting the freedom of contract of women on grounds of their civil dependency or their physical needs, as both the weaker sex and the mothers of the next generation.[23] In 1908, the famous case of *Muller v. Oregon* brought these arguments to perfection and, by restricting women's rights on categorical grounds, cleared the path for gendered social and labor legislation. This decision, upholding an Oregon ten-hour law for women workers, was notable both for its unequivocal declaration of a public interest in the employment terms of women and for its immediate impact as reformers and state courts followed its lead.[24] The case presented a choice between equal rights to contract and special needs of health. The Supreme Court acknowledged women's gains toward full legal equality, but denigrated them with the argument that "even though all restrictions on political, personal, and contractual rights were taken away, and she stood, so far as statutes are concerned, upon an absolutely equal plane with [her brother], it would still be true that she is so constituted that she will rest upon and look to him for protection." In a famous passage, the Supreme Court linked the biological characteristics of women and the health of the community, resting their case on physical difference and physical weakness and on women's vulnerability due to their responsibility for "the future well-being of the race." The inevitable conclusion to the enumeration of so many disabilities and duties was that a community interest justified the use of the police power and that, therefore, this "difference justifies a difference in legislation."[25]

As the minimum wage campaign mobilized, a year after the *Muller* decision, men's freedom of contract had been curtailed only under exceptional circumstances and where imminent danger to their health was acknowledged. Women had been recognized as a legitimate classification in social legislation, their freedom of contract as not absolute, and their health, like the public health, as a community interest. The problem remained of whether wage regulation could ever be slipped past the courts as a health measure or the courts persuaded that economic laws might embody a public interest. These constitutional factors created a mountainous obstacle to importing the British model as it stood, for low-paid workers. Minimum wagers tackled the presumption against wage legislation, and limited their risks, by conforming with existing precedents on gender. Bending their arguments to meet the constitutional recognition of gender difference, they presented the minimum wage as a measure whose protection of women was in the interest of public health and welfare.

WOMEN'S NEEDS: THE GENDERED CLAIM

Florence Kelley noted three "outstanding characteristics" of American policy, compared with British and Australasian laws: first, "its omission of men"; second, "its reference to the welfare of the people as a whole"; and "the third, which is responsible for both the others, is its subordination to the courts on grounds of constitutionality."[26] Americans used all the familiar arguments about social, economic, and organizational benefits, order in the market, and the rampant injustice of sweating. But, matching the most promising openings in constitutional law, the heart of their case concerned the inequalities of women and the interests of the state in the "mothers of the race."

Kelley and her associates rested their case on the economic, social, and physical attributes of women, while sometimes signaling a different preference. Their ambivalence ran in more than one direction. The case they made both was gendered and gave women rights as workers. Thus it clashed with their critique of industrialism and with the socialist or quasi-socialist views of some reformers, all of which grounded analysis in the economy, not in gender. Their recognition of women as workers challenged traditional gender and family roles that upheld women's domestic function. Singling women workers out as a legislative classification was inconsistent with the individualism and equality at the heart of the contemporary claim for suffrage. In face of these difficulties, anticipation of the courts ran through the minimum wagers' case, in the departures from minimum wage laws elsewhere, the language of their presentations, the lengths to which they took their argument. That argument was developed at three interrelated levels, each level presuming a gendered law, each approaching more closely the case required, it was thought, by the courts. First, American minimum wagers argued and demonstrated the *fact* of women's inequality in the economy. The second step was to prove women's *inability* to change their own fate. Minimum wagers therefore demonstrated the relative social disadvantage of women due to the circumstances of female lives and to women's own attitudes and vulnerabilities. Finally, they moved into the realm of a public interest in women's lives and health, with arguments about biology and the "mothers of the race."

The fact of economic inequality was easily demonstrated from the many surveys of women in the work force, which produced overwhelming evidence that women were segregated into poorly paid occupations or the lower echelons of trades where they earned less and had lesser prospects than men. Data undermined widely believed myths about working women—for example, that they were all teenage girls, enjoying a brief independence in the passage to their adult, womanly, roles as wives and mothers; or that they worked only to add a few luxuries to an adequate family budget.[27] The clear conclusion was that women's work life was long and necessary, if intermittent, and that they rarely made a living wage.

In Britain, such data were used to demonstrate that women were the worst-off members of a class of sweated workers. Delegations of women workers were produced for public events and parliamentary inquiries, to tug at the heartstrings of the public and shame employers as "sweaters." Gendered propaganda was used to win economic-class legislation. In the United States, the propaganda value was equal, and women's greater hardship was constantly noted. LaRue Brown compared Massachusetts's law with Britain's: "For constitutional reasons, it was thought, we had to limit ours to the employment of women. At any rate the employment of women was the field in which such legislation was badly needed, because the wages . . . were shamefully low."[28] In the United States the statistics were more than propaganda. They built the foundation of a justification of laws for women, class legislation in the technical sense of constitutionally permissible discrimination. A class for this purpose "must present the danger dealt with in a more marked and uniform degree than the classes omitted," or prove an evil either confined to this class or accepted elsewhere only "under circumstances where it is outweighed by great benefits."[29] So Mary Van Kleeck, for one, emphasized that "we are interested in the protection of women workers by wage legislation at this time, not particularly because they are women, but because they are underpaid workers and underpayment is a social menace whether the worker be a man or a woman, but it happens that the condition pressed most heavily upon women at this time, *and it seems to me that we should regard those conditions as unique to women.*"[30]

A classification need not denigrate those it singles out. But a positive case, that women could and would be equal, absent oppressive economic circumstances, was rarely made. NWTUL president Margaret Dreier Robins was one person who did not blame the victim. In her presidential address in 1913 she spoke in terms that combined women's difference from men with women's right to an equally rich life, women's exploitation at work because of gender with a straightforward economic argument for the recognition of skill, productivity, and need, regardless of gender. Women's wages, she thought, should reward their labor, not reflect their family position. Women did not "represent unintelligent, unskilled inefficient labor," as her examples, from lace-makers, doing traditional women's work as "some of the most skilled as well as the cheapest labor," to women working alongside men, as telegraph operators, bookkeepers, teachers, showed. Robins attacked the moral and financial devaluation of women's work, whether in sex-segregated or integrated occupations, and the ramshackle justifications that supported this. Furthermore, she insisted, up against the "will of the individual employer," the "girl's poverty and inexperience forces her consent" to exploitation.[31]

When Americans resorted to arguments familiar from Britain, especially the theory of sweating as a malfunction of the market mechanism and a parasite upon society (language deployed to good effect in Robins's address) they encountered both legal and ideological problems.[32] Arthur Holcombe explained to economists that two constitutional problems rendered their own professional misgivings about the minimum wage almost beside the point. These were: the current interpretation of the Fourteenth Amendment; and judges "whose economic training was received mainly from the so-called classical school of political economists." The two combined had allowed "a doctrine that is nowhere expressed therein, namely, the doctrine of freedom of contract," to creep into the Constitution. But the loophole of laws for women also disturbed Holcombe, who was not convinced that low pay was any more a social menace for women than for men. Despite his training in economics, he was less worried about malfunctioning economic process than about family roles and the fact that "upon [men] as the heads of families, the majority of women are dependent for support."[33]

Mary Van Kleeck observed that "families in which much of the burden of support fell upon the women workers" were generally families in which "the fathers were either incapacitated or dead." Given that "primarily the wages of women are family wages rather than individual wages," a minimum wage for women would be a direct contribution "to the support of families and to home life."[34] In her hands, though, the concept of the family wage was of the collective contributions of members of a shared household enterprise. Young, married, and surviving women might all contribute and should all be enabled to enter the economy on fair terms. Holcombe, by contrast, believed in "the social necessity for the maintenance of the family" and would prefer a minimum wage for men. In his hands, the family wage became patriarchal. Ideally, only *after* appropriate minima according to marital status had been ensured would a nondiscriminatory wage be considered. If then "the evidence should show that, as a matter of fact, women were oppressed to a greater degree than men by employment in the sweated trades, that would be a matter with which the enforcing authority would properly deal."[35] By his method, the facts of economic inequality would be first screened through a filter of normative gender roles and only secondarily analyzed for patterns of discrimination.

Ernst Freund had suggested that sex could not be used as a classification where the benefit at stake was the equal right of all persons to social advancement. As an example of the kind of difference that would provide a rational standard of classification, he mentioned the German Trade Code provision "that women who attend to the household are entitled to an extra half hour for the midday meal . . . here we have a social measure justified by the special duties of women, and it is perhaps possible that other cases . . . may arise."[36] Freund had criticized the *Muller* decision because of its inclination "to assign to women an inferior political status." He believed that this decision should have "pointed out that the industrial work of women, owing to the dominating influence of domestic functions or prospects, is of an adventitious rather than of a professional character and that consequently the inducement and the opportunity for organization is seriously diminished. An argument for larger control might be placed on this ground, to which women could take no just exception."[37]

It was not enough to show the courts that women *had* not helped themselves. It must be proven that they *could* not help themselves. Only then, in the eyes of the law, would the state be justified in exercising its inherent police power to protect women, and with them society, at the expense of women's abstract individual right to freedom of contract. Shifting from economic comparisons to social assumptions about women, the minimum wage campaign developed two lines of argument from women's social circumstances: women were different by virtue of their disenfranchisement and by virtue of gender roles including, but not exclusively, those within the family. As an AALL adviser, John Martin, explained, women were differentiated "by law and by custom and for social preservation."[38] Arguments about law and custom formed this second phase of the rationale for the minimum wage.

The first of Martin's factors, law, presented a difficulty. Several decades of legal reform had reduced the common law inequalities of women, so that (in a majority of states) some rights, particularly in marital relations and over property and wages, had been won. However, others remained to be fought for, and "constitutional discrimination" continued to characterize Supreme Court decisions on women's rights.[39] Faced with slow and uncertain change, many reformers had concluded that equality would not be achieved without female suffrage. "I favor this minimum wage merely because they have no vote," one (male) witness to the FIC remarked. "If they had a vote and continued to vote for the present parties they ought to suffer."[40] Most champions of the minimum wage as a special protection for women were also champions of votes for women as equals of men. But, as Holcombe warned, there were states where sweating was prevalent but where women had the vote. Legislation for women would have "no better prospect of withstanding the scrutiny of the courts than a similar bill for all adults, male and female."[41] So when Samuel Gompers, in his capacity as FIC commissioner, proposed provocatively that "if woman is to be regarded as a ward of the state, so that her wages shall be determined . . . it would be in conflict with the spirit of equality of woman with man," Josephine Goldmark of the NCL could only reply defensively. Wryly, she complimented Gompers's "solicitude lest the legislation providing for minimum wages for women if adopted might lead to some disadvantage to the political status of women," countering that "we who are suffragists are not afraid of legislation of this character."[42]

Where women could vote, Goldmark argued, legislatures continued to pass gendered protective laws. There were also laws "on the statute books to-day" protecting male workers, proving that "every man as well as every woman has to submit to restrictions on his or her personal liberty just because they are members of society and citizens."[43] Her somewhat specious argument evaded the issue of equality of restriction, which was the crux of the constitutional problem. No consistent principle of sex equality was currently apparent, either in legislation or in court decisions. But Freund could see a trend developing: "Under the operation of the Fourteenth Amendment, the legislative power is certainly not as free in this respect as it used to be . . . But classification, and therefore class legislation, has not yet been abolished, it is merely placed under judicial control."[44] Use of the due process clause by both courts and political campaigns was bringing gender distinctions under constitutional scrutiny. The pressure toward consistency felt by Goldmark was a consequence; for as Freund wrote, "The stringent exercise of judicial control will tend, and is already tending, to bring about more systematic methods of legislation."[45] This pressure to consistency worked against the flexibility favored by British reformers like Lady Dilke, whose use of arguments for gender equality or special treatment depended upon circumstances. It also worked against any use of the British class analysis, for only certain kinds of classification were constitutionally acceptable, and economic circumstance was not one of them. The "effectual limitations upon the exercise of the police power" to cases "based on time, on locality, on personal status, and on differences in acts or occupations" drove reformers to use the potentially acceptable personal status of sex.[46]

Voting might aid self-help, but suffrage arguments confused the minimum wage case. Might organization, especially in unions, enable women workers to improve their own condition? To build their case that women could not help themselves in the labor market, minimum wagers observed the fact that they had "not been able in their bargaining power to protect themselves" and argued that this was due to practical circumstances and cultural beliefs beyond their power to change.[47] This argument took them beyond Martin's realm of "law" into "custom" and into a wider discussion of the social construction of gender roles and family values.

The FIC learned from Elizabeth Dutcher, of the Retail Clerk's Union, of some structural inhibitions on organization. Dutcher spoke from experience of seasonal fluctuations in trade and employment creating a transient work force, of the low wages that made it "very hard to pay union dues out of a salary of $5 a week," and of vulnerable women who "also have bitter persecution on the part of the employers to face." Dutcher made the argument that wage boards would not displace unions: "It gives people enough money to pay their union dues. It gives them a sense of security and hope that is better than a tonic for them. They feel strengthened. They have some sort of a basis on which they can stand and come forward." The boards themselves would provide "a training in industrial self-government."[48] Pauline Newman of the ILGWU confirmed that "it is a mighty difficult thing to organize those who are at the present moment below the living level. We know it takes years and years to drill into a girl the absolute necessity for organization, the value of organization."[49] Dutcher and Newman spoke eloquently of the urgency of bringing help and dignity to working women. But their analysis of the inability of women to organize failed the test of whether "the restraint is imposed upon some while others who are in a similar position are arbitrarily exempted from it."[50] Resolute opponent Helen Marot observed: "If women need state protection on that ground why do not the great masses of underpaid, unskilled working men who show no greater appreciation of the advantages of labor organization than do women?"[51] Given the facts of sweating, including the commission's own evidence that only two-thirds of sweated workers were women, and the bias of the craft workers of the AFL against organizing unskilled workers of both sexes, this was a legally damning point.

Louis Brandeis, like Mary Van Kleeck with her statistics, tried to shade relative disadvantage into a clear-cut difference. Brandeis, fresh from an appearance as counsel in the first Supreme Court test of the minimum wage, spoke to the FIC in language that encoded certainty versus uncertainty. The difficulty of organizing applied to all women for the foreseeable future, only sometimes to men: "We know it will take a long while before women can be strong enough to protect themselves through unions," but "we have no ascertained conditions at the present time which call for this limitation upon the freedom of contract of men. In a great many instances the union has been able to take care of that."[52] Arguments about the social construction of gender roles at a particular historical moment might seem as vulnerable to change as those about inexperience and poverty. Not so to the public (or the judicial) eye, for conceptual distinctions between immutable sex and mutable gender were rarely articulated at this time. To all but a minority of feminists and socialists, the sexual division of labor between male workers and female wives and mothers seemed "natural."[53] Women's social status, beliefs, and attitudes were prominent in explanations of women's inability to solve their own economic problems.

"Custom" was Martin's label for such social constructions. Felix Frankfurter, the protegé of Brandeis who took on minimum wage cases when Brandeis was appointed to the Supreme Court in 1916, meant the same—the prevalent beliefs about gender roles and the attitudes and behavior that followed—by his description of "the weakness that tradition has imposed upon them."[54] For both men, weakness was the key to legal success. So Martin "approach[ed] this question on the assumption . . . that woman is weaker economically than man and cannot possibly ever attain in equality with men in power of competitive industry generally. Her weakness differentiates her from men."[55]

Society expected, and working women assumed, that "their work is casual labor while they wait for what they have been taught to regard as the end in life," namely marriage, an AFL study of women's unionization reported. "Normally she is in industry only for a short period and that incapacitates her for collective knowledge as man. Knowing that she will leave wage industry when she marries she will not make sacrifices for a distant benefit as a man would make who expects to be in the industry his whole life," Martin concurred.[56] Those with experience of work conditions knew that this was a false expectation for many women. John Mitchell, ex-president of the United Mine Workers, deplored "the fact that while many women do spend all their lives in industry few expect to do so." Confessing, somewhat disingenuously, that this was a new thought to him, his logic led him to the necessity of legislation: "I am afraid that unless through some legal process society can give forcible expression to its desire that women shall receive at least a sufficient wage to enable them to live healthy lives that they will not get that wage, that large numbers of them will not secure that wage."[57]

Social feminists like Kelley have been excoriated for seeking protective legislation for women that reinforced the stereotype of "the weaker sex."[58] Such women are named maternalists because of their emphasis on motherhood as the basis of gender difference. But, in arguments for the minimum wage, an economic analysis was there from the start, struggling to come out, in conflict with traditional maternalism. Margaret Dreier Robins, organizationally based in the labor movement, and Florence Kelley in the reform movement shared views in which labor realism, that women did work, and maternalist preference, the wish that women did not work or the stronger belief that they should not, combined or contested. Acknowledgment of women workers was not an alternative to a gendered explanation; minimum wagers attempted an integrated analysis of the intersections of gender, class, and economic mechanisms.

Kelley's own views exemplify the difficulty. Her comments resound with tension between an economic analysis and a case grounded in gender difference. She was caught in the contradictions between traditional views on women and the family, experience of women's working conditions, knowledge of the impact on women of the social and economic changes of recent decades, and her own socialist training and legal expertise. She endorsed the nuclear family and the women's role as wife and mother, and she spoke of her preference for a family wage. But she advocated a minimum wage that recognized and legitimated the working woman and sought to give her an adequate income. She supported gendered legislation with misgivings, not because a gendered policy was inconsistent with the facts of sweating but because it was inconsistent with maintaining unchanged the institution of the family.

A gender-neutral minimum wage could have been, Kelley believed, a means to achieve a family wage: "Why is it that we alone restrict this legislation to women? As I read the preamble to the Washington statute, I ask myself: If it is contrary to the welfare of the state of Washington that women and minors should work under conditions prejudicial to their health and morals, can it be desirable that men should work under such conditions?" She answered her own question with another (the interrogatory style perhaps a mark of her uncertainties): "Is it not true that where women and minors work for wages at all, it is ultimately because their men bread-winners are insufficiently paid?"[59] How was Kelley able to campaign for the minimum wage for women so wholeheartedly? Her age and generation, transitions in her own life, and the American political milieu all contributed to this outcome and answer for many of her contemporaries too.

Kelley's life, from 1859 to 1932, spanned a period of rapid technological and industrial change, with correspondingly sweeping social consequences for women and men. Her mother's generation justified an expanding political role as an extension of "home rule." Kelley's generation has been described as growing up "in a world governed by these words and this traditional insistence on women's innate purity and nurturance. Effortlessly, they used these old arguments to justify public roles that, in their eyes, merely carried their 'mothers'' ideas to a logical conclusion." The language of family and home was carried into a new era where it sat awkwardly with changed circumstances.[60] Kelley had both absorbed and broken away from the older tradition. Moving to Europe in 1883 and to Hull House in 1891 brought her to maturity under two great influences that formed her views in the minimum wage campaign—socialism and women's causes.

Even as a young graduate, Kelley had been predisposed to these causes. Her first publication on the exploitation of working women, when she was twenty-three, combined structural analysis with moral outrage and supported women's equal rights at work, to education and training for skilled labor and to equal pay.[61] Her plunge into European socialism and her work translating Engels gave theoretical depth to her social analysis. The near-religious commitment of the movement gave a moral flavor to her work; its condemnation of a class-structured and class-exploited society helped fuel and direct her outrage for the rest of her life. But her involvement in the German socialist movement also taught her that socialism, or at least the socialist movement, would not automatically solve working women's problems. Her biographer, Kathryn Kish Sklar, identifies a watershed in Kelley's life, when she moved, between 1888 and 1892, "from the male-dominated world of the Socialist Labor Party to the female-dominated world of women's reform organizations . . . from theory to practice . . . from the reform style of an intellectual to that of a social worker."[62] But she did not leave her earlier experiences behind; it was the cumulation of experience, not its displacement, that later made Kelley both responsive to and cross-pressured by the minimum wage for women.

Kelley's socialism predisposed her to the economic case for the minimum wage. In 1911, for example, she noted that "the institution [Minimum Wage Boards] upon which I am to report tonight rests upon recognition of the fact that one very important cause of poverty is industry."[63] She emphasized the redistributive effects of the proposal: "All industries will be standardized and none will be permitted to remain subnormal . . . With the levelling up of wages in great industries . . . a burden will be lifted which charity has borne with patient tolerance a century too long." But if the minimum wage could achieve such justice in the economic sphere, a minimum wage for women would do so at the expense of the nuclear family. As minimum wage laws multiplied, she remained dubious: "Why do we Americans refuse to face the fact that women and minors are earning wages primarily because of underpaid husbands and fathers, who would gladly keep their wives at home and their children in school? That it is precisely in the interests of the family that the wages of men should be regulated?"[64]

A minimum wage for both men and women would fit Kelley's analysis of the industrial problem *and* her preference for the family wage. Kelley, the original "half-loaf girl," regularly expressed her frustration with obstacles to the whole loaf of inclusive legislation. She railed against the courts, regarding the constitutional preemption of the issue as something to fight. She was frustrated by the confused response of state and federal courts to labor legislation. "Men are omitted from these new laws upon an arbitrary assumption that the issue would be unconstitutional if applied to men," she noted in 1914, and, with some overstatement, in 1920: "The impression is widespread that because of our Constitution American laws of this character cannot apply to men. No provision of the Constitution and no decision of a Court can, however, be cited in support of this belief."[65] Kelley never lost sight of her own ideals. But she never allowed them to paralyze her campaigns. She saw the merits of the British model of a minimum wage, but she understood the political context in which she must work. As Sklar has commented of her socialism, "When differences forced her to choose between the American and European traditions of reform, the native traditions won."[66]

Kelley committed herself to the best she could get, under the circumstances. She brought Brandeis in to defend gendered legislation in the *Muller* case and contributed NCL resources to the defense of the women's minimum wage in the courts.[67] She saw the danger of formulations that proposed that commissions include men's conditions in their inquiries, "that some crudely drawn measure may be brought before the courts, such that some court will not see its way clear to sustain the principle that underlies it. Whenever that happens, a nationwide movement, going forward as this one is now going forward, is checked." As the surest way to avert this danger, she endorsed the "right principle enunciated with unmistakable clearness" to meet the parameters of the police power, prefacing the NCL model law with the legislative declaration that "the welfare of the State of . . . demands that women and minors be protected from conditions of labor which have a pernicious effect upon their health and morals."[68]

Kelley never indulged in blaming the victim. She sympathized with the wife and mother as "she suffers the disadvantage of carrying the double burden and enduring the twofold strain of home maker and wage earner." Even as she pursued the gendered goal of protecting women, Kelley understood the genesis of the problem to lie in social structure and social change. Nonetheless, when she extended her view from individual women to the wider ramifications of women's entry into the work force, she not only made the essential public interest case for the police power but began to open the door to the rather different rationale of "social preservation." The minimum wage, she believed,

formed part of a package of legislation for women whose purpose was "to bul-
wark the family" in the community interest.[69] The "harm and only harm"
wrought by women's industrial work might lead to "increase in the number of
children who are never born," might be a "demoralizing influence for husbands" and "[press] upon the wage rate of men"; and always "her children pay
the penalty." Hence "it is ultimately the whole community which pays."[70] If
there was a community interest in the welfare of husbands and children, it
could be fulfilled by women as part of their social roles and responsibilities. But
judges could change their minds about social roles, while biological roles and
responsibilities seemed a sure and permanent foundation for arguments to the
courts in defense of gendered legislation.

Society's Need: The Maternal Claim

John Martin's final reason for legislating for women was "for social preservation." Minimum wagers required a hard and fast justification for the different
treatment of women, safe from the shifting sands of law and custom. The political instinct to go for the safest constitutional ground coincided with the tendency of legal reasoning to prefer clear categories to fuzzy distinctions. "Social
preservation" provided the clear category. The argument shifted from the be-
nevolent concern of society for the weaker sex, whether economically or socially defined, to the interest of the state in its own survival. Martin's change in
preposition, from *by* law and custom to *for* social preservation, represented a
significant change for women from being oppressed by society to being required for society. No longer simply the subject of the concern of the community, women were called to the service of the state, a shift from welfare to duty
and to a functional concept of citizenship grounded in gender difference.[71]

The role of "mothers of the race" was intended to have its own dignity. As a
political status, motherhood established reciprocal obligations between women
and the state. The obligation for women was to produce a healthy new generation. The state, in return, must safeguard its mothers (and all women were
potential mothers). But the dignity of women citizens was less visible in the
rhetoric of motherhood than was the loss of autonomy involved in subordinat-
ing the rights of workers to the responsibilities of mothers. "The state takes the
position that the payroll is a public matter and not a private interest," said
Elizabeth Glendower Evans, supporting the Massachusetts law. "The employer
is buying human life, the lives of young women who are to be the mothers of the
race. And the wages they are paid are a matter of public import."[72] Echoing the
reference in the *Muller* judgment to "the influence of vigorous health upon the
future well-being of the race," the argument that the minimum wage was for
state-mothers recurred. As Frankfurter put it, on behalf of the District of Columbia bill, in 1918, "We talk about mobilizing the resources of the country for
war. This is legislation that really mobilizes the indispensable resources of the
State, in protecting the womanhood and childhood of the country."[73]

Perhaps the fact that Congress was in session in 1918, "in the midst of war's alarms," heightened the rhetoric. At any rate, the case was made to its full extreme on the same occasion by Dr. W. C. Woodward, health commissioner for the district, who was applauded by an audience of minimum wagers:

> After all it is in marriage and the bearing of offspring that the race relies for its continuance in a proper form. So even without reference to a woman's own condition, and the maintenance of her own physical, mental and emotional health, we must bear in mind the fact that when she marries and when she bears and rears children for the coming generation, if she has been properly trained and has adequate opportunities to care for herself we shall be able as a Nation to meet the perils that confront us.

Woodward rejected the social case, based on "the need of the individual woman." "We must," he told the committee, "go beyond that need and face the fact that we are acting for the race, we are acting for the Nation, and the Nation needs all these women to be kept in the best possible condition."[74] Expressed in terms of breeding stock, this argument was the ultimate denigration. Women were objectified by their biology.

If mothers must be fit and healthy, and when the minimum wage first came before the Supreme Court this was a key point of the brief, contemporary studies showed them to be lacking. "Health is the foundation of the state," the brief in *Stettler v. O'Hara* argued: "The health of the race is conditioned upon preserving the health of women, the future mothers of the Republic."[75] Josephine Goldmark's *Fatigue and Efficiency*, based on the brief she had researched for the *Muller* case, provided data on "the special susceptibility to fatigue and disease which distinguished the female sex, *qua* female."[76] Such arguments for the primacy of the maternal role were not limited to the male experts in law and medicine. Elizabeth Glendower Evans and Margaret Dreier Robins, middle-class women whose socialist and labor connections were strong, concurred. Robins cited the British women chain-makers of Cradley Heath: "They were the mothers of those men whom the English army could not accept into its service during the Boer War because they did not come up to the physical standard demanded," she claimed, "and not only mothers of sons, they were also mothers of daughters. The mothers of girls, potential mothers of another generation, each one representing a lowered vitality and constant tend [*sic*] toward degeneracy."[77]

Linking the minimum wage to childbearing went well beyond the demands of business and labor. Motherhood was the female attribute to satisfy contemporary judicial requirements, to justify state intervention in the economy at the expense of the right to freedom of contract, and to prove the relevance of the sex classification to that overriding need. By treating wages as "a sex problem," not "a labor problem," minimum wagers believed they had found a constitutional way around the logic that what held true for women's wages held true also for men's. They could claim, with John Mitchell, that "the very fact that they are women makes it necessary in the interests of society, and in the interest of women, that they shall be protected in some ways that men are not protected."[78]

"In this country a statute is only a trial draft until the Supreme Court of the United States has passed upon it," Kelley observed.[79] Oregon provided the first test case, *Stettler v. O'Hara*. The brief for Edwin V. O'Hara, chair of the Oregon Industrial Welfare Commission, codified the diffuse arguments of years of political debate into an ordered response to the legal requirements, on the pattern of the first "Brandeis brief" of the *Muller* case. At length (706 pages), Josephine Goldmark's data demonstrated the "Bad Effect of Low Wages on the Public Health," on "Morals," and on the "Public Welfare" and then labored to justify the intervention of the state in wage fixing.[80] Constitutionally, the issue was, Frankfurter proposed when he took over from Brandeis, "simply enough" a question of the application of "Marshall's canon of constitutional construction to the complicated and extensive facts of industrial life." That is to say: "Let the end be legitimate, let it be within the scope of the constitution, and all means which are appropriate, which are plainly adapted to that end, which are not prohibited, but consist with the letter and spirit of the constitution, are constitutional." But the test case was inconclusive. The court divided evenly and left the law standing.[81]

The *Stettler* brief is of more than passing interest, however. Its orderly legal text, showing how a minimum wage for women could be justified as a police measure, demonstrated just as clearly all the legally disorderly facts of economic circumstance and family norms that contradicted the rationale for a woman's wage. Coincidentally resembling the proportions of women and men in the sweated work force, a good third of the data presented concerned men, as individual sufferers from low wages or as the implied breadwinners in a family economy. As in the political negotiations, almost all of the arguments for a minimum wage for women could equally apply to similarly situated men; only the protection of the mothers of the race and of the morals of young women clearly singled out sex as an unassailable classification. It was Frankfurter, for all his talk of women as "the indispensable resources of the state," who pointed out that the trend of social and medical evidence suggested that "there is no sharp difference in kind as to the effect of labor on men and women." He thought that a new constitutional interpretation must emerge, noting that "courts recently have followed the guidance of science, and refused to be controlled by outworn ignorance." Even as the gendered rationale for the minimum wage was perfected, Frankfurter acknowledged its bias: "Once we cease to look upon the regulation of women in industry as exceptional, as the law's graciousness to a disabled class, and shift the emphasis from the fact that they are *women* to the fact that it is *industry* and the relation of industry to the community that is regulated, the whole problem is seen from a totally different aspect."[82] Twenty years later, such a situation materialized, in the context of economic crisis, a New Deal administration, a hard-fought constitutional transition, and a differently situated women's politics. In the meantime, the wholehearted commitment to a woman's wage served at least a temporary purpose, offering escape from the impasse created by the constitutional bans on "workers" as a classification and on wages as a subject for statutory control.

THE POLICE POWER, WOMEN'S POLITICS AND THE MINIMUM WAGE

In pre-modern Europe and colonial America, "policing" was "a strategy in the regulation of populations, the ultimate objective of which [was] not the achievement of security, but happiness."[83] Christopher Tomlins has sketched the change from the original "desire of the community to order itself" to the modern meaning of policing as the imposition of order through regulatory control.[84] By the early nineteenth century, the older paradigm, with its communal and participatory associations, had been largely displaced. Modern usage, "that subspecies of state power concerned with issues of security—crime, public morality and social order," represented a change that Tomlins encapsulates as "the purge of public happiness, the stress on private security."[85] The meaning of policing and the expansion of the police power are integral to understanding women's politics and the first phase of the minimum wage campaign.

For women, particularly in the new white middle class of the early nineteenth century, the emergence of "separate spheres" of life followed change in economy, ideology, and politics. Their lives became more bounded by gendered roles and meanings, more contained within the female domestic sphere that contrasted with the male public life. In this divided world, the premodern paradigm of the policing of society did not disappear into oblivion, as Tomlins suggests. It was transported, with women, into the sphere of domestic responsibility, where it survived and flourished. The police power, which had been "coextensive with the idea of the state" in early democratic and communitarian formulations, became private and domestic.[86] The ordering of society for happiness, like the internal order and welfare of the family, was set outside of constitutional and statutory responsibility. A swathe of social functions was left to private voluntary action by women. A new view of women's roles and responsibilities as moral arbiters and social care-givers incorporated much of the previous content of "policing."[87]

The ordering of the community in its new private, domestic formulation became associated with "women's work" of mothering and caring, bound up with the domestic tasks of health, hygiene, and education, and separated from the male concerns of market and state. Later in the nineteenth century, women used these same "domestic" responsibilities as a means of and justification for their entry into the political arena. Lending themselves propriety and asserting expertise, women made up for civil inequality by politicizing their functional, female status. Paula Baker describes this empowering strategy as a new "domestication of politics."[88] Actually, women were returning to politics a whole area lost to it in the early-modern state. Their vision of a state responsive to

communitarian concerns reinvented the old notion of policing—and the realization of their vision within the bounds of American constitutionalism appropriately depended upon a revitalized and expanded police power.

The struggle to win protective legislation for women was only one of a cluster
of contemporary struggles to acquire standing in the legislative arena for claims
that had, up to this time, been defined out of the scope of deliberative public
policy. In the field of labor relations, and in the hands of organized labor as well
as in the social reform causes of women, a crucial terrain of political contest
over what constituted a *public* interest, and who decided this crucial matter,
was the law. Legal strategies were used to define and expand the scope of
politics with notable skill by groups—organized labor and women—who have
appeared more often in the history books as victims than as exploiters of the
law.[89] Minimum wagers were not only under the duress of constitutional restrictions. In formulating their case and deciding which obstacles to accept,
which to confront, in using gender difference but seeking to open the door to
state intervention in the wage bargain, the heart of the market mechanism, they
were pro-actively hoping to set the terms of future judicial consideration. Were
the courts to be persuaded that the police power extended to wage legislation,
the implications would be great. A claim that could be legislated was open to
democratic pressure, to public debate, to comprehensive policymaking rather
than the accretion of case law, to state administration and oversight and to all
the authority of a statutory basis.

Judicial decisions on the police power had written gender distinctions into
law. When the minimum wage campaign took shape, the situation was, as William Forbath describes it, "maddeningly uncertain" on the "exact borders" of
the police power but entirely clear that "broad, class-based legislation would
not pass constitutional muster." Men's right to freedom of contract overrode all
economic and most health legislation. The assertion that women either did not
possess full rights or were incapable of their exercise, had a political as well as
a legal consequence: "This constitutional segmentation of labor into a 'dependent' class of children, women, and men in certain dangerous or especially
vulnerable callings, and an 'independent' class of 'free adult workers' . . .
helped fragment not only labor legislation but also workers' group identity."[90]
The police power as a set of legal precedents bound and narrowed the vision of
minimum wagers and other champions of protective legislation. Its dictates
rejected an economic or class analysis in favor of gender, isolated women, and
tilted a gender analysis toward an essentialist, biological distinction that would
most permanently ensure the interest of the state.

The extent to which the original meaning of policing had to be fought into
the purview of the state, while aligning it with other political struggles of the
time, was a distraction from, and brought a maternalist bias to, the minimum
wage campaign. Finding police power justifications meant skewing the argument away from the economic dynamics of sweating and the class relations of
the working woman. It required an emphasis on health, on families and homes,
and on harm to society, which were symptoms, not causes, of the problem. It

turned the issue from one of economic exploitation and inequality to one of social costs and gender difference. The prejudice embodied in judicial interpretation isolated women to fight their own campaign and thereby also avoided confrontation with the same prejudices embodied in organized male labor. The police power managed simultaneously to be both a reinforcement to prejudice and an alternative strategy.

The empowerment of women by the police power was a less obvious process, more easily seen with the benefits of hindsight than by those minimum wagers who railed against the limitations of the law. The basic terms of the police power resembled to a marked degree the social responsibilities designated as women's sphere. The concept embodied both the substance of women's politics—health, welfare, and morals—and their characteristic perceptions and styles of action—community welfare and participatory, collective action. The fact that the language of policing had been appropriated for the purposes of security and control, and that this had become its dominant colloquial and legal usage, submerged rather than obliterated the older meaning. Freund's contents list, introducing the police power as simultaneously "a means of furthering the public welfare" and "a power of restraint and compulsion," exemplified the curious duality of the term.[91] Women made use of the older meaning, claimed this as their right and their proper function, and in a series of legislative and judicial battles over health, welfare, moral, and protective legislation, fought to reverse an earlier process in which community concerns had been domesticated out of the public sphere, by redomesticating politics.

The police power was no more a cause of this process than were the social and industrial changes that affected women and contributed to the development of women's political activity. Rather, it was one factor in a creative conjunction of circumstances, and a crucial one in offering women an opening into the legal discourse of political action in a constitutional culture. Baker has described how "women expanded their ascribed sphere into community service and care of dependents, areas not fully within men's or women's politics . . . not fully part of either male electoral politics and formal governmental institutions or the female world of the home and family." The unpreempted task was an opportunity, and women not only seized it in practice but took ideological possession by using their special social status: "Men and women would probably have agreed that the 'home' in a balanced social order was the place for women and children. But this definition became an expansive doctrine: home was anywhere women and children were."[92] This provided the claim to engage in municipal housekeeping and to the custody of public health, welfare, and morals, which gained constitutional authority from the original meaning of the police power.

At the same time, the massive social changes of industrialization and urbanization created a more urgent need, and the education of women created the appropriate skills, for social reform. Women's emergence in the public sphere in social reform movements may well seem overdetermined, and indeed, their "prominence in the 'social justice' wing of Progressive reform arose at least in part from the match between the social issues generated by industrial capitalism and the routine environment of their own lives."[93] In fact, as Baker points out, it is not self-evident "how and why governments took on these specific tasks," nor, as Sklar asks, how and why it was that "women's domestic responsibilities combined with their associative lives to create the phenomenon of 'municipal housekeeping,' which then extended to state and national housekeeping."[94] Part of the explanation lay in the independent agency of women themselves. Part, certainly, was because of the access afforded by the police power, an authority that women used, so far as they could, to advance their causes.

The threads of this discussion of the police power, then, variously situate the minimum wage campaign as a political strategy, as a labor strategy, as a women's strategy, and as an American strategy in contrast to the British paradigm. The latent potential of the police power, submerged for many years, matched the domestic ideal ascribed to women so well that it provided the least threatening (to men) arena for the expansion of women's political activity and may have deterred the intransigent opposition otherwise to be expected from more quarters than the AFL. The concept provided potential constitutional legitimacy, in the name of a community interest, to women whose personal standing and access to individual rights was only in the process of clarification. As well as offering claims on and access to the state, the substance of the police power lent itself to women's politics. The purpose of the ordering of the community and its collective imperative contrasted with the individualism of rights such as freedom of contract. This suited the political networks, the cooperative activity, and the democratic and inclusive impulse characteristic of much of women's politics. The policy areas identified by current interpretation of the police power enabled women to use their acknowledged responsibilities and experience and the expertise and skills gained from their voluntary work and their higher education.

The police power was an important factor in the minimum wage campaign. It was not, even at the time, an exoneration for the blindnesses and biases stemming from the determination of that campaign to treat low wages as a sex problem. This was, after all, a choice, albeit apparently one between some progress and no progress. What could not have been foreseen at the time was the speed and absoluteness with which all the positive features of the gendered strategy would turn into a trap and stall the campaign for some fifteen years.

Gender Trap

PROTECTION VERSUS EQUALITY, U.S.A., 1921–1923

THE 1920s were critical years for the development of minimum wage policy in the United States. The decade embraced two distinct periods, the turning point in 1923 marked by the Supreme Court's veto of the District of Columbia minimum wage law in April and the introduction of an Equal Rights Amendment in Congress for the first time in December. Both the tone and the substance of the minimum wage campaign differed before and after 1923. The confidence of the first period was replaced by defensiveness and demoralization in the second, the leadership of female reformers by that of male lawyers. The issue at the heart of debate before 1920 was gender at work. After 1923, it was the constitutional doctrine of due process, with gender marginalized.

The twenties were years of setbacks for the minimum wage. Differences of opinion sharpened, and legislation was nullified, underfunded, or unenforced. In 1919, laws were in place in fourteen states, the District of Columbia, and Puerto Rico. But 1919 saw the first repeal, in Nebraska. In the next decade, South Dakota passed a bill and Wisconsin revised its legislation, but two more laws were repealed and the courts struck down seven. After 1923, the failure of the test case in the Supreme Court, *Adkins v. Children's Hospital of Washington, D.C.*, left minimum wage law in limbo. Minimum wage commissions were emasculated by the fear of court cases, by budget cuts, and by loss of support.[1]

In 1920, however, optimism reigned. Florence Kelley's notes for a Thanksgiving speech were appropriately cheerful: "Wage determinations have multiplied manifold, and their beneficial effect can now be convincingly demonstrated." The future held promise: "Every year in January more than forty legislatures meet. Then the men and women work overtime who strive to carry forward, by the orderly processes of the law, new social and industrial changes. They are now drafting bills for introduction in January 1921. Their effort will be directed anew to the creation of minimum wage commissions in adjacent states over large areas." As progress was consolidated, Kelley looked forward to the final validation, "an original affirmative decision by the United States Supreme Court."[2] She knew that a test case from the District of Columbia was in the pipeline. Three years later, the minimum wage campaign had, in *Adkins*, its original decision by the Supreme Court. Kelley was bitter: "The minimum wage law of the District of Columbia has been held unconstitutional, and several thousand women have been assured of their constitutional right to starve, in the capital of our country."[3]

Also between 1921 and 1923, the National Woman's Party (NWP), a reconstituted suffrage organization, was formulating an Equal Rights Amendment to the Constitution.[4] This new strategy for bettering women's condition threatened minimum wage policy: unqualified legal equality between the sexes would contradict special protections for women. Between 1920 and 1923, debates over the minimum wage in the courts and over the ERA within women's politics became two parts of the same contest. The definition of equality for women in the postsuffrage era and the means by which to advance were at stake. Women and their legal advisers, who had reconciled the twin goals of protective legislation and suffrage before 1920, now brought the inherent contradiction between protection and equality to center stage. Without the unifying priority of suffrage, former allies polarized behind irreconcilable demands.

In May 1920, the District of Columbia Children's Hospital sought an injunction against the Minimum Wage Board. In February 1921, the NWP declared the elimination of women's legal disabilities its official goal. In April 1923, the Supreme Court ruled against the minimum wage. In December 1923, an ERA was introduced in Congress for the first time. By 1923, the two sides were neither speaking nor listening to each other. Though the ERA made little progress, its mere formulation was damaging to the minimum wage campaign. Placed on the defensive by the intellectual challenge of the ERA and rejected by the courts, minimum wagers hardened their own claim for gendered legislation from a matter of political and legal advantage to one of principle. Demoralized by the hostile court decision, after 1923 they concentrated upon reinstating what they had lost.

The relationship between female reformers and male lawyers changed at this time. The ERA and the *Adkins* case raised complex legal issues, and legal advisers inevitably gained new prominence. Women reformers and lawyers had cooperated in the early minimum wage campaign. Women primarily set the policy, and men advised on strategy and provided essential professional support. Practicing lawyers, like Brandeis and Brown in Massachusetts, carried the campaign into the male preserves of legislatures and courts.[5] In the early twenties, a separation developed between women reformers and their male legal colleagues.

Historian Sybil Lipschultz has proposed that while women evolved a new doctrine of industrial equality, male lawyers sought to reinforce traditional views of female difference. The situation was, however, more complicated than a divide between a newly social feminism and a solidifying paternalist chauvinism. Women had always sought a strategic combination of industrial equality with maternalist arguments, but now the prominence of industrial equality became heightened. Legal advisers on both labor laws and the ERA pressed the technical, constitutional conflicts between the two measures. But, as Joan Zimmerman has pointed out, they were not engaging in a different debate. The lawyers, like the women reformers, were recasting the same issues of equality and protection, in their case in professional terminology.[6]

For lawyers, the discourse of protection versus equality was an application of the contemporary contest between legal formalism and a sociological jurisprudence.[7] Formalism—the doctrine that the law consisted of a set of principles and rules and the judicial role consisted in the almost mechanical application of these rules to cases—implied an inherently conservative legal process of reference back to prior rules and precedents. If this doctrine were true, a radical end, equality for women, could be gained only by means of writing new rules—in this case by rewriting the Constitution. Lawyers for the ERA inclined to formalism, in the belief that women's future was best served by writing a new rule incorporating sex equality as a constitutional principle, to replace a multiplicity of mostly sexist concepts and declarations. Lawyer–minimum wagers Felix Frankfurter and Thomas Reed Powell, as notable examples, were more skeptical about the purity of abstractions and their neutral application in judicial decision making, more positive in their belief in the possibility of a legal process responsive to social circumstance in its application and available as an instrument of social justice. Their sociological jurisprudence espoused the view that judicial decisions not only did but should apply the corpus of legal rules with regard to current social facts and moral values. To lawyers of this sociological school, evidence of women's nature and work contributed to judicial decision making.

Lawyers had not become paternalists or simply come out of the closet as chauvinists any more than women reformers had become socialists. The prime difference between lawyers (whether formalist or sociologically inclined) and reformers at this time was that lawyers all started from a presumption of the supremacy of the rule of law. Compared with their formalist professional opponents, the outlook of minimum wage lawyers was infused with sociological realism. They sought to realign legal tradition with the changing facts of women's lives and work, but they knew too little of the magnitude of those changes to disturb their own basically maternalist ideals. Those prejudices and the legal formulations that embodied the same views served them well in preserving male privilege. But self-interest was not their sole or direct motive. Even sociologically minded lawyers retained a strong streak of formalism, an assumption that legal rules set the outer limits of possibility. Their vision of change was both technical and incremental. If women were bound, metaphorically and legally, by their Constitution, the vision of these men too was bounded by their Constitution.

The maternalists of earlier years, women and lawyers, did not abandon their faith. Indeed, by this time and with their continuing support, straightforward maternalist demands were being fulfilled through achievements such as the Children's Bureau, the Sheppard-Towner Act, and the rapid spread of mothers' pensions laws. On the equality side of the argument, too, some particularly egregious legal discriminations had been corrected, from the most obvious, the vote, to the 1922 Cable Act on married women's citizenship. Minimum wagers and ERA proponents could agree in their support of both developments. But minimum wage policy lay in the difficult area between those categorical extremes at which policy could isolate motherhood or citizenship as separable dimensions of women's identity. The minimum wage reminded that women were at the same time workers and mothers, members of an industrial class and claimants of individual rights. The earlier difficulty of reconciling these facts came to seem an impossibility in face of the absolutism of the ERA. Both women and lawyers struggled with the conceptual problem at the heart of their political causes, with the significant difference that women viewed their dilemma in the context of the woman worker's labor market situation, and men in the context of the technicalities of the law. Neither perspective made a solution easy to find.[8]

WOMEN, THE MINIMUM WAGE, AND THE ERA

The Equal Rights Amendment introduced in the House of Representatives in 1923 was to the point: "Men and women shall have equal rights throughout the United States and every place subject to its jurisdiction."[9] This was the elegant end-product of two years of intense discussion and of one hundred–plus drafts. During those two years, feminists (at the opening of the decade all those women who, in the wake of suffrage, continued to fight by many means for improvements in the condition of women) moved from compromise to irreconcilable disagreement, carrying their legal advisers, somewhat more reluctantly, with them into separate camps. The vehicle for equal rights changed from a model law hedged about with qualifications, to a succinct declaration. In the process, fundamentally different ideas of what feminism meant were revealed. Legal feminists defined equality as identity with men in the eyes of the law, and supported the ERA. Social feminists defined equality as a social as well as a legal status, defending the unequal rights of protective legislation like the minimum wage as necessary until social equality became a reality.

At the beginning of 1921, it still seemed possible that women could work for both equal rights and social change without conflict. At its February convention, the NWP, formerly a radical, conspicuous, and effective offshoot of the mainstream suffrage movement whose members had included Kelley and many other minimum wagers, committed itself to the goal of "the removal of the legal disabilities of women."[10] Soon, Kelley was recording her bafflement and anger at finding a new label, "sex discrimination," applied to "the eight hours day, the night work law, the law for minimum wage commissions . . . and all those measures for the protection, particularly the industrial protection, of women for which I have been working for thirty years."[11] By October, unity was out of the question. Kelley resigned from the NWP Advisory Committee, explaining to Alice Paul, who dominated the NWP as Kelley did the NCL, that "with every effort to give women complete political equality, I am of course in full sympathy." But the latest NWP proposal, "to introduce a blanket measure" to standardize the legal position of women and men, went too far: "Any attempt . . . affecting business or industrial relations of women, is contrary to the settled policy of this organization [the NCL] for the past twenty-two years, for the present, and for the immediate future." With her went other longtime suffragists and minimum wagers like Elizabeth Glendower Evans, who wrote regretfully to Paul: "It seems to me that the possible losses so far offset any possible gains as to make your program, were it accomplished, a very serious social injury . . . I am awfully sorry that I can't be in the camp with you, as I love you so well that my impulse to jump to your side is always difficult to resist."[12] Few took the ensuing battle as cheerfully as Elizabeth Brandeis, secretary of the District of Columbia Minimum Wage Board and daughter of Supreme Court Justice Brandeis. She told Frankfurter that "it is a merry fight."[13]

The NWP method of eliminating legal disabilities made rupture inevitable. A complex project for surveying and reforming the law of each state was soon replaced by a simplified plan for a standard "blanket bill," enumerating legal equalities, to be introduced in every state. The effect would be to repeal all "acts and parts of acts in conflict with any of the provisions of this statute."[14] Blanket bills passed during 1921 in Wisconsin and Louisiana. The Wisconsin bill tried to accommodate the priorities of both the NWP and Kelley, instituting equal rights with a proviso safeguarding "the special protections and privileges [females] now enjoy for the general welfare."[15] The idea of a constitutional amendment had obvious advantages over forty-eight blanket bills. "From the publicity and organization standpoint this procedure would be marvellous," for one thing, as would be its single-mindedness for unifying and inspiring a campaign. Paul's political instinct was that "if you are going to do anything, you have to take one thing and do it. You can't try lots and lots of reforms and get them all mixed together." Also, while legislation could easily be rescinded, an amendment was incomparably secure, and might follow the more easily on the coattails of the suffrage victory.[16]

Unlike a bill, however, a constitutional amendment must be succinct. One draft after another circulated, in a flurry of excitement. Elsie Hill reported a brainstorming session between Paul and George Washington University law professor Albert Levitt, "lasting from three until eight thirty on Sunday . . . I have never seen more continuous mental effort than those two put into this." In a wave of enthusiasm, Paul and Levitt worked out a text, Hill cashed a check, and Levitt took the midnight train to Boston to seek endorsement by Dean Roscoe Pound of Harvard.[17] A typical early draft declared that governments shall not "maintain or establish political or legal disabilities or inequalities between men and women solely on account of sex or marriage. This article shall not be interpreted as preventing legislation in the exercise of the police power or for the protection of women in industry."[18] The question was whether protective laws like the minimum wage were legal disabilities.

Dean Acheson, a Harvard graduate and young Washington lawyer, best captured the bitterness of the controversy. A mission of reconciliation left him "sat on by all sides." Mrs. Brandeis, wife of the justice, had dispatched him to talk to Paul because leading NCL members were "distressed about the waste of effort involved in a row with Alice Paul." Acheson arranged lunch, "fearing evil all the time":

> I proposed that she offer Mrs. Kelley a proviso attached to the Amendment as follows: "provided that legislation regulating conditions of labor, hours of labor, or providing minimum wage boards for women shall not be held to impose a disability or inequality within the meaning of this Amendment." [Paul] backed water at once and said that anything like this would look as though she approved of welfare legislation and would lose her supporters . . . Then I remarked that I had always believed that she was bluffing when she offered to consider safeguarding proposals and that now we all knew it. At this she accused me of insulting her & had a glorious time telling me about myself.

Acheson retired, wounded, but found that his "troubles had only started." Kelley heard of his mission, sent for him, and "gave me the devil for compromising her and the C.L. . . . It appeared that she had seen Alice Paul two days before and had told her that no proviso would be considered by the C.L. and had generally flung defiance at her." Acheson swore off "doing things for anybody—particularly when it concerns that damnable organization of Alice Paul's."[19]

To Kelley, the ERA seemed wantonly destructive of years of work by the minimum wagers, with which she had been so deeply identified. As Alice Paul became equally identified with the ERA, personal antagonisms intensified hostilities and forced everyone involved into opposing and noncommunicating camps. But the fundamental problem was not one of personalities or even of the survival of particular policies. The minimum wage was held hostage in a struggle for possession of the future of feminism. Women who were active in politics early in the 1920s, buoyed by winning the vote, all claimed the feminist label. As they argued the merits of an ERA versus those of the minimum wage, however, they were divided in three respects: first, by their concern for the immediate effect on women covered at that time by protective laws; second, by their calculation of both the tactical and symbolic costs and benefits of making social change or legal rights the next priority, a calculation that differed according to their understanding of the present social position of women; and third and fundamentally by incompatible conceptions of the meaning and ideal of gender equality.

Minimum wagers were certain that the policy had helped working women: "Our minimum wage conferences all tell of these facts. Even with the very poor wage that the wage board sets . . . we find that in 95 per cent of the cases the minimum wage raises the women's wages," Mary Anderson of the Women's Bureau wrote to Maud Younger of the NWP. She concluded that "the difference between us is that you feel this Federal amendment and the state laws will not hamper the working women and I feel the opposite."[20] Minimum wagers' simplest reaction to the ERA was anger that it ignored the plight of the sweatshop worker. Alice Hamilton, social feminist and Harvard professor of industrial medicine, could not bring herself to spoil a tea party by arguing with her old friend and leading NWP member, Edith Houghton Hooker. Later, she wrote a passionate letter: "I could not help comparing you as you sat there, sheltered, safe, beautifully guarded against even the uglinesses of life, with the women for whom you demand 'freedom of contract' . . . the women who need protection most are not politically conscious, they are not even rebels. They are just weary toilers who hold desperately to their jobs, knowing that they are not valuable, that any demand, any protest, means their discharge, and discharge means starvation for the children."[21]

Such women as Hamilton believed that harm would be done only if an ERA preceded change in the position of women in the work force or in political and legal obstacles to gender-neutral laws. The ERA was not so much inherently wrong as tactically premature. Hamilton agreed with Hooker on the importance of legal equality. But forging ahead regardless would reveal a privileged, middle-class ignorance of the way in which social class divided women: "It will be as if you began to drain a swamp by first taking down the frail bridge we have thrown over it, a bridge built by years of toil on the part of women who cared supremely about the cruel inequalities of life and wanted to make some effort to compensate for them, to at least secure for women less fortunate than themselves the right to health and some leisure and a living wage."[22]

As Kelley well knew, working women and working men shared economic deprivation and powerlessness, but women were additionally disadvantaged within their class by their sex and by a social structure constructed upon sexual difference. A sympathetic correspondent distinguished between the "political illusion" of the "right to work for less than a living wage," and the "economic reality" of low-wage workers.[23] The equality proposed by the ERA in 1921 seemed a legal fiction as illusory as the goal of a gender-neutral minimum wage in 1908. Minimum wagers were already attuned to accepting half a loaf, and their reactions to the ERA were consistent. "Working women have the world to lose and nothing to gain but their chains," wrote Clara Beyer, who had been the first secretary of the District of Columbia Minimum Wage Board, reporting a public clash of views between the factions: "They have lost these chains all too recently to be willing to be shackled again merely for the sake of a theoretical equality."[24]

Hence the difference in priorities. Both NCL and NWP were committed to equal rights in citizenship, parental, property, and divorce matters, on juries, and in public office, business dealings, and the professions. But rights, in Kelley's view, were meaningless if circumstances made it impossible to exercise them. So long as women workers lacked the social and economic freedom of men, equal rights to freedom of contract might be a symbol but could not equalize bargaining power. Worse, comprehensive implementation of the principle of legal equality would wipe out all those special protections like the minimum wage, which were supposed to compensate for social disadvantage. To grant "'equality' where there is no equality" was, in Kelley's view, entirely back to front.[25] The proper order of business placed social change first. Then legal rights would be worth winning.

Paul, on the other hand, moved from agreeing with Kelley on the ideal of a class-based, gender-neutral minimum wage to a purist position that, in its absence, an equal lack of protection was preferable to gendered laws. Paul could point to the slow and small achievement of the minimum wage campaign—laws in only fifteen states after nearly fifteen years, and none in major industrial states. She could compare the vision of comprehensive change offered by a constitutional amendment. In late 1921 she seemed to endorse the social feminist position, declaring a preference for protective legislation by trade or region "and not along sex lines . . . However, this situation should, of course, be met by raising the standard of the protective labor laws for men until they are equal to those now in existence, or desired, for women, instead of tearing down those already in existence for women."[26] But when a specific case arose in 1922, Paul distanced herself. A Massachusetts member asked whether she should be neutral on an attempt to repeal the state's minimum wage. Or, "are we to say that, if the minimum wage be good, we wish it extended to include men also, but that we take no stand on its merits?"[27] Paul's advice was that "our work should be, I think, to see that whatever legislation may be enacted is free from sex discrimination."[28] The determined single-issue politics of the NWP contrasted with the social feminist inclination to weigh and balance factors and timing. ERA supporters believed that the intended gains from an amendment were the essence of feminism, to be counted independently of any losses in the separate sphere of labor politics.

If timing had been the only problem, this destructive episode might have been avoided. But even as the ERA was abbreviated, its role was magnified. By 1923 it was no longer one way for the NWP to win equality, it had become its definition of equality for women. The third and fundamental problem between the two sides was a disagreement of principle over the nature of equality between the sexes. In NWP eyes, sex equality was a self-contained goal. Sex discrimination must be written out of all legislation, and this was the goal for a feminist organization. Theirs was a compartmentalized view of society and politics, in which categories, hierarchies, and problems were identifiable independently of each other. The NWP conceived sex equality in such a way as to make their campaign a classic case of single-issue politics: all the advantages of clarity and purpose, uninhibited by the need to reconcile conflicts of interest or to rank priorities. Single-issue politics made labor conditions the province of labor organizations, the disenfranchisement of black women an issue for racial organizations, and the cause of peace an issue for peace lobbies. Characteristically, Paul's response to pacifist women who begged the NWP to recognize peace as "the greatest feminist issue today" was not to dismiss the validity of the cause but to refer it elsewhere: "Let [the NWP] be the one place in the world today where women can work for women, and women only, while doing all sorts of other work, whatever they may wish to do so, elsewhere."[29]

Social feminists believed sex equality to be inextricably involved with other social hierarchies. They held a pluralist view of a society in which women workers must be understood simultaneously as wives, mothers, or neither, aliens or citizens, black or white, professionals or laborers, of different classes. Kelley belonged to many reform organizations. She had been a founding member of the NAACP, and at the 1921 NWP convention fought the idea that the problem of black women, prevented from exercising their right to vote, was a problem of race, not of sex. Regional and economic segregation meant that race had rarely been a consideration where minimum wage laws applied, but minimum wagers were quick to note when multi-dimensional discrimination did occur within their jurisdictions. In 1920, Clara Beyer and Elizabeth Brandeis, running the D.C. Minimum Wage Board together, stamped hard on the covert racism of an outrageously low wage proposed for laundry workers. Laundry workers were no less skilled than other low-wage workers; they were, however, black women, whose employers were willing to take advantage of the "popular belief that it cost colored people less to live than white."[30] Kelley's reiterated view encapsulated the social feminist position: "Let's not begin by meaningless words. 'Equality' where there is no equality is as terrible a thing for the defenceless workers as the cry of 'peace' where there is no peace."[31]

Women in the 1920s had different visions of feminism. By the end of the decade, the feminist label belonged to the NWP and had been ostentatiously dropped by social feminists. One view of this contested label was that feminist politics comprised women fighting for changes specifically in the condition of women. Another was that it comprised liberated women making their distinctive contribution for humanity. The first encompassed the official NWP line that a feminist organization was one working to "secure absolute equality of men and women under the law and in the administration of government." It also embraced a radical critic like Crystal Eastman who found the legalistic vision of equality inadequate. "What," she asked, " do we mean by a *feminist organization*? It does not mean mere women juries, congressmen, etc., but it means to raise the status of women, making them self-respecting persons."[32] The second view of feminist politics made women the agents of broad social change, by virtue of distinctive feminine qualities. Its most passionate adherents believed that world peace was the essential feminist issue. Peace feminists came closest to defining women by their biology, as people who "gave life—not took it."[33] The social feminists were succinctly represented by Mrs. Gill, of Illinois: "By 'feminism' we mean full social and economic freedom for women."[34]

The eventual outcome of this particular contest for control of the politics of women's equality was a reminder that such difficult political arguments take place in a world where what counts most is power. In 1923, social feminists saw defeat in the courts, and legal feminists saw the ERA reach Congress. In 1933, social feminists gained access to government positions in the Roosevelt administration and controlled the federal agenda for women until the early 1960s. The NWP, for the same long period, had to be content with the repeated introduction of the ERA to Congress in each new session, and its repeated failure to progress further through the ratification procedure.[35]

LAWYERS, THE MINIMUM WAGE, AND THE ERA

This politicized debate over the future of feminist politics had a second strand. Each side called on the legal profession to lend authority to an analysis of the relationship between an ERA and labor laws for women. In the critical months of 1921, lawyers wrote, talked, and jumped on trains for urgent discussions in offices, homes, and summer cabins. Eventually the lawyers fell into factions allied with the two groups of women. But their loyalties were as much personal as intellectual. Unlike the women, they rarely clearly disagreed on fundamentals. On the crucial matter of gender equality, most lawyers leaned toward the "equal but different" school of thought, while varying in the extent to which they emphasized biological absolutes or were primarily concerned with present social realities. They differed on legal technicalities and in their estimate of what the Supreme Court might, in the future, do. But most of them disliked the strategy of amending the Constitution, so their advice often seemed reluctant.

Kelley and Paul discussed the ERA at a rare face-to-face meeting in December 1921, during which each woman repeatedly trumped the other's legal authorities. Paul cited her own "high legal authorities," and Kelley countered with "Mr. Frankfurter and Dean Pound." Paul read a letter from Pound "of a later date than the one they had," in which he had suggested "a construing clause which he thought would protect the welfare legislation." "Their sole authority for opposing the amendment at all seemed to come down to Mr. Frankfurter," Paul accused the NCL, proceeding to imply Frankfurter's utter inadequacy on grounds of partiality and arrogance. Finally, Maud Younger, NWP legislative chairman, "turned to them and said—'Is there anyone but Mr. Frankfurter upon whom you are basing your objections?' They seemed to have no one else."[36] This capping of one lawyer with another could get out of hand, particularly when the carefully qualified style of legal opinions might be read as support for either side. The NWP was more than once accused of misrepresentation, publicly disavowed by Roscoe Pound and eminent University of Pennsylvania professor William Draper Lewis, and accused of the betrayal of confidences even by loyal Albert Levitt.[37]

Felix Frankfurter, however, was rightly perceived to be the most influential and intransigent legal opponent of the ERA. Although Frankfurter's opposition was in line with his antiformalist stance, NWP members believed he was settling old scores from suffrage days: "This attack is not made on the grounds of the amendment but on the grounds of an old hostility to the Woman's Party, dating from the days of the Shafroth Palmer Amendment."[38] An NWP member was dispatched to seek an endorsement from Alice Hamilton. Hamilton "to my amazement brought in Mrs. Frankfurter. Of course I knew at once just where Dr. Hamilton stood on our bill. However I was not over pleased as you may well imagine, to have a witness to our interview who was there, no doubt, for the express purpose of detailing to Mr. Frankfurter what went on and also to help coach Dr. Hamilton, should any point slip her memory." Hamilton was unlikely to need coaching, but she did emphasize her deference to lawyers as well as her long commitment to the cause of industrial women. She also mentioned that "at Thanksgiving dinner, our [the NWP's] amendment had been the subject of conversation, and the great danger to which we were apparently willing to expose well-fare legislation was a matter of comment. She did not say where she spent her Thanksgiving and I was wondering if it might not have been at the Frankfurters."[39]

NWP adviser Albert Levitt stayed overnight with Frankfurter while both were summering in Connecticut. They discussed the ERA "most of the time that we were not asleep," he reported to Paul, adding his own estimate of Frankfurter's position: "He favors the things which you are trying to bring about; he is flatly opposed to the method you are planning to adopt, as he is a believer in decentralization of governmental legal functions and wants each state to handle its own police power problems; he will advise against the support of any amendment which in his opinion will jeopardize any legislation looking toward the protection of women in industry." Frankfurter was, Levitt noted "temperamentally against the Federal Amendment in any form." In a prophetic summary of Frankfurter's leadership over the next decade, Levitt concluded that his desire was to perfect the case for protective legislation on which he had been working for years. His position involved no "attempt at changing the general situation within the law. It is based upon what one might call the craftsman's delight in bringing his own handiwork to a successful conclusion."[40]

The lawyers' discussions were notable first because there was no consistent disagreement on every point between pro- and anti-ERA men; and second, for their substance, in which issues of gender and equality were secondary. Key players in this formative period, Frankfurter and Dean Acheson advising the social feminists and Albert Levitt working with NWP leaders were not sharply divided on sociological-jurisprudential lines versus formalist ones. Indeed Levitt's tie to the NWP seemed more of the heart than the head. He married Elsie Hill, but was the former Harvard and Yale student when he wrote to Paul that she must "save the possibility of differentiation based on the *facts* of nature and industry."[41] These men were sensitive to the impact of legal change on the position of working women. They shared a suspicion of the strategy of amending the Constitution. On federalism, on the primary issue of whether the ERA would override or be compatible with the exercise of the police power of the state in protective legislation, and even in considering what kind of gender equality should be embodied in the law, the lawyers found common "craftsman's" ground. Their debate had the flavor of a lively seminar, a combative exchange of knowledge and problems.

Frankfurter explained his views on federalism directly to Paul. He expressed the hope, no doubt fruitlessly in view of a gratuitous comment on "minor" inequality, "that you will not dismiss these views as those of a reactionary male, and stand pat on your experience as to woman suffrage—a totally different matter." But he firmly believed that the "resort to national action on everything is bound to dry up the sources of a healthy national life—action by the states." Discrimination against women, and indeed men, displayed all manner of local variations best dealt with in their own ways by the separate states.[42] This was a consistent, lifetime position for Frankfurter. As he clarified later, "I don't give a damn about 'States' rights' but I do about states' responsibilities—the States as organs for legal control for determining most of our social relations."[43] Frankfurter may have doubted his own credentials as a feminist, but nobody doubted his credentials as an antifederalist.

This view of the federal division of powers was not logically associated with a liberal or conservative position on substantive political issues; it often has had more to do with where its proponents think particular legislation is likely to succeed, or fail. In this instance, Frankfurter, liberal counsel for the minimum wage in the *Adkins* case, was in perfect agreement with a comment from conservative George Sutherland. Sutherland, ex-senator from Utah, was a Washington lawyer in 1921 and, in 1923, the justice who wrote the *Adkins* decision. He wrote to Ethel Smith doubting "the advisability or wisdom of any federal constitutional amendment of the kind suggested. The women of every state in the Union now having been accorded the privilege of equal suffrage, I am inclined to think better results will be obtained by seeking, at the hands of the various state legislatures, such remedial legislation as may be needed in each state."[44] Likewise Levitt, citing the common view of the police power as reserved to the states, complained: "I wish I could get it into the head of Alice Paul that she is not dealing with prejudices and opinions as she was when the Suffrage Amendment was under discussion but with existing facts, laws, regulations and constitutions which are so diverse and contradictory that you cannot apply a general rule to them."[45]

Anxiety about the impact of any amendment on the historic edifice of statute and case law affected all these lawyers. The gist of their comments was that lawyers preferred incremental change, whether by the hands of judges or by those of legislators, and feared the unpredictability of an amendment. The suffrage amendment had codified the few prior laws on the one subject of the woman's vote, imposing a national rule upon a largely blank screen. An ERA, imposed upon a patchwork of existing legislation, would raise complex questions about its relationship to the police power and of the police power to the due process clause. A categorical and national declaration, politically so attractive, seemed to lawyers a dangerous morass.

The survival of minimum wage laws depended upon the entitlement of states to use their police power to set the terms of women's employment. They did so at the expense of the right of citizens, guaranteed by the due process clause, to freedom of contract. As Dean Acheson tried to spell out to Paul, the police power was "in nontechnical phrase the power of organized society to protect itself against what it considers dangerous to it."[46] An unconditional ERA could be taken as a declaration that sex discrimination in the law was itself inherently dangerous to organized society. Experts considered it probable that the ERA would stand prior to any exercise of the police power on behalf of women. An ERA ranking equal rights above police power protections would ensure rejection of gendered protective laws and do nothing to help the case for gender-neutral labor legislation.[47]

Some ERA loyalists were more optimistic. George Battle—legal adviser to Mrs. Belmont, whose fortune supported the NWP—relied on the principles enshrined in the *Muller* decision. These, he thought, "have become so firmly embedded in our jurisprudence that the enactment of this proposed amendment will not endanger [women's welfare] legislation." But Battle's distinction between biological inequality, protected by law, and civil equality, guaranteed by law, was hardly the case Paul wished to make.[48] Philadelphia lawyer Shippen Lewis was hopeful that the police power "can be exercised, where necessary, in the teeth of an apparent constitutional prohibition."[49] But when the judgment in *Truax v. Corrigan* in 1921 overturned an Arizona law on picketing, placing the rights of employers above the defense of employees, Levitt knew that the optimists were wrong: "What you have here is a definite indication on the part of the United States Supreme Court that the police power of the state is not absolute . . . that is, the very basis of the arguments presented by your [Paul's] advisors, who are saying that the present wording of the proposed amendment will not interfere with welfare legislation, is practically destroyed."[50]

"Of course, it is possible for the Supreme Court to overrule its own decisions," Lewis had qualified his advice. The argument "that the amendment of its own force obliterated all inequalities as between men and women" was certainly "a position which the Supreme Court could conceivably take, but in my opinion it would not take it."[51] The dilemma for lawyers was that, on the one hand, their advice must be inductive and professional. The range of possibilities they saw was limited by their reliance on precedent. On the other hand, they must be speculative and political about how the courts might read the same precedents in future cases. As Frankfurter reminded: "It is not how a proposed amendment should be interpreted or would be interpreted by liberal minded judges, but how an amendment *might* be interpreted by an illiberal court that matters."[52] Levitt expounded upon legal history to persuade Paul that the NWP could not simply hope for an interpretation of the ERA to suit all sides. The court had its own political cycles, in which the police power rose and fell in priority. The *Truax* decision, he believed, opened a new era in which police power claims would not hold up.[53] But Paul forged ahead, and the lawyers worked on, in search of perfectly secure language for the amendment itself or for a proviso to safeguard industrial legislation as an appropriate exercise of the police power. The drafts, and the aggravation, multiplied.

Levitt produced a paper parsing "equality" and "disabilities" in their colloquial and legal contexts. Equality, he concluded, was utterly irreconcilable with protective laws for women. Under an *equal* rights amendment, minimum wage laws "will be destroyed. For these are obviously in existence to protect women." In their basis of gender distinctions, he teased out, "you have a lack of sameness and likenesses, hence a lack of [legal] equalities, hence a presence of inequalities, hence that which the amendment as proposed forbids, and the statutes embodying those inequalities must go." Disabilities had a technical meaning, namely "the want of legal ability or capacity to exercise legal rights . . . or to do certain acts with proper legal effect, or to enjoy certain privileges or powers of free action." An amendment to eliminate disabilities would be safer than one to create equality, for "if in the exercise of the police power a state makes it illegal for certain kinds of work to be done . . . no disability is created, for the act of the legislature is constitutional and legal, and you cannot have a legal act create an illegal capacity."[54] Frankfurter disagreed. He rejected the phrase "neither political nor common law disabilities shall exist" brusquely: "I am sure that 'legal disabilities' is a dangerous phrase and their abolition would jeapordize [sic] minimum wage and like legislation." "Common law disabilities" he liked no better: "I do not believe the amendment even in this form is free from the danger of the contention that women cannot by law be treated differently from men."[55]

Frankfurter and Levitt reached the same conclusion on sex equality and on the minimum wage. Both believed that biological difference between the sexes would always have to be taken into account in the law. Levitt held out the possibility that this need not mean hierarchy between the sexes, but "men and women *are* different and *are* unequal in various biological, physiological and psychological ways. Whether men and women can be trained to an equality of function and power and ability in the future is a matter of conjecture which only time and training and education can determine." Showing himself to be no formalist in law, Levitt continued: "I am interested in a practical political matter, at the present time . . . To my mind, this matter is to be approached not from the standpoint of a theory of equality but from the standpoint of a careful knowledge of existing laws and a forecasting of what changes in these laws will produce."[56] Frankfurter distinguished two kinds of gendered laws. Protective legislation might deal with a "'disability' on account of sex," as in regulation of "the periods when a woman may work before and after confinement." But minimum wage laws, and perhaps some others, "are, in one aspect, 'disabilities,' and treated as such by the courts. But they are 'disabilities' founded upon women's peculiar relation to industry, and upon that ground sustained by the courts."[57]

Frankfurter had once argued that "there is no sharp difference in kind as to the effect of labor on men and women," and looked forward to the moment when "we cease to look upon the regulation of women in industry as exceptional, as the law's graciousness to a disabled class."[58] If Frankfurter was still edging toward that moment, Levitt had from the start tried to find a gender-free rationale even for clearly health-based laws. He hypothesized an ERA challenge to legislation banning women's employment in lead factories, "passed because of the national interest in the conservation of its human resources and not on the basis that it is a measure which protects women." Under this welfare rationale, "the existence of sex is just a circumstance and not a cause."[59] The minimum wage was a clearer case. His deduction from the *Adkins* briefs was decisively capitalized: "WOMEN DO NOT NEED TO BE IN A CLASS BY THEMSELVES TO BE PROTECTED BY A MINIMUM WAGE. THEY NEED SIMPLY TO BE EMPLOYED AT A WAGE WHICH IS BELOW THAT WHICH ALLOWS THEM TO TAKE PROPER CARE OF THEIR HEALTH TO HAVE THEIR WAGES MADE A MATTER OF PUBLIC INTEREST AND SO OF PROPER REGULATION UNDER THE POLICE POWER OF THE STATE."[60]

Levitt was clearly fond of Paul yet maddened by her obstinacy. "I am honestly of the opinion that Miss Paul is willing to sacrifice welfare legislation for the sake of putting a general theoretical principle into the Federal Constitution," he wrote to William Draper Lewis.[61] Despite coaxing with tales of "Jones and his trained Hen" (fed sawdust to test the cheapest way of raising hens, "that fool hen up and died on me and spoiled the experiment"), he could not persuade her of his belief that a "theory of the equality of the sexes" written in to the Constitution would rebound against women.[62] All the lawyers, to one degree or another, shared his view that an amendment was an inappropriate weapon for sorting out the confusion they saw between physical differences between the sexes that the law must acknowledge, legal differences that were outdated, and social differences that were open to discussion.

Lawyers were forced by the implications of the minimum wage, with its double focus on gender and labor, to declare themselves on gender equality. They did so by reference to legal principle, avoiding matters outside their immediate professional purview. Their involvement with *Adkins* focused their attention on the *Muller* definitions of women and the police power. But they also had little reason to change their own views of gender equality, which supported police power protection for women. The administration of minimum wage laws had exposed middle-class women reformers to the continuing exploitation of women workers and to changes in the labor market. Wage Board procedures were an education, as "the conferees and the interested persons who follow the . . . proceedings become convinced by a gradual process of the inadequacy of wage rates prevailing."[63] The sociological sensitivity of Frankfurter's jurisprudence may have been genuine, but it was at one remove, easier to view as an intellectual problem rather than an urgent human need. Despite their conservatism, however, legal analyses were straws in the wind, presaging two fundamental changes embodied in the *Adkins* decision: the differentiation of wage legislation from other protective laws and the declaration of women's equality.

THE ADKINS CASE

When the *Adkins* decision voiding the District of Columbia minimum wage law came down from the Supreme Court on 9 April 1923, it ended a three-year fight. In May 1920 the District Board, chaired by local lawyer Jesse Adkins, set a weekly wage of $16.50 for women employed in what Kelley, in a "new phrase," called "public housekeeping"—hotels, restaurants, apartment houses, clubs, and hospitals. An employer, the Children's Hospital, and a hotel employee, Willie Lyons, promptly went to court for an injunction to restrain the board from enforcing its order. Kelley was apprehensive about these cases from the start, pointing out that "the employees affected are largely immigrants and colored citizens. The plaintiff is a Children's Hospital alleging that hardship is inflicted upon it by the establishment of this particular standard wage rate. The sentimental appeal is fairly obvious."[64]

In May, the District court found in favor of the minimum wage and refused a temporary injunction pending an appeal. By mid-June, Elizabeth Brandeis (assistant to Clara Beyer at the board) had recruited Frankfurter while the Brandeis-Frankfurter family party sailed for a summer in Europe. Brandeis wrote home to Beyer with a mixture of business and shipboard gossip: "I have talked to Felix about our case. He is pretty keen to come into it in the Court of Appeals—says it w'd be mighty risky to let it go against us there if we can help it—though of course it's probably a slim chance anyway. Still worth trying!"[65] Frankfurter's advice was taken: "He is very anxious that the Consumers League sh'd get to work bringing the brief up to date—there is a lot to be done. He spoke of writing to Aunt Josephine [Goldmark] himself. Could you write Miss Dewson . . . Anyway do something to get them on the job."[66] The strategy was to be the same that the NCL had successfully sponsored in the *Muller* and *Stettler* cases. By presenting the facts of women's work conditions, the brief would transfer sympathy from employers nursing sick children to employees suffering the consequences of wages inadequate to maintain life and health. Molly Dewson took over the role of research assistant that had formerly belonged to Josephine Goldmark. Dewson worked full-time on the brief, on appeal and then for the Supreme Court. Her work report to the NCL noted laconically: "Wrote the factual part (453 pages) of the brief in defense of District of Columbia Minimum Wage Law; prepared copy . . . read proof, and supervised distribution of briefs." In 1923, when the Supreme Court hearing was moved forward unexpectedly, she recorded 143 and three-quarters hours of overtime in the three-week dash to complete the two-volume brief.[67]

Frankfurter duly assisted the District Counsel before the Court of Appeals in February 1921. Dewson's compendium of facts about women's employment, updated and doubled in volume from their last use in the *Stettler* case, formed the basis of the defense of the minimum wage. This time, however, the facts made less of women's weakness and more of their daily work experience: "The difference in presentation of the issue in the Oregon cases and the District of Columbia cases is that in the former brief the facts as to the need of minimum wage legislation is stressed whereas in the latter brief we have stressed the development of experience under the minimum wage laws in operation."[68]

On 6 June, the District Court of Appeals found in favor of the Minimum Wage Board. But then the case was ensnared in a procedural tangle that would be of interest only to lawyers, were not its consequences so serious. It revolved around the issue of whether a justice who because of illness had not heard the

case, could rule on a request for a rehearing, or whether that was the prerogative of the lower court judge who had substituted for him. The original bench
denied the request by a two-to-one majority, but the absentee joined the dis-
senter and had formally registered approval of a rehearing before the maneuver
was noticed. The rehearing went ahead, and the first decision was reversed in
November 1922.[69]

Such ploys contributed to an atmosphere surrounding the *Adkins* case that
was as unfriendly as that of the ERA controversy. Animosity over the ERA in
any case carried over, since counsel in the *Adkins* case were the very same
lawyers who advised on the ERA. While Frankfurter advised the District Minimum Wage Board and the NCL prepared his brief, Children's Hospital counsel ex-governor Joseph W. Folk of Missouri briefed Alice Paul. Paul privately
advised both Folk and district lawyers Challen and Wade Ellis, who used their
personal connections with the district judiciary and may have been pursuing a
personal vendetta against Frankfurter.[70] When Levitt reported that "I am at
this time [November 1921] attempting an intensive study of minimum wage
legislation so as to know how best to phrase the amendment so as to protect
minimum wage legislation," he had just spent his summer dissecting the
Adkins briefs.[71] These, he told Paul, taken together contained "a good foundation for meeting any objection on the ground of the minimum wage which may
come along."[72]

Withal, it is not surprising that Ethel Smith of the WTUL perceived a plot
when lawyer George Battle allowed the NWP to publish his endorsement of
the ERA. She thought him naive to be used in this way by opponents of the
minimum wage. He was familiar, she wrote, "with the present status of the
minimum wage law of the District of Columbia, which, after being sustained by
the District of Columbia Supreme Court and the Court of Appeals, was delayed
by rehearing before the latter court at the request of the employers." To Smith,
the checkered career of the minimum wage in the courts was a demonstration
of how lawyers and business already colluded to paralyze protective legislation.
An ERA would merely give new opportunities for their exploitation of legal
ambiguities.[73]

The atmosphere was hardly sweetened by an intemperate Appeals Court
decision on the rehearing. Justice Van Orsdel took the opportunity to add to the
standard affirmation of freedom of contract. Of the low minimum wage for
women in dead-end jobs, he proclaimed: "The equal wage paralyses ambition
and promotes prodigality and indolence." Writing in the midst of the Red Scare
of the twenties (which imperiled reforms and reformers and led to such intimi-
dations as the opening of an FBI file on Florence Kelley in 1923), he castigated
the "tendency of the times," as he saw it: "To socialize property rights under the
subterfuge of police regulation is dangerous, and if continued will prove destructive of our free institutions."[74]

The procedural delay was catastrophic for minimum wagers. Instead of an
appeal by the hospital to the Supreme Court in the fall of 1921, there was an
appeal by the Minimum Wage Board in the fall of 1922. When the case was

heard early in 1923, there were three new justices on the court. One, Justice Sutherland, wrote the majority opinion striking down the minimum wage. "I have been wondering if we were not going to receive a recirculated opinion from Sutherland after the more careful Vandevanter had gotten in his handiwork to modify some of the extreme statements," Chief Justice Taft wrote to Holmes during the deliberations.[75] The old court might well have split the same way as in *Stettler*. With a tied vote the minimum wage law would have been lost. But a tied vote and *per curiam* decision would have left the issue open for the future, whereas the five-to-three majority in *Adkins* and the strong terms of Justice Sutherland's decision ruled for the next fourteen years.[76]

In April 1923 the Supreme Court ruled against the District of Columbia minimum wage law. In 1921, Elsie Hill had quoted Governor Folk to Frankfurter, to the effect that "if the minimum wage law for women is sustained as a health, a safety or a morality measure, it also would be protected under the police power of the state in the same way as measures for hours of labor and nightwork."[77] The eventual victory of opponents of the minimum wage was in having it declared a price-fixing measure, harming employers as much as workers and doing so by deprivation of contractual rights, not injury to health. Frankfurter's earlier fear that an ERA "may bring into question a permissive field of legislation such as the minimum wage in favor of women which cannot be based solely 'on the basis of the physical constitution of women'" was realized by the *Adkins* decision.[78] The ERA had been a powerful annoyance since its inception during 1921, but its direct effect on policy was only to harden the defense of gendered laws. The *Adkins* judgment was a substantive act with serious consequences, both immediate and lasting. The D.C. board was shut down. Elsewhere, at best appropriations were cut and boards limped along hoping to avoid legal challenges. At worst, judges or politicians used *Adkins* as authority to terminate minimum wage commissions.[79] For the next decade, the energies of reformers and lawyers went into picking over the bones of the decision, trying to reinstate gendered minimum wage laws.

THE ADKINS DECISION

Sutherland's majority opinion was unequivocal on the main point. The District of Columbia minimum wage law was unconstitutional. The exercise of the police power of the state for the protection of women was no longer an acceptable reason for curtailing the constitutional "right to contract about one's affairs," whose priority under all but exceptional circumstances was simply "no longer open to question."[80] As a further blow to minimum wagers, the court added that any regulation of wage rates, for any worker on whatever pretext, was suspect to a degree that did not apply to laws dealing with such matters as hours or safety.

The decision spared no time on the rehearing muddle, and Sutherland rejected with scorn Dewson's eight hundred pages of evidence that the minimum wage was widespread (validity "cannot be aided by counting heads") and effective (the data "we have found interesting but only mildly persuasive"). Once Sutherland differentiated questions of effectiveness (matters for legislatures) and constitutionality (matters for the courts), Dewson's compilation stood no chance. But Sutherland himself made a social assumption that rendered the decision inevitable. He reported: "The appellee in the first case is a corporation maintaining a hospital for children in the District. It employs a large number of women in various capacities, with whom it had agreed upon rates of wages and compensation *satisfactory* to such employees." The entire point of the minimum wage campaign had been that there existed a category of worker for whom agreement upon wages had little, normally nothing, to do with satisfaction.[81]

Sutherland spelled out the legal basis for his foregone conclusion, in terms that left some indirect and no doubt unintended openings for the future. His premise was that free, "satisfactory" contract making was "the general rule and restraint the exception," permissible only for an appropriate use of the police power. He found no police power precedent applicable to the minimum wage, and one, gender, he removed entirely from the roster of acceptable police power applications. Summarizing *Muller*, that women differed in physical structure, by maternal function, and in a historical dependence on man, "who has established his control by superior physical strength," Sutherland pronounced that in all but physical respects the "ancient inequality of the sexes . . . has continued 'with diminishing intensity.'" In fact, the recent progress of women seemed "revolutionary," and given the "changes which have taken place since that utterance [*Muller*], in the contractual, political and civil status of women, culminating in the Nineteenth Amendment, it is not unreasonable to say that these differences have now come almost, if not quite, to the vanishing point."[82]

Dissenters pointed out the illogicality of overthrowing *Muller*, which relied heavily on physical difference, because of changes in legal status. Oliver Wendell Holmes remarked acidly that it would "need more than the Nineteenth Amendment to convince me that there are no differences between men and women," whereas Taft more temperately concluded that the "Nineteenth Amendment did not change the physical strength or limitations of women . . . [but it] did give women political power and makes more certain that legislative provisions for their protection will be in accord with their interests as they see them."[83] The debate about gender within the court replicated the debate outside, becoming similarly confused between two different dimensions of experience, the biological characteristics of the sexes and the cultural constructions of gender roles. The majority found legal sameness, the dissenters physical difference; and each side used its finding to define the scope of the police power.

Neither dissent—indeed hardly anyone involved in the debate—noted the further illogicality of the majority, of resting so much in this particular case on the winning of suffrage. The Nineteenth Amendment granted women the right to vote. But this right meant more for some than for others. For black women in the south it meant equal status with black men—in theory they could vote, but in practice white supremacy prevented them. The *Adkins* case involved the one jurisdiction, the District of Columbia, in which the Nineteenth Amendment had no effect at all. District residents were excluded from presidential elections, unrepresented in Congress, and governed locally by an appointed board of commissioners. Men and women in the district remained equally disenfranchised until the passage of the Twenty-Third Amendment in 1961.[84]

The telling blow of the *Adkins* decision against the gendered basis of the law has been seen as the historic legacy of the case. Yet the issue of gender was disposed of in just one of twenty-three pages of opinion. Following upon his declaration of equality of the sexes, Sutherland made two important distinctions: one of the circumstances under which protective laws for women might still be acceptable; the other between minimum wage and other protective laws. Thus, "while the physical differences must be recognized in appropriate cases, and legislation fixing hours or conditions of work may properly take them into account, we cannot accept the doctrine that women of mature age, *sui juris*, require or may be subjected to restrictions upon their liberty of contract which could not lawfully be imposed in the case of men under similar circumstances." Hours laws and night work bans, for reasons of health or morality, might still stand; a minimum wage, for any class of worker, would not. The main burden of Sutherland's opinion was this differentiation of wage regulation.[85]

Wages were, Sutherland declared, "the heart of the contract." They were set by freely consenting parties, each constrained by different considerations, workers only by their sense of what they could get for their services but employers by their competitive need to obtain value for the work performed. This tenet of the market was elevated to a moral law, for under minimum wage laws, "the moral requirement implicit in every contract of employment, viz, that the amount to be paid and the service to be rendered shall bear to each other some relation of just equivalence, is completely ignored." These two points, the centrality of wages and the morality guaranteed only by the freedom of the employer to negotiate, distinguished the wage bargain from all other labor conditions.[86]

Sutherland contrasted wages with hours of work, calling hours merely "incidents of the employment." An hours law burdened the employer but "leaves the parties free to contract about wages and therefore to equalize whatever additional burdens may be imposed" by statutory hours.[87] "I confess I do not understand the principle," said Holmes, of this distinction between hours and wages. Taft elaborated: "In absolute freedom of contract the one term is as important as the other, for both enter equally into the consideration given and received, a restriction as to one is not any greater in essence than the other, and is of the same kind. One is the multiplier and the other the multiplicand."[88]

Sutherland needed to make the distinction, in order to dispose of another precedent. In *Bunting v. Oregon*, the court had allowed a ten-hour law for "any person in any mill, factory or manufacturing establishment" where health might be affected. The Oregon statute had also made unprecedented provision

for time-and-a-half overtime pay. The court had refused to recognize the statute as an indirect form of wage fixing and had taken hours as a separate issue;
here Sutherland perceived his loophole.[89] He ignored, or was ignorant of, the
distinction between hours laws for all women and wages laws applying only to
industries where the disparity of bargaining power was so gross as to ensure
that "burdens" would be passed to the employees, not shared. In Sutherland's
lost world of equal parties, minimum wage laws made the employer an under-
dog. In Taft's "real" world, the assumption was that "employees, in the class
receiving least pay, are not upon a full equality of choice with their employer
and in their necessitous circumstances are prone to accept pretty much anything that is offered. . . . The evils of the sweating system and of the long hours
and low wages which are characteristic of it are well known."[90] To Taft's eyes
the difference between wages and hours was "formal rather than real."

With its rejection of gendered legislation and its contentious attempt to
maintain, and according to Taft to exaggerate, "the importance of the wage term
of the contract of employment as more inviolate than its other terms," *Adkins*
brought minimum wagers back to the long-abandoned debate about economic
mechanisms and power. Sutherland's unwitting contribution was to open the
way for the transition from the concept of a living wage into that of a fair wage,
ultimately institutionalized in the title of the Fair Labor Standards Act. For
beyond his general objection to statutory wages, he had specific objections to
the living wage calculus used by the District Board: "The price fixed by the
board need have no relation to the capacity or earning power of the employee,
the number of hours which may happen to constitute the day's work, the character of the place where the work is to be done, or the circumstances or surroundings of the employment"; it was "vague," it was "arbitrary," and it added
up to "fatal uncertainty."[91] It was, in fact, a blatant infringement of procedural
due process of law. Sutherland's alternative to this abomination was the "moral
requirement" of "some relation of just equivalence," or "a fair equivalent for the
service rendered." In his passing comment that a "statute requiring an employer . . . to pay with fair relation to the extent of the benefit obtained from
the service, would be understandable," Sutherland gave a significant hostage
to fortune.[92]

In the courts and in the construction of an Equal Rights Amendment, the
same options of equality and protection were at stake, and Sutherland's potential escape hatch was only a pointer for the future. Those involved in the
early 1920s have been labeled in more than one way: activists, leaders, women,
feminists on the one hand; and lawyers, advisors, men, sexists on the other.
Their shared intention was to find the best outcome for women, but the effort
divided women from their former colleagues, and women reformers from lawyers. As the legal debate became ever more sophisticated, it began to seem
counterproductive to political leaders. By 1922, Eleanor Brannan of the NWP
reported: "Miss Paul is not in favor of using any more of the legal opinions, as
she says that the one object of securing them was to prove that the amendment
would not interfere with 'welfare' legislation. As these opinions have failed

to satisfy our opponents in this regard, she sees no use in distributing them further, but believes that the matter must be approached from a new angle, what she did not divulge, and perhaps has not yet decided."[93] The lawyers were not so easily sidelined. Their debate was the shape of things to come, presaging their leadership of the minimum wage movement in the years following the *Adkins* decision.

The *Adkins* decision was nonetheless a shattering setback for the minimum wage movement and its legal advisers. Yet even the NWP, who hailed the decision as a victory for their principles, might have hesitated. They were, after all, just inaugurating a campaign for the elimination of legal disabilities when Sutherland announced that these very contractual, political, and civil differences had "now come almost, if not quite, to the vanishing point." The decision did mark the end of an era. It also opened a new era: it laid down a set of ground rules for a statutory minimum wage where none had existed before, and determined the form of the campaign for the next fifteen years.

Due Process

THE WELFARE OF THE ECONOMY, U.S.A., 1923–1937

THE *ADKINS* DECISION was issued on 9 April 1923. In a flurry of correspondence between the principals, despair and anger alternated. Frankfurter foresaw "terrible implications" of the adoption of the "Alice Paul theory of constitutional law." Justice Brandeis wrote privately to Frankfurter that the "fundament [*sic*] vice" of the decision was "the distortion of 'due process' 40 years ago." Newton D. Baker, president of the National Consumers' League, found it "disheartening" and spoke of picking over "the wreckage." Judge Amidon of North Dakota wrote of employers "preying upon the necessities of women," and lawyer George Alger described the judgment as a "sickening mess." Only two days later, Adkins told Frankfurter that the district commissioners, who were "decidedly unfriendly" to the board, had acted: "Yesterday without consulting us they decided to close up our work immediately and to notify us to turn over our records to them by the 15th instant."[1]

Kelley urgently convened a postmortem panel of lawyers, administrators, journalists, and reformers. They brought years of experience to their deliberations but had nothing new to offer. Kelley and Dewson listened as the group talked defensively of an educational campaign and of safeguarding the remaining laws by "non-mandatory" provisions on the notably ineffective Massachusetts model. The meeting endorsed the proposal of Governor Hart of the state of Washington that a governors' conference consider amending the Constitution. All this was wishful thinking; the only action approved was to "undertake to obtain analyses of the Supreme Court minimum wage decision by one group of authoritative economists, and by a second group of eminent constitutional lawyers."[2]

A meeting sponsored by the Women's Trade Union League in May was even less positive. Dewson captured the disarray after *Adkins*, when she told Frankfurter that "the conference was thoroughly unsatisfactory to me." There was no common view: "The A. F. of L. was there in force to tell us what they wanted: help with a blanket amendment [to safeguard the rights of labor] and the organization of working women. Anything different they were prepared to kill. . . . Besides labor, the Y.W.C.A. attended the conference in droves and talked at length. We all know that debate and generalities are their forte, and not 'A STAND' . . . The rest of the conference was made up of lawyers, each one radically differing from the other with their usual independence of judgment, a few gently bleating ewe lambs, and the glum and gloomy from the National Consumers' League."[3] For once, uncertainty overwhelmed even Kelley. She wrote to LaRue Brown in early June that "the confusion of mind both in and out of our own membership is such that I am in greater doubt than I have been in the whole twenty-four years of our work."[4]

But Dewson and Kelley had rigged the agenda of the May meeting. As Dewson somewhat disingenuously explained to Frankfurter, "It did not seem to us the moment to bring forward your plan. Your plan was not sufficiently in shape to present." The truth of the matter was that "Mrs. Kelley and I were not sure enough that it is workable to be convincing in its behalf."[5] Two separate new strategies were emerging. One, proposed by Kelley, was a radical program of bringing women to power and preempting the court with a constitutional amendment. The second, led by Frankfurter, was a plan to win new court rulings, using the openings in Sutherland's decision. If successful, this maneuver would simultaneously reinstate the minimum wage and undermine the use of the due process clauses of the Constitution against the substance of laws regulating industrial conditions. The legal ploy became the strategy of the minimum wage movement—but only after a fierce disagreement between Kelley and her legal advisers and a split that, though between the sexes, was not solely about gender.

Support for either Kelley's or Frankfurter's proposal separated women and men. This was also a division between practicing lawyers, who were men, and political activists, who were mainly women. As in the debate over the ERA, professionalism as well as gender determined the views of individuals. And now, a new pattern of leadership emerged, in which lawyers took control of the future direction of the campaign from "the ladies" (an intimidated Ben Cohen's label).[6] This reversed the previous pattern in which lawyers had taken supporting roles, lobbying or making court appearances on behalf of the women, advising rather than initiating. The question of the difference between the policy-making of (male) lawyers and (female) activists now became of more than academic interest. To what extent was this a deliberate male capture of the movement; to what extent was either side motivated by self-conscious feminism or some other goal; and how helpful or damaging was it to women's interests? Regardless of intent, what changes in the policy and its outcomes can be attributed to this change in leadership?

Feminism: Kelley's Program

In May 1923, Kelley published an angry attack on legal process: "Although the life, health and happiness of women and girls are at stake, no woman has participated in the minimum wage case at any of its stages." She resolved that "the monopoly of jurisprudence by men, must, therefore, be replaced by just representation of women."[7] Writing to a colleague, Kelley revealed more fully the radical potential of her social feminism. She simultaneously affirmed sexual difference and identified women's special political interests as revolving round motherhood (for, as well as the minimum wage, "the statutes that concern us" had to do with children and maternity) but also understood women as victims of a gendered hierarchy of power in no way implied by their maternal status: "No woman is in any way connected with this case except as the victim of the decision if this proves adverse." Kelley demanded more than judicial decisions favorable to women. She wanted the victims to take power and women to control women's affairs.[8]

Kelley contrasted legal tinkering with her gendered analysis of power: "As to my impatience with further tinkering with legislation,—what have I done but tinker for forty-one years? . . . I should have pushed a far-reaching Amendment from 1895 on, while promoting statutes and decisions. Far from being mutually exclusive both are necessary, now as then."[9] Retaining her comprehensive grasp of the social situation of women and the power structure that oppressed them, she asserted that "women need votes, and *wage* statutes, *and* unions, *and* women judges."[10] On the first anniversary of *Adkins*, she wrote to Frankfurter, reiterating her politics: "If it is not our business to study the work, and the *sources* of power of the agency that delays and may yet frustrate our long labors, I am at a loss to know who will do this studying for us, and how except by ourselves the human needs of women are to be met."[11]

At the same time, Kelley advocated restoring gendered minimum wage laws. "Wage-earning women and minors in the District of Columbia must regain what the court has taken from them," she wrote, rejecting "the inalienable constitutional right of American women to starve." Protection did not seem inconsistent with her demand for power, when she considered the practical effects of *Adkins*. She had evidence of wage cuts in the district: "In the laundry and scrubbing and cleaning industries from $16.50 to 12, 10, 9, and 8 dollars a week for 'adult ablebodied women of ordinary average ability.' On these wage rates women cannot live in health."[12]

Yet Kelley had not lost her socialist impulse to place gender within a more comprehensive structural analysis. Her egalitarianism showed in her proposal to extend the minimum wage: "No substitute has been discovered in any country for minimum wage boards for safeguarding the health of the young, the unskilled, the unorganized, the elderly who can work though not as they did in their prime, and the non-English speaking immigrant."[13] A confidential draft in her files of a constitutional amendment composed by herself and law professor Thomas Reed Powell shows her still wrestling with the question of gender-based legislation. The amendment would have safeguarded minimum wage laws from judicial scrutiny. The typed draft is altered in Kelley's own hand from "legislation forbidding the employment of women and minors at wages less than sufficient to maintain them in health . . ." to read "laws forbidding the employment of any persons. . . ." Kelley typed an annotation: "This does not imply that Mr. Powell approves our going out for an Amendment. I don't know whether he does. I showed him a very bad draft of my own and he thereupon wrote this. I think we should *not* limit it to women and minors." Again in her own hand, she added "and he agrees to this."[14]

Constitutional amendment and court reform were in the air, even apart from the looming presence of the ERA. A run of amendments had succeeded over the last decade: the authorization of income tax, direct election of senators, prohibition, and women's suffrage. Other proposals were circulating: an AFL proposal for a panoply of labor rights, drafts of a child labor amendment, and the recurrent idea that a court majority greater than five to four should be necessary to veto legislation.[15] Given the difficulties of amending the constitution and the fact that only the ERA and the Child Labor Amendment even reached Congress, however, amendment was seen by many as a last resort. Kelley felt that point had been reached.

The lawyers, bolstered by their consideration of the ERA, remained opposed. Frankfurter wrote to Kelley "about as stiffly as I know how," he confided to Ben Cohen. He told her: "For the moment I do not believe in the efficacy of the amendment movement because its realization is, for me, an extremely remote thing and I am confident that we can accomplish some important results by concentrating upon them. . . . If you and Miss Dewson go in heavily for the amendment, very, very little will be done in behalf of the requisite legislation."[16] Kelley, equally stiffly, reminded him that her "father seconded Mr. Sargent's Joint Resolution for a Suffrage Amendment in 1875 and continued to introduce it after Mr. Sargent went to the Senate until my father's death in 1889. My grandfather's aunt attended the first meeting (Seneca Falls 1848) at which votes for women were proposed in this country. I have no illusions as to speed."[17]

But Kelley found little support for her call for women on the court and a constitutional amendment to empower Congress and the states to pass wage legislation. There were doubts even within the NCL, accentuated by the failure of the Child Labor Amendment. Kelley confided to Katherine Philips Edson in 1925: "I write in deep dismay from which I have not been able to recover since our annual meeting . . . not one vote or voice could be found for approving an amendment."[18] Outside the NCL, only the small and declining Women's Trade Union League cooperated briefly. But their traditional divided loyalties drew them to the American Federation of Labor proposal for an amendment to safeguard the rights of organized labor. Kelley considered collaboration with labor, obtaining the AFL proposals by stealth. But this was premature. The AFL was barely ready to change its mind over the minimum wage when the Fair Labor Standards Act was drafted fifteen years later.[19]

Kelley was very much alone in her desire for confrontation with male power and with the Supreme Court. Her isolation was increased by the conservatism of the times. National prosperity, the Red Scare of 1921 and 1922, the divisions opening in the wake of the suffrage victory, and the mainstream educational tactics of the League of Women Voters made Kelley's lifelong radicalism seem all the more extreme. But Kelley had soon largely retired from the scene. Well before her death in 1932, the responsibility for political action for the minimum wage passed to a collectivity of her friends and former aides, including Molly Dewson, Josephine Goldmark, Frances Perkins, and Elizabeth Brandeis.[20]

The views of this group fell somewhere between Kelley and Frankfurter and represent the gradual shift from the early state minimum wage laws for women to the later federal minimum wage law, with its built-in prohibition of sex discrimination. These women were able to move into partisan and legislative politics and administrative positions, and even Kelley's closest friends went along more willingly with legal tinkering. But as insiders to the political system, they did not lose their crusading edge. Their new access absorbed their energy but did not necessarily blunt their consciences. In dialogue with minimum wage lawyers, the new generation retained an inherited modicum of Kelley's political sensitivity and feminist concern, and even of her impatience with lawyerish caution. Dewson had been Kelley's closest associate on the minimum wage. Her involvement most clearly illustrates how these women both accepted leadership from the lawyers and yet maintained a critical understanding, seemingly lacking among the lawyers, of how this strategy affected the women workers who had inspired the campaign for a minimum wage policy and, indeed, of the fact that this was a political issue and not a legal seminar: "After all this is not a case of saying this is a good law pass it. There is a frightful lot of psychology in getting the influential persons and groups interested and behind the bill."[21]

Nonetheless, the absence of discussion of sex equality by either lawyers or activists after 1923 is noticeable. Absorbed in their challenge to substantive due process, lawyers neglected the consequences for women workers. They had limited objectives; redefining the minimum wage rather than redefining its recipients. So long as Kelley had a say, the meaning of sex equality for women was that you were either for the ERA or against it. But unlike the lawyers, the women did keep an eye on the logic and the consequences of the coverage of minimum wage laws, and the issue of gendered protective legislation did not die.

Dewson once or twice raised the possibility of a minimum wage for men. When she was lobbying Roosevelt for a state law in New York, in 1928 and again in 1932, she consulted Frankfurter on the technicalities. In 1928, she wondered why existing powers of the industrial commissioner "to try to settle labor controversies amicably" could not be used: "Certainly there could be a row over unfair industrial wages even if they applied to men. Administratively why could not the Commissioner call both sides together now and get them to decide on what are fair wages," she asked, adding as an apparent afterthought, "for men and women . . . ?"[22] Dewson wrote as secretary of a new national committee for state industrial standards in 1932, making revealing handwritten alterations to a typed proposal. One goal was: "Mandatory minimum wage legislation for both women [with *both* then deleted]; and also for men if the local state labor organizations will cooperate." The letter is a record of the way that political activists were responding to the circumstances of the depression rather than the niceties of the law: "Monday morning Josephine Goldmark was undecided as to whether we should try to get legislation for men, but after listening to Leo Wolman pile facts upon facts as to the average wages of men in industries working at least 48 hours a week, she felt as I do, that it was important to have a legal minimum form the basis of the wage scale."[23]

However, after the *Adkins* case, Dewson was not naive about the law. Hours laws for men and women must have seemed a safer bet than a wage law. Even so, it was proposed to legislate for each sex separately, adding a proviso that the men's law was to be "effective during this emergency." A minimum wage for men should also "of course, be separated from the women's bill," Dewson thought. This was indeed wise. When twin bills passed the New York State legislature in 1933, the bill for men was vetoed by the governor while the women's bill survived until the Supreme Court struck it down in 1936.[24]

In 1934, Clara Beyer found herself still ahead of both her women colleagues and the legal luminaries, when she suggested that "the time was ideal 'to proceed' with the promotion of minimum wages legislation for both men and women, 'at least in some of the states.' I went on to say that several of the New England states were contemplating such action. It was then that the wrath of the drafters of the new standard for state minimum wage laws—Felix Frankfurter, Ben Cohen, Josephine Goldmark, Molly Dewson et al came down on my head." It was Frankfurter who "blasted me, 'What are you up to, a crazy idea, we've got to get the women's held constitutional before we bring the men in.'" The lawyers were adamant, but they were not alone: "Molly Dewson, my dear Molly Dewson, said she was sorry to have to, and the Goldmark sisters and all running in apologising for objecting to my proposal to cover men."[25]

Lawyers and political activists were not totally opposed. Outright disagreement about any ambitious feminist program was manifest in the flat refusal of Frankfurter to respond to Kelley's analysis of gendered power relations. The lawyers were simply not ready—or able—to contemplate the comprehensive, structural problems of the subordination of women, whether these were described in the terms of the legal feminism of the NWP or the social feminism of the minimum wagers. A compromise emerged when Kelley's successors accepted the lawyers' leadership and the cautious route to reform by means of legal tinkering. But, while abandoning any full-blooded assault on inequality, these women did retain a sensitivity to the gendered implications of their strategy and occasionally revealed their greater radicalism and frustration at cautious legalism.

If lawyers and women had somewhat different preoccupations after 1923, it is not always clear why. Were lawyers motivated by professional interest alone? Did chauvinism reinforce their absorption in the technicalities of the law, or did traditional gender views and prejudice divert the minds of male lawyers from the structural situation of women workers? Sybil Lipschultz concludes that "Felix Frankfurter . . . was one of the staunchest opponents to women's equality, in part because he was such an advocate of women's labor laws. To his legal mind, that meant stressing women's inequality."[26] The ERA debate had made clear that "women's equality" was a problematic concept for feminists and lawyers alike. The attack on due process changed the terms of the debate.

LEGALISM: THE LAWYERS' PROGRAM

Adkins reinforced Kelley's lifelong radical instinct: her reaction was to abandon compromise and "half-loaf" measures and to propose to change the system. *Adkins* also reinforced the commitments of lawyers, with very different results. They were deferential to the text of the Constitution and the structure of the court. They set out to change the Constitution by changing judicial interpretation. "The due process clauses ought to go," Frankfurter wrote in an angry editorial in the *New Republic* in 1924; but he did not mean *go* as Kelley would have meant it—that is, by changing the text of the Constitution.[27] He made the revealing remark that the minimum wage was important "not because it is in behalf of working women but because it is a measure absolutely essential to our conception [of] the greatest interests."[28] In a gathering of social reformers, perhaps he did not need to spell out his conception of the greatest interests of society; what he did reveal was that within days of the *Adkins* decision he had decided that establishing the constitutionality of the minimum wage was "absolutely essential" to constitutional, and thence at one remove to social, reform.

Frankfurter was principal author of the legal strategy. Justice Brandeis advised, as did longtime friends like LaRue Brown and younger recruits such as Dean Acheson and especially Ben Cohen. Cohen was unofficial clerk to Frankfurter on minimum wage issues. His letters full of legal advice were often quoted verbatim by Frankfurter, who also deputed him to meet with the "ladies," many of whom, like Cohen, lived in New York.[29] A cautious, staged construction of a new and solid legal foundation for the minimum wage for women developed. "I think it essential," Frankfurter wrote, "to make one more try before the Court with a law that shall seek to avoid some of the foolish notions of Sutherland and yet accomplish in practice exactly what we are after."[30]

Simply in terms of legal technicalities, however, the lawyers' cautious scheme was radical, being nothing less than to force the court to revise the prevailing interpretation of the due process clauses of the Fifth and Fourteenth Amendments. The heart of the problem for the minimum wage was, they believed, the way in which the court regularly vetoed legislation because its substance violated the requirements of due process. Due process had at one time been taken by the court only to set standards for the means by which laws were passed and implemented—procedural due process. When the court adopted the doctrine of substantive due process in reviewing economic and labor legislation, it assumed the right to review the purpose of legislation. In the case of economic and labor law, where freedom of contract became established as a right to be protected by the courts, adherence to such formal principles gained priority over the public interest in social welfare, judicial standards were set above those employed by legislatures in the name of the police power.[31]

The trend of court decisions had long concerned reform-minded lawyers and in the early 1920s began to concern them more. Ray A. Brown calculated the numbers of police power cases struck down on substantive due process grounds: "Phrased in percentages this means that from 1868 to 1912 the Court held against the legislation in a very little more than six per cent of the cases; from 1913 to 1920 in a little more than seven per cent of the cases; while since 1920 [to 1927] the Court has held against the legislature in twenty-eight per cent of the cases."[32] The "Brandeis briefs" presented in the *Muller*, *Stettler*, and *Adkins* cases, had been designed to bring social considerations into constitutional adjudication. The summary rejection of this approach in *Adkins* was the last straw for Frankfurter and his colleagues. They planned to bring about a

reappraisal of the doctrine of substantive due process, which, if they succeeded, would make legislatures the arbiter of social considerations and free
them to determine labor law. The lawyers' program was part of the perpetual
struggle between courts and legislatures to control interpretation of the constitution.

As their vehicle, lawyers hijacked the minimum wage movement. Whereas
previously the conscience and politics of reformers had defined the problem
and identified the policy, and lawyers advised on form and content, now progress became contingent upon finding an adequate legal rationale. The content
of legal discussions also changed. To justify the exercise of the police power,
lawyers as well as reformers had necessarily attended to social conditions and
gender inequalities. Reform-minded lawyers blamed the courts for forcing the
new due process strategy—Frankfurter, for example, condemning the "activity
of our courts in bending the 'conveniently vague' language of due process to the
dominant service of vested property interests."[33] But, despite such harsh
words, the social critique inherent in police power reasoning was lost when the
issue became due process. Lawyers had already suspected that the Supreme
Court was hardening its view of the priority of due process above the police
power, the formalities of contract rights and procedural correctness over legislative views on social welfare. *Adkins* confirmed the suspicions they had
voiced during their running seminar on the ERA. Finding that they faced a
systemic rather than a specific problem, they stepped back from the content of
one particular policy, to the more abstract requirements of due process and the
boundaries of judicial decision making.

LaRue Brown wrote to Kelley doubting the merit of the substantive constitutional amendments she proposed, while himself proposing a general interpretive "amendment of the 14th and 5th amendments which would limit the
power of the courts to override legislative judgment." Neither the Fifth nor the
Fourteenth Amendment, he was sure, had been intended to allow substantive
judgments on the purposes of social legislation: "Nor can I believe the revered
founders despite the all embracing clairvoyance with which they were credited
meant to limit legislative action other than by precise and specific limitations
expressed in the constitution."[34] Frankfurter likewise insisted that the future of
labor laws depended on reinterpreting the Constitution, not hanging it about
with specific provisos. He wrote crossly in reply to Kelley's objections, that
"apparently you do not seem to appreciate the destructive scope and force of
the 14th Amendment."[35] He was prepared to consider amending the Constitution, but only to clarify what he believed to be the true intention of the existing
document with regard to "the jurisdiction of the Supreme Court": "(1) by the
insistence in practice on rules which it professes, but to which it does not
adhere and (2) by cutting down its jurisdiction through a Constitutional amendment which will restrict the Fourteenth Amendment to cover only racial and
religious discriminations."[36]

The lawyers proposed to start with Sutherland's unexpectedly clear advice
on the wage-fixing formula rather than with his declaration of sex equality or his

specious differentiation of hours and wages laws. They may have hoped that the strong dissents on the latter points would be grounds enough for reconsideration at some future date, and indeed the historical record suggested that dissents were often the forerunners of new interpretations.[37] At any rate, neither issue went so directly to the issue of due process. The wage-fixing formula might seem to be a procedural question of the rules for implementation, but if Sutherland's language of a fair wage were found to be a procedurally acceptable way of setting rates, the substantive game would have been won indirectly, with the state authorized to legislate fairness in the mechanisms of the economy.

WOMEN, LAWYERS, AND THE FAIR WAGE

The new plan, on which lawyers and reformers collaborated with varying degrees of enthusiasm, was to redefine the minimum wage to meet Sutherland's criteria of due process. Sutherland had opined that a wage fixed according to some "vague" cost of living standard was "a naked, arbitrary exercise of power." The law oppressed the employer, because it extracted "an arbitrary payment for a purpose and upon a basis having no causal connection with his business, or the contract or the work the employee engages to do"; whereas "a statute requiring an employer to pay . . . the value of the service rendered, even to pay with fair relation to the extent of the benefit obtained, would be understandable."[38] Before 1923, the minimum wage had been defined as a living wage and calculated by a cost-of-living formula for a single woman. This formula itself had been problematic for feminists. It ignored the needs of the many working women with dependents, patronized women in its definition of meager necessities, yet had recognized the fact that women were independent workers, and not just members of a family unit. The concept of a fair wage, a promising opening to the lawyers, created new problems for the political wing of the minimum wage campaign.

As usual, it was Kelley who mounted the broadest and most coherent attack against hanging the whole future of the minimum wage on a legal definition of a fair wage. First, she warned that the fair wage was indefinable, that it would contradict the old but still necessary police power rationale, and that it would inflict new injuries on the workers. She was sure that "we shall be creating lasting trouble for our own future. *Fair wages* are as incapable of standard definition as *due process*." She persisted with Frankfurter, writing in 1925, for example: "What I cannot see, and certainly cannot advocate, is adopting one of Mr Sutherland's worst forms of confusion as our own and write it into even one bill anywhere. . . . [Fair wages] is as India rubber as due process itself."[39] Frankfurter himself was graphic on the tyranny of "the growingly unknown and unknowable terrors of due process," because "the meaning of phrases like 'due process of law,' and of simple terms like 'liberty' and 'property,' is not revealed within the Constitution; their meaning is derived from without."[40] But Frankfurter saw an intellectual challenge where Kelley saw a fruitless digression.

Kelley secondly feared that defining a fair wage might escape one constitutional trap only to fall into another. According to *Adkins*, the living wage failed the procedural test of due process. But its calculus of the necessities of life did fit the substantive rationale for using the police power of the state, to preserve health and welfare. The "only solid foundation of wage determinations," legally and practically, Kelley felt, remained "the health of the workers."[41] As a strategic matter, Kelley did not believe that the police power, which had sustained the minimum wage for fifteen years, should be so suddenly abandoned. Only weeks before *Adkins*, she had declared health to be the sole and exclusive ground for the policy: "We are convinced that no other defense is possible."[42] Others shared her doubts. LaRue Brown, for example, wrote in support of Frankfurter's new "fair wage" draft but added that "I agree with you that the proper foundation for minimum wage determinations is the health of the workers. I have suggested to F.F. that he ought to get some language about this into his bill somewhere."[43] Constitutionally, "health" had encoded gendered concerns, and these exchanges with Kelley underlined the way in which the debate was moving away from gender.

Kelley's third objection was that a fair wage strategy would change the balance of power in the application of the policy. The legal substitution of "fair" for "minimum" was not just clever semantics. A fair wage, in Sutherland's terms, would require "an employer to pay . . . with fair relation to the extent of the benefit obtained." Kelley balked at the implications of writing into legislation "the requirement that the financial state of the industry must be taken into account" and believed that bare-subsistence living wages would become even lower fair wages.[44] But Frankfurter argued that in practice nothing would change, that Kelley was wrong about present living-wage procedures: "Everybody knows that under the old law the wage boards did in fact take into account economic factors that had nothing to do with 'a living wage'; they did take into account other wage levels and the economic condition of business in general and the specific industry in particular. I have not a particle of doubt that under the proposed law as we have drawn it the result in practice will not be a whit different than the old type of law." And, anyway, "it may hurdle us over the Supreme Court." Frankfurter sought allies like Grace Abbott of the Children's Bureau, to convince Kelley that she was "sacrificing actualities to metaphysics."[45] He suggested that Cohen try to involve Clara Beyer: "Get her practical experience in the actual ascertainment of the awards. If she agrees that in practice your present formula will not work differently than the old law did, we will have a powerful recruit for our point of view."[46]

Lacking American allies, Kelley resurrected the British example. The comparison did little to help her. When first Frankfurter proposed to devise a fair wage, in 1923, Kelley felt "unable to enlist off hand." She cited "a long conversation with J. J. Mallon yesterday," recalling their years of association in the cause and Mallon's unparalleled experience with minimum wage policy. "I asked Mr. Mallon how the idea appealed to him of introducing into future minimum wage bills a concept of *fair wages, fair, reasonable compensation*, etc. He paused before answering, and then said 'Nothing could be more un-English.'"[47] But Frankfurter doubted the relevance of British experience: "The fact that a legislative proposal is 'un-English' does not dispose of it in this country . . . A man like Mallon simply cannot understand—no Englishman can understand—that we are concerned in this country with problems that they never have to face because they have no written Constitution."[48] Given the limited procedural meaning of due process in Britain, he was probably right when he added, to Grace Abbott, that "no Englishman can possibly understand the difficulties in which the due process clause enmeshes us."[49]

Frankfurter turned the comparison back on Kelley. The principle might be different in Britain, he argued, but the practice was much the same; "unless all the studies of the working of the minimum wage in England give an untrue picture it is just as true in England as it is true of us that minimum rates . . . (1) have *not* been fixed by an easily ascertained and easily applied formula, and (2) they *have* had regard both to the financial condition of the industry and the general wage levels in that industry." His new fair wage proposal, he thought, "merely spells out what now takes place in practice and the spelling out may serve to save the constitutionality of this legislation. With the warmest respect I venture to say that the objections which you are urging are theoretical objections and would not be found hampering in practice."[50]

Kelley, the political activist, understood how women were already disadvantaged in wage board meetings by inexperience and by their lack of information and organization. The due process merits of the fair wage smacked of metaphysics to her. Her view was that the change would replace the one criterion—their own necessities—which women workers could quantify and comprehend by means of common sense, the one figure on which they could stand against the employers. To give them only the ambiguity of fairness to defend themselves, and to place equal legitimacy and the same criterion in the hands of employers, might be legally clever but would be politically disastrous. But Kelley found little support for her only alternative, amending the Constitution. The debate soon shifted to how, not whether, to define a fair wage, and Kelley's younger colleagues worked with the lawyers to pin down the nebulous concept of fairness. But not uncritically. Elizabeth Brandeis regularly reminded Frankfurter of administrative practicalities, and Dewson kept him informed of the politics of the legislative process. Dewson's political instincts, and her grasp of the ends of the legislation and the interests of women, especially were a corrective to the lawyers' single-minded concentration on the constitutional means.

The due process strategy was embodied in two new state laws, one passed in Wisconsin in 1925 and a second in New York in 1933.[51] Both were designed to meet Sutherland's criterion for wage regulation, but they tackled the problem differently. Wisconsin defined an oppressive wage, the formula tried before, unsuccessfully, in 1911: "No wage paid or agreed to be paid by any employer to any adult female shall be oppressive. Any wage lower than a reasonable and adequate compensation for the services rendered shall be deemed oppressive and is hereby prohibited."[52] John Commons, the aging progenitor of social legislation in Wisconsin, believed his idea had finally found its moment, as the way to overcome "Justice Sutherland's objection in the *Adkins* case." It was to be "not a 'fair wage,' but merely a true 'minimum wage'—a lower limit below which no employer should be permitted to force any employee," and "analogous to a 'confiscatory rate' in public utility law."[53]

Commons disliked the fair wage. It was radical, he thought, in that it would encourage wage bargaining through claims by individual workers, destroying the laboriously constructed edifice of collective bargaining by unions. The state should keep out of such matters, its role at most to set a bottom line. The oppressive wage would do just this, defining only the outer limit of collective bargaining. Commons's concern for the labor movement was a reminder of the conspicuous absence of organized labor from the minimum wage debate in these years. Like women's organizations, labor organizations were on the defensive in the twenties. The Red Scare, the revival of repressive tactics by employers, declining membership, and their own battles with the courts, preoccupied the AFL. The textile unions had their own faction fights and were deeply divided over communism in the twenties; even with the growing prominence of Sidney Hillman and his Amalgamated Clothing Workers, and their support for state intervention, they had little impact on the reformulation of minimum wage policy at this time. Labor organizations reentered the fray only in the 1930s, when Hillman would support minimum wage legislation from a position of influence with the Roosevelt administration, while the AFL recycled its old antagonism and hostile rhetoric.[54]

The ever-practical Elizabeth Brandeis (who had become a student and associate of Commons in Wisconsin) thought Commons's reasoning failed to solve anything at all: "The problem remains, however, to determine what is an 'oppressive wage.' If cost of living is not used as a basis, what concrete measure is there?" Brandeis had no answer to her own question. "Can the statement be turned into dollars and cents?" she continued. "So far the Wisconsin Commission has made no attempt to do so. They have set no rates under the new law but continue to use those established under our old living wage law." Brandeis, both justice's daughter and former minimum wage administrator, knew that a wage formula not only must stand up in the courts but must be defined in a way that could be expressed in cash terms. She feared that Sutherland had thrown out the only standard that might work: "Cost of living (admitting the difficulty of determining that) is the only real standard that I can see. Still in view of the constitutional situation something else even though nebulous may be worth trying." By 1933, when she advised on the New York law, she was less flexible, offering Frankfurter only "my 'either or' standard," that is, "*either* prevailing wage *or* minimum cost of living."[55]

The New York branch of the NCL, led by Molly Dewson, revived interest in a minimum wage law in 1928, when the election of Franklin Roosevelt as governor placed a personal friend in power. Dewson dashed off a letter: "Dear F.F.,—We are in luck here with Roosevelt our friend Governor !!!!!!!!!" She had shed the doubts of her mentor, Kelley, and wanted to know: "Would rules with the force of law (a mandatory fair wage) be unconstitutional if what old Sutherland said about certain fair wages being understandable was carefully held in mind?" Dewson, like Commons, thought that replacing a minimum with a fair wage had radical possibilities. Unlike Commons, she liked the prospect of expanding the scope of state intervention. But she too had misgivings about how the new terminology might affect the unions. So she told Frankfurter that "I cannot reconcile myself to writing in our bill about a fair 'existence' wage or 'cost of living wage.' Is not anyone exploited who does not get a fair wage? The line in practice seems to me to have to be pricked out where the exploited group has never demonstrated the power to bargain or get reasonable wages."[56]

Cohen was sure that the courts would permit a fair wage standard only where wages were already below subsistence: "In theory the [New York] bill is not limited to those who are exploited below the margin of a fair existence but would be available to all grades of women whose wages are not considered fair in relation to the service rendered. In practice the Commission doubtless would apply it only in cases touching the margin of existence, but would it not be wise to incorporate this limitation in the bill in order to make it less frightening to a frightened court."[57] Frankfurter invented a consolidated concept—the minimum fair wage—which might reassure Sutherland *and* Dewson. But Dewson had another complaint: "BUT . . . We are all sick of the word minimum. It is a mean, hateful word. Its day has waned. If you cannot yield it because of the subtleties of the law you must find us a synonym." Frankfurter's prescient but cynical solution was that "perhaps the word 'fair' stuck in front of standards will accomplish the same thing as minimum, if that is really an offensive term to you."[58]

The New York law tried to cover every possible angle. In two steps, it defined first an offense, then a remedy. The offense was to employ a woman at "an oppressive or unreasonable wage," one "both less than the fair and reasonable value of the services rendered and less than sufficient to meet the minimum cost of living necessary for health." The remedy allowed the state to impose a wage "fairly and reasonably commensurate with the value of the service or class of service rendered." The original living wage, Kelley's health standard, Sutherland's fair wage, and Commons's oppressive wage were all incorporated. Elizabeth Brandeis's stricture that any standard must be practicable was half-met in setting the offense, where the living wage was one measure of eligibility; dodged in the remedy, where guidelines for determining fair value allowed any or all of the criteria of fair value itself, reasonable value as understood by the courts in fee disputes, and prevailing wages in the locality.[59]

As a compendium of all the ideas about wage standards that had been floated to meet Sutherland's test of due process, the New York law was comprehensive. As a way to circumvent the courts and legislate a minimum wage it proved a disaster. The Supreme Court, reviewing the legislation in 1936 and finding a living wage extant in its provisions despite the *Adkins* prohibition, used this as an excuse and refused even to look at the elaborate new provisions. The *Morehead* case was initiated by a plea of habeas corpus by a particularly unscrupulous laundry manager, Joseph Tipaldo, who was held in jail for nonpayment of the minimum wage. Tipaldo had evaded the law by paying his employees the statutory rate, receiving a signed receipt for their wages, then sending his book-keeper around the plant to collect back $4.88 from each worker. Kelley would have appreciated the public relations advantage of victims like "Anna, who lives in the Bronx and works in Brooklyn," to whom "$4.88 is the difference between 'getting along' and 'going on relief.'" But "Justice Butler, who wrote the opinion of the Court and his four associates who concurred, are not primarily concerned with the amount in Anna's pay packet on Saturday night. These gentlemen see, as their responsibility, Anna's freedom of contract."[60] The court refused to differentiate the fair wage law from the old minimum wage laws rejected in *Adkins* and refused to reconsider *Adkins*. After thirteen years of conceptual refinement, the *Morehead* decision left the lawyers' strategy in ruins.

FROM *MOREHEAD* TO *WEST COAST HOTEL*

Minimum wage policy soon rose like the proverbial phoenix from the ashes of *Morehead*. The events of 1936 and 1937 marked a change as significant as that of 1923. This time, political and constitutional change went together, and favored the minimum wage campaign. National politics, judicial decisions, and new arguments from persistent lawyers contributed. The *Morehead* case was decided on 1 June 1936. Later that year, President Roosevelt was reelected in a landslide and was ready to tackle judicial resistance to New Deal policies. A new constitutional strategy, the proposal to bring a federal minimum wage under the Commerce Clause of the Constitution, was already well in hand within his administration and was leaked to the press in the New Year.[61] On 29 March 1937, the court astonished minimum wagers by deciding the case of *West Coast Hotel v. Parrish* in their favor. *Adkins* was flatly overruled in a case about one of the original, gendered, living wage laws, the 1913 Washington State law based on the police power doctrine.[62] State laws for women were constitutional after all, Kelley's original strategy apparently vindicated.

At first glance, the *Morehead* decision left the minimum wage just where it had been in 1923. Minimum, and now fair, wage laws were unconstitutional. The judicial practice of honoring precedent and adjudicating narrowly appeared to have stalled the policy until such time as another new formula could be legislated and contested. Not for the first time, however, the dissents and even the judgment in *Morehead* did hint that the court had noted the debates which had raged around the minimum wage, and did contain seeds of change.

Especially (almost gratuitously in the wake of a prolix refusal to differentiate this law from *Adkins* and to consider its innovative fair wage), the majority opinion in *Morehead* outlined how, after all, a minimum wage might be justified, and for whom: "The Act is not to meet an emergency; it discloses a permanent policy; the increasing number of women workers suggests that more and more they are getting and holding jobs that otherwise would belong to men."[63] Minimum wagers did not want a temporary law. But they did want a law for women, and for men as well if that were possible. In its insinuation that women might no longer need protective wage laws, the court also hinted at why men might need them too: "Men in need of work are as likely as women to accept the low wages offered by unscrupulous employers. It is plain that . . . prescribing of minimum wages for women alone would unreasonably restrain them in competition with men."[64]

The "conservatives," the long-standing majority for laissez-faire, disliked women taking jobs from men but preferred them to do so, if they must, on terms of equality. They might hope that equal competition would debar women from work, but they succeeded in making the case for protective legislation for both sexes. By comparison, "liberal" (in supporting interventionist policies, at least for women) Chief Justice Hughes wrote in dissent: "The distinctive nature and function of women—their particular relation to the social welfare—has put them in a separate class. This separation and corresponding distinctions in legislation is one of the outstanding traditions of legal history."[65]

The five justices in the majority in *Morehead* were trying to have it both ways, to stand for the ideal of difference between the sexes, yet to ensure women equal rights in roles the justices actually thought proper for men, as workers. Their confusion was reminiscent of the lawyers involved in the ERA dispute in 1921, even those supporting the ERA, for whom gender difference had remained a fact, hard to reconcile with legal definitions of equality. Indeed, the *Morehead* decision was rooted not only in the same problem but in the same analysis. The National Woman's Party submitted an *amicus curiae* brief in the *Morehead* case, as it had done in *Adkins*.[66] Lawyers for Tipaldo and the state had made little of the question of the gendering of minimum wage laws. Their arguments were with wage regulation itself, not regulation specifically for women. It was the NWP brief that introduced the issue of gender, both to remind the court that it had been disposed of by *Adkins* and to explain that changes in the labor market since 1923 only reinforced the *Adkins* reasoning. The court not only noted these points but borrowed the words of the NWP brief, quoting it almost verbatim in its ruling.[67]

The NWP reminded the court that freedom of contract, the subordination of the police power to the due process clause, and, in *Adkins*, the equality of women were all established by clear precedents. Its resounding conclusion was that "the Constitution of the United States is still supreme in the United States and that the principles of constitutional liberty belong to women as well as to men. The Nineteenth Amendment gave them full political rights. The *Adkins* decision following closely thereafter gave them assurance that their fundamental liberties are recognized by the courts. It may be said that their *Magna Charta* is found in the words of Mr. Justice Sutherland."[68] The accompanying analysis of competition in the labor market was an argument for equality between workers, and the court majority responded with words that echoed the equal rights language of *Adkins*. But the justices did not write a Magna Carta. Whereas *Adkins* had simply declared the question of equality settled, *More-*

head elaborated on women's place in the economy, revealing in the process that the court would not be sorry if the equality it granted drove women out of the "jobs that would otherwise belong to men."

One year later, with the *West Coast Hotel* decision, all this appeared irrelevant. Chief Justice Hughes, for the majority, now set a flexible standard for the use of gender classifications—neither the biological absolutism of *Muller* nor the "equal rights" absolutism of *Adkins*: "The legislature 'is free to recognize degrees of harm and it may confine its restrictions to those classes of cases where the need is deemed to be clearest.' "[69] But the judgment was not just a reassertion of the "difference" theory of gender. The conclusion that "[women's] relative need in the presence of the evil, no less than the existence of the evil itself, is a matter for the legislative judgment" opened the way for minimum wage legislation to respond not only to the need of any class of victim, women or men, but to the evil of sweating itself.[70]

The *West Coast Hotel* decision also asserted the right of state legislatures to exercise their police power under a modified standard of due process: "The liberty safeguarded [by the Fourteenth Amendment] is liberty in a social organization which requires the protection of law against the evils which menace the health, safety, morals and welfare of the people. Liberty under the Constitution is thus necessarily subject to the restraints of due process, and regulation which is reasonable in relation to its subject and is adopted in the interests of the community is due process."[71] The latitude that the fair wage strategy had been designed to increase, for legislatures to make policy without substantive review, was thus granted in much fuller measure without the fair wage ever having been considered. The economic substantive due process doctrine was set aside.[72]

Due process and its corollary, freedom of contract, which had dogged the minimum wage campaign from the start—indeed had dogged the campaign against sweating since the early factory laws, such as those that Kelley had fought for and enforced in Illinois in the 1890s—had failed in the courts.[73] Yet the long-awaited triumph over constitutional doctrines that had blocked the goals of protection for both women and men turned out to be a mixed blessing. When freedom of contract lost its priority, women and workers discovered the irony that it had been a protection as well as an impediment. When the state was permitted to regulate work conditions, equality did not necessarily follow. From an equal rights perspective, Judith Baer has commented that the *West Coast Hotel* decision to permit reasonable restraints on freedom of contract meant that "the one constitutional doctrine that—whatever its validity—could have provided some measure of protection for women's rights in employment had now been abandoned. . . . Economic rights gained virtually no judicial protection after 1937. Freedom of contract could now be curtailed as long as such restriction had some reasonable relation to a legitimate government purpose."[74] Similarly labor determined during the 1940s that due process criteria could protect as well as attack their rights: "The trend of legislation changed, with numerous restrictions being imposed on unions and union practices. Faced with these enactments, labor's lawyers recalled the pre-1937 Supreme Court cases and the emphasis in them on the constitutional liberties of employees. Labor's attack, therefore, was grounded in part on due process."[75]

SWINGS AND ROUNDABOUTS: LAW AND POLICY

Florence Kelley's reluctance to see her causes held hostage to the whims, the political swings, and even the health of the courts may seem well founded. The *West Coast Hotel* case almost fell victim to the illness of Justice Stone, who missed the oral argument but participated in the decisions and prevented the case being "affirmed by a divided Court." As lawyer Ray A. Brown remarked, as he attempted to chart and explain the fluctuating court position on the police power versus due process: "Such considerations almost persuade one to abandon the further study of the cases in this field to the biographer and the psychoanalyst."[76]

Far more serious was the vulnerability of social reform to both the politics and the technicalities of the law. *West Coast Hotel* was the famous "switch in time that saved nine," the case in which Justice Roberts switched from his habitual vote with the four justices reliably against economic regulation, to voting with the four justices who normally supported regulation. Politically, the case represented the withdrawal of the Supreme Court from direct confrontation with the President, after judicial intransigence on major New Deal legislation had led to Roosevelt's court-packing proposal and given rise to unparalleled hostility between executive and judiciary. Although Roosevelt refused to comment at his next press conference, the *West Coast Hotel* decision opened the way to a resumption of his New Deal economic program.[77] The decision also inaugurated an era of judicial deference to legislative judgment and a fundamental change in control of the constitutional text. Of more immediate significance to women workers in the District of Columbia, by overturning *Adkins* the decision also opened the way for the reinstatement of the District Minimum Wage Board, whose sudden death in 1923 turned out to be only a prolonged suspension.[78]

Justice Roberts's switch has been seen as a deliberate and wise retreat from constitutional crisis. By his own account, however, his behavior was more determined by professional imperatives, "craftsman's delight," than political considerations. The new era for the court might easily have been inaugurated a year earlier by the *Morehead* decision, had it not been for Roberts's professional scruples. In *Morehead*, lawyers for the state argued that the "fair wage" criterion differed from the living wage standard reviewed in *Adkins*. Therefore their legislation could be considered without regard to the *Adkins* precedent. "The argument seemed to me disingenuous and born of timidity. I could find nothing in the record to substantiate the alleged distinction. At conference I so stated, and stated further that I was for taking the State of New York at its word. The State had not asked that the *Adkins* case be overruled but that it be distinguished."[79] Apparently, in 1936 Roberts was ready to overrule *Adkins*. Had the "switch in time" come a year sooner, it would have preceded Roosevelt's reelection and confrontation with the court. It would also have preceded Roosevelt's decision to implement Frances Perkins's plan for national wage and hours legislation.

Legal professionalism and legal technicalities were thus crucial to the development of minimum wage policy. The necessity of conforming to contemporary definitions of the police power, substantive and procedural due process, simultaneously constrained policy development and required productive clarification of its principles. But this was not a simple relationship, a didactic legal framework and a reactive and malleable policymaking process. For one thing, there was no monolithic professional position. The lawyers were engaged among themselves in a dialectic characterized by controversy, resistance, contradictions, and new ideas. The apparent finality of decisions like *Adkins* and *Morehead* was misleading, for each simply started a new stage of the debate. Also misleading was the supposed solidity of professional judgments based on the incremental accumulation of precedent, for as the *West Coast Hotel* decision showed, these could be unpredictably overthrown. Meantime, other lawyers competed to preempt judicial decisions, to determine what constitutional issue would be considered, what precedents would be called upon, which statute and which case would become the crucial test.[80]

Such fluidity, division, competition, and second-guessing within the law notwithstanding, legal decision making was not simply politics by another name. Donald Horowitz's analysis of the "attributes of adjudication" identifies factors that contributed to the separation of the legal from the women's strategy for the minimum wage.[81] Frankfurter's "craftsman's delight" always involved consideration of existing case law, which narrowed the possibilities in numerous ways. There was a certain randomness as to which cases came to court, as the strange career of the *Adkins* case attests. An argument built on precedents was built on a collection of given fragments, not on the kind of comprehensive view of the world that social feminists, for example, were seeking in the 1920s. The decision in each separate case depended heavily on the internal logic of one particular example, on the antecedent facts and the specific rights at issue. A policymaker, on the other hand, was free to consider alternatives, and costs and practicalities. The function of a court to come down with a definite resolution, yes or no, Horowitz argued, fostered "reductionist solutions."[82] Courts have always been ill-equipped to monitor the subsequent social impact of their decisions, and unintended outcomes would not be anticipated but only reckoned with in some subsequent case. Lawyers, as the development of the due process strategy confirmed, have reached their conclusions not only on a different set of facts from those available to policymakers but out of a different set of considerations.

Nonetheless, politics impinges on the process of adjudication. Minimum wage statutes were typical in being written on the basis of both technical and political judgments about their constitutionality, and anticipation of the politics of the courts that held the right of review. Statutes were set up to elicit certain constitutional responses and avoid others, and there was political calculation in the attempts of minimum wagers to bring to the courts the best possible statute from the best possible jurisdiction. When lawyers took over the leadership of the minimum wage campaign in 1923, both their political and their professional concerns led to a different kind of campaign from that envisaged by political activists like Kelley, who thought the fair wage would be a wild goose chase, like Dewson, who came to resent the political implications of their insistence that the courts would only accept subsistence wages as "fair," and like Elizabeth Brandeis, who thought that implementation of a fair wage law would not be practicable. It is also true that their legal strategy had no successes in terms of new and actively enforced laws. If women opposed the legal strategy and suffered from the absence of protection, was male insensitivity more to blame than "craftsman's delight"?

Too few women lawyers were involved to provide a comparison. When Kelley commented "as a lawyer" on the ERA in 1921, she wrote in terms very similar to the men that she was "opposed both on principle and in the light of long experience to blanket measures, and vague words in bills and constitutional amendments."[83] Two women, Burnita Shelton Matthews and Rebekah Scandrett Greathouse, presented the NWP brief in *Morehead*, but there is no way of knowing how gender or professional training may have formed their views. There were, no doubt, plenty of men in the 1920s backing away from any more demands from women and trying to get down to "politics as usual"—that is to say, male politics. The minimum wage lawyers, however, were not backing off the whole feminist program. They all supported change in marital rights and citizenship laws. But their support of protective legislation was fundamentally conservative—they wanted to carry on as before, without reconsidering the ideological basis of these laws. That would have meant reconsidering their conviction that women's legal and social position would always have to acknowledge biological difference. As equal rights lawyer Albert Levitt boldly put it to Elsie Hill (who married him some six months later), "Without regard to the question of welfare legislation . . . Your insistence that the laws based upon marriage should apply equally to husband and wife is so foolish from the standpoint of biology and physiology—upon which most law questions are really based—forgetting for the time being any psychological differences between the sexes—that you are going to lose all you have at present with little hope of getting more in the future."[84]

On the evidence of their campaigns for the minimum wage in the 1920s and 1930s, it is possible to argue that the lawyers were lawyers and not feminists but, despite Levitt's lapse, not that they were out-and-out, deliberate chauvinists. But even if they were not chauvinist in any intentional sense, their approach to minimum wage policy was gendered as well as professional. The lawyers' understanding of gender as only partly a social construction, irreducibly a biological fact, was shared by many of their social feminist women colleagues at the turn of the century. These women, however, observed and were motivated by the changing role of women in the economy and so began to grope toward new definitions of gender and equality that would reconcile the beliefs of their youth with the facts they encountered in their adult life.[85] Because they felt a bond of sisterhood with the women in the sweatshops, because they saw workplace conditions in person, because their nineteenth-century upbringings gave them a sense of female responsibility as well as an increasingly inappropriate ideal of women's family role, and because the suffrage victory opened up a new political future, women found a redefinition of their political role and their political program increasingly urgent.[86]

The altruism of minimum wage lawyers was detached, channeled by their professional interest in the technicalities of constitutional law, lacking the direct experience of women's conditions, and of course infused by an ideology of domesticity with which they were raised, as were their women colleagues, but that remained consistent with the facts of their own lives and families in a way that was not true for women. Gender and legalism together made the lawyers' view of minimum wage policy and of the broader issues of women's politics and sex equality in the twentieth century a different one from that of women campaigners.

A tension between these two groups and perspectives existed in the minimum wage campaign right from the start, in the discussions about gender and the police power in the first phase of legislation. This tension was greatest after 1920, when the conjunction of the Nineteenth Amendment, the ERA, and the *Adkins* case forced a reconsideration of gender in the public sphere. All three of these precipitating factors were constitutional events, making the lawyers' central role in the reconsideration inevitable. Their takeover of leadership, however, and the significant change of direction this brought as their attention focused on due process rather than on the social purpose of the minimum wage, was not so inevitable. The cumulation of constitutional challenges made it an opportune moment for such a change of direction. But personalities and happenstance made it possible. There was a sudden vacuum of leadership as Florence Kelley began to retire in discouragement and a tired Molly Dewson took a sabbatical.[87] Frankfurter was sympathetic to Kelley, despite their testy correspondence. As he reminded Ben Cohen, in the wake of *Adkins*: "Mrs. Kelley is a very hard customer as those of us who have been working with her for years well know. The thing to bear in mind is that she has given her life to causes before you and I were born which at the end of her whole life are largely dust and ashes." But Frankfurter's next sentence was assertive: "Of course, that doesn't mean we should allow her to run away with her own ideas and subscribe to them if we don't believe them."[88] Frankfurter's availability and the fact that he was spoiling for a campaign over due process was the other contingency that brought about the change in leadership and direction.

At the end of the period of legal leadership, in 1937, direct results were hard to see: the challenge to due process through the fair wage remained untested; a minimum wage law dating from 1913 and the old police power rationale had been upheld in an unplanned curtailment of due process; federal price and wage codes under the National Recovery Administration had been rejected by the Supreme Court; those state laws that remained on the statute books were largely unenforced. Overall, legal progress seemed almost accidental, women workers' progress nonexistent.

The record of these years can only be seen more positively from a longer-term perspective. The lawyers had laid a necessary part of the groundwork for the new federal legislation proposed in 1937, with their redefinition of fair and oppressive wages. Their crucial move from relying on the police power to posing a due process claim came to fruition in the Fair Labor Standards Act of 1938, where not the welfare of women and of the community, classic police power concerns, but the welfare of the economy was the rationale for legislation. Ben Cohen is credited with being the main draftsman of the FLSA, and his correspondence with Frankfurter between 1923 and 1933 charts the development of its minimum wage clause.[89] The lawyers had set the stage for the modern phase of minimum wage legislation.

EIGHT

Labor and Commerce

THE FAIR LABOR STANDARDS ACT, U.S.A., 1937–1938

WHY BOTHER to name an act "fair"? Who would intend anything else? The naming of the Fair Labor Standards Act of 1938, the source of modern minimum wage policy in the United States, was itself a clue that a constitutional preemptive strike as well as a political achievement was planned. Due process called for fair procedures. *Adkins* had hinted that a fair wage might be constitutional. And federal antitrust legislation had won judicial approval with the argument that the Commerce Clause of the Constitution allowed Congress to establish the rules of fair competition. Administration lawyers seeking a basis for a federal minimum wage had ample reason for placing fairness at the forefront of their case and at the head of their title. The everyday meaning of fairness as justice barely entered either legal or political debate over the act. It was a technical, constitutional sense of fairness that gave the new policy its name.[1]

The FLSA found constitutional authority in the federal power to regulate commerce between the several states. The preamble to the act declared that "the existence . . . of labor conditions detrimental to the maintenance of the minimum standard of living necessary for health, efficiency, and general well-being of workers" variously: 1) used the medium of commerce to spread such conditions more widely; 2) burdened commerce itself and inhibited its free flow; 3) constituted unfair competition; 4) led to labor disputes (with all the above lamentable secondary effects); and 5) interfered with the orderly and fair marketing of goods. This was the rhetoric of the Webbs' paradigm of sweating, seeking fair economic processes, not of the original NCL model minimum wage law: "The welfare of the State of —— demands that women and minors be protected from conditions of labor which have a pernicious effect on their health and morals."[2] The shift from police power to due process arguments after *Adkins* had diverted attention from gender issues. Passage of the FLSA completed the process as "commerce," and "employees" within commerce, became the named targets of minimum wage policy.

The FLSA apparently solved problems of definition and coverage that had dogged the campaign for the past thirty years: the act applied to "labor," not just to women or even only to sweated labor; indeed, gender discrimination was specifically barred; it was national, eliminating the need for forty-eight separate campaigns and the problems caused by the disparities between states; it set a flat-rate wage, escaping the problematic and highly political task of calculating "living" or "fair" wages; and its premise of universality meant that exemptions had to be argued out of coverage, whereas previously each occupation had been argued into coverage by state wages boards.

Appearances can be deceptive, however. Itemized exemptions and concealed biases and omissions undermined the nominal universality of the FLSA. Explicit exemptions included agriculture, executive, administrative, and professional jobs, most retailing and transport, fishing, food packing and processing, the employees of local newspapers, and, in the so-called Shirley Temple Clause, child actors. Children under sixteen were not to be employed at all, under eighteen in hazardous industries, excepting the small loophole for Shirley Temple and the large one permitting the employment of children by their parents, outside of manufacture and mining and "in periods which will not interfere with their schooling"—a euphemism for the often exploitative employment of farm children.[3] Congressman Martin Dies, seeking to kill the bill with ridicule, filed an overblown amendment during the congressional debate "calling on the Labor Department to report back to Congress within 90 days after the bill's passage on whether any worker was covered by the act."[4]

Special terms for other categories, learners, apprentices, home workers, and workers disadvantaged by age or physical or mental impairment, were left to administrative decision. The latitude for the Wage and Hour Administrator, a creation of the act, and for judges to define the boundaries of the new minimum wage was considerable.[5] The basic minimum wage clause, for example, directed that "Every employer shall pay to each of his employees who is engaged in commerce or in the production of goods for commerce" a twenty-five-cent hourly wage, rising within seven years to 40 cents an hour. Concealed in this clause were two potentially huge exclusions—that of all workers in firms unconnected with interstate commerce and that of some workers whose firms engaged in such commerce but whose own jobs might not qualify. Some such cases were obvious, others exceedingly problematic. What of the "employees of small telephone exchanges, which transmit interstate long distance calls very infrequently," or the chauffeur if we "suppose a candy manufacturing company maintains a company car . . . Is he engaged in the production of candy?"[6] Was a home worker, who was often technically a subcontractor, an employee? These lines, too, were left for administrators and judges to draw.

The effect of exemptions and interpretive openings was to bias minimum wage coverage in new ways. When contemporary standards of what was "commerce" and what was "between the states" were added to specific exemptions, it transpired that the gender discrimination of earlier laws was reversed: women were now disproportionately excluded. Furthermore, the concealed race discrimination of the first round of laws, from their absence in the southern states, was maintained by a new route: African-Americans, like women, were most likely to be in local, intrastate occupations; and one major employer of black workers, agriculture, was excluded entirely. The "labor" protected by the FLSA was principally the white, male industrial class that needed protection least. Close to the 1945 deadline for bringing wages up to the forty-cent minimum, forty cents represented a modest 35 percent of average hourly earnings in the private, nonfarm business sector.[7] Of eleven million workers formally covered when the act came into force in September 1938, only three hundred thousand earned less than the initial twenty-five-cent-an-hour legal minimum, and fewer than a million and a half earned less than the 1945 goal of forty cents an hour.[8] Meantime, expressed as median annual wages for 1939, agricultural workers made $309 and domestic workers $296, compared with the $1,009 of "Operatives and kindred workers."[9]

The FLSA was admittedly imperfect. It was in his presentation of the first draft to the House and Senate Labor Committees that Justice Department counsel Robert H. Jackson devised the concept of statutory reality, "choosing the lesser evil—and making the choice work."[10] In Britain, the shift of responsibility for minimum wage legislation from reform movement to government department had changed its emphasis from social concern to the bureaucratic mechanisms of the Trade Boards Act. The shift from state to federal government, from police power to Commerce Clause and due process authority, was of a similar order. The FLSA differed profoundly from the first phase of American minimum wage laws, in scope, in bias, and not least in its procedure of setting a single flat-rate wage, a system with administrative but also legal and political advantages and origins.

The Politics of the FLSA

By 1937, a new political environment enabled a previously unthinkable degree of wage regulation. Almost a decade of depression and mass unemployment had changed the public attitude toward an unfettered free market. Keynesian theories of economic intervention prevailed among the experts. These experts, and many of the reformers who had previously pressed for the minimum wage as outsiders, were now insiders in the vastly expanded New Deal administration. Within the labor movement, the AFL's dominance was contested by the CIO, originating in trades bordering the sweated sector and led by Sidney Hillman, a longtime advocate of state regulation of the labor market. Business interests and the AFL unions, those old allies against the minimum wage, could only delay and restrict the act. Finally, there were new constitutional arguments, and, at the crucial moment, changes in the Supreme Court. These new factors dissolved old problems but created new ones.

The FLSA was greeted by morning-after headlines about the "Wage-Hour Victory," which "promised to end sweat-shop chiseling throughout the Nation" and "fight the depression and pave the way for recovery."[11] The hyperbole, and relief at the conclusion of a hard-fought legislative passage, contrast with the many compromises made along the way. John S. Forsythe described the FLSA as "one of the most bitterly fought pieces of legislation ever to be enacted by Congress, with the true issues frequently clouded by storms of falsification and propaganda." In 1912, the novel proposal for minimum wage laws had been underestimated by opponents, and they had mobilized too little and too late. This time, the political and constitutional battles came sooner and loomed larger. This time also, the FLSA was not just another piece of labor legislation,

it was a deliberate challenge by the administration to centers of resistance to
the New Deal program. The establishment of a federal right to a minimum
wage, after years of frustration, was won when the policy was sponsored not by
outsiders on its own merits but by insiders as a means to secure their power.
Women who had led from without in earlier years now operated behind the
scenes. While NCL secretary Lucy Mason spoke for the measure in Congressional hearings, former NCL aides like Frances Perkins and Clara Beyer
watched over it within the administration. Representative Mary Norton, a New
Jersey Democrat, chaired the committee hearings after the sudden death of
William Connery in 1937—a difficult accession of power, for, she recalled, "I
was none too sure of my position, and my first meeting with the Labor Committee . . . was a terrific strain," as she came unprepared and against "an undercur-
rent of resentment" from rivals.[12] In the public battles, however, the key players were business and labor, regional interests, and pro- and anti-Roosevelt
coalitions.

The 1936 election gave Democrats 331 seats in the House, Republicans a
mere 89, and 13 to minority parties, a sweeping victory that did not ensure
passage of a Democrat President's bill. Between January 1937 and June 1938,
Congress saw ten drafts of the FLSA, each "with at least a major change from
its predecessor and most of them in the form of amendments substituting an
entirely different proposal"; twenty-five versions reached the files of the House
Labor Committee. The House vote by 216 to 198 in December 1937 to recommit the administration's bill was, James T. Patterson notes, "the clearest indication of sectional divisions of any vote to that time." It "brilliantly illuminated
the urban-rural conflicts that were dividing the Roosevelt coalition" and in
addition "revealed the dependence of the New Deal upon pressure groups":
thus "when a powerful lobby supported a bill, it usually passed . . . when a
lobby was indecisive or unenthusiastic, as labor was in this case, congressmen
were left to follow the next strongest pressures, whatever they might be."[13]
After a classic campaign of procedural obstruction in which the House Rules
Committee featured largely, the strongest pressure proved to be electoral. A
primary election in Florida in May 1938, won by Claude Pepper on a minimum
wage ticket, convinced Representatives that the public as well as the President
wanted the bill, and the way was suddenly opened for quick passage.[14]

If one factor beyond politics contributed to the new configuration of political
forces in the late thirties, it was the universal experience of the depression. The
optimism of the early twenties—when it was, perhaps, possible to believe that
a rising economic tide would float most if not all boats—had given way to a
world in which sweating seemed to characterize the whole economy. "There is
practically no industry in which some men and women are not woefully underpaid," David J. Saposs noted, replying to a 1936 Department of Labor survey
of the views of leading economists on minimum wage legislation. Twenty-five
of the twenty-eight respondents agreed that "men, women, and minors" should
all be covered. Even the three dissenters thought that the logic of economic
conditions required the eventual coverage of all workers, politically impractical
though this seemed to them at the time.[15]

By 1937, the principle of state economic management had become familiar, and the federal government had a positive, expansive view of its economic role. Secretary of Labor Frances Perkins opened her testimony to the Congressional hearings with what she presumably thought her long suit, a line of argument that smacked of the theory that the New Deal was primarily a rescue mission for capitalism: "This bill is peculiarly a measure which is to be considered as a stabilizer of employment, of income, of the market for goods, of production and production planning and marketing, a reward for efficiency. It is also a stabilizer of price, preventing the undue and disturbing fluctuations of price which so frequently lead to such downward markets as we have experienced." Paragraphs later, Perkins reached the traditional ground of "the evils of child labor, sweatshops, and low wages."[16]

Business and labor, whose opposition in the earlier period had been relatively united and uncomplicated, now presented a greater and less concerted set of views. Business divided on north-south and urban-rural lines, between large and small businesses, and between specific industries. Labor had had its dissenters and factions before. But now, with the breakaway Committee for Industrial Organization well connected with the administration, labor had neither a single view on the issue nor a single influential voice. The joint hearings conducted by House and Senate Labor committees in 1937 put all these views on record.

Business divided three ways: supporters, opponents (still the majority), and those who figured that their best strategy was to hold out for special treatment, whether by exemption, by tariffs on their competitors, or by regional differentials. These categories were never exclusive—southern businessmen, for example, often combined outright opposition with claims for any or all kinds of special treatment if the worst should happen and a bill pass. There were enough friendly businessmen to create a critical mass of support for the bill. Robert Johnson, president of Johnson and Johnson, manufacturers of surgical dressings, textile products, and baby food; the Council for Industrial Progress, representing clothing, packaging, millinery, machine parts, and building trades employers; the Portland Cement Company; the president of the Hughes Tool Company; the president of the Hormel meat-packing business—all testified in favor of the FLSA.[17] Typically, Johnson was a well-known welfare capitalist, who believed that decent labor conditions contributed to productivity and profit. Support came easily from this group anyway: most were already paying above the proposed forty-cent minimum wage. Federal Commissioner of Labor Statistics Isador Lubin tabulated average hourly earnings in major industries for the committee. Meat packing averaged 59.8 cents, cement 60.4 cents, machine tools 67.2 cents, and building construction 87.4 cents.[18]

Mass production firms like Johnson and Johnson also wanted a national market, with standardized costs and purchasing power. They realized that only the federal government could bring low-wage southern industries into line. The CIP was "preponderantly representative of the small establishment."[19] Smaller firms felt too close for comfort to the threat of competition by sweating. Concerned, for example, at the original proposal to exempt very small businesses (how small was small remained open to negotiation) they argued that "if small groups are exempt they invariably develop a situation which gives them a commercial advantage over other larger employers through the exploitation of their labor."[20] A millinery industry spokesman was emphatic: "Manufacturers either want this law enforced universally against the chiseler or they do not want it enacted. They do not want the chiseler slugging below the belt while the law ties their hands."[21] The anti-sweating argument was now claimed on behalf of "more than 52 per cent of all industrial employment in the United States."[22]

The rhetoric of the chiseler came straight from the short-lived experiment of the National Recovery Administration codes of trade practice that had operated between 1933 and 1935. That ambitious scheme had not originated from the minimum wage campaign but bequeathed to it a mixed message of the draconian measures it might take to eradicate the vigorous "poisonous creeper" of sweating.[23] The first version of the FLSA, proposing a five-person Labor Standards Board to stage the introduction of wage and hour standards, industry by industry, and time by time, would, some witnesses feared, "result in confusion comparable to that of the defunct N.R.A."[24] Supporters of legislation explained that "N.R.A. failed because we all tried to make it cover the earth," and suggested improvements.[25] Opponents quickly latched onto the impracticality of this scheme, and their "constructive" criticism was often a devious way of opposing the entire measure. The president of the U.S. Chamber of Commerce could not advocate "anything but fair wages and reasonable hours of work," but could fear that there might be some "injustice to perfectly innocent persons, and a general clog on business, in provisions of this kind." "It is easy to agree with many of [the bill's] primary objectives," James Emery testified for the National Association of Manufacturers. But, he continued, good intentions were not enough. "The pathway to eternal torment is reputed to enjoy a model pavement," and he could not support the "application of dubious and destructive legal principles or methods of administration that threaten to multiply confusion and encourage business hesitation."[26]

Mainstream business opponents argued that the bill would be unconstitutional, that it would not work, and that it was not necessary. The NAM portrayed an encouraging scene of rising employment and expanding national purchasing power, and protested "the threat of new restrictive, experimental legislation which will plunge the country into another period of doubt, uncertainty and confusion, and which might seriously impair industry's march toward more jobs for more people."[27] Other opponents were more shrill. Claudius Murchison, president of the Cotton Textiles Institute, discerned un-American behavior, which threatened democracy, free enterprise, the dignity of labor, and the "spirit of a free people." Murchison piously proclaimed that the victims of the inevitable increases in manufacturing costs would be "the agricultural workers and those who labor in occupations which are purely intrastate in character." In contravention of "an economic philosophy which accepts the presence of all functional groups in our economic system as essential to the welfare of the whole," this bill served only the interests of organized labor.[28]

But under close questioning, Murchison revealed more about the profit-related and sectional nature of the business opposition. On Lubin's figures, the average hourly earnings in cotton goods manufacturing, Murchison's constituency, were thirty-nine cents, for an average thirty-nine-hour week.[29] Murchison agreed that his members might accept the forty-hour week, but they would hold out for a thirty-cent minimum wage. The CTI was a nominally national organization, with a strong southern bias, and the "majority of the industry believes that legislative action should take due cognizance of what it regards as a normal economic differential and take no steps which would serve artificially to eliminate this differential."[30]

The low-wage, anti-union economy of the southern states stood to lose its advantage if national labor standards were imposed.[31] Try as they would to phrase it in other terms—those of equality ("Why should such favors be held from workers on the farms, in the kitchen, and in other places where fewer people are employed?"), of federalism ("This means ... another stupendous subtraction from the rights and powers of both the States and the individuals thereof"), and of practicality ("another tremendously big and growing army of assistants, comprising secretaries, attorneys, examiners, regional directors, special consultants, experts and others" at the taxpayers' expense)—southern employers were defending their competitive position. Any system of uniform wage rates would wipe southern products out of national markets. Cross-examined, John E. Edgerton, of the Southern States Industrial Council, revealed the substance of the South's advantage. At his own textile mill the average work week was forty hours, but he could not say how many worked overtime. No one worked for less than thirteen dollars a week. That is, he admitted, except for unnumbered learners, casual labor employed by the hour for around twenty-five cents, those on piecework rates, and a category who were "philanthropically employed": "We had a group in our mill of old women, grandmothers most of them, who could not do much work. We had a certain job. For instance, we reserved for these old women, usually the mothers and the grandmothers of employees, who wanted to make some contribution to the family pot, we had a certain job that was easy that they could do, but they could not do very much and they got very low wages." Edgerton's grandmothers made six dollars for a forty-hour week—fifteen cents an hour.[32]

Southerners claimed "differences in types of industries predominating in each section" and that "living costs are lower in rural communities." To higher wage employers, their predicament simply looked like sweating. The cost-of-living argument met with particular scorn. Edgerton prevaricated about the quality of life for a family of four on sixteen dollars a week: "He may be a fellow that cannot think of a living standard unless he has four glasses of beer a day or some wine . . ."[33] When southern representatives voted down a draft, the Atlanta branch of the ILGWU passed a resolution "proposing that salaries of Southern Congressmen be reduced 20 per cent because of sectional differences in living expenses."[34] But southern business interests fought to the bitter end for regional wage differentials. When it became evident that a bill would pass, "behind the scenes a quiet but intensive campaign was reported under way to muster support for a Senate filibuster." The best they could do was to win a little time; the Wage and Hour Board was given discretion to bring in the rates over seven years.[35]

When Southern manufacturers were forced into such a last-ditch defense of their interests, the limits of their power were revealed. By contrast, agriculture gave a fine demonstration of political power, in its ability to remove itself from the agenda even before the drafting of legislation. The definition of "employee" in the first draft of the Wages and Hours bill already excluded "any person employed . . . as an agricultural laborer."[36] Knowing that the farm bloc would be bitterly opposed and could stop any bill in Congress, the administration had agreed a trade-off. Roosevelt announced the labor bill together with one to maintain farm prices: "The two go hand in hand."[37] Senator Black of Alabama, sponsor of the FLSA, had already consulted state farm organizations and promised a "measure which wholly excludes farming."[38] The bargain was kept, the administration holding the farm bill hostage to receipt of the votes of agricultural states for the wages and hours bill. Producers scrambled to prove their agricultural bona fides, turpentine "manufacturers" a classic and successful example.[39]

Section 3(f) of the FLSA defined agriculture, including "commodities defined as agricultural commodities in section 15(g) of the Agricultural Marketing Act as amended." This confirmed that the Turpentine Farmers Association, among others, had won. The consequences were considerable. Agricultural employers had admitted that their employees were on piecework rates, that employment was seasonal, and that children as young as ten might work as much as fifty hours a week: the "average daily wage of one of those men . . . is possibly $10 a week," while children might make only a dollar a day.[40] But, a Georgia farmer promised, "We feed them through the winter months, we furnish them houses, we furnish them wood and we furnish them water, we get them doctors if they are sick, we buy them medicine, and we bury them when they are dead."[41] Everything, in fact, except a living wage with which to make their own provision. Agricultural labor may have been "the most shamefully disregarded section of our working population."[42] Against the procession of producers of turpentine, fruit, lumber, dairy products, and the processors, canners, shippers, and sellers of agricultural products who claimed to be inseparably linked with agriculture, agricultural workers had only one advocate in the congressional hearings. Gardner Jackson, chairman of the National Committee on Rural and Social Planning, "an organization of college professors, social workers, trade unionists, farm laborers, and sharecroppers," made a detailed case against "the convincing myth [of the family farm] which the agricultural lobby has, over the decades, built so systematically that it has all the appearance of reality." His data on rural poverty and the sweating practices of large farm employers, which helped put the family farm out of business, received only polite attention.[43]

The deep split that had opened between AFL and CIO [Committee for Industrial Organization] was apparent in labor's response to the FLSA. The AFL still spoke in 1937 in its language of 1913. But it had no credibility as a single voice for organized labor. CIO leaders John L. Lewis and Sidney Hillman supported the principle of federal wage and hour standards. The CIO represented just those unskilled male workers neglected by the AFL and by the first minimum wage laws. When men with similar disadvantages to women workers (poverty, lack of skills, scattered workplaces) were organized, as with Hillman's Amalgamated Clothing Workers, they had often turned to arbitration to settle disputes. They accepted expert help to redress their lack of organizational strength; management cooperation came in those industries most threatened by an anarchic sweated sector. This experience of conciliatory settlement by intermediaries was better preparation for accepting a federal minimum wage than the AFL history of collective bargaining from industrial strength.[44]

Lewis disliked the complex administrative proposals of the first bill. But he believed that it marked "the beginning of an industrial bill of rights for workers as against industry, just as the so-called Bill of Rights in our political Constitution guarantees personal and civil liberties of the citizen."[45] Hillman, who knew more than most about sweated labor from a lifetime of organizing the garment trades, was the most enthusiastic labor spokesman. He was already pushing for such legislation in 1932, using his influence with the new Democratic administration. In March 1938, on returning from a convalescence in Florida, his first visits were to members of Congress and of the CIO-sponsored Labor's Non-Partisan League to lobby for the "Pay-Hour Bill."[46]

Enmity between AFL and CIO complicated the passage of the FLSA. The administration consulted with both. But, as the *New York Times* remarked at the time of a crucial House vote: "William Green, president of the A.F. of L., is bitterly opposed to the creation of another board to deal with labor affairs and the fact that the measure as it stands has the endorsement of John L. Lewis, leader of the C.I.O., probably does not lessen his opposition."[47] Though the AFL publicly maintained outright opposition to a minimum wage for men, it also worked at narrowing the scope of any wage that might be legislated. Green persuaded the House Committee to amend the 1937 bill to safeguard union agreements, and even argued for the priority of union agreements for lower than minimum wages: "I should rather preserve the principle of industrial democracy than to yield a right to the Board to interfere in the free exercise of collective bargaining." Even so, Green received an unprecedented reprimand at the fall convention of the AFL for conceding too much.[48]

In December 1937, Green could add enough northern Democrat votes to the southern/Republican bloc to recommit the administration bill. But he could not pass his own.[49] The AFL was forced to negotiate. In January 1938, it was said that the AFL would accept only an hours law, the CIO only one with a minimum wage. Lewis had already impressed on the administration that statistical investigations and elaborate codes were not what he sought: "[Lewis] is against any regulation so far as wages and hours are concerned except the part relating to a floor and a ceiling," Jackson was reminded.[50] The *New York Times* reported in March that "Green Yields Point" and might settle for a (low) fixed wage; in April, that the AFL had opened war on the CIO for supporting the administration bill; that Congress had offered to implement Lewis's solution of a single fixed wage; and Green was quoted as saying that the House Labor Committee "seems to have arrived at the A.F. of L. viewpoint."[51] This was face-saving, though untrue. The act did require industry committees (charged with bringing the minimum rates in over seven years) to consider existing collective labor agreements, among other factors. But the AFL had conceded almost every point of principle, especially its thirty-year insistence on the insulation of men from minimum wage laws.

CONSTITUTIONAL STRATEGY AND THE FLSA

Minimum wage policy was deeply implicated in major constitutional changes developing alongside the political dramas of the FLSA. The process of constitutional change was a longer and a more calculated development than the visible moment of Justice Roberts's conversion in the *West Coast Hotel* case might suggest. Its ramifications went far wider than just for minimum wage policy, although minimum wage cases, from *Morehead* to *West Coast Hotel* to Supreme Court approval of the FLSA in *U.S. v. Darby* in 1941, were landmarks.

By the early thirties, before the well-known judicial attack on New Deal legislation that earned the court its reactionary reputation, and before the famous "switch in time" of mid-1937, there were, David Currie has noted, signs that "the Court seemed well on the way to making peace with the modern social state."[52] The newly permissive attitude of the Supreme Court to legislation regulating industries "affected with a public interest" was one such sign.[53] From 1933 onward, lawyers in academia and within the administration discussed specifically how to legitimate new functions of federal government. The authority of Constitution and court in relation to public policy and the legislature became a matter of public debate when, two years into the first Roosevelt administration, the court seemed to be at war with his legislative program. Minimum wagers had been preparing for this moment ever since 1923. Now their efforts became part of a wider constitutional critique. Once again, the preemption of judicial decision making was the deliberate goal. The extent of the change achieved in only a few years was such that one legal scholar has described the outcome as constitutional amendment by public colloquy: "The New Deal Democrats amended the Constitution by provoking a complex constitutional dialogue between the voters at large and institutions of the national government." The outcome was what had been sought by minimum wagers since the early twentieth century, "the legitimation of the activist regulatory state."[54]

In 1933, Edward S. Corwin wrote of the "striking failure to date of spontane-
ous recuperative forces to manifest themselves in the field of business and
industry." This, he argued as Roosevelt took office, "has produced a widespread
and growing conviction that the National Government must within the immediate future, and for some time to come, take a large hand in social and economic reconstruction." The question was, "What is the constitutional basis
upon which it may operate?"[55] Robert L. Stern, coming fresh from Harvard
Law School to the Petroleum Administrative Board, worked out the answer
when he found himself conducting one of the first defenses of New Deal economic regulation. In an influential article, Stern argued that "any one but a
constitutional lawyer would immediately agree" that in the present economic
crisis, "because of the integrated character of the national economic structure
action by the states separately would be impracticable and ineffectual." He
challenged the courts' narrow definition of interstate commerce as only the
literal movement of goods and transactions across state lines, with another
question: "Does the commerce clause, which is the integrating factor in the
union of states, . . . permit the economic treatment of the union as a whole—or,
by merely devitalizing the separate units without substituting any positive central authority, has it become the agency which will bring about their ruin?"[56]
The minimum wage campaign had tested the right of any government to regulate labor conditions, and the authority of the state in defining the relationship
between gender and work. With the FLSA, minimum wagers entered a third
contested area of constitutional authority: the boundaries between state and
federal power.[57] The federal structure had institutionalized local difference,
with the result, Florence Kelley had graphically observed, that in progress with
labor legislation, the "48 States suggest the legs of a centipede, some going
forward and some paralyzed."[58] Now legal experts sought both a rationale and
an opportunity for federal legislation.

Frances Perkins, Frankfurter, and Dewson hatched a plan in February 1933,
involving Roosevelt and Governor Lehman of New York. Roosevelt was to
meet state governors immediately after his inauguration. His advisers suggested that the agenda include "industrial labor standards as a part of the attack
on the depression." They drafted a letter from Roosevelt, urging the governors
to consider "how to effect appropriate and harmonious action by the states
under the police power for the regulation of labor and industry"; and from
Lehman a reply, in which he would be "greatly heartened." He would then
propose that "the federal government may help the state governments in three
ways," one being that "the Commerce Clause of the constitution should be
invoked whereby the Federal Trade Commission will prevent unfair methods
of competition by unfair wage cutting and long hours."[59]

Frankfurter was studying the history of the Commerce Clause. Despite his
instinct that massive national planning was undesirable, he made a political
case for an expansive federal role. He believed that "the commerce clause, by
its own force and without national legislation, puts it into the power of the

Court to place limits upon state authority." The court was narrowing the application of the Commerce Clause, striking down major Roosevelt initiatives like the National Recovery Act. But Frankfurter quoted Justice Holmes: "History sets us free and enables us to make up our minds dispassionately whether the survival which we are enforcing answers any new purpose when it ceases to answer the old." When the court blocked New Deal legislation, he argued, it departed from a more generous original intent. In the 1820s, Chief Justice Marshall himself had "conveyed some general attitudes towards the Constitution which readily yielded authority in support of Congressional power, when the time eventually did come for its more aggressive employment."[60]

In frustration, some lawyers had revived the idea of a constitutional amendment as the only sure way around the court. A draft in circulation would have given Congress the power "to legislate in all cases for the general interests of the Union," and especially in those "to which the States are separately incompetent." But "the fundamental objections to Constitutional amendments," the difficulty of passage, and the uncertainty of future interpretation were well known, especially to those who had participated in the ERA debate.[61] This one would require the consent of three-quarters of the states to a potentially huge increase in federal power. Justice Department lawyers, puzzling over the question "By what legal method can Congress regulate wages and hours in the nation's industry?" were dismissive. Constitutional amendment, a memo noted, was "an admission of a bankruptcy of constitutional scholarship."[62] The constitutional definition of commerce and the distinction between commerce within a state and commerce between the states drew a boundary between state and federal sovereignty. Shifting this boundary in one direction or the other by using carefully constructed legislation to finesse the courts was a better alternative. Success would have the wider consequence that *the jurisdiction of Federal legislation over business would be vastly extended.*"[63]

This was the context in which the FLSA became a head-on challenge to the courts to renounce their recent habit of rejecting national economic regulation, to redefine federalism, and to acknowledge the legislative implementation of a popular mandate for wages and hours laws and other economic regulation.[64] The hope was that the Commerce Clause would allow the regulation of economic activity even indirectly affecting interstate commerce, and, also or alternatively, allow a federal police power to prohibit the sale across state lines of goods made under substandard conditions. Drafting the act was part of Roosevelt's challenge to the Supreme Court. His intention was flagged in the press: "A result of such an act would be to put most of the constitutional issues involved in the old NRA before courts again, and with them the question raised by the President in his annual message to Congress of whether the judiciary will join the legislative and executive branches in making the Constitution, as now framed, serve the present-day needs of the nation or suffer a curtailment of its powers."[65] And the opening speaker at the congressional hearings on the FLSA was not Secretary of Labor Perkins but Assistant Attorney General Robert H. Jackson.

The purpose of the bill, Jackson declared, was "to recognize the fundamental interests of free labor." His constitutional strategy was to overwhelm the court with an onslaught of different reasonings, to "consolidate in a single bill all hopeful approaches to constitutionality, each complete in itself, so that if one or more falls at the hands of the Court, we will not be left for an interval while a new bill is being adopted. The result is that there is some overlapping in its provisions but no inconsistency in its operation or its objectives."[66] Jackson's statement revived the economic critique of sweating, which perfectly fitted the Commerce Clause's requirement that the object of concern of either regulatory or police powers be the economy. Sweating disrupted fair competition: "The factual basis for this view is that by prohibiting the use of substandard labor conditions by those who compete with employers who use fair labor standards, the great majority of employers who really desire to treat labor fairly are thereby protected against the unfair methods of competition of those who utilize sweatshop methods to gain an unfair advantage."[67]

The "fair," "fairly," and "unfair" criteria of that sentence signaled the new constitutional direction. If the policy could be shifted from state to national responsibility, then its authority might depend on the rather shaky concept of a national police power *and* on the untested opening of the "fair" wage suggested in the *Adkins* decision *and* on a long line of interpretation of the due process clause of the Fourteenth Amendment as it applied to existing federal antitrust, or fair competition, legislation.[68] A different standard of fairness from the Sutherland notion of a fair wage was involved, though both rested on the same premise that a fair government intervention was one that could be shown to be reasoned and appropriate, the opposite of arbitrary. The view that due process required legislation to be fair in its deprivation of liberty or property was first propounded in a dissent to the *Slaughter-House Cases* of 1873. In subsequent decisions, the matching of fair intervention against unfair corporate practices—unfair competition—became the accepted basis for federal regulation. Thus due process, articulated as procedural fairness in the market, had long been accepted as the constitutional ground for antitrust law, outlawing market-rigging, monopoly agreements, and other restraints of trade. Minimum wage lawyers sought to have employment at below-subsistence wages recognized as detrimental to economic well-being. As drafting commenced, a Justice Department memorandum suggested "a comprehensive *Fair Competition Act*" that would codify previously designated unfair practices and add some new items, sweating included, "now generally recognized by economists and commercial experts as contrary to the existing standards of fairness."[69]

The preamble to the FLSA, declaring that sweating burdened, obstructed, and interfered with commerce, completed the shift in minimum wage policy from concern about the welfare of women to concern about the welfare of the economy. A federal police power, another arm of the strategy, lacked the direct attention to community welfare or to women of the state police power. Following a handful of existing precedents, lawyers predicated the contaminating effect on competition and the national market of goods produced in substandard conditions. Gender issues took on a new form. When Jackson argued that "it was not intended to leave Congress free to prohibit traffic between States in lottery tickets and strong drink, but not to prohibit the interstate shipment of 'the product of ruined lives,'" he introduced the one Commerce Clause case in which women had appeared—but defined not as workers but as the contaminating product. Women transported across state lines for immoral purposes shared the legal standing of lottery tickets and adulterated eggs as objects rather than subjects in economic transactions.[70]

The FLSA and Women's Work

Advocates of the FLSA did not intend to patronize or discriminate. Gender differentials were officially abandoned in the act. Perkins was surprised when Congressmen raised the question, and reiterated her belief that "the minimum wage should be fixed for the occupation and not according to the age or sex of the employee."[71] John L. Lewis presaged the Equal Pay Act of 1963 with his testimony that "Secretary Perkins . . . suggested a further industrial right, which I believe the committee should add to the bill, namely, that women doing the same work as men should receive the same pay as men."[72] In the early months of 1937, when the FLSA was in draft and the court unexpectedly upheld legislation for women, the President himself confirmed the gender-neutral approach: "That [*West Coast Hotel*] is women only. I think it should include everybody, men and women." "Why not go the whole hog?" he asked the press corps, answering for himself, "Men and women. It is all right."[73]

But discrimination emerged in practice when statutory reality, legislation written to meet political and constitutional requirements, met social reality, the actual dimensions of poverty and distribution of different social groups in the work force. For one thing, the notional universality of the category of "employee" concealed discrimination. Neither home workers nor members of families were sure even to be defined as employees. They might instead be subcontractors, or, as testimony to Congress had revealed, children, or grandmothers. Home workers and family members helping out on farms were most often women. When the Conference Committee narrowed the coverage of the FLSA by a small change in wording to apply to each employee, rather than to each firm, in interstate commerce, bias was accentuated. The production-line worker in a steel plant was certainly covered, the file clerk, telephonist or janitor arguably. Arbitration of such open questions, critical for women and minority workers, was left to judicial and administrative decision.[74]

Nor was "interstate commerce" a neutral category. Major cases over what was, or what directly affected, interstate commerce had before 1938 involved agriculture and sugar production, navigation and railroads, steel, coal mining and oil extraction, poultry slaughtering—all male and (excepting agriculture) heavily white occupations. In 1933, Frankfurter (briefed by Ben Cohen) had pointed out the limitations of a federal minimum wage, to calm the doubts of Governor Lehman. Frankfurter reminded Perkins that while Lehman's "concern is over the competitive handicaps that such a measure may impose upon New York," there was another problem: "I wonder if you could not marshal materials to show the wide range of occupations which should be affected by the Minimum Wage Law that are wholly local in their incidence, even assuming that minimum standards would involve a handicap as against cut-throat or run-away competition outside the state. What about all the laundry workers and scrubwomen and waitresses and whatnot who do not compete over state lines?"[75]

Few individuals kept sight of this point. Perkins, and Lucy Randolph Mason for the NCL, were alone in telling Congress that the FLSA would not be a universal panacea. Perkins acknowledged state sensibilities with an assurance that the FLSA would not displace state measures: "It will supplement [state law]; that is all."[76] Optimists like Clara Beyer saw the need for both state and federal law, the constitutional issues as quite separate, and the time ripe to progress from that "for which they have fought in the past." She could hardly overlook this, since frequent complaints landed on her desk in the Labor Department: "From laundry workers, hotel workers, store clerks come innumerable letters . . . asking why they must continue to work 12 hours a day for 10 or 15 cents an hour, when their neighbours work a reasonable day in a factory for at least 30 cents an hour. Telling them that they are not covered by the Federal law does not solve their problem." Beyer used her government position to press the states for action before, during and after the passage of the FLSA.[77] Frankfurter had mentioned laundry workers, scrubwomen, and waitresses—groups who epitomized women's service role and society's financial valuation of that role; figures provided for the hearings on the FLSA showed that hotels (29.9 cents) and laundries (37.7 cents) ranked among the very lowest hourly wages, but "none of them probably would come under this act."[78] Local retailing, hospitals, service industries, state and local government employees (including teachers), and domestic service (at that time the main source of employment for black women) were also excluded. Even where the national minimum wage applied, when it raised wages in southern states for example, it might have discriminatory effects. The fate of pecan-shellers and embroiderers in Texas, according to Julia Kirk Blackwelder was that the "guaranteed wage meant fewer jobs for Chicanas because it destroyed their advantage in the national market without affecting the pattern of discrimination that excluded them from other jobs."[79]

Domestic workers were the extreme case of the distance between the principle of universal entitlement and its realization in practice. As Phyllis Palmer has shown, domestic workers held a unique social status in which every conceivable constitutional, political, and cultural factor contrived to exclude them from such protections as the minimum wage. Under the Commerce Clause, their work was local. Under any political authority, their individual workplaces created the ultimate administrative nightmare, supposing, as was not usual in minimum wage history, that enforcement was taken seriously. The cultural value placed on the privacy of the home militated against public intrusion. Even Clara Beyer justified this exclusion: "But when you come to the households, it's much more difficult. You can't have inspectors on that."[80] Gendered stereotypes of women's service in the home placed domestic employment outside of "labor" and "industry." On any scale of the "truly needy," domestic workers ranked high. But few voices were raised on their behalf. One was Eleanor Roosevelt's, who advocated "extension of the law to define some standard of employment for domestic servants and farm laborers." But her husband later reminded journalists, in response to rumors in the South that housewives would be forced to "pay your negro girl eleven dollars a week," that "no law ever suggested intended a minimum wages and hours bill to apply to domestic help." The fact that the President thought of these women as help, not as labor, sums up their problem.[81] What farm employers created by persistent and vigilant political action, domestic employers acquired as a gift from social norms: legitimation, in public policy, of a unique status for the occupation, implying a different quality of the work itself and of relationships within the workplace from those in commerce.

When the rights of workers came into conflict with family values, workers generally lost. The confusion of the minimum wage with the family wage survived in 1937, though sometimes with ambivalence. Having proposed equal pay for equal work, John L. Lewis also asserted his belief that "normally, a husband and father should be able to earn enough to support his family. This does not mean, of course, that I am opposed to the employment of women, or even of wives, when this is the result of their own free choice. But I am violently opposed to a system which by degrading the earnings of adult males, makes it economically necessary for wives and children to become supplementary wage earners."[82] Though long disproven, it was still believed that men had dependents, women did not, that men needed a family wage and that married women need not work. As late as 1936, Paul Douglas, a supporter of an expansive policy, worried: "If we include men, we shall have a real problem on our hands in determining how many dependents are to be supported by the wage of the male earner."[83]

Legal terminology, a gender-segregated economy, and lasting cultural prejudices, combined to create discrimination. But legal terminology also left open a loophole. Robert L. Stern resorted to the etymology of "commerce among." After consulting the dictionaries available to the Founding Fathers, he concluded that the original intent of the Commerce Clause matched the New Deal plan for its application: "'Commerce among the several states' may therefore be clumsily paraphrased as 'the interrelated business transactions of the several states'—which would naturally contrast with the purely local business transactions." Toward the end of his argument, speculating about what occupation might incontestably not be an "interrelated business transaction," Stern presaged future developments. He contrasted coal miners with barbers. Miners' wages must be nationally set, or their competition would threaten economic stability. "Barbers in different states, on the other hand, do not compete." But then, "the wages of barbers are just as important to the national purchasing power as the wages of miners or railroad conductors." And thus, perhaps, a court might even find that the barber affected interstate commerce.[84]

THE FLSA AFTER 1938

The FLSA minimum wage applied to workers—a victory for the principle of equity. But as to equity in practice, data collected by the Labor Department in 1939 confirm the discriminatory impact of the act, even within interstate commerce. Both the text of the FLSA and the early effects of its implementation indicate who exercised to greatest effect power over the formulation of the act.

A White House memo conceded that "to make it acceptable to labor" the bill "should be limited in its application to the low-paid, long-hour industries."[85] Organized labor, although not powerful enough to write itself out, had won exemption in fact. In October 1939, when the automatic increase from twenty-five cents to thirty cents an hour came into effect, 650,000 workers out of 12,300,000 covered by the act would receive raises. They doubled the 300,000 who had gained a twenty-five-cent wage in 1938. Some 2.4 million would become eligible for the time-and-a-half overtime rate, as the standard work week dropped to forty-two hours.[86] A relatively small proportion of workers thus stood to benefit in practice. Both AFL and CIO had won much of what they wanted, including a flat-rate wage.

Agriculture also had demonstrated its clout, gaining exemption even before the act was drafted. Agriculture was at this time the major employer of black men, at rock-bottom wages. Though racially neutral in language, the FLSA thus had a racial bias in effect. On the other hand, black workers in covered southern industries, clustered in the lowest-paying jobs, did benefit: in July 1939, 45.3 percent of black laborers in the South earned the minimum of twenty-five cents and stood to gain from the October rise to thirty cents, compared with 23.9 percent of white laborers. Also noted was the fact that since "it has sometimes been alleged that the position of the Negro would be jeopardized by minimum-wage legislation, it is significant to note that Negroes constituted a slightly higher percentage of the common labor sample in 1939 than in 1938."[87]

Winners and losers in the business sector were clear. Southern industrial interests were reduced to mounting an eleventh-hour stand for regional wage differentials. They lost, both in the terms of the act and in its implementation. More northern workers benefited in sheer numbers, but the proportion of the work force affected was far greater in the South—"three-fourths of all the wage earners in southern sawmills," 80 percent in the animal feed, and two-thirds in the fertilizer business, for example.[88] It is not surprising that the southern lumber industry, with the lowest hourly entrance rate (25.9 cents) and the highest differential from northern rates (27.3 cents lower), brought the test case to the Supreme Court in 1941.[89]

Powerful opponents were unable to block the principle of an expanded, federal, and nondiscriminatory minimum wage but were able to protect themselves to a considerable degree. The losers were the neediest workers, African-Americans, women, children, and the marginal, unskilled, less-organized workers—home workers a striking example—who were exempted or technically covered but at the mercy of administrative fiat. The worst-off were also least organized and least able to fight for the delivery of benefits. As the administrative process of defining coverage proceeded, the Labor Department compared bakeries, wherein only 70 percent of wage earners came under the act, with the typical heavy industry wherein 95 to 98 percent were covered. Furthermore: "Reports from establishments manufacturing confectionery, ice cream, beverages, and shirts and collars indicated about the same proportion of workers subject to the act as in the case of bakeries." Bakers, candy workers, garment workers—the familiar characters of the earlier struggle for labor laws—were still losing out.[90] Labor had safeguarded their own position and also maintained their separation from the problems of the most disadvantaged sector of the work force.

Minimum wagers had come closer to achieving their goal. They were a new generation, in new and advantageous positions inside government. Times had changed, public opinion had changed, political alignments and the courts had changed. Drafting the FLSA as a direct challenge to the judicial mind culminated a minimum wage campaign dominated by constitutional strategy. The FLSA was soon endorsed by the Supreme Court, as that institution itself changed radically, first with the new majority created by Justice Roberts's vote in *West Coast Hotel* and then with a sequence of vacancies that allowed Roosevelt eight new appointments between 1937 and 1941, elevating to the bench such sympathizers as Hugo Black (1937), Felix Frankfurter (1939), and Robert H. Jackson (1941).

The constitutionality question was decided in 1941, in the *Darby* case.[91] The decision, written by newly elevated Chief Justice Stone, settled issues that had dogged the minimum wage campaign: the prerogative of the legislature to decide the proper purposes of the regulation of commerce; the demarcation of state and federal power so that states might regulate commerce in the absence of federal law, but Congress might regulate intrastate activities "where they have a substantial effect on interstate commerce" regardless of state law; removal of the impediment of the child labor case restriction on regulation to the shipment of goods harmful in themselves, which "should be and now is overruled." The court accepted that substandard labor conditions in any jurisdiction could be regulated as unfair competition. On the means of regulating unfair competition, the court affirmed the *West Coast Hotel* decision, "that the fixing of a minimum wage is within the legislative power and that the bare fact of its existence is not a denial of due process under the Fifth more than the Fourteenth Amendment." And, finally, procedural due process was met: "The Act is sufficiently definite to meet constitutional demands." The single flat-rate wage not only pleased opponents like the AFL. A single rate, fixed by Congress, respected the due process ban on delegating fundamental decisions to unelected personnel.

There remained, however, many gaps and discrepancies in minimum wage policy. The old, inadequate, gendered state policies remained the only recourse for many low-paid workers, especially for many women workers.[92] Workers on the margins of the economy, those specifically exempted, and large sectors such as employees of the states, remained beyond reach. Over the next decades, the fight continued to end exclusion and discrimination in minimum wage policy. Two lines of struggle were pursued, both dependent on constitutional arguments—legal claims, and political action in the name of and by groups of victims of discrimination. Administrators (many women), lawyers, and now the would-be clients themselves were the key players.

The *Darby* decision was augmented by an ostensibly unrelated decision on farm crop quotas, which confirmed almost unlimited federal economic oversight. In 1942, the newly elevated Justice Jackson declared that even a small and self-sufficient farmer, who used his own produce without entering the market, had (like Stern's hypothetical barber) an impact on interstate commerce through his very decision not to buy and sell.[93] Interstate commerce was so much expanded by this decision that thereafter most judicial rulings were matters of "statutory delineation, not constitutional power." Cases like *Borden Co. v. Borella* abounded, in which maintenance employees in a building occupied by a national firm were brought under the FLSA.[94]

Case-by-case decisions made small advances. A series of amending statutes, from 1949 through 1974, clarified and (usually) extended the coverage of the law, progressively eliminating more exemptions and encroaching on territory assumed, even after *Wickard*, to remain with the states. Formal power to control home work was given in 1949. In 1955, it was decreed that the act would cover employees *in industries* engaged in interstate commerce—not just employees themselves engaged in interstate commerce. The major exemptions collapsed somewhat later, with the first inclusion of agricultural workers in 1966, domestic workers in 1974. In 1966, Congress brought employees in public schools, nursing homes, laundries, and the entire construction industry under the FLSA—in 1972 professional, executive, and administrative workers; in 1974 all nonsupervisory employees of federal, state, and local governments. The retail industry continually tried to renegotiate the criteria of size that determined its inclusion. After 1966, agriculture played the same game of trying to define boundaries to its own advantage. The sum of all these changes was that by the end of the 1970s about 90 percent of the nonsupervisory work force was covered, and the most glaring race and sex discrimination concealed within the original terms of the FLSA had been wiped out.[95]

THE POLITICS OF RIGHTS

Exemption for agriculture and domestic service was ended by a new kind of minimum wage campaign, the assertion of a "rights consciousness" by and on behalf of the excluded themselves.[96] These were claimants in the name of equity, not of need. Phyllis Palmer has observed that the inclusion of agriculture and domestic service coincided with the height of activism of the civil rights and the women's movements. The story of the expansion of the FLSA, she argues, is one of new alliances, new attacks on ideologies of labor that devalued their work, and persistent political action by previously excluded social groups.[97] In politics and in constitutional law, a process was emerging described by John Kincaid as "displacing places to benefit persons."[98] The issues of place, state or federal, North or South, factory, farm, or home, which been written into minimum wage legislation, were settled in favor of inclusiveness. Issues of persons, black, female, young, tackled the discrimination written between the lines of the law. The focus of activism, and of constitutional interpretation, turned to guaranteeing the rights of individuals and groups. For workers deprived of benefits by the nuances of "commerce between the states" and by the regional structures of the labor market, recognition of the priority of individual rights was the opening they needed.

Farm workers, principally black and Hispanic men and women, had been excluded from virtually all New Deal labor legislation. After the Second World War, organized labor turned its attention to what it now began to label "industrialized agriculture," proposing that this be brought under the FLSA. The task of organizing a dirt-poor, widely scattered, multilingual, maybe undocumented migrant population, even without their exclusion from the National Labor Relations Act, was daunting. By the 1960s, however, agribusiness no longer had farm politics under control. The civil rights movement, the political "discovery" of rural poverty, and the labor movement, further unsettled by indigenous organization like that of Cesar Chavez and the United Farm Workers, all threatened the status quo.[99] Agribusiness dropped the indefensible image of the family farm but continued to claim the uniqueness and vulnerability of agriculture, the impracticality of administration of labor law on farms, the unconstitutionality of congressional regulation of something that was not commerce and was anyway a state concern. But the opposition was making a different case: "The accent was on justice, equality under the law, and on denying there was any rational basis for the exemption." The 1966 amendments to the FLSA began the process of bringing farm workers into coverage. A legislative history claimed that, with these amendments, "for the first time in its history, the law protected almost two-thirds of black workers and almost three-quarters of women workers."[100]

Some 2,063,000 domestic workers still remained outside the law, the only major industry shown in congressional data as having *no* workers covered.[101] The inclusion of domestic service, still the major occupation of black women in the 1960s, also came from a conjunction of favorable circumstances. The civil rights movement was one. The mobilization of the women's movement was another. The campaign for the Equal Pay Act of 1963, an act that was itself an amendment to the FLSA, was crucial. The Equal Pay Act was a compromise; for example, it applied only where the FLSA applied, to interstate commerce, not to exempted occupations. Equal pay was understood to be a different and complementary measure to the minimum wage, but there was a logic in associating the two under the umbrella of the FLSA, and a practical advantage of sharing the established enforcement machinery of the FLSA. Nonetheless, given the sex-segregated labor market, the Equal Pay Act (toned down from "comparable" work to "work requiring equal skill, effort, responsibility, and in similar working conditions") would improve the wages of very few women. Most of all, it would be hard to apply to the minimum wage jobs at the bottom of the scale, including domestic workers, which were often the most segregated and the hardest to match with "equal" male jobs. But it did go a step beyond nonprescriptive gender-neutrality, to begin to specify the parameters of gender equality.[102]

For domestic workers, the significance of the Equal Pay Act was that it brought middle-class, professional women in search of equal pay into the same political arena as less-skilled working-class women, more often minorities, seeking the most basic protections. The new self-consciousness of the former group helped bring them into alliance with the latter. One of the first victories of this alliance came in the 1966 amendments to the FLSA, with the inclusion of workers in public schools, nursing homes, hospitals, and laundries. Many of the workers brought under the act in 1966 were black women, and many of the tasks they performed were commercial versions of work domestics had done previously in private homes. This was a crucial step toward having women's work defined as "work," labor on a par with industrial labor, a strategy developed more explicitly in FLSA congressional hearings in 1971 and 1973, justifying the claim of equality typically expressed by the National Committee on Household Employment: "The household worker works with and for people, and must have many skills in human relations. [She] also must manipulate many machines, tools, and materials in her performance of even the most basic tasks. She, or he, like every other American worker deserves a minimum wage and maximum hour protection."[103]

The definition of domestic service as work rather than service was one step, the mobilization of political power the second. Labor had begun to acknowledge domestic workers in the early 1970s. The resurgent women's movement, reviving the Equal Rights Amendment, could not see the advantages of a coalition with anti-ERA labor unions. Witnesses like Pauli Murray, representing the ACLU in 1970, raised the plight of black women in employment as "dual victimization by race and sex-based discrimination," reading into the record of hearings on sex discrimination in education, the professions, and federal employment a Women's Bureau study of the plight of domestic workers.[104] In 1973, the winning coalition was achieved by the determination of

Congresswoman Shirley Chisholm: "Civil rights coalitions, social action groups, church groups, labor unions, women's groups, consumer groups . . . all joined their legions, an exciting new conglomerate in the ongoing history of Congressional alliances."[105] The coalition made a powerful double appeal, on grounds of need and of discrimination, expressed forcefully by Representative Martha Griffiths: "For anyone . . . to come in and say, 'Let them work for nothing; they are not entitled to a minimum wage' is a sort of sex discrimination that is beyond my imagination."[106] In its 1974 amendments to the FLSA, Congress recognized domestic workers as workers and brought them under the act. The Constitution was not a problem: "The Committee found that domestics and the equipment that they use in their work are in interstate commerce." To make doubly sure, or perhaps because Congress could see the somewhat tenuous nature of this argument, an unprecedented addition was made to the preamble to the FLSA, the "Findings and Declaration of Policy," that "Congress further finds that the employment of persons in domestic service in households affects commerce."[107]

There was one last postscript to this story of expansion. Federalism continued to rankle, and the states continued to guard their own employment policies from intervention. Defenders of states' autonomy won a notable victory in 1976, when, for the first time in forty years, the Supreme Court held a federal use of the Commerce Clause to be unconstitutional, rejecting the extension of the FLSA to state employees. The states' victory was short-lived. Within ten years, the court decided to "revisit [the] issue raised" in its 1976 decision and to reverse its position. The 1985 *Garcia* decision affirmed the federal right to regulate state employment and the individual citizen's right to federal protection in the giving and receiving of state services.[108] Compared with the defining identities of the first phases of minimum legislation, the functional citizen—the mother, the worker—was fully displaced by the individual bearer of rights. The equal rights approach of the formalists of the twenties displaced the special case arguments with which the campaign had begun almost eighty years before. But if the NWP principle was vindicated by the march toward universalism on rights grounds, the expansion of minimum wage coverage had come only with the evolution of new sociolegal meanings of terms like *work* and *commerce*, new understandings of women's work, and continuing social change in the economy and the possession of political power. Florence Kelley's stand against the illusion of "equality where there is no equality" was also vindicated, by both the policy gains of the late twentieth century and the problems that remained. The limits of constitutionalism, even of a constitutionalism of ostensible universalism, lie in the gap between skeletal principle and social complexity, legal language and social meaning, statutory reality and social reality. The gaps that have distorted minimum wage policy have changed and often narrowed along the road from *Muller* to *Garcia*, but they have not entirely disappeared.

Conclusion

THE MINIMUM WAGE IN THE 1990S

As the 1990s opened, what had come of the long endeavor to create a universal and equitable minimum wage policy? By comparison with Britain, with its record of pragmatism and inertia, Americans had won much in principle. More than 90 percent of American workers were covered by minimum wage legislation, compared with only 10 percent in Britain.[1] Examined in practice, however, this achievement fades. In each nation, minimum wage rates were low compared with average earnings, in each only a small minority of the work force actually benefited from the statutory wage rates, and in each a majority of those who benefited were women.

In 1992, the American minimum wage of $4.25 an hour was approximately 40 percent of the average wage of industrial workers.[2] In Britain, where rates in 1992 were still set industry by industry, the average Wages Council hourly rate of approximately £2.80 was just over 37 percent of average earnings.[3] How far below the average should the minimum sit? By the old criterion of parasitic industries, no lower than the cost of subsistence for the worker. But it remains true, as James J. Mallon observed in 1914, that "is there anything harder than to affirm a standard of well-being generally applicable to great populations?"[4] In 1980, a British study defined "low pay" at approximately the level of entitlement to income supplements for impoverished families; Wages Council rates for a comparable week's work brought in some 75 percent of this figure. Likewise, American estimates suggest that the minimum rate has usually been at or below the poverty line.[5] In neither country have minimum wages met NASL's modest demand for "a wage upon which at any rate life can be maintained."[6]

In Britain, the intention was only ever to cover a minority of workers. Twenty-six industries, 10 percent of the work force, were designated in 1992; 96 percent of the 2.5 million people involved were employed in a few service industries, especially catering, and in clothing manufacture. In the United States, the difference between 90 percent covered in principle and 10 percent benefiting in practice was achieved by different means. The single flat-rate wage set by Congress, though rising from twenty-five cents in 1938 to $4.25 in 1993, has always been so low that the majority of workers already earn as much or more. Business interests jealous of profits and control, organized labor jealous of bargaining prerogatives, have been able to ensure this outcome.[7] The fact that, in both nations, upward of two-thirds of those benefiting have been women is testimony to the survival of gendered norms and structures in the labor market. Women have remained disproportionately clustered in low-paid occupations and so have disproportionately received the meager benefits of minimum wage policy.[8]

Does this mean that American constitutionalism has made little difference to the problems—poverty, low pay, exploited women in the labor market—first identified by minimum wagers? Or that differences attributable to the constitutional factor have been merely symbolic? Consider two examples of people who in the United States are covered by the policy and in Britain were not: domestic workers and young people. Their circumstances and options exemplify some potentialities of constitutional politics. In Britain, domestic workers were never covered or ever proposed for inclusion.[9] Domestic workers in America were not covered by the FLSA, despite Eleanor Roosevelt's plea. But their inclusion was won in 1974 by a coalition of civil rights and women's organizations, pressing claims of equity in the face of race and sex discrimination. In the Wages Act of 1986, British workers between the ages of sixteen and twenty-one were removed from all Wages Council coverage. A "youth sub-minimum wage," proposed in the U.S. in 1981, fell victim to politics before draft legislation had even moved out of committee, but not before it had attracted opposition on grounds of age discrimination.[10] British domestic workers and British young people had no claim for inclusion in minimum wage policy, except of need.

As those young people discovered (their exclusion, unlike that of domestic workers, was at least contested), the level of need could be disputed. Alternatively, their need could be construed as for more jobs at lower wages; their families could be held responsible for their well-being; or the competing need for employers or the economy to hire low-wage labor could be deemed more urgent.[11] A debate in the Lords illustrated how easily a case based solely on need and effect could reach stalemate. A challenge, "[young people's] pay has declined sharply with no noticeable benefit to the economy," drew a government reply that "I believe that those statistics prove the positive effect" and a comment from an eminent economist, who did "not pay very much attention to the empirical results because . . . they are inconclusive. One has to start with an intuition." Without some statutory ground for claims of discrimination or injustice, the interests of young people could be forwarded only with more of the scorned statistics, by new intuitions, or by moral judgments. Despite the plea that "when did we ever consider that pay should depend on family income or on need? . . . Pay has to be for the job done," all the old arguments about need, family dependency, and benefit to the economy, which were made about women's work at the beginning of the century, were dusted off and displayed inconclusively once more.[12] Constitutional politics offered the American counterparts of such excluded groups three related advantages, absent in the British debate: an uncomplicated baseline for their grievance, a claim of rights, and a degree of dignity.

The Fair Labor Standards Act created a single, flat-rate, minimum wage, set by Congress. This had two purposes. It satisfied organized labor that government would keep out of the negotiating territory of unions, the details of pay and differentials within each industry. And it met due process requirements for a clear formula and open decision making. Due process could not guarantee any particular value to the minimum wage, as the perennially low rates demonstrated. But wages represent a bargained compromise and an index of power. They are a social as well as a monetary valuation of the worth of individuals, social groups, skills, and occupations. Effective participation in bargaining wages requires some comprehension of the broader picture. The clear and public formula decreed by the FLSA has created a "value consciousness." Everyone knows the going minimum wage. Knowing where you stand is the beginning of the ability to gauge complex wage relativities, to evaluate options, to compare women with men, work with welfare, in fact to comprehend inequality. "And it's not a minimum wage job," can be said with a note of pride. Armed with the minimum wage baseline, the poor (largely without access to economic information) possess a vital piece of information about their own economic and social standing.[13]

Compare this with the "relative deprivation" of the British, revealed in a survey taken in the 1960s, a time when rights claims were multiplying in the United States. These British workers knew their own wage and that of their neighbor, or the foreman one step up in the hierarchy of the workplace. But they lacked a standard outside of personal experience by which to situate themselves. "Almost all of them imply a comparison close to the actual situation of the respondent. None could be termed in any sense 'class-conscious,' and most of them suggest or, sometimes, directly state a comparison based on a particular feature of the respondent's personal situation."[14] This was a recipe for low aspirations, and acquiescence in minor amendments to the status quo. British minimum wage law, untrammeled by due process requirements that legislatures be specific in their decisions and in their delegation of power, offered nothing to enlarge this narrow vision. A law with no criterion of value represented a degree of legislative irresponsibility unthinkable in America. The single rate of the American minimum wage hardly begins to measure the complexity of the labor market, but at least it sets an accessible starting point for the estimation of worth and justice. It has a democratic flavor and potential lacking in the decisions made in privacy in Britain by corporatist Wages Councils, handed down in codes so specific as to ensure their purely parochial relevance.

Constitutional politics also gave excluded groups in the United States claims of rights and of the equal protection of the law. Minimum wagers knew from experience that the politics of rights was a double-edged sword. The right to suffrage was a contradiction to the claim for protection; citizens of the state could not be wards of the state. When women gained the standing of equal citizens, minimum wagers had next to wrestle with the meaning of equal rights in a world of inequality. Florence Kelley, fearing that women had gained only the constitutional right to starve, and skeptical of the India rubber concept of due process, has been echoed by recent critics of the use of constitutional claims of rights as a strategy for enhancing social justice. These critics have claimed that rights "are indeterminate, rights limit our imaginations, rights inhibit political and social change."[15] Those who can take their own rights for granted know that rights have not solved every problem. But they may be missing a point, understood by the minimum wagers and labor organizations who struggled for decades to bring their concerns within constitutional rather than common law, and to minority and disadvantaged groups attempting to realize constitutional promises. For them, "the language of rights is liberating and empowering, not enervating—a source of solidarity, not paralysis."[16]

A constitutional guarantee of rights also carries a dignity that claims of needs have lacked. When the minimum wage debate has been framed in terms of needs, the definition of need has rarely been anything the experts would care to live by themselves. The model budgets of the first phase of minimum wage law made moral judgments about appropriate expenditure. When laundry employers confronted the District of Columbia Minimum Wage Board in 1920, their none-too-subtle hint was that black workers could live on less than white. When southerners defended their low wage economy to Congress in 1937, they made snide asides about workers enjoying four glasses of beer a day. When a woman Cabinet minister announced that abolition of the British minimum wage would affect mainly women "in households with at least one other source of income," a parliamentary colleague waited "with bated breath . . . for the Secretary of State for Employment and all her female colleagues to declare themselves as mere subsidiaries and . . . to take a cut in their salaries on the same grounds."[17] One reason that the politics of rights has attracted underprivileged groups is simply the difference in spirit between the recognition of equality and the definition of need.

The minimum wage in Britain and America has been a social policy, not a social right. Inspired particularly by the classic discussion by T. H. Marshall in his essay "Citizenship and Social Class," in which he proposed a historical sequence from civil to political to social rights in the creation of a truly egalitarian society, the benefit of transmuting social policy into social rights has become an issue.[18] The difference described here between a minimum wage policy backed by guaranteed civil and political rights, and one without, suggests that the question of how any social provision, once enacted in any form, can be made equitable and effective may be more important than that of the distinction between policy and right.

Provided that prior constitutional rights authorize claims and constraints upon policy, social "rights" need not be all of a kind with them in constitutional status. But the proviso is important. The difference between written guarantees of fairness and cultural norms of fair play is considerable. Americans used written promises of fairness and equality to constrain and then correct a social policy. Without equivalent formal guarantees, the British had no civil or political rights that gave them such claim on the content of social policy. This allowed the flexibility that so intrigued Dicey, Bryce, and Lowell. At the turn of the century, British commentators tended to complacency. "A typical example of English practical empiricism," Sidney Webb said in appreciation of the history of factory legislation; "We began with no abstract theory of social justice or the rights of man. We seem always to have been incapable of taking a general view of the subject we were legislating upon." "Our legislative patchwork of eccentricities," Sir Charles Dilke noted fondly, observing with some pride that Britain "passed Acts in advance of other nations, before we began to look for the doctrines which underlay our action, and long before we possessed the knowledge on which it was said to be based."[19] The early introduction of the British minimum wage endorses this pride in the freedom to experiment. But in the long stretch from 1909 to 1993, the policy demonstrates how easily flexibility capitulates to power. The clientele of Trade Boards could rely no more on nominally socialist, political-insider, labor organizations or the Labour Party than on paternalistically inclined Conservatives to protect their interests. The unfinished developments of 1993 may be more a harbinger of change than a demonstration of effectiveness, but they are one last source of evidence of the difference a constitutional politics may make.

THE MINIMUM WAGE ABOLISHED

In the summer of 1993, the British minimum wage was abolished. Conservative governments had taken two earlier steps toward this goal. In 1985, the International Labor Organization was informed that Britain would withdraw from a 1928 convention binding its signatories to provide minimum wage machinery.[20] In 1986, a Wages Act curtailed minimum wage policy. Three main provisions removed young people from Wages Council jurisdiction, limited Wages Councils to setting a single hourly rate and a single overtime rate for each industry, and simplified the procedures for termination of Wages Councils.[21] Two years later, a formal consultation on abolition aroused more opposition from lobbies for the low-paid than support from business interests.[22] Regardless, in 1992 a reelected Conservative government introduced the necessary legislation.

"Wages Councils ... have no part to play in the 1990s," pronounced Employment Secretary Gillian Shephard. Her reasons were several: Britain was abandoning "traditional industry-wide collective bargaining which fixes pay without any regard to the skills and performance of individual employees or the need to contain costs in order to create jobs"; "eighty per cent of people in Wages Councils industries live in households with at least one other source of income"; and most businesses fell into one of two groups, paying above the minimum wage—making the law irrelevant, or paying "more than they can afford" when forced by Wages Councils. The new legislation would, Shephard promised, both "strengthen the rights of the individual" and "increase the competitiveness of the economy."[23]

These arguments would have been familiar to the Merchants and Manufacturers of Massachusetts, campaigning against the minimum wage in 1916. The counterarguments—that the individuals in question were powerless to exercise an individual right to contract; that the pin-money theory of women's work as a supplement to the household economy was long disproved; and that these were industries where wages were characteristically forced down regardless of costs—would have been equally familiar to Winston Churchill, introducing the British legislation in 1909. Indeed Churchill was much called upon in the 1993 debates. But the rehearsal of tired dogmas was unlikely to change the result. Abolition was never in doubt; a parliamentary majority ensured that the government would have its way.

The debate in 1993 was different from that in 1909 in but one respect. Using evidence of bias in Wages Council sector employment, minimum wagers introduced claims of discrimination and of rights.[24] Wages Councils covered approximately 2.5 million workers. About 80 percent were women (women were 43 percent of the employed work force).[25] An argument could be made that this larger proportion of women would also be affected more than men by the loss of Wages Councils. Prior to the Equal Pay Act of 1970, Wages Councils could and did set lower rates for women workers. After 1970, women were entitled to equal pay for the same work, but, in a labor market where women and men traditionally performed different tasks, Wages Councils might still perpetuate sex-based differentials. An unintended consequence of the 1986 Wages Act was that the single rate for a whole industry leveled out such differentials. As a result, "In 1992 the female:male earnings ratio for wages councils industries was higher than the ratio for all industries. That was particularly marked in the lower decile of weekly earnings."[26]

Many of these women workers were members of ethnic minorities as well. Ethnic bias also became an issue and a claim upon the future of Wages Councils. By 1993, the ethnic proportion of the work force had risen to an estimated 4.9 percent. "One in four of the ethnic minorities who are lucky enough to have a job find that they are confined to wages sector industries," according to one M.P., compared to one in ten of the whole population.[27] Clustered both regionally and in the garment and catering trades, ethnic workers were, as an ethnic population became a presence in the British labor market, discriminated against not by the functional definition of minimum wage coverage but by racism in the labor market. The prospect of abolition drew attention to their disproportionate presence in these low-wage sectors and, for the first time in British minimum wage history, racial as well as gender bias was a concern. Home workers in the Yorkshire garment trade published information and campaign advice in Punjabi, Gujerati, Bengali, Chinese, and Urdu; the EOC (Equal Opportunities Commission) noted that low pay "bears particularly heavily on black and ethnic minority groups, where women are clustered in low paid, zero prospects jobs"; parliamentarians that many of the workers "are women and many are from ethnic minority groups . . . they are among the most vulnerable workers and that is why they need some form of state protection."[28]

A moral argument, based on prima facie evidence of "the most vulnerable workers," had been tried before. But, as Baroness Lockwood reminded the House of Lords, women, at least, could now make a different claim. If indeed it was true that "the wages councils have performed a positive and unrecognised role in eliminating discrimination in pay between the sexes," then defenders of the policy detected a possible "infringement of the European Community's equal pay legislation."[29] Since 1973, membership of the European Community had imposed external standards on British law. Clauses of the Treaty of Rome and EC Directives were binding upon Parliament and a constraint upon national legislation—fragments, at least, of a written constitution. The European Court of Justice became a new forum for the redress of grievances. With reference only to sex, and not to attributes like race or age, Article 119 of the Treaty of Rome made equal pay for equal work a right; binding EC Directives subsequently required equal treatment and equal conditions and placed a responsibility on member states to provide "effective means" to ensure that the objectives were honored.[30] In these provisions, minimum wagers have found a possible lifeline for the policy. For "women and men who are on the statutory minimum, the wages council system has the effect of providing a legal guarantee of equal pay. It is this legal guarantee which the Government is removing, so that market forces can determine how low pay should fall." Even before the legislation was passed, minimum wagers, led by the TUC and endorsed by a vote of the European Parliament, were preparing to ask the European Commission to lodge a complaint against the British government, for contravening the requirement to maintain "effective means" of ensuring equal pay.[31]

"The EOC supports the principle of [a Statutory Minimum Wage] because of its simplicity and the public awareness and understanding of rights which will result," a policy document declared in 1992.[32] The political as well as the legal advantages of rights had been learned, and, as in the United States, the attractions of a constitutional politics and of claims of rights seemed greater to the receivers than to the givers of policy. In 1989, the British government was still selectively repealing remnants of gender-specific protective legislation to comply with EC requirements. At the same time, and with more enthusiasm, it was repealing equal protections to fulfill its own vision of a free market.[33] It was the ironic conjunction of these two trends—the removal of a nominally equal provision, or, as Florence Kelley might have put it, of equality where there is no equality—that invited the claim that "the abolition of the wages councils is likely to have a disproportionate impact on women and so is likely to be indirectly discriminatory in its effects."[34]

Constitutionalism made a difference in the United States independently of particular institutional forms. So it undoubtedly will in Britain. How the imperatives of legal craftsmanship, the content of new constitutional documents, and the superimposing of constitutional politics on an older and antithetical parliamentary tradition will interact with the demands of citizens remains to be seen. Britain's "legislative pattern of eccentricities" has already been placed under siege by the suprastatutory, systematizing, equality clauses of EU law, but the count has only just begun. Since gender equality at work was written into the original European documents, women have been among the first to use judicial review and rights claims to advance their political agenda; their tactics in seeking test cases and establishing new principles in the courts begin to bear some resemblance to the American model. But only up to a certain point: British women share Florence Kelley's ambivalence about forced choices between gender equality and gender difference; the advantage of preexisting constitutional axioms of work equality is offset by the greater difficulties of access to British and European political and judicial institutions.[35] Thus far, British constitutional politics has been mainly reactive, to inequities in existing law. The creative plowing of fresh acreage on the constitutional terrain, as Bryce observed the habit of Americans, the anticipation and furtherance of new policies with constitutional authority, has yet to develop.[36]

FOR AND AGAINST CONSTITUTIONALISM

The answer to the question of whether a constitutional framework changes the nature of social policy has never been in doubt—it does. The question of this study has been *how*: in what ways, by what means, and with what limitations? The evidence of this book works both for and against the written constitution. Compared with the development of the British minimum wage, the American constitutional framework forced an open debate on matters of definition and required the specification in law of rules and procedures. It guarded against equivocation on fundamental issues of purpose and against the private exercise of public power in implementing the policy, which such evasion has allowed in Britain. Its presence facilitated access to the political contest for those without major economic clout: the police power legitimated politics by and for women, and the declarations of rights and promises of equality were inspirational in the mobilization of political movements. The Constitution not only gave political standing to claimants for benefit from the policy but eventually enabled claims to be based on dignified grounds of right rather than demeaning terms of need.

Minimum wagers in America certainly saw advantages to constitutionalizing policy: advantages to expanding the police power to bring the whole sphere of workplace relations out of private, individual bargaining and common law remedies, into statute law and under constitutional guarantees of due process; advantages to expanding the Commerce Clause to allow national regulation of the most local transaction; advantages in using constitutional guarantees of equality. American women acquired constitutional legitimation for their political activity, first from the police power and then from claims of rights. We may differ about the kinds of politics these constitutional precepts encouraged, but not, by comparison with Britain, about the advantages of such legitimacy and standing. But none of these advantages were unproblematic.

The record of state intervention in labor affairs has not been one of benevolence. Yet excluding the state from "private" relationships gave the nod to the private abuse of power. Hence the domain of privacy in the workplace in the United States gradually succumbed to demands for public jurisdiction, and for expansive definitions of publicly recognized "work" to include domestic "help" and "family" farming. The contest has emerged in reverse in Britain, where "bold reformers" in the Conservative government (whom Dicey would have recognized at once), seek to return work conditions and labor relations to the private sphere and to individual negotiation, abolishing the minimum wage and opting out of the Social Chapter treaty obligations of the European Union. This "deregulation" of the workplace is, meanwhile, contested by British women learning to use the European constitutional framework and to go to court as a political strategy.[37]

The constitutional framework meant that even with activists well versed in the law, political contests could become technical and inaccessible. The minimum wage campaign after 1923 was an example of the disappearance of even the vestiges of representation of the views of sweated workers themselves and of arguments about the policy as empowerment, the opposite to the empowering rights claims of the sixties. The demarcations made by the courts, the skeletonization of facts in legal argument, skewed the policy from a labor problem to a sex problem, leaving some third of sweated workers unprotected. The same necessities later reversed the process, defining a labor problem and thereby reinforcing sex discrimination.

The results of a constitutionalized minimum wage policy for American women have been paradoxical. They have been gainers. Relative to Britain their dual identity and double burden have been open issues. The continuing argument between recognition of gender difference and gender equality has, over time, led to women's comprehensive inclusion in such redistributive public policies as the minimum wage. But the redistributive potential of the right to both living and fair wages was shrunk by the political power of those who would lose in the process, while the judiciary, adept at ruling on civil rights questions of who should receive, avoided determination of the fairness of what should be received. And at many points in the historical narrative, particular women have been losers, have starved in the meantime, as Pauline Newman warned, while lawyers and courts refined and reversed the constitutional terms of policy, bringing whole groups into or out of coverage with a flourish of the pen.

Constitutionalizing the policy, in the hands of even the most sociological or realist practitioners, has always meant imposing an artificial order on the disorderly and complex structure of work; the choices embodied in "statutory reality" have never matched the circumstances. The law compartmentalized the dual identity of women workers, and the prejudices and inequalities embedded in culture and the structure of the labor market have been amended, not annihilated, by constitutional politics. But the constitutional choices have been different from choices determined by political or economic power, as British empiricism again can attest. It is easy but wrong, however, to assume constitutionalism and politics as either separate categories or alternatives. This study shows the limitations of constitutionalism alone. Constitutionalism did not, cannot, and indeed should not shut the politics out of policymaking. Brought to bear on a minimum wage policy borrowed from a system with no such framework, constitutional terms and judicial review created new political actors, political prizes, and new arenas for political struggle while at the same time imposing new constraints and requiring different formulations. The constitutional factor changed, not eliminated, the politics of the minimum wage. The imposition of a framework of legal, formal requirements, a rule of law for the making of policy, did not bring about a utopia of justice and fairness. The more careful formulation in the United States could not ensure fair practice. To expect such results without profound change in the structures of wage labor, of the family, and in the distribution of power that reinforces existing inequalities, would be expecting miracles of the Constitution. And to expect law to be the major vehicle, let alone the only one, for bringing about social change would be equally unrealistic.

The comparison with Britain, however, suggests that the absence of constitutional limitations may bring about even less desirable results, even less attention to the real problem, and even less representation of the interests of potential beneficiaries against greater play for those of self-defined and powerful losers. If mixed blessings, lesser evils, and modest changes seem disappointing answers to the question of what difference a written constitution may make to social policy, then E. P. Thompson's historical observation may fittingly sum up the comparison and remind of their importance nonetheless: "There is a difference between arbitrary power and the rule of law. We ought to expose the shams and inequities which may be concealed beneath this law. But the rule of law itself, the imposing of effective inhibitions upon power and the defence of the citizens from power's all-intrusive claims, seems to me to be an unqualified human good."[38]

Archive collections are cited in the endnotes by the following abbreviations:

AALL Papers	American Association for Labor Legislation Papers. Microfilm ed. Ann Arbor: University Microfilms, 1974.
Cabinet Papers	Great Britain, Cabinet Papers. Public Record Office, London.
CLM Papers	Consumers' League of Massachusetts Papers. Schlesinger Library, Radcliffe College, Cambridge, Massachusetts.
CMB Papers	Clara Mortenson Beyer Papers. Schlesinger Library, Radcliffe College, Cambridge, Massachusetts.
CWD Papers	Sir Charles Wentworth Dilke Papers. British Museum, London.
EBR Papers	Elizabeth Brandeis Raushenbush Papers. Schlesinger Library, Radcliffe College, Cambridge, Massachusetts.
FF Microfilm	Felix Frankfurter Papers. Microfilm ed. Photoduplication Service, Library of Congress, Washington, D.C.
FF Papers	Felix Frankfurter Papers. Library of Congress, Washington, D.C.
JRM/LSE Papers	James Ramsay MacDonald Papers. British Library of Political and Economic Science, London School of Economics, London.
JRM/PRO Papers	James Ramsay MacDonald Papers. Public Record Office, London.
LRB Papers	[Herman] LaRue Brown Papers. Harvard Law School Library, Cambridge, Massachusetts.
MTN Papers	Mary T. Norton Papers. Rutgers University, New Brunswick, New Jersey.
MWD Papers	Mary W. Dewson Papers. Franklin D. Roosevelt Library, Hyde Park, New York.
NCF Papers	National Civic Federation Papers. New York Public Library, New York.
NCL Microfilm	National Consumers' League Papers. Microfilm ed. Photoduplication Service, Library of Congress, Washington, D.C.
NCL Papers	National Consumers' League Papers. Library of Congress, Washington, D.C.
NWP Papers	National Woman's Party Papers. Microfilm ed. Sanford, N.C.: Microfilming Corporation of America, 1979.
NYWTUL Papers	Women's Trade Union League of New York Papers. New York State Department of Labor Library, New York.
OWH Papers	Oliver Wendell Holmes Papers. Harvard Law School Library, Cambridge, Massachusetts.
PWTUL	Papers of the Women's Trade Union League and Its Principal Leaders. Microfilm ed. Woodbridge, Ct.: Research Publications, 1981.
RHJ Papers	Robert H. Jackson Papers. Library of Congress, Washington, D.C.
TGC Papers	Thomas G. Corcoran Papers. Library of Congress, Washington, D.C.
VG Papers	Viscount Gladstone Papers. British Museum, London.
WEIU Papers	Women's Educational and Industrial Union Papers. Schlesinger Library, Radcliffe College, Cambridge, Massachusetts.
WTUL Papers	Women's Trades Union League Papers. Microfilm ed. Trades Union Congress Library, London.

PREFACE

1. Elizabeth Brandeis to Clara Mortenson, 11 July 1920, EBR Papers; "Address by Mrs. Glendower Evans," *City Club Bulletin* (Philadelphia) 6 (27 January 1913): 204.

2. State of New York, *Fourth Report of the Factory Investigating Commission, 1915* (Albany: J. B. Lyon, 1915), vol. 5, p. 2871.

CHAPTER ONE
CONSTITUTIONAL POLITICS

1. James Bryce, *The American Commonwealth*, 2 vols. (London: Macmillan, 1891); A. V. Dicey, *Lectures on the Relation between Law and Public Opinion in England during the Nineteenth Century* (1914; reprint, London: Macmillan, 1962); and A. Lawrence Lowell, *The Government of England*, 2 vols. (New York: Macmillan, 1908). See also J. W. Burrow, "Some British Views of the United States Constitution," in R. C. Simmons, ed., *The United States Constitution: The First 200 Years*, Fulbright Papers no. 6 (Manchester: Manchester University Press, 1989), 116–37; Richard A. Cosgrove, *Our Lady the Common Law: An Anglo-American Legal Community* (New York: New York University Press, 1987); and David P. Crook, *American Democracy in English Politics, 1815–1850* (Oxford: Clarendon Press, 1965).

2. Dicey, *Law and Public Opinion*, 305–6. Cosgrove, *Our Lady the Common Law*, discusses the admiration of legal scholars at this time for the common law.

3. Bryce, *American Commonwealth*, vol. 1, 350.

4. Ibid.

5. Lowell, *Government of England*, vol. 1, 5, 9, 11. See also Geoffrey Marshall, "Due Process in England," in J. Roland Pennock and John W. Chapman, eds., *Due Process*, nomos 18 (New York: New York University Press, 1977), 69–89; and Katherine O'Donovan and Erika Szyszczak, *Equality and Sex Discrimination Law* (Oxford: Blackwell, 1988), 24–27.

6. The seminal discussion of social benefits as rights is T. H. Marshall, *Citizenship and Social Class* (Cambridge: Cambridge University Press, 1950).

7. Lowell, *Government of England*, vol. 1, 6.

8. Bryce, *American Commonwealth*, vol. 1, 381.

9. *Muller v. Oregon*, 208 U.S. 412 (1908); *Adkins v. Children's Hospital of Washington, D.C.*, 261 U.S. 525 (1923); and *West Coast Hotel Co. v. Parrish*, 300 U.S. 379 (1937).

10. Studies of social policy framed by analysis of judicial decisions include Judith A. Baer, *The Chains of Protection: The Judicial Response to Women's Labor Legislation* (Westport: Greenwood Press, 1978); and Donald L. Horowitz, *The Courts and Social Policy* (Washington, D.C.: Brookings Institution, 1977). Among many discussions of the desirability of a judicial role in policymaking, two authors may serve to introduce the complex theoretical and value-laden issues of democracy and control involved: Ronald Dworkin, *Law's Empire* (London: Fontana, 1986), and *Taking Rights Seriously* (London: Duckworth, 1978); and Theodore J. Lowi, *The End of Liberalism: Ideology, Policy, and the Crisis of Public Authority* (New York: Norton, 1969).

11. Clifford Geertz, *Local Knowledge: Further Essays in Interpretive Anthropology* (New York: Basic Books, 1983), 170.

12. Kim Lane Scheppele, "Constitutionalizing Abortion," a paper prepared for the meetings of the American Political Science Association, Chicago, September 1992. See also Horowitz, *Courts and Social Policy*, chap. 2, "The Attributes of Adjudication." Recent controversy over the political uses of rights claims is relevant; as a sample of a continuing debate, see defenses of a politics of rights from Wendy Kaminer, *A Fearful Freedom: Women's Flight from Equality* (Reading, Mass.: Addison-Wesley, 1990); Stuart Scheingold, *The Politics of Rights: Lawyers, Public Policy, and Political Change* (New Haven: Yale University Press, 1974); Patricia A. Williams, *The Alchemy of Race and Rights* (Cambridge: Harvard University Press, 1991); critiques and alternatives offered by Mary Ann Glendon, *Rights Talk: The Impoverishment of Political Discourse* (New York: Free Press, 1991); Martha Minow, *Making All the Difference: Inclusion, Exclusion, and American Law* (Ithaca: Cornell University Press, 1990); and Cass R. Sunstein, *After the Rights Revolution: Reconceiving the Regulatory State* (Cambridge: Harvard University Press, 1990).

13. "Memorandum," n.d. (c. 1937), 6, RHJ Papers, box 80.

14. Christopher L. Tomlins, *The State and the Unions: Labor Relations, Law, and the Organized Labor Movement in America, 1880–1960* (Cambridge: Cambridge University Press, 1985), 58. See also James B. Atleson, *Values and Assumptions in American Labor Law* (Amherst: University of Massachusetts Press, 1983); Karl E. Klare, "Critical Theory and Labor Relations Law," in David Kairys, ed., *The Politics of Law: A Progressive Critique* (New York: Pantheon, 1982), 65–88; Karl E. Klare, "Judicial Deradicalization of the Wagner Act and the Origins of Modern Legal Consciousness, 1937–1941," *Minnesota Law Review* 62 (November–March 1977–78): 265–339; and Katherine Van Wezel Stone, "The Post-War Paradigm in American Labor Law," *Yale Law Journal* 90 (June 1981): 1511–80.

15. Robin West, "Jurisprudence and Gender," in Katherine T. Bartlett and Rosanne Kennedy, eds., *Feminist Legal Theory: Readings in Law and Gender* (Boulder: Westview Press, 1991), 202–3, 207. This collection provides an introduction to the debate. See also Lisa C. Bower, "'Mother' in Law: Conceptions of Mother and the Maternal in Feminism and Feminist Legal Theory," *Differences: A Journal of Feminist Cultural Studies* 3 (1991): 20–38; Diane Polan, "Toward a Theory of Law and Patriarchy," in Kairys, ed., *The Politics of Law*, 294–303; and Debra Ratterman, "Liberating Feminist Jurisprudence," *off our backs* 19 (August–September 1989): 22–24.

16. Ben Cohen to Felix Frankfurter, 8 January 1932, FF Papers, box 45.

17. The same shift from common to statute law was taking place in Britain, as a matter of parliamentary will. According to Dicey, in 1898 "the active use of parliamentary sovereignty" had recently become the established mode of action: "Laws are with us created and changed in two different ways—that is, either by Act of Parliament, or by judicial legislation arising from the action of the Courts in deciding the particular cases which come before them. Even at the present day the greater part and the most important of the laws by which Englishmen are governed are in reality judge-made law, and this was much more obviously the case at the beginning of the nineteenth century." Dicey, *Law and Public Opinion*, 165–66. See also Cosgrove, *Our Lady the Common Law*.

18. Jennifer Nedelsky, *Private Property and the Limits of Constitutionalism: The Madisonian Framework and Its Legacy* (Chicago: University of Chicago Press, 1990), 2.

19. Karen Orren, *Belated Feudalism: Labor, the Law, and Liberal Development in the United States* (Cambridge: Cambridge University Press, 1991), 31. See also Robert J.

Steinfeld, *The Invention of Free Labor: The Employment Relation in English and American Law and Culture* (Chapel Hill: University of North Carolina Press, 1991).

20. See Leon Fink, "Labor, Liberty, and the Law: Trade Unionism and the Problem of the American Constitutional Order," *Journal of American History* 74 (December 1987): 904–25; William E. Forbath, *Law and the Shaping of the American Labor Movement* (Cambridge: Harvard University Press, 1991); Victoria C. Hattam, *Labor Visions and State Power: The Origins of Business Unionism in the United States, 1806–1896* (Princeton: Princeton University Press, 1993); Orren, *Belated Feudalism*; and Martin J. Sklar, *The Corporate Reconstruction of American Capitalism, 1890–1916: The Market, the Law, and Politics* (Cambridge: Cambridge University Press, 1988).

21. See Norma Basch, *In the Eyes of the Law: Women, Marriage, and Property in Nineteenth-Century New York* (Ithaca: Cornell University Press, 1982); and Michael Grossberg, *Governing the Hearth: Law and the Family in Nineteenth-Century America* (Chapel Hill: University of North Carolina Press, 1985); for British parallels, Mary Lyndon Shanley, *Feminism, Marriage, and the Law in Victorian England, 1850–1895* (Princeton: Princeton University Press, 1989).

22. Felix Frankfurter, "Hours of Labor and Realism in Constitutional Law," *Harvard Law Review* 29 (February 1916): 365. Emphasis in original.

23. See a study of modern reform groups attempting to control the "legal stimuli" presented to judges and bring about legal change: Lee Epstein and Joseph F. Kobylka, *The Supreme Court and Legal Change: Abortion and the Death Penalty* (Chapel Hill: University of North Carolina Press, 1992).

24. The uncertain fate of women workers under minimum wage law has brought criticisms of sexist intent, especially from later commentators. In the strongest version, the British Trade Boards Act has been seen as covert discrimination, a means, if not a plot, by which male businessmen and workers could isolate women in the few designated and controlled occupations covered by the law, and the gender-based American laws as overtly fulfilling the same purpose. On Britain, see Jenny Morris, *Women Workers and the Sweated Trades: The Origins of Minimum Wage Legislation* (Aldershot: Gower, 1986); on the U.S.A., Mimi Abramowitz, *Regulating the Lives of Women: Social Welfare Policy from Colonial Times to the Present* (Boston: South End Press, 1988), chap. 6; Susan Lehrer, *Origins of Protective Legislation for Women, 1905–1925* (Albany: State University of New York Press, 1987); and Joseph F. Tripp, "Law and Social Control: Historians' Views of Progressive-Era Labor Legislation," *Labor History* 28 (Fall 1987): 447–83.

The role of women as policymakers as well as clients has raised questions about their own class interests, especially the desire of middle-class women benevolently to protect mothers in their own image, however unrealistic for working women, or less kindly to impose their own moral vision. Major contributions to the growing literature on maternalism are Seth Koven and Sonya Michel, eds., *Mothers of a New World: Maternalist Politics and the Origins of Welfare States* (New York: Routledge, 1993); Seth Koven and Sonya Michel, "Womanly Duties: Maternalist Politics and the Origins of Welfare States in France, Germany, Great Britain, and the United States, 1880–1920," *American Historical Review* 95 (October 1990): 1076–1108; Sonya Michel and Robyn Rosen, "The Paradox of Maternalism: Elizabeth Lowell Putnam and the American Welfare State," *Gender and History* 4 (Autumn 1992): 364–86; Ann Shola Orloff, "Gender in Early U.S. Social Policy," *Journal of Policy History* 3 (Fall 1991): 249–81; and Theda Skocpol, *Protecting Soldiers and Mothers: The Political Origins of Social Policy in the United States* (Cambridge: Harvard University Press, 1992).

The role of British women minimum wagers has been underestimated by historians, and these latter arguments have attached particularly to American women, whose "maternalism" has even been contrasted with British "paternalism." See Theda Skocpol and Gretchen Ritter, "Gender and the Origins of Modern Social Policies in Britain and the United States," *Studies in American Political Development* 5 (Spring 1991): 36–93.

25. On race and social policy in the early twentieth century, see, for example, Eileen Boris, "The Power of Motherhood: Black and White Activist Women Redefine the Political," in Koven and Michel, *Mothers of a New World*, 213–45; Linda Gordon, "Black and White Visions of Welfare: Women's Welfare Activism, 1890–1945," *Journal of American History* 78 (September 1991): 559–89; Gwendolyn Mink, "The Lady and the Tramp: Gender, Race, and the Origins of the American Welfare State," in Linda Gordon, ed., *Women, the State, and Welfare* (Madison: University of Wisconsin Press, 1990), 92–102; and Dorothy Salem, *To Better Our World: Black Women in Organized Reform, 1880–1920* (Brooklyn, N.Y.: Carlson, 1990).

26. Deborah Rhode, *Justice and Gender: Sex Discrimination and the Law* (Cambridge: Harvard University Press, 1989), chap. 8, "Equality in Form and Equality in Fact: Women and Work."

27. Robert H. Jackson in Congressional testimony. Congress, Senate, Committee on Education and Labor (75th Congress, 1st session, 2–22 June 1937), *Fair Labor Standards Act of 1937. Joint Hearings before the Committee on Education and Labor, U.S. Senate, and the Committee on Labor, House of Representatives*, 2.

CHAPTER TWO
NO SWEAT

1. Trade Boards Act 1909, 9 Edw. 7, c. 22.

2. H. J. Tennant, junior minister at the Board of Trade, introducing the second reading of the Trade Boards Bill, 28 April 1909. *Parliamentary Debates* (Commons), 5th ser., 4 (1909): col. 344.

3. Ibid., col. 345.

4. See Derek Fraser, *The Evolution of the British Welfare State* (London: Macmillan, 1973); Bentley B. Gilbert, *The Evolution of National Insurance in Great Britain: The Origins of the Welfare State* (London: Michael Joseph, 1966); J. R. Hay, *The Origins of the Liberal Welfare Reforms, 1906–1914* (London: Macmillan, 1975); and Pat Thane, *The Foundations of the Welfare State* (London: Longmans Green, 1982). Samuel H. Beer, *British Politics in the Collectivist Age*, 2d. ed. (New York: Random House, 1969), explains the politics and philosophy of collectivism, which allowed Liberals and Labour to ally.

5. See Linda Gordon, "The New Feminist Scholarship on the Welfare State," in Linda Gordon, ed., *Women, the State, and Welfare* (Madison: University of Wisconsin Press, 1990), 9–35; Carole Pateman, "The Patriarchal Welfare State," in Amy Gutmann, ed., *Democracy and the Welfare State* (Princeton: Princeton University Press, 1988), 231–60; and, on gender implications in specific British policies, Harold Benenson, "The 'Family Wage' and Working Women's Consciousness in Britain, 1880–1914," *Politics and Society* 19 (March 1991): 71–108; Seth Koven and Sonya Michel, "Womanly Duties: Maternalist Politics and the Origins of Welfare States in France, Germany, Great Britain, and the United States, 1880–1920," *American Historical Review* 95 (October 1990): 1076–1108; Susan Pedersen, "The Failure of Feminism in the Making of the British Welfare State," *Radical History Review* 43 (1989): 86–110, and "Gender, Welfare, and

Citizenship in Britain during the Great War," *American Historical Review* 95 (October 1990): 983–1006; and Theda Skocpol and Gretchen Ritter, "Gender and the Origins of Modern Social Policies in Britain and the United States," *Studies in American Political Development* 5 (Spring 1991): 36–93.

6. See Robert Gray, "Factory Legislation and the Gendering of Jobs in the North of England, 1830–1860," *Gender and History* 5 (Spring 1993): 56–80; and essays by Lea S. Vandervelde and Eileen Boris in Christopher L. Tomlins and Andrew J. King, eds., *Labor Law in America: Historical and Critical Essays* (Baltimore: Johns Hopkins University Press, 1992).

7. Charles Kingsley, *Alton Locke, Tailor and Poet: An Autobiography* (London: Macmillan, 1889). First published in 1849, this book immortalized "the Sweater's Den." "Cheap Clothes and Nasty," published by Kingsley under the pseudonym of Parson Lot, appears as a preface to this edition of *Alton Locke*; see esp. xix. Accounts of sweating include Duncan Bythell, *The Sweated Trades: Outwork in Nineteenth-Century Britain* (London: Batsford Academic, 1978); Jenny Morris, *Women Workers and the Sweated Trades* (Aldershot: Gower, 1986); and James A. Schmiechen, *Sweated Industries and Sweated Labor: The London Clothing Trades 1860–1914* (London: Croom Helm, 1984).

8. Richard Mudie-Smith, ed., *Sweated Industries: Being a Handbook of the "Daily News" Exhibition* (London: Bradbury, Agnew, 1906), 8.

9. NASL handbill, in author's possession.

10. See Martin Bulmer, Kevin Bales and Kathryn Kish Sklar, eds., *The Social Survey in Historical Perspective, 1880–1940* (Cambridge: Cambridge University Press, 1991); and Michael J. Lacey and Mary O. Furner, eds., *The State and Social Investigation in Britain and the United States* (Cambridge: Woodrow Wilson Center Press and Cambridge University Press, 1993). Morris, *Women Workers*, 9–10, notes especially Royal Commissions on Labour and Housing, and the Annual Reports of the Factory Inspectorate. From 1893, a Woman Inspectorate drew attention to the female work force; see Adelaide Mary Anderson, *Women in the Factory: An Administrative Adventure, 1893–1921* (London: John Murray, 1922); and Mary Drake McFeely, *Lady Inspectors: The Campaign for a Better Workplace, 1893–1921* (Oxford: Blackwell, 1988).

11. Morris, *Women Workers*, 8.

12. Ibid., 8, 10. See also Sally Alexander, "Women's Work in Nineteenth Century London: A Study of the Years 1820–1950," in Juliet Mitchell and Ann Oakley, eds., *The Rights and Wrongs of Women* (Harmondsworth: Penguin, 1976), 59–111; and Nancy Grey Osterud, "Gender Divisions and the Organization of Work in the Leicester Hosiery Industry," in Angela V. John, ed., *Unequal Opportunities: Women's Employment in England, 1800–1918* (Oxford: Blackwell, 1986), 45–68.

13. The Interdepartmental Committee on the Employment of Schoolchildren, 1890, quoted in Edward Cadbury and George Shann, *Sweating* (London: Headley Brothers, 1907), 62.

14. "The total number of aliens in the United Kingdom in 1901 was 286,925 in a population of 41 million"; see Cadbury and Shann, *Sweating*, 85. See also Sir Charles Dilke's assessment that the problem was more of women and children than aliens, *Women's Trades' Union Review*, no. 54 (July 1904): 4; and the *Anti-Sweater*, no. 8 (February 1887): 1, on "Hebrew" victims of sweating. On the broader issues of prejudice against aliens and the restrictive Aliens Act of 1905 see Bernard Gainer, *The Alien Invasion: The Origins of the Aliens Act of 1905* (London: Heinemann, 1972); and John A. Garrard, *The English and Immigration, 1880–1910* (Oxford: Oxford University Press, 1971).

15. *Parliamentary Papers* (Lords), "Fifth Report from the Select Committee of the House of Lords on the Sweating System," 1890, vol. 17, no. 169, xlii.

16. *Parliamentary Papers* (Commons), "Report from the Select Committee on Home Work," HC 1907, vol. 6, no. 290, 136. Hereafter cited as *Select Committee 1907*.

17. Mary Agnes Hamilton, *Mary Macarthur: A Biographical Sketch* (London: Leonard Parsons, 1925), 64.

18. Cadbury and Shann, *Sweating*, 25–34. Forty-two trades averaged between 6s and 10s a week, thirteen trades less than 6s, and the remainder more than 10s. Wages tabulated in Mudie-Smith, *Sweated Industries*, 120–23, cluster around a similar mean of 7s to 9s.

19. Cadbury and Shann, *Sweating*, 76–77. See also Edward Cadbury, M. C. Matheson, and George Shann, *Women's Work and Wages* (London: Fisher Unwin, 1906).

20. Cadbury and Shann, *Sweating*, 20, 14–15.

21. Department of Employment and Productivity, *British Labour Statistics: Historical Abstract, 1886–1968* (London: HMSO, 1971), tables 1, 4, 6. The higher figures were usually for London.

22. Cadbury and Shann, *Sweating*, 25–34.

23. *Parliamentary Papers* (Commons), "Report from the Select Committee on Home Work," HC 1908, vol. 8, no. 246, 85–99, esp. 92. Hereafter cited as *Select Committee 1908*.

24. *British Labour Statistics*, tables 1, 4, 6. Many home workers spent time fetching work, like the chair-caners who had to "go a long way to the factories" and "carry the chairs to and fro." Cadbury and Shann, *Sweating*, 43.

25. Schmiechen, *Sweated Industries*, 42.

26. Ibid., 52.

27. Morris, *Women Workers*, 9.

28. *Select Committee 1907*, 141.

29. Sidney Webb and Beatrice Webb, *Industrial Democracy* (New York: Longmans Green, 1911), 662.

30. H. J. Tennant, *Parliamentary Debates* (Commons), 5th ser., 4 (1909): col. 344.

31. James Ramsay MacDonald, "Arbitration Courts and Wages Boards in Australasia," *Contemporary Review* 93 (March 1908): 325.

32. Evidence of Mrs. Ramsay MacDonald, *Select Committee 1907*, 213; and Cadbury and Shann, *Sweating*, 75.

33. *Select Committee 1907*, 1–19. And see his interrogation by Liberal M.P. Leo Chiozza-Money, *Select Committee 1907*, 288–307.

34. B. L. Hutchins and A. Harrison, *A History of Factory Legislation*, 2d ed. (London: P. S. King, 1911), ix.

35. Ibid., viii. Emphasis added.

36. A. Amy Bulley and Margaret Whitley, *Women's Work* (London: Methuen, 1894), 166. See also Margaret MacDonald's 1907 "Report on Enquiry into Conditions of Work in Laundries," in Ellen Mappen, ed., *Helping Women at Work: The Women's Industrial Council, 1889–1914* (London: Hutchinson, 1985), 69–83.

37. Hutchins and Harrison, *Factory Legislation*, 203, 65. Their account remains the best history of protective legislation. See discussions of the principle of protective legislation by Sally J. Kenney, *For Whose Protection? Reproductive Hazards and Exclusionary Policies in the United States and Britain* (Ann Arbor: University of Michigan Press, 1992), 11–41; Jane Lewis and Celia Davies, "Protective Legislation in Britain, 1870–1990: Equality, Difference and Their Implications for Women," *Policy and Politics* 19

(January 1991): 13–25; Ann P. Robson, *On Higher than Commercial Grounds: The Factory Controversy, 1850–1853* (New York: Garland, 1985), esp. 26; Fraser, *British Welfare State*, 21–27; on the parallel struggle for equal rights in marriage, Mary Lyndon Shanley, *Feminism, Marriage, and the Law in Victorian England, 1850–1895* (Princeton: Princeton University Press, 1989).

38. Hutchins and Harrison, *Factory Legislation*, 203.

39. Clementina Black, *Sweated Industry and the Minimum Wage* (London: Duckworth, 1907), 194.

40. H. J. Tennant, *Parliamentary Debates* (Commons), 5th ser., 4 (1909): col. 345.

41. "The Case for a Legal Minimum Wage. By the Fabian Society," in Beatrice Webb, B. L. Hutchins, and the Fabian Society, *Socialism and National Minimum* (London: A. C. Fifield, 1909), 66.

42. *Women's Trades' Union Review*, no. 48 (January 1903): 11.

43. "Sweated Industries and the Minimum Wage," *Quarterly Review* 210 (January 1909): 67–85, esp. 68–69, 85. The article was unsigned.

44. Webb and Webb, *Industrial Democracy*, 749.

45. Ibid., 751.

46. Ibid., 750, 751.

47. George Shann, "The Effect of the Non-Living Wage upon the Individual, the Family, and the State," in *The Industrial Unrest and the Living Wage: Being a Series of Lectures Given at the Inter-Denominational Summer School Held at Swanwick, Derbyshire, June 28th–July 5th, 1913* (London: P. S. King, 1914), 87–105, esp. 100, 103.

48. *Select Committee 1908*, xiv.

49. *Parliamentary Debates* (Commons), 5th ser., 4 (1909): col. 345.

50. Skocpol and Ritter, "Gender and the Origins," 36.

51. Hay, *The Origins*, 52–53.

52. Sir Charles Dilke to Herbert Gladstone, 15 February 1908, VG Papers, Add. Mss. 46065. Dilke was a leading radical Liberal in 1885, when he was named in a divorce case and forced out of public life. Mrs. Emilia Pattison nevertheless announced her engagement to Dilke and married him. He returned to Parliament in 1892 and became a spokesperson for labor legislation and unions. Dilke later attributed the invention of the minimum wage to his friend John Stuart Mill, in his "principal book on economy, published in the Forties." *Select Committee 1908*, 173. For biographical information on women, see Olive Banks, *The Biographical Dictionary of British Feminists, Volume 1: 1800–1930* (New York: New York University Press, 1985); and see David Marquand, *Ramsay Macdonald* (London: Jonathan Cape, 1977); Betty Askwith, *Lady Dilke: A Biography* (London: Chatto and Windus, 1969); Stephen Gwynn and Gertrude Tuckwell, *The Life of the Rt. Hon. Sir Charles W. Dilke*, 2 vols. (London: John Murray, 1918); and Roy Jenkins, *Victorian Scandal: A Biography of the Right Honourable Gentleman Sir Charles Dilke* (New York: Chilmark Press, 1965). See also Pat Jalland, *Women, Marriage and Politics, 1860–1914* (Oxford: Oxford University Press, 1988).

53. Morris, *Women Workers*, chaps. 8 and 9; and Hamilton, *Mary Macarthur*, 65.

54. Sir Charles W. Dilke, "Prospects of Wages Boards," *Woman Worker*, no. 1 (April 1908): 145.

55. Webb and Webb, *Industrial Democracy*, 766–84.

56. See, for example, the 1895 "Act to amend and extend the Law Relating to Factories and Workshops," described in Hutchins and Harrison, *Factory Legislation*, 195, 203, an attempt to patch up earlier laws, and Dilke's criticism of its failure, *Parliamentary Debates* (Commons), 4th ser., 74 (1899): col. 225.

57. Quoted in Gwynn and Tuckwell, *The Life*, vol. 2, 345. See also Charles Wentworth Dilke, *Greater Britain: A Record of Travel in English-Speaking Countries during 1866 and 1867* (London: Macmillan, 1869), part 3. Contemporary accounts of the development of minimum wage laws in Australia and New Zealand include Black, *Sweated Industry*, 230–59; George W. Gough, "The Wages Boards of Victoria," *Economic Journal* 15 (September 1905): 361–73; Rev. John Hoatson, "Victorian Minimum Wage System," in NASL, *Report of a Conference on a Minimum Wage Held at the Guildhall, London, on October 24th, 25th, and 26th, 1906* (London: Co-operative Printing Society, 1907), 75–85; MacDonald, "Arbitration Courts"; and William Pember-Reeves, "The Minimum Wage Law in Victoria and South Australia," *Economic Journal* 11 (September 1901): 334–44.

58. Testimony of Sir Charles Dilke, *Select Committee 1908*, 174. Deakin subsequently became premier of a federated Australia.

59. Alfred Deakin to Dilke, 10 October 1900, CWD Papers, Add. Mss. 43877.

60. *Women's Trades' Union Review*, no. 4 (15 January 1892): 18.

61. Ibid., no. 12 (January 1894): 7.

62. Figures quoted in Harold Goldman, *Emma Paterson* (London: Lawrence and Wishart, 1974), 110, 108. See also Gladys Boone, *The Women's Trade Union Leagues in Great Britain and the United States of America* (New York: Columbia University Press, 1942); Barbara Drake, *Women in Trade Unions* (London: Labour Research Department, 1920; reprint, London: Virago, 1984); and Norbert C. Soldon, *Women in British Trade Unions, 1874–1976* (Dublin: Gill and Macmillan, 1978).

63. See the preface by Lady Dilke to Bulley and Whitley, *Women's Work*, v–xiii. Dilke was a friend of Emma Paterson, long involved with the WTUL. Another friend recalled her as the wife of Mark Pattison, rector of Lincoln College, Oxford, using the college hall for a meeting to form the Oxford branch of the Women's Protective Provident League, the original name of the WTUL; M. Nettleship to Sir Charles Dilke (n.d), CWD Papers, Add. Mss. 43918. See also Askwith, *Lady Dilke*; and Jenkins, *Victorian Scandal*.

64. See the pen portrait by J. J. Mallon, *Woman Worker*, no. 13 (28 August 1908): 323; and Hamilton, *Mary Macarthur*.

65. Drake, *Women in Trade Unions*, 15–18.

66. On women's political organization for labor issues, see Christine Collette, *For Labour and for Women: The Women's Labour League, 1906–1918* (Manchester: Manchester University Press, 1989), chap. 1; Morris, *Women Workers*, chap. 5; and Pat Thane, "Women in the British Labour Party and the Construction of State Welfare, 1906–1939," in Seth Koven and Sonya Michel, eds., *Mothers of a New World: Maternalist Politics and the Origins of Welfare States* (New York: Routledge, 1993), 343–77. On WIC, see Ellen Mappen, *Helping Women at Work*. On women's organizations within political parties, see Linda Walker, "Party Political Women: A Comparative Study of Liberal Women and the Primrose League, 1890–1914," in Jane Rendall ed., *Equal or Different: Women's Politics, 1800–1914* (Oxford: Blackwell, 1987), 165–91. On the Women's Co-operative Guild see Naomi Black, *Social Feminism* (Ithaca: Cornell University Press, 1989), chaps. 6–7.

67. *Women's Trades' Union Review*, no. 22 (July 1896): 15; and no. 25 (April 1897): 1.

68. WTUL, *Annual Report, Presented to the Committee, February, 1901* (London: Co-operative Printing Society, 1901), 11.

69. *Women's Trades' Union Review*, no. 47 (October 1902): 3.

70. WIC, *What the Council Is and Does* (London: Morton and Burt [printers], January 1909), in Mappen, *Helping Women at Work*, 67.

71. J. Ramsay MacDonald, "Diary of American Tour 1897," JRM Papers/PRO, PRO

30/69/923, Monday (16 August), Thursday (21 October). Margaret MacDonald's diary is in the same collection.

72. Mrs. M. E. MacDonald, "A Bill for the Better Regulation of Home Industries," in Mudie-Smith, *Sweated Industries*, 27.

73. "Memorandum of Evidence on Home Work, by Mrs. J. R. MacDonald" (n.d), JRM Papers/PRO, PRO 30/69/1369.

74. Clementina Black, quoted in Mappen, *Helping Women at Work*, 17.

75. Ibid., 26.

76. Hamilton, *Mary Macarthur*, 75.

77. *Select Committee 1907*, 148–49.

78. Dilke to Gladstone, 23 May 1907, VG Papers, Add. Mss. 46064.

79. The WTUL endorsed Beatrice Webb's insistence that the Factory Acts "must *make the giver-out of work legally responsible for the sanitary and other conditions under which the work is executed.*" *Women's Trades' Union Review*, no. 13 (May 1894): 5. Emphasis in original.

80. Ibid., no. 19 (October 1895).

81. Helen Marot to Margaret E. MacDonald, 6 August 1907, JRM Papers/PRO, PRO 30/69/1205.

82. MacDonald, "A Bill," 26.

83. J. J. Mallon, "Portrait Gallery. Mrs. Margaret MacDonald," *Woman Worker*, n.s., no. 2 (12 June 1908): 3. Typical of her strong feelings is a printed memo circulated to a meeting she could not attend: Margaret E. MacDonald, "To the Members of the National Council of Women of Great Britain and Ireland," 8 October 1908, JRM Papers/PRO, PRO 30/69/1369.

84. Black, *Sweated Industry*.

85. MacDonald to Black, 27 November 1908, JRM Papers/LSE, vol. 1.

86. WIC, "How to Deal with Home Work," in Mappen, *Helping Women at Work*, 95. See also the printed text of "Bill for the Better Regulation of Homework," n.d., JRM Papers/PRO, PRO 30/69/1369: "The object of this Bill is to protect the public against the dissemination of disease and dirt by wearing apparel, and other articles, made in insanitary dwelling places, and to protect the workers themselves against unhealthy and vicious conditions over which they can exercise no control."

87. *Times* (22 January 1909): 4. The council compromised, and later published a pamphlet, *The Case For and Against a Legal Minimum Wage for Sweated Workers* (London: WIC, 1909). MacDonald had difficulty finding an author to write "for." B. L. Hutchins wrote withdrawing from the project, 12 March (1909), JRM Papers/LSE, vol. 1. The split was barely papered over; see James Ramsay MacDonald, *Margaret Ethel MacDonald* (London: Swarthmore Press, 1912), 136, where her resignation is presumably wrongly dated as 1907, and Collette, *For Labour and For Women*, 119, where she is noted as resigning with other Women's Labour League members in 1910.

88. Denise Riley, *"Am I That Name?" Feminism and the Category of "Women" in History* (Basingstoke: Macmillan, 1988), esp. 49–66, " 'The Social,' 'Woman,' and Sociological Feminism," discusses other examples of the implicit gendering of society and politics at this time.

89. See Linda Gordon's analysis of the politics of family violence, and the choice of some victims of violence to call in outside help and turn "interference" to their own advantage: *Heroes of Their Own Lives: The Politics and History of Family Violence, Boston 1880–1960* (New York: Viking, 1988). Essays in Eileen Boris and Cynthia R. Daniels, eds., *Homework: Historical and Contemporary Perspectives on Paid Labor at*

Home (Urbana: University of Illinois Press, 1989), discuss the balance of benefits to women, and the powerful disadvantages.

90. All quotations from the preface by Emilia F. S. Dilke, in Bulley and Whitley, *Women's Work*, v–xiii.

91. This combination was more familiar in Britain than in the United States, as Holton notes: "It could not be argued for Britain, as DuBois does for America, that 'the suffrage movement grew out of a critique of what we are calling women's culture,' if that is to be understood in terms of the concepts 'female world' and 'female consciousness.' Rather it seems likely that it derived much of its strength and potency from these." Sandra Stanley Holton, *Feminism and Democracy: Women's Suffrage and Reform Politics in Britain, 1900–1918* (Cambridge: Cambridge University Press, 1986), 20. Holton refers to Ellen Carol DuBois, *Feminism and Suffrage: The Emergence of an Independent Women's Movement in America, 1848–1869* (Ithaca: Cornell University Press, 1978). See also Black's analysis of the pro-suffrage Women's Co-operative Guild, *Social Feminism*, chap. 6; and Robin Miller Jacoby, "Feminism and Class Consciousness in the British and American Women's Trade Union Leagues, 1890–1925," in Berenice A. Carroll, ed., *Liberating Women's History: Theoretical and Critical Essays* (Urbana: University of Illinois Press, 1976), 137–60. Kenney, *For Whose Protection?*, 322, concludes that British feminists have always been more open to the recognition of gender difference and to conditional categorizations than have Americans.

92. Tuckwell's views are described in Banks, *Biographical Dictionary of British Feminists*, 214–16. Black, *Sweated Industries*, 274.

93. *Select Committee 1907*, 116–17. See also the testimony of Thomas Holmes, that sweated home workers were "the most industrious, sober and honest class of the community . . . in fact, their goodness appals me." *Select Committee 1908*, 13; and Thomas Holmes, *London Home Industries and the Sweating of Women* (London: Headley Brothers, [1907]), esp. 28.

94. Hamilton, *Mary Macarthur*, 17. Bondfield was then assistant general secretary of the National Union of Shop Assistants, for which Sir Charles Dilke spoke in Parliament.

95. Drake, *Women in Trade Unions*, chap. 11, esp. 105. See also Wilfred B. Whitaker, *Victorian and Edwardian Shop Workers* (Newton Abbot: David and Charles, 1973).

96. Jill Liddington and Jill Norris, *One Hand Tied behind Us: The Rise of the Women's Suffrage Movement* (London: Virago, 1978), chap. 8, esp. 125, 127.

97. Hamilton, *Mary Macarthur*, 42.

98. Ibid., 45.

99. Eileen Boris discusses the use of this poster in the U.S., in "Regulating Industrial Homework: The Triumph of 'Sacred Motherhood,'" *Journal of American History* 71 (March 1985): 750.

100. Quoted by Drake, *Women in Trade Unions*, 45.

101. Quotations from J. J. Mallon, reprinted in Hamilton, *Mary Macarthur*, 93, 72. A lace-makers' association lobbied for enforcement of factory laws and won one of the first trade boards.

102. *Woman Worker*, n.s., no. 6 (10 July 1908): 165.

103. Ibid., no. 30 (23 December 1908): 740.

104. *Select Committee 1907*, 140.

105. Ibid., 134.

106. The most detailed source for her life remains, despite its fulsome sentimentality, the memorial by her husband: MacDonald, *Margaret Ethel MacDonald*. But see, for a partial corrective, Jalland, *Women, Marriage and Politics*, esp. 126–29. There is no sim-

ple relationship between women reformers' views and their family status. Tuckwell never married, Dilke's first unhappy and childless marriage was followed by her second happy and childless marriage to Sir Charles. MacDonald married in her midtwenties and had six children. Macarthur put her work before marriage when Will Anderson proposed in 1903, but she married him in 1911 and had two children, one stillborn.

107. *Select Committee 1907*, 227.

108. *For and Against a Legal Minimum Wage*, 11. Similarly, Tuckwell testified that with a Wages Board, "you would call the workers together to choose the workpeople who are going to represent them; and in that way they will instantly form a nucleus of an organisation." *Select Committee 1907*, 118.

109. *Select Committee 1907*, 215.

110. Ibid., 226.

111. MacDonald, *Margaret Ethel MacDonald*, 216. Home work for MacDonald herself was undertaken at the big black table in her happily chaotic home, "she looking over her arm every now and again and joining in the baby ripplings, whilst the sun poured down upon both from the wide-open windows," and the artist friend who came to sketch the baby, Sheila, who "was with the little nurse when I arrived." Ibid., 121.

112. Ibid., 191.

113. Quoted in ibid., 177.

114. *Select Committee 1907*, 214, 228.

115. Ibid., 221.

116. MacDonald, *Margaret Ethel MacDonald*, 90–91, 105–6; see also Jane Lewis, "The Place of Social Investigation, Social Theory and Social Work in the Approach to Late Victorian and Edwardian Social Problems: The Case of Beatrice Webb and Helen Bosanquet," in Bulmer, Bales, and Sklar, *The Social Survey*, 158.

117. A. V. Dicey, *Lectures on the Relation between Law and Public Opinion in England during the Nineteenth Century* (London: Macmillan, 1962), 66. This combination of maternalism and structuralism remained central to socialist women's thought in the twentieth century, according to Pat Thane. See "Visions of Gender in the British Welfare State: The Case of Women in the British Labour Party and Social Policy, 1906–1945," in Gisela Bock and Pat Thane, eds., *Maternity and Gender Policies: Women and the Rise of the European Welfare States, 1880s–1950s* (London: Routledge, 1991), 93–118; see also Seth Koven, "Borderlands: Women, Voluntary Action, and Child Welfare in Britain, 1840–1914," in Koven and Michel, *Mothers of a New World*, 94–135; and Jane Lewis, *Women and Social Action in Victorian and Edwardian England* (Aldershot: Edward Elgar, 1991), e.g., her comment on p. 5 that the "image of the upright Victorian figure, confidently directing the business of her own home and extending her rule to the homes of the poor . . . dissolves into a more complicated series of problems and contradictions."

118. Unsigned review of the Webbs' *Industrial Democracy*, *Women's Trades' Union Review* 28 (April 1898): 16–17. Black's views, delivered to the Royal Patriotic Club, are reported in "Women's Work and Wages," *Times* (23 January 1909): 2. Black's reply to Admiral the Hon. Sir E. R. Fremantle, who "contended that the work in the home, the tact and influence there to be exercised, offered the best field for women's effort. If they were first in the home they could not claim to have a foremost part in the work outside," was not reported.

119. Carroll Smith-Rosenberg, *Disorderly Conduct: Visions of Gender in Victorian America* (New York: Oxford University Press, 1985), 263, 264.

120. Black, *Social Feminism*, 11.

121. *Select Committee 1908*, Macarthur's witnesses, 85–99, Vynne, 119, and Vynne's witnesses, 122–30, esp. 126.

122. Testimony of Miss Edith Lawson, Hon. Secretary, National Home-Workers League. Ibid., 130.

123. *Select Committee 1907*, 148.

124. Clementina Black, questioned by Sir Thomas Whittaker. Ibid., 148.

CHAPTER THREE
LOW-PAID WORKERS

1. *Parliamentary Debates* (Commons), 4th ser., 152 (1906): col. 529. See I. Bealey and H. Pelling, *Labour and Politics, 1900–1906* (London: Macmillan, 1958); Samuel H. Beer, *British Politics in the Collectivist Age*, 2d ed. (New York: Random House, 1969); Elie Halevy, *A History of the English People in the Nineteenth Century*, vol. 6: *The Rule of Democracy, 1905–1914* (London: Ernest Benn, 1934); and Kenneth O. Morgan, *The Age of Lloyd George: The Liberal Party and British Politics, 1890–1929* (London: Allen and Unwin, 1971).

2. NASL, *First Annual Report Adopted at the Annual Meeting Held 18th July, 1907* (London: Co-operative Printing Society, 1908), 5.

3. Richard Mudie-Smith, ed., *Sweated Industries: Being a Handbook of the "Daily News" Exhibition* (London: Bradbury, Agnew, 1906), 7–8.

4. Jenny Morris, *Women Workers and the Sweated Trades: The Origins of Minimum Wage Legislation* (Aldershot: Gower, 1986), 198.

5. Mudie-Smith, *Sweated Industries*, 7.

6. Mary Agnes Hamilton, *Mary Macarthur: A Biographical Sketch* (London: Leonard Parsons, 1925), 65–66.

7. WTUL, "Minutes of Executive Committee, 1903–1921"; "Minutes," 8 February 1906, 8 March 1906; "Extraordinary Committee Meeting, March 15th, 1906"; and "Extraordinary Committee Meeting. March 21st 1906," WTUL Papers. The minutes report only decisions; it can be deduced, for example, from Liberal M.P. H. J. Tennant's dissent that cooperation with a radical group like the SDF was the problem.

8. James Ramsay MacDonald, "Sweating and Wages Boards," *Nineteenth Century* 64 (November 1908): 748; and James Ramsay MacDonald, *Margaret Ethel MacDonald* (London: Swarthmore Press, 1912), 147.

9. NASL, *Report of Conference on a Minimum Wage Held at the Guildhall, London, October 24th, 25th, & 26th, 1906* (London: Co-operative Printing Society, 1907), 86–89; *Parliamentary Papers* (Commons), "Report from the Select Committee on Home Work," HC 1907, vol. 6, no. 290, 228. Hereafter cited as *Select Committee 1907*.

10. NASL, *First Annual Report, 1907*, 3.

11. Ibid., esp. 8, 9.

12. Dorothy Gladstone to Gertrude Tuckwell, 5 January 1908, CWD Papers, Add. Mss. 43967. See Pat Jalland, *Women, Marriage and Politics, 1860–1914* (Oxford: Oxford University Press, 1986), part 3; Jane Lewis, *Women and Social Action in Victorian and Edwardian England* (Aldershot: Edward Elgar, 1991); and Jane Rendall, ed., *Equal or Different: Women's Politics, 1800–1914* (Oxford: Blackwell, 1987), esp. essays by Dorothy Thompson and Linda Walker.

13. Dr. Gore, quoted in Stephen Gwynn and Gertrude M. Tuckwell, *The Life of the Rt. Hon. Sir Charles W. Dilke, Bart., M.P.* (London: John Murray, 1918), vol. 2, 363.

14. WTUL, *Annual Report and Balance Sheet, April, 1909* (London: W. Speaight,

1909), 4; and WTUL, *35th Annual Report and Balance Sheet, April, 1910* (London: Speaight, 1910), 12.

15. NASL, *Fifth Annual Report Adopted at the Annual Meeting Held July 27th, 1911* (Manchester: William Morris Press, 1911), 10.

16. NASL, *Report of Conference*, 5.

17. *Woman Worker*, no. 30 (23 December 1908): 740.

18. NASL, *First Annual Report*, 3–4; and NASL, *Report of Conference*, 4.

19. NASL, *Report of Conference*, 85.

20. Quotations from Tuckwell's paper, in ibid., 33–37.

21. Ibid., 41–43.

22. See "Table II: Analysis of Principal Trade Unions," in Barbara Drake, *Women in Trade Unions* (London: Labour Research Department, 1920; reprint, London: Virago, 1984), following 237; and Morris, *Women Workers*, chap. 4 and 220–24.

23. James Ramsay MacDonald, "Arbitration Courts and Wages Boards on Australasia," *Contemporary Review* 93 (March 1908): 311, 324. See also William Forbath, "Law and the Shaping of Labor Politics in the United States and England," in Christopher L. Tomlins and Andrew J. King, eds., *Labor Law in America: Historical and Critical Essays* (Baltimore: Johns Hopkins University Press, 1992), esp. 214–22.

24. Ibid., 325.

25. NASL, *Report of Conference*, 87–88.

26. Ibid., 88.

27. Hamilton, *Mary Macarthur*, 68.

28. NASL, *First Annual Report*, 4.

29. Gwynn and Tuckwell, *Sir Charles Dilke*, vol. 2, 552.

30. Question from Mr. O'Grady (Leeds East), *Parliamentary Debates*, 4th ser., 159 (1906): cols. 1636–37. A Royal Commission, appointed by the government, is a prestigious panel of distinguished and expert citizens.

31. Parliamentary question from Leo Chiozza-Money, *Parliamentary Debates*, 4th ser., 161 (1906): col. 476; NASL, *First Annual Report*, 5.

32. Sir Charles W. Dilke, "Prospects of Wages Boards," *Woman Worker*, no. 1 (April 1908): 145.

33. Sidney Low, "Anti-Strike Legislation in Australasia," *Fortnightly Review*, n.s., 91 (1 April 1912): 585. A typical positive assessment is "The Success of the Victorian Act," in Beatrice Webb, B. L. Hutchins, and the Fabian Society, *Socialism and National Minimum* (London: A. C. Fifield, 1909), 73–75. The most devious evasions were unfortunately credited to Chinese employers and "the cunning of the yellow man" (ibid., 73); a foreign work force was not a major issue in Britain, but wherever it was raised there was little to choose between radicals and conservatives in their racism.

34. Ernest Aves, "Report to the Secretary of State for the Home Department on the Wages Boards and Industrial Conciliation and Arbitration Acts of Australia and New Zealand," Cd. 4167 (1908), and Aves's testimony, *Parliamentary Papers* (Commons), "Report from the Select Committee on Home Work," HC 1908, vol. 8, no. 246, 158–73. Hereafter cited as *Select Committee 1908*. Margaret E. MacDonald to the members of the National Council of Women of Great Britain and Ireland, 8 October 1908. JRM/ PRO, PRO 30/69/1369; and MacDonald, *Margaret Ethel MacDonald*, 148.

35. For example, MacDonald, "Sweating and Wages Boards," 761.

36. Ernest Aves, *Select Committee 1908*, 163, 165.

37. Margaret E. MacDonald to Clementina Black, 27 November 1908, JRM Papers/ LSE, vol. 1.

38. "The Sweated Industries Bill," a memorandum from Herbert J. Gladstone, February 1908, Cabinet Papers, CAB 37/91.

39. The historians' consensus on Gladstone's character, according to Roger Davidson, "Llewellyn Smith, the Labour Department and Government Growth," in Gillian Sutherland, ed., *Studies in the Growth of Nineteenth-Century Government* (London: Routledge, 1972), 228.

40. NASL, *First Annual Report*, 6.

41. *Select Committee 1907*, iii.

42. A. G. Gardiner to Herbert Gladstone, 22 May 1907, VG Papers, Add. Mss. 46064.

43. Dilke to Gladstone, 23 May 1907, VG Papers, Add. Mss. 46064. Dilke declined to serve on the committee himself.

44. *Select Committee 1908*, iii.

45. Gladstone, "Sweated Industries Bill," CAB 37/91.

46. Dilke encouraged Gladstone to put the text of his bill before the committee, but only after he had "waited to consult Miss Tuckwell, regarded by me as the real author of the Bill." Dilke to Gladstone, 15 February 1908, VG Papers, Add. Mss. 46065.

47. *Select Committee 1908*, xviii.

48. Ibid., iii, xi, xiv, xii. *Woman Worker*, no. 21 (23 October 1908): 524; and no. 22 (28 October 1908): 549.

49. Ibid., n.s., no. 6 (10 July 1908): 165.

50. Thomas P. Whittaker, "A Minimum Wage for Home Workers," *Nineteenth Century* 64 (September 1908): 522.

51. Richard Arthur Goddard, *Select Committee 1907*, 84–85.

52. Whittaker, "A Minimum Wage," 522.

53. *Select Committee 1907*, 114.

54. Whittaker, "A Minimum Wage," 522.

55. Ibid., 523.

56. *Select Committee 1908*, iv.

57. Leo Chiozza Money unsuccessfully moved that Wages Boards should not be "the only line of effort which should be adopted by Parliament in this connection. . . . we believe that the eradication of the sweating evil would be greatly furthered by the reform of the Poor Law, by suitable legislation to mitigate the distress arising from want of employment, and by old age and invalidity pensions." *Select Committee 1908*, xlvii–xlviii.

58. The gendered and familial assumptions of the "living wage" debate are well represented in *The Industrial Unrest and the Living Wage: Being a Series of Lectures Given at the Inter-Denominational Summer School Held at Swanwick, Derbyshire, June 28th–July 5th, 1913* (London: P. S. King, 1914); see especially George Shann, "The Effect of the Non-Living Wage upon the Individual, the Family, and the State." See also Michelle Barrett and Mary McIntosh, "The Family Wage: Some Problems for Socialists and Feminists," *Capital and Class* 11 (1980): 51–72; Jane Humphries, "The Working Class Family, Women's Liberation, and Class Struggle: The Case of Nineteenth Century British History," *Review of Radical Political Economics* 9 (Fall 1977): 25–41; Hilary Land, "The Family Wage," *Feminist Review* 6 (1980): 55–78; and, in an American context, Alice Kessler-Harris, *A Woman's Wage: Historical Meanings and Social Consequences* (Lexington: University Press of Kentucky, 1990).

59. Anna Davin, "Imperialism and Motherhood," *History Workshop* (Spring 1978): 9–65. See also Jane Lewis, *The Politics of Motherhood: Child and Maternal Welfare in England, 1900–1939* (London: Croom Helm, 1980); Jane Lewis, ed., *Labour and Love: Women's Experience of Home and Family, 1850–1940* (Oxford: Blackwell, 1986).

60. Whittaker, "A Minimum Wage," 517.

61. *Select Committee 1908*, vi.

62. *Woman Worker*, n.s., no. 6 (10 July 1908): 165.

63. *Select Committee 1908*, iii.

64. Ibid., xv.

65. Draft letter, Margaret E. MacDonald to the editor of the *Morning Post*, 11 February 1909; MacDonald to Black, 27 November 1908; JRM Papers/LSE, vol. 1. Macarthur had the same information and regarded the narrow majority as "the one blot on the recommendations." *Woman Worker*, no. 30 (23 December 1908): 740.

66. *Select Committee 1908*, xiv.

67. "The explanation for the origins of minimum wage legislation in [Britain] lies in the concern of one section of the ruling class with the maintenance of the existing social order and their recognition of the harmful effect of sweated labour on social stability." Morris, *Women Workers*, 225. But the motivation of social control, unless conceived as a deliberate and conscious conspiracy to cry reform while intending domination, is an undiscriminating theory, capable of absorbing all the ostensible motivations of minimum wagers and making for a tautological account insofar as the moderation of any social problem presumably contributes to stability. See also J. R. Hay, "Employers' Attitudes to Social Policy and the Concept of 'Social Control,' 1900–1920," in Pat Thane, ed., *The Origins of British Social Policy* (London: Croom Helm, 1978), 107–25.

68. Webb, *Socialism and National Minimum*, 36–37. See also Gosta Esping-Anderson, *The Three Worlds of Welfare Capitalism* (Princeton: Princeton University Press, 1990).

69. Edward Cadbury and George Shann, *Sweating* (London: Headley Brothers, 1907), 11.

70. *Select Committee 1908*, 30.

71. Gladstone, "The Sweated Industries Bill," CAB 37/91, 5.

72. José Harris, "The Transition to High Politics in English Social Policy, 1880–1914," in Michael Bentley and John Stevenson, eds., *High and Low Politics in Modern Britain* (Oxford: Clarendon Press, 1983), esp. 61; Randolph S. Churchill, *Winston S. Churchill: Volume II, 1901–1914, Young Statesman* (London: Heinemann, 1967), chap. 9.

73. Adelaide Mary Anderson, *Women in the Factory: An Administrative Adventure, 1893–1921* (London: John Murray, 1922), chap. 3; Mary Drake McFeely, *Lady Inspectors: The Campaign for a Better Workplace* (Oxford: Blackwell, 1988).

74. See Roger Davidson and R. Lowe, "Bureaucracy and Innovation in British Welfare Policy, 1870–1945," in W. J. Mommsen, ed., *The Emergence of the Welfare State in Britain and Germany, 1850–1950* (London: Croom Helm, 1981); Davidson, "Llewellyn Smith"; Hubert Llewellyn Smith, *The Board of Trade* (London: Putnam's, 1928); and Jill Pellew, *The Home Office, 1848–1914: From Clerks to Bureaucrats* (Rutherford, N.J.: Fairleigh Dickinson University Press, 1982).

75. Llewellyn Smith to Churchill, 11 August 1908, in Randolph S. Churchill, *Winston S. Churchill: Volume II, Companion, Part 2, 1907–1911* (London: Heinemann, 1969), 834.

76. Gladstone to Churchill, 18 December 1908, in Churchill, *Companion*, 864.

77. See Roger Davidson, *Whitehall and the Labour Problem in Late-Victorian and Edwardian Britain* (London: Croom Helm, 1985). Davidson demonstrates the highly political nature of these statistics and their inadequacies as a basis for policy. In particular, data on out-workers, home workers, and women was largely borrowed from impressionistic surveys published by voluntary organizations. Their own wages and earnings data "related almost entirely to organised labour" (154).

78. Winston S. Churchill, "The Untrodden Field in Politics," *Nation* (London) 2 (7 March 1908): 813. See also Churchill's compilation of his own speeches, *Liberalism and the Social Problem* (London: Hodder and Stoughton, 1909).

79. Mary Macarthur, *Woman Worker*, no. 30 (23 December 1908): 740.

80. Gladstone to Churchill, 18 December 1908, in Churchill, *Companion*, 864.

81. H. H. Asquith to Edward VIII, 26 January 1909, Cabinet Papers, CAB 41 32/1.

82. H. H. Asquith to Churchill, 27 December 1908, in Churchill, *Companion*, 861–62. For May Tennant's career, see McFeely, *Lady Inspectors*.

83. Churchill to Gladstone, 30 December 1908, in Churchill, *Companion*, 865; Churchill to Asquith, 12 January 1909, in ibid., 870.

84. On the autonomous role of state institutions in policymaking, see Peter B. Evans, Dietrich Rueschemeyer, and Theda Skocpol, *Bringing the State Back In* (Cambridge: Cambridge University Press, 1985); and Ann Shola Orloff and Theda Skocpol, "Why Not Equal Protection? Explaining the Politics of Public Social Spending in Britain, 1900–1911, and the United States, 1880s–1920," *American Sociological Review* 49 (December 1984): 726–50.

85. Stephen Toulmin, Liberal M.P. for Bury, on the second reading of the Sweated Industries Bill, 21 February 1908, *Parliamentary Debates* (Commons), 4th ser., 184 (1908): col. 1196.

86. See, for example, the comments of Alfred Lyttelton, Liberal M.P. for St. Georges, Hanover Square, *Parliamentary Debates* (Commons), 5th ser., 4 (1909): col. 351.

87. NASL, *First Annual Report*, 10.

88. Churchill to Asquith, 12 January 1909, in Churchill, *Companion*, 870.

89. Winston S. Churchill, Cabinet memorandum, 26 January 1909, in Churchill, *Companion*, 880. Also his comment on the role of the public representatives, *Parliamentary Debates* (Commons), 5th ser., 4 (1909): col. 386.

90. NASL, *First Annual Report*, 11.

91. *Parliamentary Debates* (Commons), 5th ser., 4 (1909): col. 352.

92. Ibid., 374.

93. Ibid., 388.

94. NASL, *First Annual Report*, 10. Percentages calculated from Morris, *Women Workers*, 9 (based on the 1891 census).

95. Schedule by Sir H. Llewellyn Smith, attached to Churchill's Cabinet memorandum, 27 January 1909, Cabinet Papers, CAB 37/97.

96. *Parliamentary Debates* (Commons), 5th ser., 4 (1909): col. 404. Three-quarters of chain-makers hand-hammering the cheapest chains were women, making one-third of the wages earned by men in the trade. The men worked in factories and were unionized; the women worked in home workshops, where a long campaign resulted in the formation of the Hammered Chain Branch of the NFWW, led by Mary Macarthur, in 1907. See Cadbury and Shann, *Sweating*, 31 and 38–40; R. H. Tawney, *Studies in the Minimum Wage, No. 1: The Establishment of Minimum Rates in the Chain-Making Industry under the Trade Boards Act of 1909* (London: G. Bell and Sons, 1914), esp. 25.

97. Quoted by R. H. Tawney, *Studies in the Minimum Wage*, 21. See also *Parliamentary Debates* (Commons), 5th ser., 4 (1909): cols. 366–69.

98. Cadbury and Shann, *Sweating*, 39. Compare the earlier campaign against women coal miners engaged in "men's work," Angela V. John, *By the Sweat of Their Brow: Women Workers at Victorian Coal Mines* (London: Routledge, 1984).

99. Tawney, *Studies in the Minimum Wage*, xi.

100. NASL, *First Annual Report*, 10. The Webb's clinical proposal was a minimum

"to prevent bodily deterioration." Sidney Webb and Beatrice Webb, *Industrial Democracy* (London: Longmans Green, 1911), 774–75.

101. NASL handbill, in possession of the author.

102. Churchill, Cabinet memo, 12 March 1909, in Churchill, *Companion*, 880.

103. Churchill to Clementina Churchill, 28 April 1909, in Churchill, *Companion*, 887.

104. Irish members wanted Ireland exempted to protect its distinctive rural economy; see *Parliamentary Debates* (Commons), 5th ser., 4 (1909): cols. 377–83, 396–400; and ibid., no. 5 (1909): 976. To some, this meant the low wages and evasion of labor laws practiced there; see McFeely, *Lady Inspectors*, chaps. 10–12. Between the Act of Union of 1800 and the Government of Ireland Act of 1920, Ireland was fully incorporated in the United Kingdom. Legislation applied throughout the U.K., except in a few cases such as religious establishment. Although Ireland was nominally included in the Trade Boards Act, confrontation was avoided by allowing separate Irish boards within scheduled industries. The history of the minimum wage in Ireland is outlined in Gerard V. McMahon, "Ireland and Britain—Minimum Wages in the Poor Nations of Europe," *Low Pay Review* 30 (Summer 1987): 13–20.

105. *Parliamentary Debates* (Commons), 5th ser. 4 (1909): col. 350.

106. NASL, *Third Annual Report*, 5.

107. Ibid., 5.

108. J. W. Hills to Dilke, 30 March 1909, CWD Papers, Add. Mss. 43921.

109. NASL, *Fifth Annual Report*, 4.

110. Quoted in Mary McDowell, "The National Women's Trade Union League," *Survey* (16 October 1909): 105.

111. McDowell, "The National Women's Trade Union League," 105.

112. Trade Boards Act, clause 4 (1).

113. Dorothy Sells, *British Wages Boards: A Study in Industrial Democracy* (Washington, D.C.: Brookings Institution, 1939), 27. See also F. J. Bayliss, *British Wages Councils* (Oxford: Blackwell, 1962).

114. The "ambulance" image is from Bayliss, *British Wages Councils*, 13.

115. See Fraser P. Davidson, *A Guide to the Wages Act 1986* (London: Financial Training Publications, 1986); Anne E. Morris and Susan M. Nott, *Working Women and the Law: Equality and Discrimination in Theory and Practice* (London: Routledge, 1991), esp. chap. 6; and Low Pay Network, *Save Wages Councils: A Briefing Paper on the Abolition of Wages Councils* (London: Low Pay Unit, [1992]).

116. McDowell, "National Women's Trade Union League," 105.

117. American Federation of Labor, *Report of Proceedings of the Twenty-Ninth Annual Convention, Held at Toronto, Ontario, November 8 to 20, 1909* (Washington, D.C.: Law Reporter Printing, 1909), 155.

Chapter Four
A Sex Problem

1. James J. Mallon, "The Case for Wages Boards," 359–449, Mme E. [*sic*] Kelley, "Le Travail a Domicile et la Ligue d'Acheteurs en Amerique," 449–55, esp. 449, in *Première Conférence Internationale des Ligues Sociales d'Acheteurs, Genève, les 24, 25 et 26 Septembre, 1908* (Fribourg, Switzerland, 1909). Kelley's trip reported in Executive Committee minutes, 16 October 1908, NCL Papers, series A, box 1.

2. Emilie Hutchinson, "Women's Wages: A Study of the Wages of Industrial Women and of Measures Suggested to Increase Them" (Ph.D. dissertation, Columbia Univer-

sity, 1919), 80. Hutchinson had taught at Mount Holyoke, Wellesley, and Barnard; her Columbia supervisor for this doctoral dissertation, Henry Seager, was an NCL adviser on the minimum wage.

3. Clara M. Beyer, *History of Labor Legislation for Women in Three States*, Bulletin of the Women's Bureau, no. 66 (Washington, D.C.: GPO, 1929), 55. Beyer was the first secretary of the District of Columbia Minimum Wage Board, 1918–21, a lobbyist for the NCL in New York State in the 1920s, and joined the Children's Bureau and then the Labor Department in 1933 as associate director of the Division of Labor Standards, where she was again a key minimum wager. Beyer cited: Congress, Senate, *Report on Condition of Women and Child Wage-Earners in the United States*, vols. 1–12 (Washington, D.C.: GPO, 1910–11); Elizabeth B. Butler, *Women and the Trades* (New York: Russell Sage Foundation, 1909); Edith Abbott, *Women in Industry* (New York: Appleton, 1910); Annie M. MacLean, *Wage-Earning Women* (New York: Macmillan, 1910); Louise M. Bosworth, "The Living Wage of Women Workers," *Annals of the American Academy of Political and Social Science* 37 (Supplement; May 1911): 1–90.

4. See Eileen Boris, *Home to Work: Motherhood and the Politics of Industrial Homework in the United States* (Cambridge: Cambridge University Press, 1994), chap. 2; I am grateful for an early sight of the manuscript. On the garment industry, see Christine Stansell, "The Origins of the Sweatshop: Women and Early Industrialization in New York City," in Michael H. Frisch and Daniel J. Walkowitz, eds., *Working-Class America: Essays on Labor, Community, and American Society* (Urbana: University of Illinois Press, 1983), 78–103; David Montgomery, *The Fall of the House of Labor* (Cambridge: Cambridge University Press, 1987), 116–23; and Steven Fraser, *Labor Will Rule: Sidney Hillman and the Rise of American Labor* (New York: Free Press, 1991), 23–39.

5. Urban population grew dramatically between 1850 and 1900: in Massachusetts from 25 percent to 75 percent, and in New York from 25 percent to nearly 70 percent. Britain's urban population grew from 50 percent in 1850 to 72 percent in 1891. New York City's population tripled between 1880 and 1900; London tripled over sixty years. See U.S. Census Office, *Statistical Atlas of the United States, 1900* (Washington D.C.: U.S. Census Office, 1903), plates 20, 23; and Adna F. Weber, *The Growth of Cities in the Nineteenth Century* (New York: Macmillan, 1899; reprint, Ithaca: Cornell University Press, 1963), 46–47.

6. William D. P. Bliss, ed., *Encyclopedia of Social Reform* (New York: Funk and Wagnalls, 1897), 1299.

7. Helen L. Sumner, "Social and Economic Conditions: Women and Child Labor," in *The American Labor Year Book, 1916* (New York: Rand School of Social Science, [1916]), esp. 265.

8. New York, *Fourth Report of the Factory Investigating Commission, 1915* (Albany, N.Y.: J. B. Lyon, 1915), vol. 5, 2543; hereafter cited as *FIC* 5. See, for women's labor market position, Valerie Kincade Oppenheimer, *The Female Labor Force in the United States: Demographic and Economic Factors Governing its Growth and Composition* (Berkeley: Institute of International Studies, University of California, 1970), 3; for economic factors, Claudia Goldin, *Understanding the Gender Gap: An Economic History of Women* (New York: Oxford University Press, 1990); and discussion in Ava Baron, ed., *Work Engendered: Toward a New History of American Labor* (Ithaca: Cornell University Press, 1991).

9. *FIC* 5.2543; child labor figures from William D. P. Bliss et al., eds., *New Encyclopedia of Social Reform* (New York: Funk and Wagnalls, 1908), vol. 2, 1180. See also Edna D. Bullock, ed., *Selected Articles on Child Labor*, 2d ed. (White Plains, N.Y.: H. W. Wilson, 1915).

10. *FIC* 5.2542–43. Boris finds ethnic differences in garment industry employment between factories and tenements, machine and handwork, skilled and less skilled: Boris, *Home to Work*, chap. 2. The minimum wage was rarely discussed in relation to immigration. In 1910, Father John Ryan claimed that cheap immigrant labor was a cause of low wages; see "A Minimum Wage and Minimum Wage Boards," *Proceedings of the National Conference of Charities and Correction* (1910): 457–75. Minimum wage laws as a form of immigration control were proposed by Paul U. Kellogg; see "An Immigrant Labor Tariff," *Survey* (7 January 1911): 529–31; "The Minimum Wage and Immigrant Labor," *Proceedings of the National Conference of Charities and Correction* (1911): 165–77; "Communications, Minimum Wage and Immigration Restriction," *Survey* (4 February 1911): 789–92; and "Immigration and the Minimum Wage," *Annals of the American Academy of Political and Social Science* 48 (July 1913): 66–77.

11. On black women in the labor force, see Jacqueline Jones, *Labor of Love, Labor of Sorrow: Black Women, Work, and the Family, from Slavery to the Present* (New York: Basic Books, 1985); Debra Lynn Newman, "Black Women Workers in the Twentieth Century," *Sage* 3 (Spring 1986): 10–15; on domestic service, Elizabeth Ross Haynes, "Negroes in Domestic Service in the United States" (1923), in Darlene Clark Hine, ed., *Black Women in United States History: The Twentieth Century* (Brooklyn, N.Y.: Carlson, 1990), vol. 2, 507–65; on home work, Eileen Boris, "Black Women and Paid Labor in the Home: Industrial Homework in Chicago in the 1920s," in Eileen Boris and Cynthia R. Daniels, eds., *Homework: Historical and Contemporary Perspectives on Paid Labor at Home* (Urbana: University of Illinois Press, 1989), 33–52. A rare instance when race was directly discussed in minimum wage history is described in Vivien Hart, "Feminism and Bureaucracy: The Minimum Wage Experiment in the District of Columbia," *Journal of American Studies* 26 (April 1992): 13–14. Black women's work situation gave rise to their own political activity; see Sharon Harley, "When Your Work Is Not Who You Are: The Development of a Working Class Consciousness among Afro-American Women," in Noralee Frankel and Nancy S. Dye, eds., *Gender, Class, Race, and Reform in the Progressive Era* (Lexington: University Press of Kentucky, 1991), 42–55.

12. Mrs. Katherine Philips Edson, addressing the Minimum Wage Conference of the National Civic Federation, 25 February 1915, NCF Papers, box 135A.

13. See Maud Nathan, *The Story of an Epoch-Making Movement* (New York: Doubleday, 1926).

14. See George G. Kirstein, *Stores and Unions: A Study of the Growth of Unionism in Dry Goods and Department Stores* (New York: Fairchild Publications, 1950). H. J. Conway, secretary of the Retail Clerks' International Protective Association, served on an NCF "committee to take up the minimum wage question," from 1913–16. See transcripts of meetings in 1913 and 1914, NCF Papers, box 135A; and correspondence leading to Conway's endorsement of the committee's hostile report on the minimum wage: Gertrude Beeks to Conway, 30 December 1915; Conway to Beeks, 29 January 1916; and Beeks to Conway, 8 February 1916, NCF Papers, box 135A. On women's employment in retailing, see Susan Porter Benson, *Counter Cultures: Saleswomen, Managers, and Customers, 1890–1940* (Urbana: University of Illinois Press, 1986). On Britain, see Wilfred B. Whitaker, *Victorian and Edwardian Shopworkers* (Newton Abbot: David and Charles, 1973).

15. *FIC* 5.2544–46; Mary Van Kleeck's evidence, ibid., 2628–40, esp. 2632.

16. Ibid., 2621. The issue of the individual or family basis of women's budgets was the same in the U.S.A. as in Britain. See Alice Kessler-Harris, *A Woman's Wage: Historical Meanings and Social Consequences* (Lexington: University Press of Kentucky, 1990);

Leslie Woodcock Tentler, *Wage-Earning Women: Industrial Work and Family Life in the United States, 1900–1930* (New York: Oxford University Press, 1979).

17. Cynthia R. Daniels, "Between Home and Factory: Homeworkers and the State," in Boris and Daniels, eds., *Homework*, 15, 16. See Hilary Silver, "The Demand for Homework: Evidence from the U.S. Census," in ibid., on measuring the incidence of home work.

18. U.S. Bureau of the Census, *Historical Statistics of the United States, Colonial Times to the Present* (Washington, D.C.: GPO, 1976), series D 765–78.

19. Lawyer Manfred W. Ehrich, *FIC* 5.2922.

20. Legislation was enacted in Massachusetts (1912); California, Colorado, Minnesota, Nebraska, Oregon, Utah, Washington, and Wisconsin (1913); Arkansas and Kansas (1915); Arizona (1917); D.C. (1918); North Dakota, Texas, and Puerto Rico (1919); and South Dakota (1923). Nebraska repealed (1919); Texas repealed (1921); and courts struck down legislation in D.C. (1923), in Puerto Rico and Wisconsin (1924), in Arizona, Kansas, and Minnesota (1925), and in Arkansas (1926). See the chronology in Department of Labor, *Growth of Labor Laws in the United States* (Washington, D.C.: GPO, 1967), 93–97; and Elizabeth Brandeis, "Labor Legislation," in John R. Commons, ed., *History of Labor in the United States, 1896–1932* (New York: Macmillan, 1935), vol. 3, 501–39. The Supreme Court case was *Adkins v. Children's Hospital of Washington, D.C.*, 261 U.S. 525 (1923).

21. Florence Kelley, "Minimum Wage Laws," *Journal of Political Economy* 20 (December 1912): 999.

22. Beyer, *History of Labor Legislation*, 1–2.

23. Massachusetts shared many social characteristics with Britain; see Ann Shola Orloff and Theda Skocpol, "Why Not Equal Protection? Explaining the Politics of Public Social Spending in Britain, 1900–1911, and the United States, 1880s–1920," *American Sociological Review* 49 (December 1984): 726–50. Accounts of some crucial states include Beyer, *History of Labor Legislation*, for Massachusetts, New York, and California; for California, Jacqueline R. Braitman, "Katherine Philips Edson: A Progressive Feminist in California's Era of Reform" (Ph.D. dissertation, University of California at Los Angeles, 1988); for Oregon, Sister Miriam Theresa (Caroline J. Gleason), *Oregon Legislation for Women in Industry*, Bulletin of the Women's Bureau, no. 90 (Washington, D.C.: GPO, 1931); Edwin V. O'Hara, *A Living Wage by Legislation: The Oregon Experience* (Salem: State Printing Department, 1916); and for Washington State, Joseph F. Tripp, "Toward an Efficient and Moral Society: Minimum-Wage Legislation in Washington State, 1913–1925," *Pacific Northwest Quarterly* 67 (1976): 97–112.

24. See Susan M. Kingsbury, ed., *Labor Laws and Their Enforcement, with Special Reference to Massachusetts* (New York: Longmans Green, 1911). For the reform culture of Massachusetts, see Arthur Mann, *Yankee Reformers in the Urban Age: Social Reform in Boston, 1880–1900* (New York: Harper Torchbooks, 1954).

25. See Sarah Deutsch, "Learning to Talk More like a Man: Boston Women's Class-Bridging Organizations, 1870–1940," *American Historical Review* 97 (April 1991): 379–404.

26. *Twenty-Ninth Annual Report of the Women's Educational and Industrial Union, Boston, Massachusetts, January 1908* (Boston: WEIU, 1908), 21, WEIU Papers.

27. Deutsch, "Learning to Talk," 396.

28. Kathryn Kish Sklar, "*Hull House Maps and Papers*: Social Science as Women's Work in the 1890s," in Martin Bulmer, Kevin Bales, and Kathryn Kish Sklar, eds., *The Social Survey in Historical Perspective, 1880–1940* (Cambridge: Cambridge University

Press, 1991), 129. See also Ellen Fitzpatrick, *Endless Crusade: Women Social Scientists and Progressive Reform* (New York: Oxford University Press, 1990).

29. Kingsbury, *Labor Laws*, was vol. 2 of the Studies in Economic Relations of Women of the WEIU; "Commission on Woman's Work," AALL Papers, reel 61.

30. The Massachusetts Commission was indebted to "professors Emily G. Balch and Susan M. Kingsbury for their personal inquiries into the working of the English minimum wage law during their sojourn in England last summer," Commonwealth of Massachusetts, *Report of the Commission on Minimum Wage Boards*, House no. 1697 (Boston: Wright and Potter Printing, 1912), 7; Nathan, *Epoch-Making Movement*, chap. 5; Morton Keller, "Anglo-American Politics, 1900–1930," *Comparative Studies in Society and History* 22 (1980): 458–77; Kenneth O. Morgan, "The Future at Work: Anglo-American Progressivism 1890–1917," in H. C. Allen and Roger Thompson, eds., *Contrast and Connection: Bicentennial Essays in Anglo-American History* (London: Bell, 1976), 245–71; and C. L. Mowat, "Social Legislation in Britain and the United States in the Early Twentieth Century: A Problem in the History of Ideas," *Historical Studies* 7 (1969), 81–96.

31. Minutes, 14 October 1908, CLM Papers, box 1.

32. *Tenth Annual Report of the Consumers' League of Massachusetts* (Boston: Lincoln and Smith Press, 1908), 3. Earlier discussions of wage standards are reported in CLM minutes, e.g., 24 May 1898, 10 October 1906, 13 March 1907, and 12 June 1907, CLM Papers, box 1.

33. *Eleventh Annual Report of the Consumers' League of Massachusetts* (Boston: A. T. Howard, [1909]), 3.

34. "Address by Mrs. Glendower Evans," *City Club Bulletin* (Philadelphia) 6 (27 January 1913): 203.

35. Ibid.; NWTUL, *Third Biennial Convention of the National Women's Trade Union League of America, Boston, June 12 to 17, 1911, Inclusive*, 22. Evans attended the 1909 Labour Party conference and visited and befriended Bruce and Katherine Glasier, members of the Independent Labor Party who lived in principled poverty. On her return to the States, Evans established a trust fund for the Glasiers; their first child, born in 1910, was named John Glendower Bruce Glasier. See L. Thompson, *The Enthusiasts: A Biography of John and Katherine Bruce Glasier* (London: Gollancz, 1971), 159–61.

36. Minutes of the National Conference of the NWTUL, Norfolk, Virginia, 13 November 1907, PWTUL, reel 1. The founding of the NWTUL in Boston in 1903, during an AFL convention, is recounted in Philip S. Foner, *Women and the American Labor Movement: Colonial Times to the Eve of World War I* (New York: Free Press, 1979), 298–302.

37. National Executive Board meeting, 20 May 1910, Boston WTUL report, PWTUL, reel 1.

38. Beyer, *History of Labor Legislation*, 56.

39. NWTUL, *Third Biennial Convention*, 5; *Life and Labor* 1 (March 1911): 93.

40. "Address by Mrs. Glendower Evans," 203.

41. According to the Boston report to the NWTUL Executive Board meeting, 20 May 1910, "The League called a conference of unionists and social workers to consider bringing in a minimum wage board bill. After much conferring and upon the urgent advice of Mr. Brandeis, the League decided to postpone legislative work for another year." PWTUL, reel 1; Louis Brandeis to Emily Greene Balch, 3 February 1911, in Melvin I. Urofsky and David W. Levy, eds., *Letters of Louis D. Brandeis* (Albany, N.Y.: State University of New York Press, 1972), vol. 2, 403; H. LaRue Brown to Elizabeth Glendower Evans, 1 September 1926; "Transcript of Taped Reminiscences," 18,

LRB Papers, box 16; H. LaRue Brown, "Massachusetts and the Minimum Wage," *Annals of the American Academy of Political and Social Science* 48 (July 1913): 13–21. Brown, like Brandeis, was born in Louisville, trained at Harvard Law School, and practiced law in Boston. He married Dorothy Kirchwey, sister of *Nation* editor Freda Kirchwey. See references in Sara Alpern, *Freda Kirchwey: A Woman of the Nation* (Cambridge: Harvard University Press, 1987).

42. Massachusetts, *Report*, 6.

43. Mary W. Dewson, "Mrs. Glendower Evans," annotated as "An Address by Miss M. W. Dewson, Member SSB, Boston, Jan. 28, 1938, Memorial Service at Ford Hall, Boston," MWD Papers, box 9. On Dewson, see James T. Patterson, "Mary Dewson and the American Minimum Wage Movement," *Labor History* 5 (Spring 1964): 134–52; and Susan Ware, *Partner and I: Molly Dewson, Feminism, and New Deal Politics* (New Haven: Yale University Press, 1987), chap. 3. See also Evans's speech to the NWTUL in response to an ovation for her appointment, *Third Biennial Convention*, 21–22.

44. Massachusetts, *Report*. See Elizabeth Glendower Evans, "The Minimum Wage for Women," *Twentieth Century Magazine* 6 (1912): 65–69, for a justification of the commission's recommendations.

45. Brown to Evans, 17 July 1912 and 23 July 1912; Evans to Brown, 19 July 1912, LRB Papers, box 9. Brown suggested a fee of one thousand dollars, half of which he waived; the other half was paid by Evans. Brown's papers record his public lobbying and private negotiation on behalf of the bill. See H. La Rue Brown, *The Wages Board Act: A Statement of Its Scope and Purpose and a Reply to Its Opponents* (1912); Brown to Evans, 20 April 1912; Brown to Brandeis, 23 May 1912; Brown to Rep. James F. Cavanaugh, 15 April 1912, LRB Papers, box 9; and "Transcript of Taped Reminiscences," 18, LRB Papers, box 16.

46. *Life and Labor* 1 (March 1911): 93; Beyer, *History of Labor Legislation*, 57.

47. Beyer, *History of Labor Legislation*, 2–3, 57. The effectiveness of organized women textile workers in Britain was relative; see Joanna Bornet, "Lost Leaders: Women, Trade Unionism and the Case of the General Union of Textile Workers, 1875–1914," in Angela V. John, ed., *Unequal Opportunities: Women's Employment in England, 1800–1918* (Oxford: Blackwell, 1986), 207–33; Barbara Drake, *Women in Trade Unions* (London: Labour Research Department, 1920; reprint, London: Virago, 1984), 118–40.

48. NWTUL, *Third Biennial Convention*, 39.

49. "Synopsis of Activities of Consumers' League of Massachusetts, 1897–1907" (typescript), 6, 12, CLM Papers. For the contested legal position of union labels as a form of labor boycott, see William E. Forbath, *Law and the Shaping of the American Labor Movement* (Cambridge: Harvard University Press, 1991), 90–94.

50. "Minutes, 1897–1909," 23 September 1897; "Synopsis of Activities," 18, 24 May 1898; references to local discussion and communication with the National Consumers' League on reluctance to "enter into the question of wages," "Minutes of Meetings of the Consumers' League of Massachusetts," 10 October 1906, 13 March 1907, 12 June 1907; minutes, 13 March 1907, CLM Papers, box 1.

51. Beyer, *History of Labor Legislation*, 59.

52. Brown, *The Wages Boards Act*, 7.

53. H. LaRue Brown to Representative James F. Cavanaugh, 15 April 1912, LRB Papers, box 9. See Stuart D. Brandes, *American Welfare Capitalism, 1880–1940* (Chicago: University of Chicago Press, 1976).

54. NWTUL, *Third Biennial Convention*, 22.

55. "Address by Mrs. Glendower Evans," 203.

56. Beyer, *History of Labor Legislation*, 60.

57. *The Minimum Wage: A Failing Experiment* (Boston: Executive Committee of the Merchants and Manufacturers of Massachusetts, 1916), 5.

58. Brown to Evans, 14 June 1912, LRB Papers, box 9.

59. Sue Ainslie Clark to Mrs. Robins [January 1912], PWTUL, reel 1. See also Henry F. Bedford, *Socialism and the Workers in Massachusetts, 1886–1912* (Amherst: University of Massachusetts Press, 1966), chap. 8; Ardis Cameron, "Bread and Roses Revisited: Women's Culture and Working-Class Activism in the Lawrence Strike of 1912," in Ruth Milkman, ed., *Women, Work and Protest: A Century of U.S. Women's Labor History* (Boston: Routledge, 1985), 42–61.

60. Edwin F. McSweeney to John B. Andrews, 29 November 1912, AALL Papers, reel 8.

61. Brown to Rep. James F. Cavanaugh, 15 April 1912, LRB Papers, box 9.

62. Edwin F. McSweeney to John B. Andrews, 29 November 1912, AALL Papers, reel 8. See also "Address by Hon. H. La Rue Brown, Esq.," *City Club Bulletin* (Philadelphia) 6 (27 January 1913): 199: "It was passed by a Republican legislature, under some pressure, perhaps, from the political conditions which were obtaining . . . last spring," with unanimous Democratic support.

63. Beyer, *History of Labor Legislation*, 60. Louis D. Brandeis to Arthur N. Holcombe, 5 April 1912, in Brandeis, *Letters*, vol. 2, 576. See Philippa Strum, *Louis D. Brandeis: Justice for the People* (Cambridge: Harvard University Press, 1984), for Brandeis's vision of a nonconflictual, decentralized "industrial democracy."

64. Brown, *The Wage Boards Act*, 4.

65. Kelley, "Minimum-Wage Laws," 1002–3.

66. Massachusetts, *Report*, 25–26. Emphasis added.

67. Evans, "The Minimum Wage for Women," 67.

68. Mary Morton Kehew to Brown, 15 March 1911, LRB Papers, box 9.

69. Brandeis to Holcombe, 5 April 1912, Brandeis, *Letters*, vol. 2, 576.

70. The national campaign was a classic example of what Theda Skocpol calls "widespread federated interests" promulgating social policy agendas at this time. See Theda Skocpol, *Protecting Soldiers and Mothers: The Political Origins of Social Policies in the United States* (Cambridge: Harvard University Press, 1992), 55–57; Theda Skocpol et al., "Women's Associations and the Enactment of Mothers' Pensions in the United States," *American Political Science Review* 87 (September 1993): 686–701. For contemporary note of the multiplication of group interests, see Arthur F. Bentley, *The Process of Government* (Chicago: University of Chicago Press, 1908; reprint, ed. Peter H. Odegard, Cambridge: Harvard University Press, 1967).

71. Florence Kelley to Dr. Jessica B. Peixotto, 15 April 1912, NCL Papers, series B, box 11.

72. "Address of the President, Mrs. Raymond Robins," NWTUL, *Fourth Biennial Convention of the National Women's Trade Union League of America, Saint Louis, June 2 to 7, 1913, Inclusive*, 2. Elizabeth Anne Payne, *Reform, Labor, and Feminism: Margaret Dreier Robins and the Women's Trade Union League* (Urbana: University of Illinois Press, 1988), is in part a biography of Robins; see also Mary E. Dreier, *Margaret Dreier Robins: Her Life, Letters, and Work* (New York: Island Press Cooperative, 1950).

73. See Foner, *Women and the American Labor Movement*; Fraser, *Labor Will Rule*, esp. chap. 3 on the NWTUL and labor relations in the Chicago garment trades; Colette A. Hyman, "Labor Organizing and Female Institution-Building: The Chicago Women's Trade Union League, 1904–24," in Milkman, *Women, Work, and Protest*, 22–41.

74. Mary McDowell, "The National Women's Trade Union League," *Survey* (16 October 1909): 107.

75. Ibid. Nancy Schrom Dye, *As Equals and as Sisters: Feminism, the Labor Movement, and the Women's Trade Union League of New York* (Columbia: University of Missouri Press, 1980), argues that the league introduced a legislative strategy around 1913, contrary to feminist and working women's needs. Recent studies find an earlier commitment to legislation; see Diane Kirkby, *Alice Henry: The Power of Pen and Voice* (Cambridge: Cambridge University Press, 1991), esp. chap. 5; and Payne, *Reform, Labor, and Feminism*, 99.

76. Illinois efforts reported by Mrs. Robins to the AFL convention; see AFL, *Report of Proceedings of the Thirty-First Annual Convention of the American Federation of Labor. Held at Atlanta, Georgia, November 13 to 25, 1911, Inclusive* (Washington, D.C.: Law Reporter Printing, 1911), 179; NWTUL, *Third Biennial Convention*, 6.

77. 1903 insignia, reproduced in Payne, *Reform, Labor, and Feminism*, plates between 116 and 117.

78. See Kessler-Harris, *A Woman's Wage*, chap. 1; Martha May, "Bread before Roses: American Workingmen, Labor Unions, and the Family Wage," in Milkman, *Women, Work, and Protest*, 1–21. Father John Ryan of Minnesota, whose book *A Living Wage: Its Ethical and Economic Aspects* appeared in 1906, was a leading exponent of women's dependency; he participated in the Minnesota minimum wage campaign and on NCL committees. Although he claimed to be a founding father of the campaign his strong, inegalitarian views on gender roles did not determine the form of legislation. John A. Ryan to Florence Kelley, 4 June 1923, NCL Papers, series B, box 12. On Catholic labor activism, see Marc Karson, *American Labor Unions and Politics, 1900–1918* (Carbondale: Southern Illinois University Press, 1958); and David Montgomery, *Fall of the House of Labor*, 306–10.

79. NWTUL, *Fourth Biennial Convention, 1913*, 6.

80. "Minutes of the National Conference of the NWTUL, Norfolk, Va., November 13, 1907," PWTUL, reel 1. "It was moved that Miss Mary Macarthur be invited to come to America for six months to stir up interest in the organization of women. After much discussion the motion was laid on the table." "Minutes of the Annual Meeting of the NWTUL, April 18th, 1907." PWTUL, reel 1.

81. Kirkby, *Alice Henry*, chaps. 1–2.

82. Ibid., 20, 151. Kirkby discusses Henry's socialist and feminist experience, chaps. 1–2, and 120–23. Compare an American feminist's migration to Australia and back: Hester Eisenstein, *Gender Shock: Practicing Feminism on Two Continents* (Boston: Beacon Press, 1991). The influence of the Australasian model was usually by way of Britain, but see the report of a trip to the Antipodes by Henry Demarest Lloyd, "A Living Wage by Law," *Independent* 52, part 2 (1900): 2330–32; and academic writing, for example, Victor S. Clark, "The Labor Party and the Constitution in Australia," *Journal of Political Economy* 19 (June 1911): 479–90; Matthew B. Hammond, "The Minimum Wage in Great Britain and Australia," *Annals of the American Academy of Political and Social Science* 48 (July 1913): 22–36, and "Judicial Interpretation of the Minimum Wage in Australia," *American Economic Review* 3 (June 1913): 259–86. See also Peter J. Coleman, *Progressivism and the World of Reform: New Zealand and the Origins of the American Welfare State* (Lawrence: University Press of Kansas, 1987).

83. Kirkby, *Alice Henry*, 119.

84. Payne, *Reform, Labor, and Feminism*, 127.

85. Maurine Weiner Greenwald, "Working-Class Feminism and the Family Wage

Ideal: The Seattle Debate on Married Women's Right to Work, 1914–1920," *Journal of American History* 76 (June 1989): 118–49, esp. 141.

86. Nathan, *Epoch-Making Movement*, 23. Nathan's appendix G reports on each state branch; and Florence Kelley, "Aims and Principles of the Consumers' League," *American Journal of Sociology* 5 (November 1899): 289–304. See also Kathryn Kish Sklar, "Two Political Cultures in the Progressive Era: The National Consumers' League and the American Association for Labor Legislation," in Linda Kerber, Alice Kessler-Harris, and Kathryn Kish Sklar, eds., *American History as Women's History* (Chapel Hill: University of North Carolina Press, forthcoming); Sklar discusses the collaborative culture and fostering of local branches within the NCL; Boris, *Home to Work*, chap. 3, discusses the NCL and the theory of consumer politics.

87. Constitution of the New York Consumers' League, in Nathan, *Epoch-Making Movement*, 26. Emphases added.

88. Ibid., 38.

89. See Josephine Goldmark, *Impatient Crusader* (Urbana: University of Illinois Press, 1953); Kathryn Kish Sklar, *Florence Kelley and Women's Political Culture: Doing the Nation's Work, 1830–1930*, vol. 1: *1830–1900* (New Haven: Yale University Press, 1994); Kathryn Kish Sklar, "Hull House in the 1890s: A Community of Women Reformers," *Signs* 10 (Summer 1985): 658–77; *The Autobiography of Florence Kelley: Notes of Sixty Years*, ed. Kathryn Kish Sklar (Chicago: Charles H. Kerr, 1986).

90. Nathan, *Epoch-Making Movement*, 25.

91. "The Work of the National Consumers' League during the Year Ending March 1, 1910," *Annals of the American Academy of Political and Social Science* (Supplement; September 1910): 21; NCL, *Eighth Annual Report, Year Ending March 5, 1907* (no imprint), 12.

92. *FIC* 5.2819.

93. NCL Council minutes, 2 March 1909, NCL Papers, series A, box 7.

94. Chaired by Professor Emily Greene Balch of Wellesley, members were Henry Seager of Columbia, Herbert Mills of Vassar, and Holcombe and Ryan. With Balch distracted by other interests and Holcombe ill, Seager's preference for delay on Balch's bill, which "would apply to trades largely employing women and children," weighed large. Seager's opinion was "that it would be advisable to delay further action in this matter till English experience could be used to influence the American judicial mind." NCL Executive Committee minutes, 21 May 1909, 1 March 1910, and 21 October 1910, NCL Papers, series A, box 1.

95. "Report of the Special Committee on Minimum Wage Boards," "The Minimum Wages Bill Pending in Wisconsin," NCL, *Twelfth Report, Year Ending February 7, 1911* (no imprint [1911]), 51–52.

96. "Report of the Special Committee on Minimum Wages Boards," NCL, *Thirteenth Report, Year Ending January 19, 1912* (no imprint), 41.

97. "A Minimum Wage Commission Bill," NCL, *Fourteenth Report* (no imprint [1913]), 52–57.

98. Reprinted in Nancy F. Cott, *The Grounding of Modern Feminism* (New Haven: Yale University Press, 1987), 242.

99. *The Minimum Wage: A Failing Experiment*, 5, 13. Emphasis in the original.

100. See Irwin Yellowitz, *Labor and the Progressive Movement in New York State, 1897–1916* (Ithaca: Cornell University Press, 1965), chaps. 3–4; on the NCCC and the *Survey*, Clarke A. Chambers, *Paul U. Kellogg and the Survey: Voices for Social Welfare and Social Justice* (Minneapolis: University of Minnesota Press, 1971); on the AALL,

Sklar, "Two Political Cultures"; and Skocpol, *Protecting Soldiers and Mothers*, esp. chap. 3.

101. Goldmark, *Impatient Crusader*, 68.

102. Sklar, "Two Political Cultures."

103. Goldmark, *Impatient Crusader*, 152–59.

104. Minutes, Executive Committee meeting, 29 December 1909, 2; meeting of the General Administrative Council, Chicago, 11 June 1910, 3; AALL Papers, reel 61.

105. See Mitchell's testimony to the FIC 5.2721–28.

106. Florence Kelley to Dr. Jessica B. Peixotto, 15 April 1912, NCL Papers, series B, box 11.

107. Gwendolyn Mink, *Old Labor and New Immigrants in American Political Development: Union, Party, and State, 1875–1920* (Ithaca: Cornell University Press, 1986), describes how the AFL boxed itself into a defensive and conservative relation with industry and the state, out of fear of the consequences of mass immigration. See also Montgomery, *Fall of the House of Labor*, esp. chap. 6; and Fraser, *Labor Will Rule*, chap. 4 on the origins and early years of the ACWA.

108. Florence Kelley to Amy G. Maher, 29 October 1920, NCL Papers, series B, box 718. See also Robins's personal recollections of Gompers, in Payne, *Reform, Labor, and Feminism*, esp. 94–108; and Foner, *Women and the American Labor Movement*, chap. 26.

109. Typescript, annotated in Kelley's hand (dated "1921?" and written "as of the date Thanksgiving 1920"), NCL Papers, series D, box 1.

110. Quoted from *American Federationist* (April 1898): 24, by Mollie Ray Carroll, *Labor and Politics: The Attitude of the American Federation of Labor toward Legislation and Politics* (Boston: Houghton Mifflin, 1923), 57.

111. Samuel Gompers, "Should the Wife Help to Support the Family?" *American Federationist* 13 (January 1906): 36.

112. AFL, *Report of Proceedings of the Thirty-Fourth Annual Convention of the American Federation of Labor. Held at Philadelphia, Pa., November 9 to 21, 1914, Inclusive* (Washington, D.C.: Law Reporter Printing, 1914), 58.

113. AFL, *Report of Proceedings of the Thirty-Second Annual Convention of the American Federation of Labor. Held at Rochester, New York, November 11 to 23, 1912, Inclusive* (Washington, D.C.: Law Reporter Printing, 1912), 94.

114. AFL, *Report of the Proceedings of the Thirty-Third Annual Convention of the American Federation of Labor. Held at Seattle, Washington, November 10 to 22, 1913, Inclusive* (Washington, D.C.: Law Reporter Printing, 1913), 63.

115. Yellowitz, *Labor and the Progressive Movement*, 136.

116. *American Federationist* 21 (March 1914): 231–34; 21 (May 1914): 383–84; 21 (June 1914): 472; and 21 (July 1914): 544.

117. Mildred Gordon, *The Development of Minimum-Wage Laws*, Bulletin of the Women's Bureau, no. 61 (Washington, D.C.: GPO, 1928), 11, 273, 318.

118. See Marguerite Green, *The National Civic Federation and the American Labor Movement, 1900–1925* (Washington, D.C.: Catholic University of America, 1956); on the NCF relationship with the AFL, Mink, *Old Labor and New Immigrants*, esp. chap. 5; and Montgomery, *Fall of the House of Labor*, chap. 6.

119. Beeks to Porter, 12 January 1916, NCF Papers, box 135A. Porter was president of the Shredded Wheat Company of Niagara Falls. Other members were H. J. Conway of the Retail Clerks, Lee K. Frankel of Metropolitan Insurance, Percy Straus of Macy's, Miss Thalia Newton Brown of Marconi, and Mrs. Van Rensselaer from the NCF

Women's Department. Marie Obenauer, who wanted a balanced report, had compiled official statistics for the Oregon Minimum Wage Commission and worked temporarily on statistics for the NCF inquiry, but she turned down several offers of longer employment. See NCF Papers, box 135A.

120. Beeks to Abram Elkus, 8 October 1913, NCF Papers, box 121.

121. Straus to Beeks, 4 March 1917; Wood to Beeks, 20 March 1916, NCF Papers, box 135A.

122. See *FIC* 5.2546, 2548–49, 2954–55; and Bloomingdale to Beeks, 28 October 1913, NCF Papers, box 121.

123. "Meeting Held under the Auspices of the Minimum Wage Commission of the NCF," 25 February 1915, 1–80, NCF Papers, box 135A. Ralph M. Easley to Samuel Gompers, 16 February 1915, NCF Papers, box 220.

124. *The Minimum Wage: A Failing Experiment*, 13, 17, 18. Emphases in the original.

125. Rome G. Brown, "The Statutory Minimum Wage," *Case and Comment* (22 June 1915): 285. Brown represented Stettler in the first case to reach the Supreme Court, *Stettler v. O'Hara*, 243 U.S. 629 (1917), and published *The Minimum Wage: With Particular Reference to the Legislative Minimum Wage under the Minnesota Statute of 1913* (Minneapolis, [1914]). Described by Walter Lippmann as "a kind of specialist in the business of finding fault with the minimum wage," his views attracted public rebuttal, for example, Walter Lippmann, "The Campaign against Sweating," *New Republic* 2 (27 March 1915): 1–8, esp. 2; and Harris Weinstock, "Justifying the Minimum Wage," *Industrial Outlook* (January 1915): 7–8.

126. Roy Lubove, *The Progressives and the Slums: Tenement House Reform in New York City, 1890–1917* (Pittsburgh: University of Pittsburgh Press, 1962), 133 and appendixes 3 and 4. See also Daniels, "Between Home and Factory"; and Leon Stein, *The Triangle Fire* (Philadelphia: J. B. Lippincott, 1962). On the reform tradition in New York, see Richard L. McCormick, *From Realignment to Reform: Political Change in New York State, 1893–1910* (Ithaca: Cornell University Press, 1981); and Robert F. Wesser, *Charles Evans Hughes: Politics and Reform in New York, 1905–1910* (Ithaca: Cornell University Press, 1967).

127. Thomas J. Kerr, IV, "The New York Factory Investigating Commission and the Minimum Wage Movement," *Labor History* 12 (Summer 1971): 373–91; and Stein, *Triangle Fire*, 207–11.

128. Belle L. Israels to Paul Kennaday, 12 November and 14 November 1912, AALL Papers, reel 8. Israels, who married Henry Moskowitz in 1914, was involved in reform and arbitration activities, and subsequently in Democratic politics; see Elisabeth Israels Perry, *Belle Moskowitz: Feminine Politics in the Age of Alfred E. Smith* (New York: Oxford University Press, 1987).

129. State of New York, *Third Report of the Factory Investigating Commission, 1914* (Albany: J. B. Lyon, 1914), v.

130. Abram I. Elkus to Dr. H. B. Woolston, 9 October 1913, commissioning "Dr. John B. Andrews or some one under his direction to make a report to the Commission on minimum wage legislation," AALL Papers, reel 10; Irene Osgood Andrews to Abraham [*sic*] I. Elkus, 4 March 1914, submitting her report, AALL Papers, reel 11; for her correspondence to state experts on details for the report, see, for example, Andrews to Father John A. Ryan, 26 January 1914, Mrs. Katherine Philips Edson, 7 February 1914, AALL Papers, reel 11. John Andrews and other leading reformers were on the advisory committee for the minimum wage inquiry; see Elkus to Andrews, 15 September 1913, AALL Papers, reel 10.

131. *FIC* 5.2735, 2740–41.

132. Payne, *Reform, Labor, and Feminism*, 106. See also Dye, *As Equals and as Sisters*, 146–48; Yellowitz, *Labor and the Progressive Movement*, 129–36; Mari Jo Buhle, *Women and American Socialism, 1870–1920* (Urbana: University of Illinois Press, 1981), chap. 5.

133. Dye, *As Equals and as Sisters*, esp. chap. 5; see also Meredith Tax, *The Rising of the Women: Feminist Solidarity and Class Conflict, 1880–1917* (New York: Monthly Review Press, 1980), chap. 5, "Leonora O'Reilly and the Women's Trade Union League."

134. On working women and the suffrage see Ellen Carol DuBois, "Working Women, Class Relations, and Suffrage Militance: Harriot Stanton Blatch and the New York Woman Suffrage Movement, 1894–1909," *Journal of American History* 74 (June 1987): 34–58; and Dye, *As Equals and as Sisters*, chap. 6.

135. NYWTUL, "Minutes of Meeting of Executive Board Held June 27th, 1912," NYWTUL Papers, reports, minutes, and proceedings file.

136. Yellowitz, *Labor and the Progressive Movement*, chaps. 8, 10. Woolston wrote to John Andrews when the Republicans took control of the Assembly: "It seems that in planning a nine months investigation, the fact that a Republican majority might overturn plans for a continuation was not taken into account." 9 February 1914, AALL Papers, reel 11. The FIC was continued for another year but wound up abruptly in 1915.

137. NYWTUL, "Minutes of Meeting of Executive Board Held November 24th, 1914"; "Minutes of League Meeting Held December 7th, 1914"; "Minutes of Meeting of League Held January 4th, 1915," NYWTUL Papers, reports, minutes, and proceedings file.

138. Dye, *As Equals and as Sisters*, 124.

139. Yellowitz, *Labor and the Progressive Movement*, 89, 127.

140. Paula Baker, "The Domestication of Politics: Women and American Political Society," *American Historical Review* 89 (June 1984): 620–47; Sonya Michel and Robyn Rosen, "The Paradox of Maternalism: Elizabeth Lowell Putnam and the American Welfare State," *Gender and History* 4 (Autumn 1992): 364.

141. Brandeis, "Labor Legislation," 512–13; the 1911 proposal printed in full in NCL, *Twelfth Report*, 51–52. See also William L. Crow, "History of Legislative Control of Wages in Wisconsin," *Marquette Law Review* 16 (April 1932): 188–98; John R. Commons, *Myself* (New York: Macmillan, 1934), 153–57; David P. Thelen, *The New Citizenship: Origins of Progressivism in Wisconsin, 1885–1900* (Columbia: University of Missouri Press, 1972), esp. chap. 5.

142. Quoted in Crow, "Legislative Control," n. 29.

143. State of Ohio, *Proceedings and Debates of the Constitutional Convention* (Columbus, Ohio: F. J. Heer Printing, 1913), vol. 2, 1328–38, 1784–87. See also James M. Cox, *Journey through My Years* (New York: Simon and Schuster, 1946), chaps. 9–11; Hoyt Landon Warner, *Progressivism in Ohio, 1897–1917* (Columbus: Ohio State University Press, [1964]), chaps. 11–14.

144. Irene Osgood Andrews to Thomas Gibbons, 31 January 1914, Gibbons to Andrews, 3 February 1914, AALL Papers, reel 11.

145. Brandeis, "Labor Legislation," 519, emphasis added; Governor Cox's message to the Legislature, quoted in James Boyle, *The Minimum Wage and Syndicalism* (Cincinnati: Stewart and Kidd, 1913), 70.

146. Nathan, *Epoch-Making Movement*, 196.

147. Theda Skocpol and Gretchen Ritter, "Gender and the Origins of Modern Social Policies in Britain and the United States," *Studies in American Political Development* 5 (Spring 1991): 36.

CHAPTER FIVE
POLICE POWER

1. State of New York, *Fourth Report of the Factory Investigating Commission, 1915* (Albany: J. B. Lyon, 1915), vol. 1, 33. Hereafter cited as *FIC*. See also Thomas J. Kerr IV, "The New York Factory Investigating Commission and the Minimum Wage Movement," *Labor History* 12 (Summer 1971): 373–91.

2. For example, the 1909 AFL convention where J. R. Clynes, a visiting Labour M.P., hailed the new "Wages Boards bill . . . that singles out what we call our sweated trades, trades in which girls and women, and men and boys as well, are employed at slaves' wages." AFL, *Report of the Proceedings of the Twenty-Ninth Annual Convention, Held at Toronto, Ontario, November 8 to 20, 1909, Inclusive* (Washington, D.C.: Law Reporter Printing, 1909), 155.

3. "Address by Mrs. Glendower Evans," *City Club Bulletin* (Philadelphia) 6 (27 January 1913): 204. J. B. Andrews to Sophie Sanger, 23 April 1914, AALL Papers, reel 11.

4. Executive Committee minutes, 21 October 1910, NCL Papers, series A, box 1. Many minimum wagers were also involved in the child labor campaign, which did attempt a new constitutional strategy. A federal child labor law, proposed by Senator Beveridge in 1906 and passed in 1916, used the Commerce Clause to claim a federal police power. The court had upheld the authority to prohibit shipment across state lines of products regarded as harmful in themselves (lottery tickets, adulterated eggs, prostitutes); the legislation banned shipment of goods in themselves harmless but produced in harmful circumstances, e.g., by children. This was rejected by the Supreme Court (but not until ten years after the minimum wage course was set) in *Hammer v. Dagenhart*, 247 U.S. 251 (1918). There is no record that the same strategy was contemplated for the minimum wage until the 1930s. See Grace Abbott, *The Child and the State* (Chicago: University of Chicago Press, 1938), vol. 1, 461–563; John Braeman, "The Square Deal in Action: A Case Study in the Growth of the 'National Police Power,'" in John Braeman, Robert H. Bremner, and Everett Walters, eds., *Change and Continuity in Twentieth-Century America* (Columbus: Ohio State University Press, 1964), 35–80; and Stephen B. Wood, *Constitutional Politics in the Progressive Era: Child Labor and the Law* (Chicago: University of Chicago Press, 1968).

5. Quoted by Susan Ware, *Beyond Suffrage: Women in the New Deal* (Cambridge: Harvard University Press, 1981), 100. This was a description of Frances Perkins, who, it was said, had learned from Kelley while lobbying for the NYCL in 1912.

6. Ernst Freund, *The Police Power: Public Policy and Constitutional Rights* (Chicago: Callaghan, 1904; reprint, Buffalo: William S. Hein, 1981), iii. Freund was professor of jurisprudence and public law at the University of Chicago, first on the political science faculty, then in the Law School from 1902, and an adviser to the NCL on the minimum wage and other legislative campaigns. Ellen Fitzpatrick, *Endless Crusade: Women Social Scientists and Progressive Reform* (New York: Oxford University Press, 1990), 44–46, describes Freund's influence on reform also through students like Sophonisba Breckenridge.

7. *Lochner v. New York*, 198 U.S. 45 (1905).

8. Freund, *Police Power*, iii.

9. *In re Jacobs*, 98 N.Y. 98 (1885). The defense brief quoted by Eileen Boris, *Home to Work: Motherhood and the Politics of Industrial Homework in the United States* (Cambridge: Cambridge University Press, 1994), chap. 1.

10. Quoted in Elizabeth Faulkner Baker, *Protective Labor Legislation: With Special*

Reference to Women in the State of New York (New York: Columbia University Press, 1925), 27.

11. *Allgeyer v. Louisiana*, 165 U.S. 578 (1897); and *Holden v. Hardy*, 169 U.S. 366 (1898).

12. See Paul Kens, *Judicial Power and Reform Politics: The Anatomy of "Lochner v. New York"* (Lawrence: University Press of Kansas, 1990). On the intellectual and legal background to this development, see Sidney Fine, *Laissez-Faire and the General-Welfare State: A Study of Conflict in American Thought, 1865–1901* (Ann Arbor: University of Michigan Press, 1956); and Morton J. Horwitz, *The Transformation of American Law, 1870–1960: The Crisis of Legal Orthodoxy* (New York: Oxford University Press, 1992). For the line of descent from the Fourteenth Amendment with reference to gender see Barbara Allen Babcock et al., *Sex Discrimination and the Law: Causes and Remedies* (Boston: Little, Brown, 1975), chap. 1; and Joan Hoff, *Law, Gender, and Injustice: A Legal History of American Women* (New York: New York University Press, 1991), chap. 5. Judith A. Baer, *The Chains of Protection: The Judicial Response to Women's Labor Legislation* (Westport: Greenwood Press, 1978), gives an important critical evaluation of the moral issues involved.

13. Baker, *Protective Labor Legislation*, 27.

14. In 1908, twelve states regulated sweated industries by licensing and inspection of tenement and home premises. Public health concerns were central. Massachusetts and New York had the most extensive licensing laws. "These laws usually prohibit the manufacture, repair, alteration, or finishing of apparel for wear or adornment, and the manufacture of purses, cigars, cigarettes or umbrellas in rooms or apartments in tenement- or dwelling-houses except under certain prescribed conditions. . . . The factory inspectors are required to visit and inspect the sanitary condition of rooms or apartments coming within the scope of the laws and to enforce the provisions of the laws, and in some cases to report insanitary conditions, infectious or contagious diseases, etc., to the health officers." William D. P. Bliss et al., eds., *The New Encyclopedia of Social Reform* (New York: Funk and Wagnalls, 1908), vol. 2, 1180–81.

15. "Standard of Living and Labor. Report for the Committee—A Retrospect and a Look Ahead," *Proceedings of the National Conference of Charities and Correction* (1913), 225.

16. H. A. Millis, "Some Aspects of the Minimum Wage," *Journal of Political Economy* 22 (February 1914): 153.

17. Freund, *The Police Power*, 303–4. See also O. H. Myrick, "Statutory Regulation of Wages," *Central Law Journal* 65 (20 December 1907): 468–74.

18. Freund, *The Police Power*, 299.

19. See the full text of *Lochner*, reprinted in Kens, *Judicial Power*, 174, 175.

20. The possibility of characterizing Lochner's subjects as *either* bakers *or* grown men is a classic example of the vulnerability of judgments based upon malleable or interpretable social facts. See the discussion of this problem, especially in papers by David P. Currie, H. N. Hirsch, and Cheryl B. Welch, in Vivien Hart and Shannon C. Stimson, eds., *Writing a National Identity: Political, Economic, and Cultural Perspectives on the Written Constitution*, Fulbright Papers no. 11 (Manchester: Manchester University Press, 1993); and H. N. Hirsch, *A Theory of Liberty: The Constitution and Minorities* (New York: Routledge, 1992).

21. Boris, *Home to Work*, chap. 1, analyzes this case and gives a detailed account of the confusion in social norms and legislative and judicial decisions from *Jacobs* to the present day, over gender and family, home and work. See also Eileen Boris, "'A Man's

Dwelling House Is His Castle': Tenement House Cigarmaking and the Judicial Imperative," in Ava Baron, ed., *Work Engendered: Toward a New History of American Labor*
(Ithaca: Cornell University Press, 1991), 114–41.

22. Nancy S. Erickson, "*Muller v. Oregon* Reconsidered: The Origins of a Sex-Based
Doctrine of Liberty of Contract," *Labor History* 30 (Spring 1989): 232.

23. *Slaughter-House Cases*, 83 U.S. 36 (1873). The one exception, the Illinois case of
Ritchie v. People (155 Ill. 98, 1895), in upholding women's equality to contract upheld their
equality not to be subjected to an eight-hour law. See Baer, *Chains of Protection*, 53–54,
77–79; Frances Olsen, "From False Paternalism to False Equality: Judicial Assaults on
Feminist Community, 1869–1895," *Michigan Law Review* 84 (June 1986): 1518–1541.

24. *Muller v. Oregon*, 208 U.S. 412 (1908). Muller is also known for its massive "Brandeis brief," 2 pages of argument and 113 of medical and social evidence. Erickson shows
that it was not the first use of such evidence in legal argument, but its scale put it in a
new league, and its compilation by Josephine Goldmark of the NCL started that organization in a new line of business. See Erickson, "*Muller v. Oregon* Reconsidered," 229;
Louis D. Brandeis and Josephine Goldmark, *Women in Industry* (New York: National
Consumers' League, [1909]; reprint, New York: Arno Press, 1969), contains the brief and
judgment; and see Babcock, *Sex Discrimination and the Law*, 37–39, "The Litigative
Strategy of the National Consumers' League." On the difficulties of attaining any general hours restrictions for men, see Ernst Freund, "Constitutional Aspects of Hours
Legislation for Men," and the ensuing "General Discussion," *American Labor Legislation Review* 4 (1914): 129–37.

25. Brandeis and Goldmark, *Women in Industry*, 7. Justice Brewer, who wrote the
opinion, held particularly rigid views on the sanctity of freedom of contract and was most
likely to stress the biological difference as a way of guarding against future claims of
exception, according to Baer, *Chains of Protection*, 61–65.

26. Florence Kelley, "Status of Legislation in the United States," *Survey* 33 (6 February 1915): 487.

27. Dr. Howard Woolston, testimony to *FIC* 5.2562, succinctly concluded that "the
'pin-money' idea is pretty well knocked in the head." It was said that "many women work
for pin-money. They haven't anything to do, and so they go into the factory or store, and
spend the money they earn on dress and amusement." Of three hundred women living
at home, he had found that 75 percent turned over all their wages to their families, and
a further 20 percent paid much of their wages as board. Florence Kelley observed the
change in the age of the female work force with her observation that "we habitually
spoke, in the nineteenth century, of working girls, not of working women." "Minimum-
Wage Laws," *Journal of Political Economy* 20 (December 1912): 1003; with an edge of
nativism, she blamed immigrants ignorant of "the American tradition that men support
their families."

28. H. LaRue Brown, "Transcript of Taped Reminiscences," 18, LRB Papers, box 16.

29. Freund, *The Police Power*, 755.

30. *FIC* 5.2801. Emphasis added.

31. "Address of the President, Mrs. Raymond Robins," *Fourth Biennial Convention of
the National Women's Trade Union League of America, Saint Louis, June 2 to 7, 1913,
Inclusive* (no imprint), 2–3. Robins had made similar arguments, more briefly, to the
AFL convention in 1911, as fraternal (*sic*) delegate from the WTUL; see AFL, *Report of
Proceedings of the Thirty-First Annual Convention of the American Federation of Labor,
Held at Atlanta, Georgia, November 13 to 20, 1911, Inclusive* (Washington: Law Re-
porter Printing, 1911), 179.

32. So familiar was the Webbs' theory that Holcombe thought only a footnote to an American article was needed: "The economic reasoning underlying proposals to establish minimum standards of remuneration and conditions of employment generally is familiar to economists, and requires no further elaboration in this place. The student who desires to pursue further the economic argument . . . should consult the Webbs' *Industrial Democracy*, part III, chap. iii." A. N. Holcombe, "The Legal Minimum Wage in the United States," *American Economic Review* 2 (March 1912): 33.

33. Ibid., 25, 26, 27.

34. *FIC* 5.2802, 2801. See also Alice Kessler-Harris, *A Woman's Wage: Historical Meanings and Social Consequences* (Lexington: University Press of Kentucky, 1990).

35. Holcombe, "Legal Minimum Wage," 27.

36. Freund, *The Police Power*, 299.

37. Freund, "Constitutional Limitations," 619.

38. John Martin, self-described as "a publicist, a member of the Board of Education and of the Advisory Council of the Association for Labor Legislation," *FIC* 5.2743.

39. See Hoff, *Law, Gender, and Injustice*, chap. 5, "Constitutional Discrimination, 1872–1908," and pp. 127–35 on earlier changes in the status of married women.

40. Benjamin C. Marsh, a New Yorker with connections to the Henry Street Settlement, *FIC* 5.2848. On the relationship between suffrage and labor movements, see Ellen Carol DuBois, "Working Women, Class Relations, and Suffrage Militance: Harriot Stanton Blatch and the New York Woman Suffrage Movement, 1894–1909," *Journal of American History* 74 (June 1987): 34–58; Eileen Lorenzi McDonagh, "The Significance of the Nineteenth Amendment: A New Look at Civil Rights, Social Welfare, and Woman Suffrage Alignments in the Progressive Era," in Naomi B. Lynn, ed., *Women, Politics, and the Constitution* (New York: Harrington Park Press, 1990), 59–94.

41. Holcombe, "The Legal Minimum Wage," 26.

42. *FIC* 5.2724, 2772, 2773.

43. Ibid., 2773.

44. Freund, *The Police Power*, 755.

45. Ibid., 754.

46. Ibid., 705.

47. Louis Brandeis, testifying to *FIC* 5.2889.

48. Ibid., 2834–35. Belief in an educational role for minimum wage boards was one source of Kelley's disappointment with proposals for industrial commissions or boards with appointed members and no worker representation, as "they are alarmingly undemocratic"; in "Minimum Wage Legislation," *Survey* 30 (5 April 1915): 9.

49. *FIC* 5.2871.

50. Freund, *The Police Power*, 705.

51. Helen Marot, "Trade Unions and Minimum Wage Boards," *American Federationist* 22 (November 1915): 966.

52. *FIC* 5.2890, 2891. Brandeis was counsel until his nomination to the Supreme Court, in the test of the Oregon law, finally decided as *Stettler v. O'Hara*, 243 U.S. 629 (1917).

53. "Feminism in my working definition presupposes that women's consciousness is socially constructed, that is historically shaped by human social usage . . . Although the concept has only recently been given vocabulary in the distinction of gender from the biological category of sex, the perception that women's status vis-à-vis men . . . has been purposefully shaped and thus can be reconstructed has long been essential to efforts to gain women's rights or freedoms." Nancy F. Cott, *The Grounding of Modern Feminism* (New Haven: Yale University Press, 1987), 4.

54. Congress, House of Representatives (65th Congress, 2d session), *Minimum Wage for Women and Children: Hearings before the Subcommittee of the Committee on the District of Columbia* (Washington D.C.: GPO, 1918), 9.

55. *FIC* 5.2743.

56. AFL, *Report of the Proceedings of the Thirty-Fourth Annual Convention of the American Federation of Labor, Held at Philadelphia, Pa., November 9 to 21, 1914, Inclusive* (Washington D.C.: Law Reporter Printing, 1914), 58.

57. *FIC* 5.2725–26. Mitchell had been a member of the AALL Committee on Woman's Work, which recommended minimum wage legislation in 1910 ("Meeting of the General Administration Council, Chicago, June 11, 1910," AALL Papers, reel 61, organizational materials, 1906–42), and had supported it in NCF discussions and no doubt elsewhere long before 1915.

58. I use the *social feminist* label because it does, from custom and usage, identify this particular group of women at this particular time, because it may have shed some of the pejorative load it bore in the 1970s and 1980s, and, laying historiography aside, because in this account it refers to women who were feminists and whose causes lay in social reform. See Nancy F. Cott, "What's in a Name? The Limits of 'Social Feminism'; or, Expanding the Vocabulary of Women's History," *Journal of American History* 76 (December 1989): 809–29; Naomi Black, *Social Feminism* (Ithaca: Cornell University Press, 1989). Many labels exist for the groups emerging among women at this time, e.g., hard-core, legal, and rights feminists for the National Woman's Party; and social, labor law, maternal, and relational feminists for the NCL and allies. The distinction was originally made between "hard-core feminists" and "social feminists" by William L. O'Neill, "Feminism as a Radical Ideology," in A. F. Young, ed., *Dissent: Explorations in the History of American Radicalism* (DeKalb: Northern Illinois University Press, 1968), 275–300.

The harm done to women whom protective legislation was supposed to help is widely noted, even where credit is given for good intentions. Elizabeth Faulkner Baker gave one of the earliest and clearest accounts, in *Protective Labor Legislation*, chap. 7, "The Controversy." Strongly critical examples elsewhere include "These reformers strove to make women healthier and happier crypto-slaves," Baer, *Chains of Protection*, 180; and "[Protective laws] confirmed women's 'alien' status as worker," Heidi Hartmann, "Capitalism, Patriarchy, and Job Segregation by Sex," *Signs* 1 (Spring 1976, part 2): 165; typical of more moderate comments: "[Protective legislation] therefore bears some of the responsibility for successfully institutionalizing women's secondary labor force position," Alice Kessler-Harris, *Out to Work: A History of Wage-Earning Women in the United States* (N.Y.: Oxford University Press, 1982), 181. Estimates of the actual consequences for women include the contradictory findings of Elizabeth M. Landes, "The Effect of State Maximum Hours Laws on the Employment of Women in 1920," *Journal of Political Economy* 88 (June 1980): 476–94; Claudia Goldin, "Maximum Hours Legislation and Female Employment: A Reassessment," *Journal of Political Economy* 96 (February 1988): 189–205; and Alice Kessler-Harris, "The Debate over Equality for Women in the Workplace," in Laurie Larwood, Ann H. Stromberg, and Barbara A. Gutek, eds., *Women and Work: An Annual Review* (Beverly Hills: Sage, 1985), vol. 1, 141–61.

59. Florence Kelley, "Minimum Wage Laws," *Proceedings of the National Conference of Charities and Correction* (1913): 233–34.

60. Carroll Smith-Rosenberg, *Disorderly Conduct: Visions of Gender in Victorian America* (New York: Oxford University Press, 1985), 264.

61. Florence Kelley, "Need Our Working Women Despair?" *International Review* 13 (December 1882): 517–27.

62. *The Autobiography of Florence Kelley: Notes of Sixty Years*, ed. Kathryn Kish Sklar (Chicago: Charles H. Kerr, 1986), 10. My account of Kelley is much informed by the forthcoming biography by Sklar, *Florence Kelley and Women's Political Culture: Doing the Nation's Work, 1830–1930*, vol. 1: *1830–1900* (New Haven: Yale University Press, 1994). I am grateful for an early sight of the manuscript.

63. "Standards of Living and Labor. Report of the Committee, by Mrs. Florence Kelley, Secretary of the National Consumers' League, Chairman." *Proceedings of the National Conference of Charities and Correction* (1911): 148, 156. Organized socialism played little part in the minimum wage campaign, though socialist women did, particularly in the WTUL; see Mari Jo Buhle, *Women and American Socialism, 1870–1920* (Urbana: University of Illinois Press, 1981), chap. 5.

64. Florence Kelley, *Modern Industry: In Relation to the Family, Health, Education, Morality* (New York: Longmans Green, 1914), 32–33.

65. Ibid., 32; typescript, annotated in Kelley's hand (dated '1921?" and written "as of the date Thanksgiving 1920"), NCL Papers, series D, box 1.

66. *Autobiography of Florence Kelley*, 7.

67. *Stettler v. O'Hara*, 243 U. S. 629 (1917); and *Adkins v. Childrens Hospital of Washington, D.C.*, 261 U.S. 525 (1923). See Joan Zimmerman, "The Jurisprudence of Equality: The Women's Minimum Wage, the First Equal Rights Amendment, and *Adkins v. Children's Hospital*, 1905–1923," *Journal of American History* 78 (June 1991): 188–225, for Kelley's jurisprudential theory and an important discussion of law, overly detached from the political circumstances, but endorsing the view of Kelley as using the law as a political opportunity.

68. Kelley, "Minimum Wage Laws," *Proceedings* (1913): 231–32.

69. Kelley, *Modern Industry*, 5.

70. Florence Kelley, "Married Women in Industry," *Academy of Political Science Proceedings* 1 (1910–11): 90–91.

71. See Wendy Sarvasy's discussion of "functionally based" citizenship in the U.S. at this time, "Beyond the Difference versus Equality Policy Debate: Postsuffrage Feminism, Citizenship, and the Quest for a Feminist Welfare State," *Signs* 17 (Winter 1992): 329–62; and in Britain, Susan Pedersen, "Gender, Welfare and Citizenship in Britain during the Great War," *American Historical Review* 95 (October 1990): 983–1006.

72. "Report of Activities of the Chicago League," *Life and Labor* 4 (May 1914): 156–57.

73. Congress, *Minimum Wage for Women and Children*, 9.

74. Ibid., 30.

75. Supreme Court of the United States. October term, 1914. Nos. 507 and 508. *Frank C. Stettler v. Edwin V. O'Hara et al., Brief for Defendants in Error*, 92.

76. Josephine Goldmark, *Fatigue and Efficiency: A Study in Industry* (New York: Charities Publication Committee, 1912), 39, 40. See a discussion of Goldmark's work in Martha Banta, *Taylored Lives: Narrative Productions in the Age of Taylor, Veblen, and Ford* (Chicago: University of Chicago Press, 1993), 128–30, 140–47.

77. NWTUL, *Fourth Biennial Convention*, 5.

78. *FIC* 5.2724.

79. Kelley, "Minimum Wage Laws," *Proceedings* (1913): 230.

80. Brandeis later remarked to Dean Acheson that the brief represented "What Any Fool Knows." Acheson to Felix Frankfurter, 16 November 1920, FF Papers, box 19. Morals, here as generally in the debate, were dealt with cursorily compared with other police power categories. The brief suggested that low wages encouraged girls to seek larger incomes from prostitution. Testifying to the FIC, minimum wagers tried not to

depend on such an argument: "I think there is not a great difference between the effect of low wages on men and low wages on women, that for both it means a lower moral tone" (Mary Van Kleeck, *FIC* 5.2806); "We have too high an opinion of working women to think that they turn readily to that. As investigator after investigator has shown, the wonder of it is how good they remain under temptation, but it is an unfair premium put on goodness" (Josephine Goldmark, ibid., 2778).

81. Supreme Court of the United States. October term, 1916. Nos. 25 and 26. *Frank C. Stettler v. Edwin V. O'Hara et al., Brief for Defendants in Error upon Reargument*, A7. Also published as *Oregon Minimum Wage Cases* (New York: National Consumers' League, [1917]). Goldmark's compilation filled pp. 77–783.

82. Felix Frankfurter, "Hours of Labor and Realism in Constitutional Law," *Harvard Law Review* 29 (February 1916): 367. See also the overoptimistic view that "who shall say that within the next fifteen years some learned court of last resort may not declare . . . that children have fathers as well as mothers, and that the impaired vitality of the father . . . means inherited weakness or disease for the child." Louis M. Greeley, "The Changing Attitude of the Courts toward Social Legislation," *Illinois Law Review* 5 (November 1910): 222–32.

83. Christopher L. Tomlins, "Law, Police, and the Pursuit of Happiness in the New American Republic," *Studies in American Political Development* 4 (1990): 5. See also his *Law, Labor, and Ideology in the Early American Republic* (Cambridge: Cambridge University Press, 1993).

84. Ibid., 19.

85. Ibid., 25.

86. Ibid., 19.

87. Tomlins notes the importance of the familial metaphor in the prerevolutionary discourse about "policing"; ibid., 14–15.

88. Paula Baker, "The Domestication of Politics: Women and American Political Society, 1780–1920," *American Historical Review* 89 (June 1984): 620–47. See also Suzanne Lebsock, "Women and American Politics, 1880–1920," in Louise A. Tilly and Patricia Gurin, eds., *Women, Politics, and Change* (New York: Russell Sage Foundation, 1990), 35–62.

89. See a narrative with a broad brush, of struggles between the 1890s and 1930s of excluded groups to expand the state: Alan Dawley, *Struggles for Justice: Social Responsibility and the Liberal State* (Cambridge: Harvard University Press, 1991); and see also, particularly with regard to property and labor, William Forbath, *Law and the Shaping of the American Labor Movement* (Cambridge: Harvard University Press, 1991); Victoria C. Hattam, *Labor Visions and State Power: The Origins of Business Unionism* (Princeton: Princeton University Press, 1993); Jennifer Nedelsky, *Private Property and the Limits of American Constitutionalism: The Madisonian Framework and Its Legacy* (Chicago: University of Chicago Press, 1990); and Karen Orren, *Belated Feudalism: Labor, the Law, and Liberal Development in the United States* (Cambridge: Cambridge University Press, 1991).

90. Forbath, *Law and the Shaping of the American Labor Movement*, 52–53.

91. Freund, *The Police Power*, contents, vii. This duality may also illuminate the debate about whether ostensibly well-intentioned humanitarian proposals, including the minimum wage, were "really" measures of social control. In the older sense of public order as welfare, they were; given the elision of the two meanings into one legal and political concept they may often have become inextricably linked also in motivation and argument.

92. Baker, "The Domestication of Politics," 625, 631.

93. Kathryn Kish Sklar, "Two Political Cultures in the Progressive Era: The National Consumers' League and the American Association for Labor Legislation," in Linda Kerber, Alice Kessler-Harris, and Kathryn Kish Sklar, eds., *American History as Women's History* (Chapel Hill: University of North Carolina Press, forthcoming).

94. Baker, "The Domestication of Politics," 78; and Sklar, "Two Political Cultures."

CHAPTER SIX
GENDER TRAP

1. Mildred Gordon, *The Development of Minimum Wage Laws in the United States, 1912 to 1927*, Bulletin of the Women's Bureau, no. 61 (Washington, D.C.: GPO, 1928), is the best source on implementation problems in these years.

2. Typescript annotated in Kelley's hand (dated "1921?" and written "as of the date Thanksgiving 1920"), NCL Papers, series D, box 1.

3. Kelley to Mrs. John Blair, 1 May 1920, NCL Papers, series C, box 1. On the Adkins case, see Judith A. Baer, *The Chains of Protection: The Judicial Response to Women's Labor Legislation* (Westport: Greenwood Press, 1978), 91–101; Sybil Lipschultz, "Social Feminism and Legal Discourse, 1908–1923," in Martha Albertson Fineman and Nancy Sweet Thomadsen, eds., *At the Boundaries of Law: Feminism and Legal Theory* (New York: Routledge, 1991), 209–25; and Joan G. Zimmerman, "The Jurisprudence of Equality: The Women's Minimum Wage, the First Equal Rights Amendment, and *Adkins v. Children's Hospital*, 1905–1923," *Journal of American History* 78 (June 1991): 188–225.

4. See Susan D. Becker, *The Origins of the Equal Rights Amendment: American Feminism between the Wars* (Westport: Greenwood Press, 1981); Joan Hoff-Wilson, ed., *Rights of Passage: The Past and Future of the ERA* (Bloomington: Indiana University Press, 1986); and Christine A. Lunardini, *From Equal Suffrage to Equal Rights: Alice Paul and the National Woman's Party, 1910–1928* (New York: New York University Press, 1986), which, despite its title, is mainly a study of the suffrage campaign preceding the ERA. Studies of the 1920s equality/protection debate include William H. Chafe, *The Paradox of Change: American Women in the Twentieth Century* (New York: Oxford University Press, 1991); Nancy F. Cott, *The Grounding of Modern Feminism* (New Haven: Yale University Press, 1987); and J. Stanley Lemons, *The Woman Citizen: Social Feminism in the 1920s* (Urbana: University of Illinois Press, 1973).

5. These were not entirely separate categories. Lawyers were reformers and women often legal experts in their own right. Among leading women, Kelley took a law degree at Northwestern University, graduating in 1895 (Kathryn Kish Sklar, *Florence Kelley and Women's Political Culture: Doing the Nation's Work, 1830–1930*, vol. 1: *1830–1900* [New Haven: Yale University Press, 1994], chap. 10); Crystal Eastman graduated from New York University Law School (Edward James et al., eds., *Notable American Women* [Cambridge: Harvard University Press, 1971], vol. 1, 544); Alice Paul was studying at the Washington College of Law and George Washington University Law School (Zimmerman, "Jurisprudence of Equality," 217, n. 50); and see Albert Levitt to Paul, 13 July and 20 July 1921, with advice on her course credits, NWP Papers, reel 9); Elsie Hill completed a year of law school in 1921 (Becker, *The Origins*, 32). In 1910, however, "women constituted only one percent of the legal profession," according to Albie Sachs and Joan Hoff-Wilson, *Sexism and the Law: A Study of Male Political Beliefs and Judicial Bias* (Oxford: Martin Robertson, 1978), 188.

6. Lipschultz, "Social Feminism and Legal Discourse," esp. 210–12; Zimmerman, "Jurisprudence of Equality," esp. 188–93.

7. "The close relationship between the *Adkins* decision and the emergence of the ERA . . . illustrates how specific reforms can intersect with legal doctrines and principles." Zimmerman, "Jurisprudence of Equality," 193. See Laura Kalman, *Legal Realism at Yale, 1927–1960* (Chapel Hill: University of North Carolina Press, 1986), on the three-way divide between formalists, upholding a traditional and conservative view of law as a set of guiding principles, and of judicial decision making as solely the interpretation of those principles; sociological jurisprudentialists (including Frankfurter and some of his Harvard colleagues), who sought recognition of social facts in judicial determinations and saw a proper social purpose in the application of legal principle to specific situations; and the realists (whose base became the Yale Law School), who at the extreme rejected the notion of fixed rules and concepts, believing that the certainty of formalism was continually undermined by the psychology of judges and the sociology of their environment. See also Morton J. Horwitz, *The Transformation of American Law, 1870–1960: The Crisis of Legal Orthodoxy* (New York: Oxford University Press, 1992).

8. See Wendy Sarvasy, "Beyond the Difference versus Equality Policy Debate: Postsuffrage Feminism, Citizenship, and the Quest for a Feminist Welfare State," *Signs* 17 (Winter 1992): 329–62. A focus on the minimum wage rather than on Sarvasy's example of mothers' pensions confirms that many women sought a synthesis between difference and equality, to connect "the achievement of women's full citizenship to the needs of the most vulnerable women" (Sarvasy, 361), but finds more divisiveness when the subject is the problematic identity of woman/worker. Accounts of specific policies include Sophonisba P. Breckenridge, *Marriage and the Civic Rights of Women: Separate Domicil and Independent Citizenship* (Chicago: University of Chicago Press, 1931); Joanne Goodwin, "An Experiment in Paid Motherhood: The Implementation of Mothers' Pensions in Early Twentieth Century Chicago," *Gender and History* 4 (Autumn 1992): 323–42; Mark Leff, "Consensus for Reform: The Mothers' Pension Movement in the Progressive Era," *Social Service Review* 47 (September 1973): 397–417; Robyn Muncy, *Creating a Female Dominion in American Reform, 1890–1935* (New York: Oxford University Press, 1991); and Theda Skocpol, *Protecting Soldiers and Mothers: The Political Origins of Social Policy in the United States* (Cambridge: Harvard University Press, 1992), chap. 8.

9. Amendments and riders put to Congress from 1923 to 1972 are given in "Appendix: Various Attempts to Define Equal Rights for Women," in Hoff-Wilson, ed., *Rights of Passage*, 121–25.

10. "Stenographic Report: National Convention of the National Woman's Party, February 15, 16, 17, 18, 1921," 106, NWP Papers, reel 115.

11. Kelley to Elsie Hill, 21 March 1921, NWP Papers, reel 7. Correspondence in this collection is arranged chronologically, regardless of subject.

12. Kelley to Alice Paul, 14 October 1921, NWP Papers, reel 10; Elizabeth Glendower Evans to Paul, 21 December 1921, NWP Papers, reel 11.

13. Elizabeth Brandeis to Frankfurter, 21 September 1921, FF Papers, box 153.

14. "Proposed Blanket Bill,"n.d., NWP Papers, reel 10.

15. Lemons, *The Woman Citizen*, 187; Maud Younger to Kelley, 15 October 1921, NWP Papers, reel 10.

16. Hill to Mary Winsor, 14 May 1921, NWP Papers, reel 8; Paul quoted in "Alice Paul: From Dilemma to Decision," by Amelia R. Fry, a paper presented at the Berkshire Conference on the History of Women, Smith College, June 1984, 4–5; Hill to Mrs. De Angelis, 16 May 1921, NWP Papers, reel 8.

17. Hill to Mary Winsor, 14 May 1921, NWP Papers, reel 8. Pound soon claimed that he had commented, not endorsed, that protective laws must be safeguarded, and that "I told the emissaries of the Woman's Party that this clause was vital. They act in gross bad faith when they eliminate it and then quote me." Roscoe Pound to Frankfurter, 3 February 1922, FF Papers, box 90. Pound, dean of Harvard Law School from 1916 to 1936, had taken an early stand against formalism, although he was a cautiously conservative legal thinker. In the later twenties, he was opposed by Frankfurter in a feud over appointments and policy at Harvard. See Kalman, *Legal Realism*, chap. 2; and David Wigdor, *Roscoe Pound* (Westport: Greenwood Press, 1974). Albert Levitt was assistant professor at George Washington University Law School in 1920–21, and at the University of North Dakota the following year. In a varied career, he taught philosophy and medical jurisprudence and was a special assistant to attorneys general in 1923–24 and from 1933 to 1937; he ran as an independent Republican for governor of Connecticut in 1932 and a Republican for the Senate in California in 1950. With degrees from Harvard and Yale, he had a foot in the camps of both sociological jurisprudence and realism. Levitt and Elsie Hill, chairman of the NWP from 1921 to 1925, caused a sensation by marrying while at a legal convention in Chicago in December 1921, a sensation to which Hill further contributed by deciding to keep her maiden name. Given Levitt's misgiving about the ERA, this connection and the interest in the intellectual problems of the ERA that shows in his letters and papers may explain his persistence with Paul, whose single-mindedness and cavalier use of Pound's comments clearly annoyed him. See *Who Was Who in America: Volume 5, 1969–1973* (Chicago: Marquis Who's Who, 1973).

18. Albert Levitt to Paul, Tuesday afternoon [May 1921], NWP Papers, reel 8.

19. Dean Acheson to Frankfurter, 7 December 1921, FF Papers, box 19. See also "Mr. Acheson's draft" of a proviso, annotated "rejected by Miss Paul." FF Papers, box 153. The NWP kept a record of the meeting between Paul and Kelley, "Conference Held December 4, 1921," NWP Papers, reel 11.

20. Mary Anderson to Maud Younger, 20 October 1921, NWP Papers, reel 10.

21. Quoted in Barbara Sicherman, *Alice Hamilton: A Life in Letters* (Cambridge: Harvard University Press, 1984), 256.

22. Ibid.

23. George W. Alger to Kelley, n.d. [April 1923], FF Papers, box 153.

24. Clara Mortenson Beyer, "What Is Equality?" *Nation* 116 (31 January 1923): 116.

25. "Stenographic Report," 79, NWP Papers, reel 115.

26. Paul to Mrs. Clarence M. Smith, 29 November 1921, NWP Papers, reel 11.

27. Eleanor Brannan, quoted in Paul to Brannan, 9 December 1922, NWP Papers, reel 19.

28. Paul to Brannan, 9 December 1922, NWP Papers, reel 19.

29. See the discussion of the politics of the ERA as single-issue politics in the 1970s, by Jane Mansbridge, *Why We Lost the ERA* (Chicago: University of Chicago Press, 1986), chap. 1; Nancy F. Cott, "Feminist Politics in the 1920s: The National Woman's Party," *Journal of American History* 71 (June 1984): 43–68; "Stenographic Report," 111, 115, NWP Papers, reel 115.

30. See "Stenographic Report," 78–79, NWP Papers, reel 115, for Kelley's demand for attention to "colored and white women alike"; "The White Woman's Burden," *Nation* 112 (16 February 1921): 257–58; Cott, "Feminist Politics in the 1920s," 50–55 (quoting Kelley that the NWP had "welshed on the Negro question," 54); *Third Annual Report of the District of Columbia Minimum Wage Board for the Year Ending December 31, 1920* (Washington, D.C.: GPO, 1921), 16–17; and Vivien Hart, "Feminism and Bureaucracy:

The Minimum Wage Experiment in the District of Columbia," *Journal of American Studies* 26 (April 1992): 8–17.

31. "Stenographic Report," 79, NWP Papers, reel 115.

32. Mrs. Morey, chairman of the Massachusetts branch of the NWP, "Stenographic Report," 62–63, Crystal Eastman, 129, NWP Papers, reel 115.

33. Mrs. Laskey, Oklahoma delegate, "Stenographic Report," 119, NWP Papers, reel 115.

34. "Stenographic Report," 130, NWP Papers, reel 115.

35. See Susan Ware, *Beyond Suffrage: Women in the New Deal* (Cambridge: Harvard University Press, 1981); Cynthia Harrison, *On Account of Sex: The Politics of Women's Issues, 1945–1968* (Berkeley and Los Angeles: University of California Press, 1988); Leila Rupp and Verta Taylor, *Survival in the Doldrums: The American Women's Rights Movement, 1945 to the 1960s* (New York: Oxford University Press, 1987); Judith Sealander, "Moving Painfully and Uncertainly: Policy Formation and 'Women's Issues,' 1940–1980," in Donald T. Critchlow and Ellis W. Hawley, eds., *Federal Social Policy: The Historical Dimension* (University Park: Pennsylvania State University Press, 1988), 79–96.

36. "Conference Held December 4, 1921," NWP Papers, reel 11.

37. The NWP claim of support from two anonymous Supreme Court justices was too much for Levitt: Levitt to Paul, Tuesday morning (July 1921), Levitt to Paul, Thursday night [July/August 1921], NWP Papers, reel 9. One of the justices was Oliver Wendell Holmes. Paul also cited Roscoe Pound, whose opinion both sides subsequently used. Pound wrote to Ethel Smith of the WTUL: "The draft amendment as shown to me by the committee of the National Woman's Party seemed to me as well drawn as it could be if such an amendment is advisable. As I told them, in the present temper of the courts it is hard to draw up *anything* that may not be used to defeat social legislation. Their draft seems to me, if fairly construed, to cover the case well. But I am doubtful whether anything will be fairly construed in such connections in the next few years." Enclosed with Frank Walsh to Paul, 14 November 1921, NWP Papers, reel 11. He later accused the NWP of "gross bad faith." Pound to Frankfurter, 3 February 1922, FF Papers, box 90. In December 1921, Paul had to apologize to Dean William Draper Lewis of the University of Pennsylvania for a published report of his endorsement of the ERA, actually made by Shippen Lewis, a member of the Pennsylvania Bar. See also Mary Anderson to Maud Younger, 20 October 1921; and the series of letters solicited from Washington lawyers by the NWP, filed at the end of the correspondence for November 1921, NWP Papers, reel 11.

38. Maud Younger to Mrs. Genevieve Allen, 28 November 1921, NWP Papers, reel 11. The Shafroth-Palmer Amendment, proposed in 1914, would have required states to hold binding referenda on suffrage if 8 percent of their existing electorate so requested. It was intended to mollify states' rights hostility to a federal amendment and to make it much easier to force a decision; Mari Jo Buhle and Paul Buhle, eds., *Concise History of Woman Suffrage* (Urbana: University of Illinois Press, 1978), 422–23.

39. Katherine Morey Pinkham to Paul, 3 December 1921, NWP Papers, reel 11. But Marion Frankfurter was dogged by ill health and did not take an active part in her husband's affairs or in organizations like the NCL. See Michael E. Parrish, *Felix Frankfurter and His Times: The Reform Years* (New York: Free Press, 1982).

40. Levitt to Paul, Tuesday morning [July 1921], NWP Papers, reel 9.

41. Levitt to Paul [May 1921], NWP Papers, reel 8.

42. Frankfurter to Paul, 30 June 1921, NWP Papers, reel 8.

43. Frankfurter to Herbert Croly, 8 January 1925, FF Papers, box 50, criticizing the proposed Child Labor Amendment. He concluded crossly: "If the women really cared as much as businessmen cared *they* could get similar results from the states and the process of such an effort would give us a very different body of citizens than we now have." Pinkham summed him up as "not only a states rights man but a city and town and small separate community rights man. He is the worst I ever saw." Katherine Morey Pinkham to Paul, 19 November 1921, NWP Papers, reel 11.

44. Sutherland to Ethel M. Smith, 24 December 1921, NWP Papers, reel 11. See J. F. Paschal, *Mr. Justice Sutherland: A Man against the State* (Princeton: Princeton University Press, 1951). When southern states commandeered states' rights arguments to defend racism and reactionary social policy, liberals assumed that federal government and courts were their best hope; recently, with a more conservative Supreme Court, there has been a revival of interest in the states; see Stanley H. Friedelbaum, ed., *Human Rights in the States: New Directions in Constitutional Policymaking* (New York: Greenwood Press, 1988), and Paul Finkelman and Stephen E. Gottlieb, eds., *Toward a Usable Past: Liberty under State Constitutions* (Athens: University of Georgia Press, 1991).

45. Levitt to Hill, Saturday [26 September 1921], 2 P.M., NWP Papers, reel 10.

46. Acheson to Paul, 16 July 1921, NWP Papers, reel 9.

47. *Bunting v. Oregon*, 243 U.S. 426 (1917), appeared to overturn the decision in *Lochner v. New York*, 198 U.S. 45 (1905), which had rejected the police power argument for labor laws for men for all but exceptional cases. The suspicion that Bunting was not a reliable precedent was justified: "Although the Court did not mention Lochner, the ruling in effect overturned its specific holding. But the Lochner philosophy survived for another two decades." Gerald Gunther, *Cases and Materials on Constitutional Law*, 10th ed. (Mineola, N.Y.: Foundation Press, 1980), 524.

48. George Gordon Battle to Ethel M. Smith, 16 December 1921, NWP Papers, reel 11. Battle was, according to Smith, "Mrs. Belmont's personal attorney and manager of her estates. Perhaps that explains his stupidity(?)" Smith to Frankfurter, 27 January 1922, FF Papers, box 153.

49. "Statement of Mr. Shippen Lewis, LL.B. University of Pennsylvania, Member of the Pennsylvania Bar," n.d., NWP Papers, reel 8.

50. Levitt to Paul, 21 December 1921, NWP Papers, reel 11. In *Truax v. Corrigan*, 257 U.S. 312 (1921), the court ruled that peaceful picketing of restaurant premises infringed the Fourteenth Amendment rights of the owners to due process and equal protection of the laws.

51. "Statement of Mr. Shippen Lewis," NWP Papers, reel 8.

52. Frankfurter, "Memorandum on the Proposed Amendment to the United States Constitution presented by the National Woman's Party" [July 1921], NWP Papers, reel 9.

53. Levitt to Paul, 21 December 1921, NWP Papers, reel 11. He believed this era would run for the length of the new chief justice's tenure. Chief Justice Taft resigned in 1930. See David P. Currie's assessment that between 1930 and 1934 the court began to shift toward acceptance of "the new social state." *The Constitution in the Supreme Court: The Second Century, 1888–1986* (Chicago: University of Chicago Press, 1990), 208.

54. [Albert Levitt], "Argument against the Proposed Amendment to the United States Constitution" [August 1921], NWP Papers, reel 9.

55. Frankfurter, "Memorandum on the Proposed Amendment." The interpretation of equality and disability was the main but not the only interest. Levitt was seized with

"a happy idea . . . I suggest . . . equal rights with men shall not be denied to women, nor abridged, *unless the abridgement shall promote the general welfare*, . . . the underscored phrase will protect the minimum wagers because the general welfare is the basis of their case . . . the opponents of the minimum wage cannot use it because it allows the abridgement of women's rights when the general welfare calls for such abridgement . . . it conserves the police power for 'safety, health and morals' are protected because of the general welfare." Levitt [to Elsie Hill?], 18 June 1921, NWP Papers, reel 8. Writing the police power directly into the amendment would have specified a power previously only inferred, defined through case law, and whose status as state or federal power had never been agreed. See Roscoe Pound to Levitt, 27 May 1921, NWP Papers, reel 8; and Levitt's parallel of the applicability of the Fifth Amendment to the states, Levitt to Paul, 13 July 1921, NWP Papers, reel 9. Solving their problems by giving the court a free hand to interpret vague concepts like the general welfare or the police power did not seem to the lawyers to solve anything at all.

56. Levitt to Hill, 26 September 1921, NWP Papers, reel 10.

57. Frankfurter to Ethel Smith, 8 September 1921, NWP Papers, reel 10.

58. Felix Frankfurter, "Hours of Labor and Realism in Constitutional Law," *Harvard Law Review* 29 (February 1916): 367.

59. Levitt to Pound, 25 May 1921, NWP Papers, reel 8.

60. Levitt, "Copy, Minimum Wage Board of Washington D.C. *Reply to Argument by Governor Folk*" [July 1921], NWP Papers, reel 8.

61. 5 December 1921, NWP Papers, reel 11.

62. Levitt to Paul [May 1921], NWP Papers, reel 8.

63. Clara Mortenson [Beyer], "The Minimum Wage at Work in the District of Columbia," *Proceedings of the National Conference of Social Work* (1920): 299. LaRue Brown, "Transcript of Taped Reminiscences," LRB Papers, box 16, 18–20, describes the educational effect of Massachusetts Commission proceedings.

64. Typescript annotated in Kelley's hand (dated "1921?" and written "as of the date Thanksgiving 1920") NCL Papers, series D, box 1. See *Third Annual Report of the Minimum Wage Board of the District of Columbia, for the Year Ending December 31, 1920* (Washington, D.C.: GPO, 1921), 24. The case is chronicled in the 1920, 1921, and 1922 annual reports. The board did not survive long enough after the *Adkins* decision to issue a 1923 report.

65. Elizabeth Brandeis to Clara Mortenson [Beyer], 16–20 June 1920, EBR Papers. Clara Mortenson married Otto Beyer in 1920, surprising Brandeis by sending the news to her in England.

66. Ibid.

67. "Summary (*) of the Work of Mary W. Dewson," NCL Papers, series C, box 1; Mary W. Dewson to Kelley, 10 February 1923, NCL Papers, series C, box 1. Frankfurter later admitted to his shame that he had "entered on collaboration with her with unconscious misgivings, due to no cause other than the fact that Josephine was such a superb co-worker." Frankfurter to Kelley, 28 February 1921, FF Papers, box 157.

68. John R. Shillady, NCL executive director, to Elsie Hill, 9 July 1921, NWP Papers, reel 9. Shillady's suggestion that the change reflected the fact that for the first time there was practical experience to recount need not contradict the view of Lipschultz, "In Defense of Industrial Equality," but may redress the balance between Lipschultz's ideological emphasis and simple pragmatism.

69. Events described in Chief Justice Smyth's dissent to the second decision of the Court of Appeals; *Washington Law Reporter*, 50 (17 November 1922): 726.

70. Zimmerman quotes Burnita Shelton Matthews of the NWP that Challen Ellis bore a grudge against Frankfurter from Harvard Law School days and may have pursued the case more tenaciously once Frankfurter was brought in. "Jurisprudence of Equality," 209–12.

71. Levitt to Mildred Gordon, 28 November 1921, NWP Papers, reel 11.

72. Levitt to Paul, Tuesday morning [July 1921], NWP Papers, reel 9. Levitt concluded from his study that "Folk is entirely fallacious in his method of approach and that Frankfurther [sic] did not see what to my mind was [sic] the most obvious flaws in the argument made by Folk." Levitt to Paul, 13 July 1921, NWP Papers, reel 9.

73. Zimmerman, "Jurisprudence of Equality," 211–12, 219–21; Ethel Smith to George Gordon Battle, 15 December 1921; and Battle to Smith, 16 December 1921, NWP Papers, reel 11.

74. Smyth, *Washington Law Reporter*, 725.

75. Chief Justice Taft to Justice Holmes, 4 April 1923, bound with the decision in *Justice Holmes Opinions, October Term 1922*, OWH Papers. Sutherland blamed his defeat in the 1916 Utah Senate race on women voters; his law office was in the same building as those of the Ellises, attorneys for the Children's Hospital (Zimmerman, "Jurisprudence of Equality," 219–20). Elsie Hill wrote in 1921 that "I have had two conferences with former Senator Sutherland, of Utah, about the effect of the amendment upon industrial legislation for women. He is, as you probably know, the man who is considered in political circles in Washington as the person most likely to receive the next appointment to the Supreme Court . . . He said that this legislation for women could be thrown out now as unconstitutional under the 5th and 14th amendments in the same way that such legislation has been thrown out for men, if the court desires to throw it out." Hill to Mrs. John Winters Brannan, 26 September 1921, NWP Papers, reel 10. This draft is amended in Hill's hand to represent the "concensus of opinion among the lawyers whom we have consulted." Later in 1921, Sutherland wrote to Ethel Smith of the WTUL that he doubted the wisdom of an ERA, believing that remedial legislation should be left to the states: "Of course, no one can predict what construction the courts will put upon the proposed amendment. I think they would struggle to give it a reasonable interpretation, and to save the state laws relating to the eight hour day for women, and so on. But . . . might take the view that the amendment meant precisely what is said, and that a law which gave unequal *advantages* to women was as obnoxious to the amendment as one which was unequally to their *disadvantage*." 24 December 1921, NWP Papers, reel 11.

76. Justice Brandeis withdrew, as he had in *Stettler v. O'Hara*, this time because his daughter was secretary of the board involved. Clara Beyer later recalled that "he could have done such wonderful work. I dare say he did do a little bit on the side really, because he knew everybody who was anybody." "Conversation between Clara Mortenson Beyer and Vivien Hart, Washington, D.C., November 14, 1983," 8, transcript in CMB Papers; Adkins and Frankfurter speculated about whether Elizabeth should resign to enable her father's participation; see Jesse Adkins to Frankfurter, 24 September 1921, FF Papers, box 153.

77. Hill to Frankfurter, n.d. [June 1921], NWP Papers, reel 8.

78. Frankfurter to Elsie Hill, 7 June 1921, NWP Papers, reel 8.

79. See Jesse Adkins to Frankfurter, 11 and 14 April 1923; Frankfurter to Adkins, 16 April 1923, FF Papers, box 153, on the options for the board; for its revival in 1937, see *Annual Report of the Minimum Wage Board of the District of Columbia for the Period June 10, 1937 to December 31, 1937* (no imprint). "[Since 1923] the laws of Arkansas, District of Columbia, Kansas, and Wisconsin . . . Arizona and Porto Rico . . . have been

declared unconstitutional, and such doubt has been thrown on the validity of all these laws, except the nonmandatory Massachusetts act, as to cause almost complete cessation of work in some States and to retard work seriously in all." Gordon, *The Development*, 319.

80. *Adkins*, 545.

81. Ibid., 559–60, 542.

82. Ibid., 553.

83. *Adkins*, quotations by Holmes, 570, and Taft, 567. Dissents were written by Taft with Sanford, and by Holmes.

84. The irony was rarely noted, but see Adkins himself, to Frankfurter, complaining: "But the constitutional amendment has made no change in the District of Columbia." 14 April 1923, FF Papers, box 153; Thomas Reed Powell: "Just how the Nineteenth Amendment affects the civil, political, or any other status of women in the District of Columbia, it is hard to see." "The Judiciality of Minimum-Wage Legislation," *Harvard Law Review* (March 1924), reprinted in *The Supreme Court and Minimum Wage Legislation*, compiled by the NCL (New York: New Republic, 1925), 23.

85. *Adkins*, 553.

86. Ibid., 554, 558.

87. Ibid., 554.

88. *Adkins*, quotations by Holmes, 569, and Taft, 564.

89. *Bunting v. Oregon*, 243 U.S. 426 (1917).

90. *Adkins*, 562.

91. Ibid., 557.

92. Ibid., 558–59.

93. Eleanor Brannan to Lavinia Egan, 18 August 1922, NWP Papers, reel 17.

CHAPTER SEVEN
DUE PROCESS

1. Felix Frankfurter to Jesse Adkins, 16 April 1923, FF Papers, box 153; Frankfurter to Kelley, 10 April 1923, box 157; Louis D. Brandeis to Frankfurter, 11 April 1923, box 26; Newton D. Baker to Kelley, 10 April 1923, NCL Papers, series C, box 1; Charles F. Amidon to Frankfurter, 12 April 1923, FF Papers, box 20; George W. Alger to Kelley, n.d., box 153; and Jesse C. Adkins to Frankfurter, 11 April 1923, box 153.

2. "People Invited to Conference Friday Morning," "Stenographic Report of Minimum Wage Conference Called by National Consumers' League, April 20, 1923," and "For Release Morning Papers April 21, 1923," NCL Papers, series C, box 1.

3. Dewson to Frankfurter, 25 May 1923, FF Papers, box 153.

4. Kelley to Brown, 8 June 1923, NCL Papers, series C, box 2. The reference is to her twenty-four years as secretary of the NCL.

5. Dewson to Frankfurter, 25 May 1923, FF Papers, box 153.

6. Ben Cohen to Frankfurter, 8 January 1932; he refers repeatedly to "our ladies" and "the ladies." FF Papers, box 45.

7. "The Minimum Wage—What Next?" a typescript in NCL Papers, series C, box 1.

8. Kelley to Mrs. John Blair, 1 May 1923, NCL Papers, series C, box 1. "This case" referred to the test of the Sheppard-Towner Maternity Act, also before the court in this session; Kelley's foreboding that this legislation too would be lost was unnecessary; in June 1923 the court dismissed the case "for want of jurisdiction and without ruling on the constitutionality of the act." J. Stanley Lemons, *The Woman Citizen: Social Feminism in the 1920s* (Urbana: University of Illinois Press, 1973), 171–72.

9. Kelley to Frankfurter, 26 May 1923, FF Papers, box 157.

10. Kelley to Mrs. Katherine Philips Edson, 4 May 1923, NCL Papers, series C, box 3.

11. Kelley to Frankfurter, 3 April 1924, FF Papers, box 157.

12. "The Minimum Wage—What Next?"; Kelley to Mrs. John Blair, 1 May 1923, NCL Papers, series C, box 1.

13. "The Minimum Wage—What Next?"

14. Undated paper among 1923 correspondence, NCL Papers, series C box 2.

15. See Mary Frances Berry, *Why ERA Failed: Politics, Women's Rights, and the Amending Process of the Constitution* (Bloomington: Indiana University Press, 1986), chap. 5. In 1924, Kelley's old friends in the Progressive party took up the same problems. Their platform demanded: "Abolition of the tyranny and usurpation of the courts, including the practice of nullifying legislation in conflict with the political, social or economic theories of the judges. . . . Removal of legal discriminations against women by measures not prejudicial to legislation necessary for the protection of women and for the advancement of social welfare." Kirk H. Porter and Donald Bruce Johnson, *National Party Platforms, 1840–1964* (Urbana: University of Illinois Press, 1966), 256.

16. Frankfurter to Kelley, 31 May 1923, FF Papers, box 157.

17. Kelley to Frankfurter, 26 May 1923, FF Papers, box 157. William D. Kelley was a Republican Congressman from Pennsylvania for more than twenty years; see Kathryn Kish Sklar, *Florence Kelley and Women's Political Culture: Doing the Nation's Work, 1830–1930*, vol. 1: *1830–1900* (New Haven: Yale University Press, 1994).

18. Kelley to Edson, 2 December 1925, NCL Papers, series C, box 3.

19. "Ethel Smith's Study Program," "Ethel Smith's Manifesto," "Extract from Proceedings of Forty-Second Annual Convention of the American Federation of Labor," containing draft of their proposed amendment, marked in Kelley's hand "Precious Keep Safe FK." NCL Papers, series C, box 2. In a letter to Frankfurter on 29 May 1923, Kelley had written that "I am trying to extract through Ethel Smith a trial draft of the Federation omnibus Amendment. Our hope is that when our leaders see the hugeness of *that* undertaking, they may consider more favorably a specific Amendment." FF Papers, box 157.

20. See Joseph P. Lash, *Dealers and Dreamers: A New Look at the New Deal* (New York: Doubleday, 1988), chap. 4; Susan Ware, *Partner and I: Molly Dewson, Feminism, and New Deal Politics* (New Haven: Yale University Press, 1987), chaps. 7–9.

21. Dewson to Frankfurter, 5 December 1928, FF Papers, box 157.

22. Ibid.

23. Dewson to Frankfurter, 14 December 1932, FF Papers, box 153. As her biographer points out, Dewson was born the year after the depression of 1873; the letter concludes: "The American Federation of Labor is impotant [*sic*] and levels are crashing right and left. The situation of the workers has not been so bad since the early seventies. I always marvel why I was so interested in this problem, but now I understand that I was birthmarked by it." See Ware, *Partner and I*, 4.

24. *Morehead v. New York ex rel. Tipaldo*, 298 U.S. 587 (1936).

25. "Conversation between Clara Mortenson Beyer and Vivien Hart, Washington, D.C., November 14, 1983," 15, transcript in CMB Papers.

26. Sybil Lipschultz, "Social Feminism and Legal Discourse, 1908–1923," in Martha Albertson Fineman and Nancy Sweet Thomadsen, eds., *At the Boundaries of Law: Feminism and Legal Theory* (New York: Routledge, 1991), 217.

27. Felix Frankfurter, "The Red Terror of Judicial Reform," in Philip B. Kurland, ed., *Felix Frankfurter on the Supreme Court: Extrajudicial Essays on the Court and the Con-*

stitution (Cambridge: Harvard University Press, 1970), 167. This appeared as an unsigned editorial in the *New Republic* of 1 October 1924.

28. NCL, "Stenographic Report," 2.

29. See Cohen to Frankfurter, 7 February 1933, FF Papers, box 153, on the effect of a federal law on local employment, used by Frankfurter in his letter to Frances Perkins, 9 February 1933, FF Microfilm, reel 94; Dewson thought Cohen lacked political instincts, begging Frankfurter, 5 December 1928, FF Papers, box 157: "Please do not turn me over to Mr. Cohen who is a very fine fellow whose zeal and interest I appreciate 100%." On the legal community involved, see also Lash, *Dealers and Dreamers*, esp. chap. 4; Michael E. Parrish, *Felix Frankfurter and His Times: The Reform Years* (New York: Free Press, 1982), 159–69; and the somewhat conspiratorial picture of this legal circle drawn by Bruce Allen Murphy, *The Brandeis/Frankfurter Connection* (Garden City, N.Y.: Anchor Books, 1983), chap. 3. See also the contributors to the volume on *Adkins* (twelve out of sixteen condemning the decision) compiled by the NCL and published as *The Supreme Court and Minimum Wage Legislation: Comment by the Legal Profession on the District of Columbia Case* (New York: New Republic, 1925).

30. Frankfurter to Cohen, 5 June 1923; Frankfurter to Kelley, 31 May 1923, FF Papers, box 157.

31. For a clear summary of this "formalist" period, see William M. Wiecek, *Liberty under Law: The Supreme Court in American Life* (Baltimore: Johns Hopkins University Press, 1988), chap. 5; see also Charles A. Miller, "The Forest of Due Process of Law: The American Constitutional Tradition," in J. Roland Pennock and John W. Chapman, eds., *Due Process*, nomos 18 (New York: New York University Press, 1977), 3–68; and William E. Nelson, *The Fourteenth Amendment: From Political Principle to Judicial Doctrine* (Cambridge: Harvard University Press, 1988).

32. Ray A. Brown, "Due Process, Police Power, and the Supreme Court," *Harvard Law Review* 40 (May 1927): 944–45. Frankfurter was already focused on this problem; for example, Harold Laski wrote to Holmes in 1918, "Felix is going to write a book . . . He'll write on the 14th Amendment." Quoted in Parrish, *Felix Frankfurter*, 159.

33. Frankfurter, "The Red Terror," 163.

34. Brown to Kelley, 10 May 1923, NCL Papers, series C, box 2. Brown was unable to attend the *Adkins* postmortem in April, but he discussed the decision in a chance meeting in Washington with Jesse Adkins and had written before to Kelley. See Brown to Kelley [April 1923]: "I dined with F.F. on Wednesday night and his views, as I understood them, are mine"; NCL Papers, series C, box 1; Brown to Kelley, 11 June 1923, NCL Papers, series C, box 2; Adkins to Frankfurter, 14 April 1923, FF Papers, box 153. Lawyers took the basic problem to be the Fourteenth Amendment, imposing the requirement of due process on the states where virtually all law regulating industrial and social conditions was made. The *Adkins* judgment, referring to federal law for the District of Columbia and thus ruled by the Fifth Amendment, was assumed to be a direct precedent for what would normally be Fourteenth Amendment cases.

35. Frankfurter to Kelley, 3 April 1924, FF Papers, box 157.

36. Frankfurter to Kelley, 30 March 1924, NCL Papers, series C, box 2. See the discussion of the interpretation of the Fourteenth Amendment with reference to both discrimination and economic regulation in Wiecek, *Liberty under Law*, 96–139.

37. Especially in the case of substantive due process itself, traced back to the dissents of Justice Bradley in the Slaughter-House Cases of 1873. See Wiecek, *Liberty under Law*, 116.

38. *Adkins v. Children's Hospital of Washington, D.C.*, 261 U.S. 525 (1923), 555, 559.

39. Kelley to Frankfurter, 3 November 1925, FF Papers, box 157.

40. Frankfurter, "The Red Terror," 164, 163.

41. Kelley to Frankfurter, 26 May 1923, FF Papers, box 157.

42. Kelley to Mildred Chadsey, 8 March 1923, NCL Papers, series C, box 2.

43. Brown to Kelley, 11 June 1923, NCL Papers, series C, box 2. Several correspondents, especially lawyers, reiterated their support for the health argument and their doubts about Frankfurter's strategy; see, for example, Prof. Irving Fisher to Kelley, 8 June 1923, Myrta Jones to Kelley, n.d., NCL Papers, series C, box 2.

44. Kelley to Frankfurter, 5 June 1923, FF Papers, box 157. Minimum wagers' experience of the downward pull of industry demands by boards' and commissions' fixing of wage levels gave Kelley cause for this belief. See, for example, the role played by industry representatives in the District of Columbia, detailed in the annual reports of the board and summarized in Vivien Hart, "Feminism and Bureaucracy: The Minimum Wage Experiment in the District of Columbia," *Journal of American Studies* 26 (April 1992): 1–22.

45. Frankfurter to Grace Abbott, 5 June 1923, FF Papers, box 157.

46. Frankfurter to Ben Cohen, 5 June 1923, FF Papers, box 157. On Beyer's work at the District of Columbia board, see Hart, "Feminism and Bureaucracy"; her own account of its opening years, Clara E. Mortenson, "The Minimum Wage at Work in the District of Columbia," *Proceedings of the National Conference of Social Work* (1920): 298–304; her reminiscences in "The Work Got Done: An Interview with Clara Mortenson Beyer," in Meg McGavran Murray, *Face to Face: Fathers, Mothers, Masters, Monsters* (Westport: Greenwood Press, 1983), 203–32; and in "Conversation between Beyer and Hart."

47. Kelley to Frankfurter, 29 May 1923, FF Papers, box 157. The NCL had recently published a summary of the British government report on Trade Boards, *The Cave Report on the British Trade Board Acts, 1909–1922: The Success of Minimum Wage Legislation* (New York: Steinberg Press, [1922]). See also Vivien Hart, "No Englishman Can Understand: Fairness and Minimum Wage Laws in Britain and America, 1923–1938," in Brian Holden Reid and John White, eds., *American Studies: Essays in Honour of Marcus Cunliffe* (London: Macmillan, 1991), 249–69.

48. Frankfurter to Kelley, 31 May 1923, FF Papers, box 157.

49. Frankfurter to Abbott, 5 June 1923, FF Papers, box 157.

50. Frankfurter to Cohen, 5 June 1923, Frankfurter to Kelley, 6 June 1923, referring to published evidence by Tawney, Bulkley, and the Cave Committee, FF Papers, box 157.

51. See Elizabeth Brandeis, "Labor Legislation," in John R. Commons, ed., *History of Labor in the United States, 1896–1932* (New York: Macmillan, 1935), vol. 3, 505, 512–13. On Wisconsin, Elizabeth Brandeis, "The Wisconsin Minimum Wage Law," typescript, March 1933, NCL Papers, series B, box 2; William L. Crow, "History of Legislative Control of Wages in Wisconsin," *Marquette Law Review* 16 (April 1932): 188–98. On New York, "Constitutionality of the New York Minimum Wage Law," *Yale Law Journal* 42 (June 1933): 1250–59.

52. Quoted in Brandeis, "Labor Legislation," 505, n. 15.

53. Brandeis to Kelley, 20 June 1929. NCL Papers, series C, box 1. Brandeis was authorized to speak for Commons; see John R. Commons to Kelley, 25 June 1929, NCL Papers, series C, box 1. See also Jack Barbash, "John R. Commons: Pioneer of Labor Economics," *Monthly Labor Review* 112 (May 1989): 44–49; and John R. Commons, *Myself* (New York: Macmillan, 1934), 153–60.

54. See Irving Bernstein, *The Lean Years: A History of the American Worker, 1920–1933* (Boston: Houghton Mifflin, 1960); Felix Frankfurter and Nathan Greene, *The*

Labor Injunction (New York: Macmillan, 1930); Steven Fraser, *Labor Will Rule: Sidney Hillman and the Rise of American Labor* (New York: Free Press, 1991), esp. 189–97 and chap. 8; David R. Roediger and Philip S. Foner, *Our Own Time: A History of American Labor and the Working Day* (London: Verso, 1989), chap. 10; Christopher L. Tomlins, *The State and the Unions: Labor Relations, Law, and the Organized Labor Movement in America, 1880–1960* (Cambridge: Cambridge University Press, 1985), 74–95. Compare the policy statement in AFL, *Report of Proceedings of the Thirty-Third Annual Convention of the American Federation of Labor. Held at Seattle, Washington, Nov. 10 to 22, 1913, Inclusive* (Washington, D.C.: Law Reporter Printing, 1913), 63; and William F. Green's testimony, "Any such proposal to deal with the fixing of general minimum wage standards by a government fiat for men in private industry would be strenuously opposed." Congress, Senate, Committee on Education and Labor (75th Congress, 1st session), *Fair Labor Standards Act of 1937, Joint Hearings before the Committee on Education and Labor, U.S. Senate, and the Committee on Labor, House of Representatives* (Washington, D.C.: GPO, 1937), 219.

55. Brandeis to Kelley, 20 June 1929; Brandeis to Frankfurter, 16 January 1933, FF Papers, box 153.

56. Dewson to Frankfurter, 27 November 1928, FF Papers, box 157.

57. Cohen to Frankfurter, 30 November 1928, FF Papers, box 157.

58. Frankfurter to Dewson, 10 December 1928, MWD Papers; Dewson to Frankfurter, 5 December 1928, FF Papers, box 157; Lash, *Dealers and Dreamers*, 43.

59. *Morehead*, 587.

60. Beulah Amidon's description of the legislation and the background to the case, reprinted from *Survey-Graphic* 25 (July 1936) in Egbert Ray Nichols and Joseph H. Bacchus, eds., *Selected Articles on Minimum Wages and Maximum Hours* (New York: H. W. Wilson, 1937), 175.

61. See, for example, "New NRA Mapped by the President in Single Statute," *New York Times* (29 January 1937): 1.

62. *West Coast Hotel v. Parrish*, 300 U.S. 379 (1937).

63. *Morehead*, 615.

64. Ibid., 616–17.

65. Ibid., 629.

66. See Joan G. Zimmerman, "The Jurisprudence of Equality: The Women's Minimum Wage, the First Equal Rights Amendment, and *Adkins v. Children's Hospital*, 1905–1923," *Journal of American History* 78 (June 1991): 220–21.

67. Compare the NWP brief: "More men are affected by [low wages] than women since there are more men workers than women, and consequently more people dependent upon men's earnings than upon women's." *In the Supreme Court of the United States, October Term—1935, No. 838 . . . Brief as Amici Curiae on Behalf of the National Woman's Party . . .* , 26, with the opinion of Justice Butler: "Men in greater number than women support themselves and dependents and because of need will work for whatever wages they can get." *Morehead*, 616.

68. NWP, *Brief as Amici Curiae*, 34.

69. *West Coast Hotel*, 400.

70. See also J. Kennard Cheadle, "The Parrish Case: Minimum Wages for Women and, Perhaps, for Men," *University of Cincinnati Law Review* 11 (May 1937): 307–26.

71. *West Coast Hotel*, 391.

72. See Robert L. Stern, "The Problems of Yesteryear—Commerce and Due Process," *Vanderbilt Law Review* 4 (1951): 446–68; Robert G. McCloskey, "Economic Due Process and the Supreme Court: An Exhumation and Reburial," *Supreme Court Review*

34 (1961): 34–62. The doctrine of economic substantive due process continued to be applied by state courts. See Monrad G. Paulsen, "The Persistence of Substantive Due Process in the States," *Minnesota Law Review* 34 (January 1950): 91–118; John A. C. Hetherington, "State Economic Regulation and Substantive Due Process of Law," *Northwestern University Law Review* 53 (1958): 226–51. Substantive due process in areas other than economic regulation has again become an issue, with the same concern over the relation of judiciary and legislature. See, for example, essays in Stanley H. Friedelbaum, ed., *Human Rights in the States: New Directions in Constitutional Policymaking* (New York: Greenwood Press, 1988); and Richard A. Epstein, "Substantive Due Process by Any Other Name: The Abortion Cases," *Supreme Court Review* (1973): 159–85.

73. See *The Autobiography of Florence Kelley: Notes of Sixty Years*, ed. Kathryn Kish Sklar (Chicago: Charles H. Kerr, 1986), 12–13, 77–89.

74. Judith A. Baer, *The Chains of Protection: The Judicial Response to Women's Labor Legislation* (Westport: Greenwood Press, 1978), 100–101.

75. Paulsen, "The Persistence," 114.

76. See the memorandum written by Justice Roberts about the circumstances of the case, in Kurland, *Felix Frankfurter on the Supreme Court*, 521. Ray A. Brown, "Police Power—Legislation for Health and Personal Safety," *Harvard Law Review* 42 (May 1929): 868.

77. "Q: If you find that the Adkins law is back on the statute books, if you get such an opinion from the Attorney General, would you explore the possibility of having other laws, such as N.R.A. and A.A.A.— THE PRESIDENT (interposing): You are getting too 'iffy.'" Franklin D. Roosevelt, "Presidential Press Conference Number 356 (March 30, 1937)," in *The Complete Presidential Press Conferences* (New York: Da Capo Press, 1972), vol. 9, 232.

78. Roosevelt immediately consulted the attorney general over whether overruling *Adkins* meant that the district law was simply back on the books. He transmitted official confirmation of this to Congress on 3 April 1937. A board was appointed on 10 June, and on 1 July "began business in room 502 [of the District Building], the one occupied by the former Board in 1918." *Annual Report of the Minimum Wage Board of the District of Columbia for the period June 10, 1937 to December 31, 1937* (no imprint), 8. See also Roosevelt, *Press Conferences*, vol. 9, 231–32; Franklin D. Roosevelt, *The Public Papers and Addresses of Franklin D. Roosevelt, 1937 Volume: The Constitution Prevails* (New York: Macmillan, 1941), "37: The President Transmits the Attorney-General's Opinion on the Status of the Minimum Wage Law of the District of Columbia. April 6, 1937," 146–50. The board is still in business.

79. Roberts, quoted in Kurland, *Felix Frankfurter on the Supreme Court*, 520.

80. Minimum wage lawyers were always on the lookout for the best test case; it was a tactic that could be taken too far, as by opponents in California, whose case was dismissed when they were shown to have paid a young woman to bring suit against the California law. Katherine Philips Edson to Kelley, 7 January 1925, NCL Papers, series C, box 3.

81. Donald L. Horowitz, *The Courts and Social Policy* (Washington, D.C.: Brookings Institution, 1977), chap. 2.

82. Ibid., 23.

83. Kelley to Maud Younger, 19 October 1921, NWP Papers, reel 10.

84. [Levitt to Hill], Saturday [June 1921], NWP Papers, reel 8. But perhaps Hill had replied by the time Levitt wrote to Paul that " marriage will always involve 'disabilities'

. . . Men and women both are subject to them . . . The other factors involved, such as the headship of the home and family are matters of fact and not matters of law. (On this last sentence there is much good authority against me!!)." Levitt to Paul, 13 July 1921, NWP Papers, reel 9.

85. See Carroll Smith-Rosenberg, *Disorderly Conduct: Visions of Gender in Victorian America* (New York: Oxford University Press, 1985), 264–65, on this transitional generation; the differences in law between approaches based on gender and those based on sex, and their frequent confusion, are criticized by Joan C. Williams, "Deconstructing Gender," in Katherine T. Bartlett and Rosanne Kennedy, eds., *Feminist Legal Theory: Readings in Law and Gender* (Boulder: Westview Press, 1991), 95–123, esp. 110–12.

86. See also Naomi Black, *Social Feminism* (Ithaca: Cornell University Press, 1989), for an analysis in sympathetic terms of this reconceptualization of feminism and politics.

87. See Ware, *Partner and I*, chap. 7, esp. 102–3; and also my comment on Dewson's career as an aide rather than a leader, in Vivien Hart, "Review Essay: Behind Every Successful Man?" *Journal of American Studies* 23 (1989): 91–94.

88. Frankfurter to Cohen, 5 June 1923, FF Papers, box 157.

89. Joseph Rauh, quoted in Lash, *Dealers and Dreamers*, 335: "The bill had lots of 'kibitzers,' Corcoran, Jackson, Ambrose Doskov, Frankfurter, Jerry Reilly, even yours truly, but Ben was *the* draftsman."

CHAPTER EIGHT
LABOR AND COMMERCE

1. Marcus Cunliffe pointed out that politicians always think their legislation is fair but rarely go to the length of labeling it thus, a provoking observation that shaped this analysis.

2. See Congress (75th Congress, 3d session), *Statutes at Large 1938* (Washington, D.C.: GPO, 1938), vol. 52, chap. 676, 1060–69. Sidney Webb and Beatrice Webb, *Industrial Democracy* (London: Longmans Green, 1897), 749–65; and "Report for the Special Committee on Minimum Wages Boards, by the General Secretary, Mrs. Florence Kelley," in NCL, *Fourteenth Report, 1913* (New York: NCL, 1914), 53. The final text of the FLSA differed markedly from the 1937 draft, for which see *New York Times* (25 May 1937).

3. See Katharine Du Pre Lumpkin, "The Child Labor Provisions of the Fair Labor Standards Act," *Law and Contemporary Problems* 6 (Summer 1939): 391–405; and Jeremy P. Felt, "The Child Labor Provisions of the Fair Labor Standards Act," *Labor History* 11 (Fall 1970): 467–81.

4. Sar A. Levitan and Richard S. Belous, *More than Subsistence: Minimum Wages for the Working Poor* (Baltimore: Johns Hopkins University Press, 1979), 41.

5. Delegation was a due process issue in itself. See Morton J. Horwitz, *The Transformation of American Law, 1870–1960: The Crisis of Legal Orthodoxy* (New York: Oxford University Press, 1992), chap. 8. Precise guidelines for delegated decisions were required. Thus, the administrator was to set up industry boards to supervise the transition to the forty-cent wage and to consider exemptions, with due regard to competitive conditions, collective labor agreements, and existing minimum wage levels, and without classification of workers by age or sex. The administrator had also to resolve problems that Congress had compromised or evaded, like the legal status of home workers, discussed in Eileen Boris, *Home to Work: Motherhood and the Politics of Industrial Homework* (Cambridge: Cambridge University Press, 1994).

6. Examples from Frank E. Cooper, "The Coverage of the Fair Labor Standards Act and Other Problems in Its Interpretation," *Law and Contemporary Problems* 6 (Summer 1939): 336, n. 26 (quoting a Wage and Hour Division release, subsequent issues of which implied that all telephone operators would be covered), and 337.

7. Minimum Wage Study Commission, *Report of the Minimum Wage Study Commission, May 1981* (Washington, D.C.: MWSC, 1981), vol. 1, fig. 4.3, 72. This is the 1947 figure, which subsequently has rarely topped 55 percent of average hourly earnings.

8. John C. Turnbull, C. Arthur Williams, Jr., and Earl F. Cheit, *Economic and Social Security*, 4th ed. (New York: Ronald Press, 1973), 638. As the nickname of the FLSA revealed, this was a Wages and Hours Act. It eliminated the anomaly of the separate, often contradictory, development of wages and hours laws. The hours provision set a maximum forty-hour week, eased in by two annual steps to forty-four- and forty-two-hour weeks. The wage provisions were reinforced by an overtime rule that excess hours must be paid "at a rate not less than one and one-half times the regular rate at which he is employed."

9. Ben J. Wattenberg, ed., *The Statistical History of the United States from Colonial Times to the Present* (New York: Basic Books, 1976), 304.

10. Congress, Senate, Committee on Education and Labor (75th Congress, 1st session), *Fair Labor Standards Act of 1937. Joint Hearings before the Committee on Education and Labor, U.S. Senate, and the Committee on Labor, House of Representatives* (Washington, D.C.: GPO, 1937), 219. Cited hereafter as *FLSA Hearings*. Robert H. Jackson became attorney general and was appointed to the Supreme Court in 1941; see Robert H. Jackson, *The Struggle for Judicial Supremacy: A Study of a Crisis in American Power Politics* (New York: Knopf, 1941; reprint, New York: Octagon Books, 1979), for his account of relations between the Roosevelt administration and the court.

11. *CIO News* (18 June 1938): 1.

12. Mary T. Norton (unpublished autobiography), 140, and chap. 8. MTN Papers, folder Mss Autobiography. I am grateful to Eileen Boris for this source. See also Barbara Sicherman et al., eds., *Notable American Women: The Modern Period* (Cambridge: Harvard University Press, 1980), 511–12.

13. James T. Patterson, *Congressional Conservatism and the New Deal: The Growth of the Conservative Coalition in Congress, 1933–1939* (Lexington: University of Kentucky Press, 1967), 196–97.

14. John S. Forsythe, "Legislative History of the Fair Labor Standards Act," *Law and Contemporary Problems* 6 (Summer 1939): 474. See also Paul Douglas and Joseph Hackman, "The Fair Labor Standards Act of 1938," *Political Science Quarterly* 53 (December 1938): 491–515, and 54 (March 1939): 29–55; *Law and Contemporary Problems* 6 (Summer 1939): 321–491, a special issue on "The Wage and Hour Law"; Orme Wheelock Phelps, *The Legislative Background of the Fair Labor Standards Act: A Study of the Growth of National Sentiment in Favor of Governmental Regulation of Wages, Hours and Child Labor* (Chicago: University of Chicago Press, 1939); Jonathan Grossman, "Fair Labor Standards Act of 1938: Maximum Struggle for a Minimum Wage," *Monthly Labor Review* 19 (June 1978): 22–30. Drafting began in January 1937, a bill went to the House in May, June saw joint hearings by House and Senate Labor Committees, and an amended version passed the Senate in July. The House Rules Committee stalled until the recess, but in November the President called a special session, with the bill on the agenda. In December the bill was discharged from the Rules Committee. The House rejected both an alternative promoted by the AFL and the administration bill. On 3 January 1938, the President again requested passage, and his advisers produced a much-

simplified text. On 28 April, the House Labor Committee reported out this bill, but a minority report from the committee proposed an alternative. On 29 April, the Rules Committee refused to report either bill. The Florida primary was on 3 May; on 6 May, a petition to discharge the administration bill from the Rules Committee succeeded within hours; on 24 May, the House rejected the minority report and passed the administration version. A Conference Committee briefly deadlocked, but a compromise was found. On 25 June, the President signed the FLSA.

15. NCL Microfilm, reel 54, FLSA correspondence 1930–37.

16. *FLSA Hearings*, 173, 174. Anthony J. Badger, *The New Deal: The Depression Years, 1933–1940* (London: Macmillan, 1990), introduces the historiography of the New Deal. Recent interpretations include Steve Fraser and Gary Gerstle, eds., *The Rise and Fall of the New Deal Order, 1930–1980* (Princeton: Princeton University Press, 1989), part 1; Stanley Vittoz, *New Deal Labor Policy and the American Industrial Economy* (Chapel Hill: University of North Carolina Press, 1987), who sees a new social vision, shared to some degree by business and labor, rather than a capitalist plot; and studies emphasizing the role of the state, Theda Skocpol, "Political Response to Capitalist Crisis: Neo-Marxist Theories of the State and the Case of the New Deal," *Politics and Society* 10 (1980): 155–202; Theda Skocpol and Kenneth Finegold, "State Capacity and Economic Intervention in the Early New Deal," *Political Science Quarterly* 97 (Summer 1982): 255–78; and Margaret Weir and Theda Skocpol, "State Structures and the Possibilities for 'Keynesian' Responses to the Great Depression in Sweden, Britain, and the United States," in Peter B. Evans, Dietrich Rueschemeyer, and Theda Skocpol, eds., *Bringing the State Back In* (Cambridge: Cambridge University Press, 1985), 107–63.

17. *FLSA Hearings*, 91–154, 243–61, 371–80. On Robert Johnson and his cooperation with Sidney Hillman in the FLSA campaign, see Steven Fraser, *Labor Will Rule: Sidney Hillman and the Rise of American Labor* (New York: Free Press, 1991), 392.

18. *FLSA Hearings*, 338–40. Fifty-six cents for the clothing industry seems high but probably represented the skilled garment trade, with sweatshops and home workers eluding the census takers. Average hours clustered around the proposed forty-hour mark; without knowing the range of hours around the average, the likely overtime bills cannot be calculated.

19. Ibid., 126.

20. *New York Times* (25 May 1937): 20, sec. 6 (a) of the draft bill; *FLSA Hearings*, 134.

21. *FLSA Hearings*, 456.

22. Testimony of John G. Paine, chairman of the Management Group of the Council for Industrial Progress, ibid., 126.

23. Under the National Recovery Act of 1933, wage and price codes were imposed on specific industries, as part of the emergency effort to stabilize the economy. Old minimum wage hands who had moved into the Labor Department were involved, but the economist and lawyer Brains Trusters of the Roosevelt administration were the prime source; see Peter H. Irons, *The New Deal Lawyers* (Princeton: Princeton University Press, 1982), chaps. 1–5; and Joseph P. Lash, *Dealers and Dreamers: A New Look at the New Deal* (New York: Doubleday, 1988), chap. 10. Studies of the NRA include Donald R. Brand, *Corporatism and the Rule of Law: A Study of the National Recovery Administration* (Ithaca: Cornell University Press, 1988); Ellis W. Hawley, *The New Deal and the Problem of Monopoly* (Princeton: Princeton University Press, 1966); and Vittoz, *New Deal Labor Policy*, chaps. 4–6.

24. Testimony of Paul S. Hanway of the National Fibre, Can and Tube Association, *FLSA Hearings*, 143.

25. See, for example, Frances Perkins's comments on the laudable goals and administrative lessons of the NRA, ibid., esp. 173–87.

26. Ibid., 936, 624, 626.

27. Quoted from a National Association of Manufacturers bulletin, *New York Times* (24 May 1937): 7.

28. *FLSA Hearings*, 808, 809. A representative of the Ohio Chamber of Commerce claimed that the bill rendered all the sacrifices of Americans in the War of Independence, the Civil War, *and* the First World War in vain; ibid., 871.

29. Ibid., 339–40.

30. Ibid., 813.

31. This was part of a larger struggle between southern industries, especially textiles, and national forces; see Fraser, *Labor Will Rule*, chap. 14, on Sidney Hillman and the Textile Workers' Organizing Committee.

32. John E. Edgerton, *FLSA Hearings*, 762, 763, 765, 781–82.

33. Ibid., 765, 766, 788.

34. *New York Times* (16 January 1938): 19.

35. Ibid. (15 May 1938): 2. The *New York Times* headlined the southern strategy: "Wage Bill Change Threatens Senate with a Filibuster" (9 June 1938), 1; "Wage Bill Is Sped by a Compromise Aimed to Suit South" (11 June 1938), 1; and on 19 June 1938, p. 6E reported the final compromise.

36. Ibid. (25 May 1937): 20, sec. 2 (7). See Rena G. Alpert, "Legislative Protection for the Agricultural Laborer," *George Washington Law Review* 8 (May 1940): 1060–69; William T. Ham, "The Status of Agricultural Labor," *Law and Contemporary Problems* 4 (October 1937): 559–72; Austin P. Morris, "Agricultural Labor and National Labor Legislation," *California Law Review* 54 (December 1966): 1939–89. On farm politics, see Richard S. Kirkendall, "The New Deal and Agriculture," in J. Braeman, R. H. Bremner and D. Brody, *The New Deal*, vol. 1: *The National Level* (Columbus: Ohio State University Press, 1975), 83–109; Grant McConnell, *The Decline of Agrarian Democracy* (Berkeley and Los Angeles: University of California Press, 1959); and Theodore Saloutos, *The American Farmers and the New Deal* (Ames: Iowa State University Press, 1982). The classic discussion of the power to keep topics *off* the political agenda is Peter Bachrach and Morton S. Baratz, "The Two Faces of Power," *American Political Science Review* 56 (December 1962): 947–52.

37. See Roosevelt's message to Congress accompanying the bill, 24 May 1937, in Roosevelt, *The Public Papers*, 1937 vol., esp. 210.

38. Senator Hugo Black to Mr. C. W. Rittenour, 21 July 1937. Copy in TGC Papers, box 25. Hugo Black's career went from Ku Klux Klan member to Democratic senator from Alabama and sponsor of labor legislation, to liberal Supreme Court justice from 1937 to 1971. See Virginia Van Der Veer Hamilton, *Hugo Black: The Alabama Years* (Baton Rouge: Louisiana State University Press, 1972); Elizabeth Black, ed., *Mr. Justice and Mrs. Black: The Memoirs of Hugo L. Black and Elizabeth Black* (New York: Random House, 1986); and on his time on the court, see Howard Ball and Phillip J. Cooper, *Of Power and Rights: Hugo Black, William O. Douglas, and America's Constitutional Revolution* (New York: Oxford University Press, 1992); and James F. Simon, *The Antagonists: Hugo Black, Felix Frankfurter and Civil Liberties in Modern America* (New York: Simon and Schuster, 1990).

39. See testimony of Harley Langdale, president of the American Turpentine Farmers Association; J. Leonard Rountree, turpentine producer, Summit, Ga.; C. F. Speh, Bureau of Chemistry and Soils, Department of Agriculture; and Jay Ward, Department of Agriculture; *FLSA Hearings*, 1164–90.

40. Ibid., esp. 1170–76.

41. Ibid., 1181.

42. Ibid., 1196.

43. Ibid., 1196–97.

44. See Fraser, *Labor Will Rule*, 55–113, on Hillman's early association with Progressives including the WTUL, and the arbitration movement.

45. *FLSA Hearings*, 273. On labor and the New Deal, including the crucial battle for organizing rights, see Irving Bernstein, *Turbulent Years: A History of the American Worker 1933–1941* (Boston: Houghton Mifflin, 1971); Christopher L. Tomlins, *The State and the Unions: Labor Relations, Law, and the Organized Labor Movement* (Cambridge: Cambridge University Press, 1985).

46. *New York Times* (30 March 1938): 15. On Hillman's leadership of the textile workers and support for government regulation of the more anarchic sectors of the economy, see Fraser, *Labor Will Rule*; on passage of the FLSA, 391–94; on labor mobilization on the issue, Elizabeth Brandeis, "Organized Labor and Protective Labor Legislation," in Milton Derber and Edwin Young, eds., *Labor and the New Deal* (New York: Da Capo Press, 1972), 217–30; Melvyn Dubofsky and Warren Van Tine, *John L. Lewis: A Biography*, abridged ed. (Urbana: University of Illinois Press, 1986), esp. chap. 14; Steve Fraser, "Dress Rehearsal for the New Deal: Shop-Floor Insurgents, Political Elites, and Industrial Democracy in the Amalgamated Clothing Workers," in Michael H. Frisch and Daniel J. Walkowitz, eds., *Working-Class America: Essays on Labor, Community, and American Society* (Urbana: University of Illinois Press, 1983), 212–55.

47. *New York Times* (13 December 1937): 12.

48. *FLSA Hearings*, 226; AFL, *Report of the Proceedings of the 57th Annual Convention of the American Federation of Labor, Denver, Colorado, 4 Oct.–15 Oct. 1937* (Washington, D.C.: Judd and Detweiler, 1937), 500–502.

49. The AFL-sponsored bill was defeated, on 12 December 1937, by 162 votes to 131; on 17 December the administration bill was recommitted by a vote of 216 to 198.

50. Walter L. Pope, "Memorandum for Mr. Jackson," 8 June 1937, RHJ Papers, box 80.

51. *New York Times* (9 January 1938): 4; (26 March 1938): 2; (3 April 1938): 3; (14 April 1938): 1; and (16 April 1938): 2. In his "Memorandum for Assistant Attorney General Jackson" of 12 July 1937, Justice Department official Walter L. Pope attributed the idea of a flat-rate wage to John L. Lewis, not to the AFL; RHJ Papers, box 80.

52. David P. Currie, *The Constitution in the Supreme Court: The Second Century, 1888–1986* (Chicago: University of Chicago Press, 1990), 208. Currie's chap. 7 summarizes the relevant legal developments. See also R. A. Maidment, *The Judicial Response to the New Deal: The United States Supreme Court and Economic Regulation* (Manchester: Manchester University Press, 1991), who argues, from a formalist standpoint, that precedents for new interpretations of economic regulation were already set in the early thirties. On the antagonisms between administration and court, and the emergence of a new majority permitting economic regulation and labor laws, see Leonard Baker, *Back to Back: The Duel between FDR and the Supreme Court* (New York: Macmillan, 1967); Irons, *New Deal Lawyers*, chap. 13; Felix Frankfurter, "Mr. Justice Roberts," in Philip Kurland, ed., *Felix Frankfurter on the Supreme Court: Extrajudicial Essays on the Court and the Constitution* (Cambridge: Harvard University Press, 1970), 516–24.

53. Especially *Nebbia v. New York*, 291 U.S. 502 (1934), in which Justice Roberts wrote, upholding the regulation of milk prices.

54. Bruce Ackerman, "Constitutional Politics/Constitutional Law," *Yale Law Journal* 99 (December 1989): 459.

55. Edward S. Corwin, "Congress's Power to Prohibit Commerce a Crucial Constitutional Issue," *Cornell Law Quarterly* 18 (June 1933): 477. See also Edward S. Corwin, *The Commerce Power versus States' Rights* (Princeton: Princeton University Press, 1936). On the nationalization of policy and the role of the state, see Alan Brinkley, "The New Deal and the Idea of the State," in Fraser and Gerstle, eds., *Rise and Fall of the New Deal Order*, 85–121.

56. Robert L. Stern, "That Commerce which Concerns More States than One," *Harvard Law Review* 47 (June 1934): 1335, 1337. See also Stern, "The Commerce Clause and the National Economy, 1933–1946," *Harvard Law Review* 59 (May 1946): 653–58; and Irons, *New Deal Lawyers*, esp. 46–54. Major Commerce Clause precedents wavered between a narrow interpretation of the nature of interstate commerce, as in *United States v. E. C. Knight Co.*, 156 U.S. 1 (1895), the Sugar Trust case, and a more generous one as in *Houston E. and W. Texas Ry. Co. v. U.S.*, 234 U.S. 342 (1914), the Shreveport Rate case. The most important anti–New Deal cases were *Schechter Poultry Corp. v. U.S.*, 295 U.S. 495 (1935), striking down the NRA on grounds that the federal government could regulate only goods in the stream of commerce, not the conditions under which they were processed or sold; and *Carter v. Carter Coal Co.*, 298 U.S. 238 (1936): "Mining brings the subject matter of commerce into existence. Commerce disposes of it." In Carter, the court specifically rejected the argument that the importance of coal production to the national economy justified government regulation.

57. David Currie argues that even as the FLSA gathered momentum, the claim to expand federal power was already won, for "constitutional federalism had died in 1937," with the *West Coast Hotel* and *NLRB v. Jones and Laughlin Steel Corp.*, 301 U.S. 1 (1937), decisions. See Currie, *Constitution in the Supreme Court*, 238. On the constitutional history of federal powers, see Ball and Cooper, *Of Power and Right*, chap. 11; and Louis Fisher, *Constitutional Structures: Separated Powers and Federalism* (New York: McGraw-Hill, 1990), 371–96.

58. Extract from Kelley's testimony to the House Committee on Labor in 1914, reprinted in Grace Abbott, *The Child and the State* (Chicago: University of Chicago Press, 1938), vol. 1, 482.

59. Frances Perkins to Raymond Moley, 16 February 1933, with draft agenda item, letter to governors, suggested statement for Governor Lehman to make at the governors' conference, 6 March 1933, FF Microfilm, reel 94, subject file/Labor Department. Despite the suggestion, Roosevelt's speech and the discussion were on banking, taxation, and relief; *New York Times* (8 February 1933): 1; (6 March 1933): 1; and (7 March 1933): 1. Following passage of Lehman's New York minimum wage bill in April, Roosevelt did write to other governors urging them to follow suit; *New York Times* (13 April 1933): 1. See also Frances Perkins, *The Roosevelt I Knew* (New York: Viking Press, 1946), chap. 21, esp. 249. Black had upstaged the incoming team by introducing, in December 1932, a thirty-hour bill; he argued that its strength was its new and necessary interpretation of the Commerce Clause. See Hamilton, *Hugo Black*, 214–21; and *New York Times* (31 March 1933): 3.

60. Felix Frankfurter, *The Commerce Clause under Marshall, Taney and Waite* (Chapel Hill: University of North Carolina Press, 1937), 18, 2, 39.

61. "Wages and Hours—What Is Practical Now," memo, Sam [?] to Tommy [Corcoran], 17 June 1936, on Securities and Exchange Commission letterhead, TGC Papers, box 255.

62. "Memorandum," n.d. [c. 1936–37], RHJ Papers, box 80.

63. "Memorandum," n.d. [c. 1937], RHJ Papers, box 80, 5.

64. In addition to the 1936 election result, opinion polls confirmed support for wages and hours regulation: 61 percent in favor in May 1937 was the lowest figure; George H.Gallup, *The Gallup Poll: Public Opinion, 1935–1971* (New York: Random House, 1972), 60.

65. *New York Times* (29 January 1937): 1.

66. *FLSA Hearings*, 2.

67. Ibid., 3. Jackson's statement filled ninety pages of small print. Frankfurter wrote applauding "an altogether advisable statement . . . I congratulate you on its wisdom and for its rightness." Felix Frankfurter to Jackson, 3 June 1937, RHJ Papers, box 80.

68. A package of strategies summarized by Jackson's assistant, Walter L. Pope, as "the 'anti *Hammer v. Dagenhart*' approach, the 'Wagner Act' approach, the 'Ashurst-Summers' approach and the 'unfair competition' approach." "Memorandum for Assistant Attorney General Jackson," 12 July 1937, RHJ Papers, box 80. In the FLSA, the Wagner Act approach of preventing industrial strife, and Ashurst-Summers referring to the conditions under which goods in interstate commerce were produced, had been abandoned. *Hammer v. Dagenhart* (on child labor) was overruled in *United States v. Darby*.

69. "Memorandum," n.d. [c. 1937], RHJ Papers, box 80. The Slaughterhouse Cases, 83 U.S. 36 (1873), gave the first Supreme Court judgment on the Fourteenth Amendment privileges and immunities, equal protection, and due process clauses. See William M. Wiecek, *Liberty under Law: The Supreme Court in American Life* (Baltimore: Johns Hopkins University Press, 1988), on the majority opinion and racial equality, 96–109; and on the dissents, economic regulation and the foundations of the doctrine of substantive due process, 115–39. Federal legislation on fair competition included the Interstate Commerce Act of 1887, and Sherman and Clayton Antitrust Acts of 1890 and 1914. See also my discussion of fairness in minimum wage policy, "No Englishman Can Understand: Fairness and Minimum Wage Laws in Britain and America, 1923–1938," in Brian Holden Reid and John White, eds., *American Studies: Essays in Honour of Marcus Cunliffe* (London: Macmillan, 1991), 249–69.

70. Jackson, *FLSA Hearings*, 4–5. Jackson was trying to preempt the ruling child labor decision, *Hammer v. Dagenhart*, which prohibited regulation of the conditions under which goods were made prior to their shipment in interstate commerce. There had been discussions within the Justice Department about either reviving or avoiding this issue; see, for example, "Memorandum Concerning the Wagner Act Decision on a Basis for Legislation Regulating Child Labor, Wages and Hours," n.d. [c. 1937], RHJ Papers, box 80. In three crucial cases for incorporating the concept of a national police power into the Commerce Clause, the court upheld a prohibition on the interstate shipment of lottery tickets in *Champion v. Ames*, 188 U.S. 321 (1903); allowed the seizure of adulterated eggs even after they had reached a local point of sale in *Hipolite Egg Co. v. United States*, 220 U.S. 45 (1911); and, in *Hoke v. United States*, 227 U.S. 308 (1913), upheld the Mann Act, which prohibited the interstate transportation of women for immoral purposes.

71. *FLSA Hearings*, 187. See also William Green, *FLSA Hearings*, 218, 233; and Representative Luce, ibid., 844, on the costs of training short-term female employees.

72. Ibid., 273.

73. Franklin D. Roosevelt, *The Complete Presidential Press Conferences* (New York: Da Capo Press, 1972), 30 March 1937, vol. 9, 230–32.

74. See Cooper, "Coverage of the Fair Labor Standards Act," 335–37.

75. Cohen to Frankfurter, 7 February 1933, FF Papers, box 153; Frankfurter to Frances Perkins, 9 February 1933, FF Microfilm, reel 94.

76. *FLSA Hearings*, 196. Lucy Randolph Mason became general secretary of the NCL in 1932. The NCL was concentrating on wage standards and Mason worked closely with Clara Beyer. Beyer was associate director of the Division of Labor Standards in the Labor Department from 1933. Mason resigned from the NCL in May 1937, frustrated by funding problems, but represented them in the FLSA hearings in June. She became a CIO and Textile Workers', Organizing Committee staffer; see John A. Salmond, *Miss Lucy of the CIO: The Life and Times of Lucy Randolph Mason, 1882–1959* (Athens: University of Georgia Press, 1988). Mason's testimony, *FLSA Hearings*, 403–10. See also her FLSA correspondence, NCL Microfilm, reel 54.

77. See Department of Labor, Division of Labor Standards, *Why a State Wage-Hour Law Now?* Bulletin no. 47 (Washington: GPO, 1941), 4; Beyer's letter to an official of the Louisiana YWCA, in Gerald Markowitz and David Rosen, eds., *"Slaves of the Depression": Workers' Letters about Life on the Job* (Ithaca: Cornell University Press, 1987), 159–60; and her account of coaxing state officials, in "Conversation between Clara Mortenson Beyer and Vivien Hart, Washington, D.C., November 14, 1983," 14, 35, transcript in CMB Papers. Cooperation with states was both necessary and problematic during the New Deal, whether in attempts to dovetail policy development, or joint funding or implementation. See especially James T. Patterson, *The New Deal and the States* (Princeton: Princeton University Press, 1969); also Anthony J. Badger, "The New Deal and the Localities," in Rhodri Jeffreys-Jones and Bruce Collins, eds., *The Growth of Federal Power in American History* (Edinburgh: Scottish Academic Press, 1983); and William R. Brock, *Welfare, Democracy, and the New Deal* (Cambridge: Cambridge University Press, 1988).

78. *FLSA Hearings*, 338.

79. Julia Kirk Blackwelder, "Texas Homeworkers in the 1930s," in Eileen Boris and Cynthia R. Daniels, eds., *Homework: Historical and Contemporary Perspectives on Paid Labor at Home* (Urbana: University of Illinois Press, 1989), 88.

80. "Conversation between Beyer and Hart," 30. I owe the example of domestic work to Phyllis M. Palmer, *Domesticity and Dirt: Housework and Domestic Service in the United States, 1920–1945* (Philadelphia: Temple University Press, 1989); esp. chap. 6 on public policy. Many state laws covered only women "employed in trade and industry"; some specifically excluded domestic workers; only Wisconsin included all female wage workers; see Melvin Sims, *Legal Aspects of Labor Problems—Minimum Wages* (Washington, D.C.: Office of National Recovery Administration, Division of Review, 1936), esp. 37, 106, 133–34.

81. *New York Times* (27 May 1937): 4; Roosevelt, *Presidential Press Conferences*, 8 April 1938, vol. 9, 297. See also Susan Tucker, "A Complex Bond: Southern Black Domestic Workers and Their Employers," in Darlene Clark Hine, ed., *Black Women in United States History: The Twentieth Century* (Brooklyn, N.Y.: Carlson, 1990), vol. 4, 1187–1204; and on the language of female work, Linda K. Kerber, "Separate Spheres, Female Worlds, Woman's Place: The Rhetoric of Women's History," *Journal of American History* 75 (June 1988): 28.

82. *FLSA Hearings*, 275.

83. Paul H. Douglas to Charles O. Gregory, 31 December 1936, NCL Microfilm, reel 54. This was Douglas's response to the Labor Department survey of economists, copies of which were sent to the NCL by Marion Stitt, director of the Division of Minimum Wage in the Women's Bureau. See also Winifred D. Wandersee, *Women's Work and Family Values, 1920–1940* (Cambridge: Harvard University Press, 1981); and Lois Scharf, *To Work and to Wed: Female Employment, Feminism, and the Great Depression*

(Westport: Greenwood Press, 1980); sec. 213 of the 1932 Economy Act required the spouse of a federal employee to be first fired or last hired by the federal government.

84. Stern, "That Commerce," 1346–47, 1365.

85. "Wage and Hour Bill," unsigned and undated note in a White House speech material file, TGC Papers, box 232.

86. "Second Year of the Wage and Hour Act," *Monthly Labor Review* 49 (July–December 1939): 1439, 1444.

87. Edward K. Frazier and Jacob Perlman, "Entrance Rates of Common Laborers, July 1939," ibid., 1454–55. On judicial mediation of New Deal and later labor law with regard to African-American workers, see Herbert Hill, *Black Labor and the American Legal System: Race, Work, and the Law* (Madison: University of Wisconsin Press, 1985). See also Harvard Sitkoff, *A New Deal for Blacks: The Emergence of Civil Rights as a National Issue*, vol. 1: *The Depression Decade* (Oxford: Oxford University Press, 1978).

88. "Second Year," 1443–44.

89. Frazier and Perlman, "Entrance Rates," 1456–57. *United States v. Darby*, 312 U.S. 100 (1941).

90. "Second Year," 1440. Bakers were the subject of the major Supreme Court decision in *Lochner v. New York*, 198 U.S. 45 (1905), which ruled against labor laws for men; candy makers featured largely in several of the early minimum wage investigations, especially in Massachusetts in 1911.

91. *United States v. Darby*, 312 U.S. 100 (1941).

92. Currie, *The Constitution in the Supreme Court*, 238.

93. *Wickard v. Filburn*, 317 U.S. 102 (1942).

94. Stern, "The Commerce Clause and the National Economy, 1933–1946," 891–92; *Borden Co. v. Borella*, 325 U.S. 679 (1945).

95. Changes summarized from the following sources: Phyllis Palmer, "Outside the Law: Agriculture and Domestic Workers under the Fair Labor Standards Act," a paper presented at the OAH convention, Reno, Nevada, 1988, revised version, 1993; Minimum Wage Study Commission, *Report of the Minimum Wage Study Commission* (Washington, D.C.: MWSC, 1981), vol. 1, 1–5; U.S. Laws, Statutes (Fair Labor Standards Act of 1938), *1977 Minimum Wage Law: Fair Labor Standards Act with 1977 Amendments, Explanation . . . Joint Explanatory Statement of Committee of Conference . . . Text of FLSA as Amended* (Washington, D.C.: Bureau of National Affairs, 1977). Amendments were passed in 1949, 1955, 1961, 1966, 1974, 1977, and 1989.

96. See the symposium on "Rights Consciousness in American History," *Journal of American History* 74 (December 1987): 795–1034; see also Stanley N. Katz, "The Strange Birth and Unlikely History of Constitutional Equality," *Journal of American History* 75 (December 1988): 747–61.

97. Palmer, "Outside the Law," 3.

98. John Kincaid, "Constitutional Federalism: Labor's Role in Displacing Places to Benefit Persons," *PS* 26 (June 1993): 172–77.

99. See Sitkoff, *A New Deal for Blacks*, esp. chap. 2; Gavin Wright, *Old South, New South: Revolutions in the Southern Economy Since the Civil War* (New York: Basic Books, 1986); Morris, "Agricultural Labor"; Cletus E. Daniel, *Bitter Harvest: A History of California Farmworkers, 1870–1941* (Ithaca: Cornell University Press, 1981); and Michael Harrington, *The Other America* (New York: Macmillan, 1962).

100. Occasions such as Senate Subcommittee hearings on Migratory Labor in 1965 and 1966 brought the issue into the open; see Morris, "Agricultural Labor," esp. 1983. I owe to Phyllis Palmer a later reference: "Migrant Workers Are Employees under

FLSA, Seventh Circuit Says," *Current Developments* (Washington, D.C.: Bureau of National Affairs, 11 January 1988): A-6.

101. Congress, Senate, Subcommittee on Labor of the Committee on Labor and Public Welfare (94th Congress, 2d session), *Legislative History of the Fair Labor Standards Act Amendments of 1974* (Washington, D.C.: GPO, 1976), 484, table 3, 129.

102. For this discussion of the Equal Pay Act I am indebted to Cynthia Harrison, *On Account of Sex: The Politics of Women's Issues, 1945–1968* (Berkeley and Los Angeles: University of California Press, 1988), esp. chaps. 3 and 6. For details of how the act worked, see the Bureau of National Affairs, *Equal Pay for Equal Work* (Washington, D.C.: BNA, 1963). See also Paul Burstein, *Discrimination, Jobs, and Politics: The Struggle for Equal Employment Opportunity in the United States since the New Deal* (Chicago: University of Chicago Press, 1985); Claudia Goldin, *Understanding the Gender Gap: An Economic History of American Women* (New York: Oxford University Press, 1990), chap. 7; and Alice Kessler-Harris, *A Woman's Wage: Historical Meanings and Social Consequences* (Lexington: University Press of Kentucky, 1990), chap. 4.

103. Many of the state employees covered in the 1966 amendments carried out the public housekeeping functions that domestic servants performed in private households. In *Maryland v. Wirtz*, 392 U.S. 183 (1968), the Supreme Court confirmed their place in the stream of commerce, making the extension to domestic servants logical. Testimony of Edith B. Sloan and Geneve Reid, of the NCHE; Congress, House of Representatives, Committee on Education and Labor (93d Congress, 1st session), *Fair Labor Standards Act Amendments of 1973: Hearings* (Washington, D.C.: GPO, 1973), 206–8

104. Congress, House of Representatives, Special Subcommittee on Education of the Committee on Education and Labor (91st Congress, 2d session, 17, 19, 26, 29, and 30 June 1970), *Discrimination against Women*, "Statement of Dr. Pauli Murray," 333, "Women Private Household Workers Fact Sheet," 357–62.

105. Susan Tolchin and Martin Tolchin, *Clout: Womanpower and Politics* (New York: G. P. Putnams, 1976), 137. See Shirley Chisholm, *Unbought and Unbossed* (New York: Avon Books, 1970); Paula Giddings, *When and Where I Enter: The Impact of Black Women on Race and Sex in America* (New York: William Morrow, 1984), 337–40; and Tolchin and Tolchin, *Clout*, chap. 5; on other women's organization at the time, Joyce Gelb and Marian Lief Palley, *Women and Public Policies*, rev. ed. (Princeton: Princeton University Press, 1987); and Kay Lehman Schlozman, "Representing Women in Washington: Sisterhood and Pressure Politics," in Louise A. Tilly and Patricia Gurin, eds., *Women, Politics, and Change* (New York: Russell Sage Foundation, 1990), 339–82.

106. Quoted in Tolchin and Tolchin, *Clout*, 144.

107. Taking the Wickard principle to the extreme, Congress noted that vacuum cleaners were produced in only six states, soap moved in interstate commerce, and all in all household work "created a tremendous flow in commerce." Congress, *Legislative History*, 500–501. *1977 Minimum Wage Law*, "Fair Labor Standards Act as Amended," sec. 2 (a), 101.

108. *National League of Cities v. Usery*, 426 U.S. 833 (1976); and *Garcia v. San Antonio Metropolitan Transit Authority*, 469 U.S. 528 (1985). These two cases sparked a debate about the future of federalism if individual rights were automatically to override states' rights. See, for example, Robert F. Nagel, "Federalism as a Fundamental Value: *National League of Cities* in Perspective," *Supreme Court Review* (1981): 81–109; Frank I. Michelman, "States' Rights and States' Roles: Permutations of 'Sovereignty' in *National League of Cities v. Usery*," *Yale Law Journal* 86 (May 1977): 1165–95; Laurence

Tribe, "Unraveling *National League of Cities*: The New Federalism and Affirmative Rights to Essential Government Services," *Harvard Law Review* 90 (April 1977): 1065–1104; and Andrzej Rapaczynski, "From Sovereignty to Process: The Jurisprudence of Federalism after *Garcia*," *Supreme Court Review* (1985): 341–419.

CHAPTER NINE
CONCLUSION

1. Low Pay Network, *Save Wages Councils: A Briefing Paper on the Abolition of Wages Councils* (London: [LPN, 1992]), 1, using 1988 figures, the latest available. Trade Boards were renamed Wages Councils in the Wages Councils Act of 1945; see F. J. Bayliss, *British Wages Councils* (Oxford: Blackwell, 1962).

2. "Average Hourly Earnings of Production or Nonsupervisory Workers on Private Non-Farm Payrolls," *Monthly Labor Review* 115 (September 1992): table 15, 69.

3. LPN, *Save Wages Councils*, appendix 2; Department of Employment, *New Earnings Survey 1992* (London: HMSO, 1992), tables 1, 2, 171.

4. *The Industrial Unrest and the Living Wage: Being a Series of Lectures Given at the Inter-Denominational Summer School, Held at Swanwick, Derbyshire, June 28th–July 5th, 1913* (London: P. S. King, 1914), 144.

5. Low Pay Unit, *Minimum Wages for Women: An Examination of Women's Earnings in Industries Covered by Wages Councils* (London: Low Pay Unit and Equal Opportunities Commission, 1980), 22–24. These were figures for family earnings; the same report dismissed the old "pin-money" hypothesis for women's earnings. For a comparable American discussion, see a review and analysis concluding that raising the minimum wage would lift significant numbers out of officially defined poverty, by Ronald B. Mincy: "Raising the Minimum Wage: Effects on Family Poverty," *Monthly Labor Review* 113 (July 1990): 18–25.

6. NASL handbill, in author's possession.

7. In 1939, only 5 percent of those workers technically covered by the FLSA benefited from the new thirty-cent rate, "Second Year of the Wage and Hour Act," *Monthly Labor Review* 49 (July–December 1939): 1439. In 1980, 6.2 percent of the entire work force was actually earning the minimum wage; Minimum Wage Study Commission, *Report* (Washington, D.C.: MWSC, 1981), vol. 1, 9, and fig. 4.3.

8. The Low Pay Network estimates that upward of 80 percent of Wages Councils workers were women. LPN, *Save Wages Councils*, 12.

9. Employment in private households is exempted from legislation on employment rights and discrimination, including the Sex Discrimination Act of 1986.

10. See Congress, Senate (97th Congress, 1st session), *Youth Opportunity Wage Act of 1981: Hearings before the Subcommittee on Labor of the Committee on Labor and Human Resources, March 24 and 25, 1981* (Washington, D.C.: GPO, 1981). For example, p. 17, Senator Harrison Williams: "These proposals would establish a subclass of workers who are not deserving of the dignity or protection accorded to all other classes of workers in our society . . . [and] set a dangerous precedent for the discriminatory treatment of other classes of workers."

11. *New Earnings Survey, 1992*, table 9, reports average hourly earnings for domestic work at 387 pence, just above counterhands and catering assistants at 377 pence. Fraser P. Davidson, *A Guide to the Wages Act 1986* (London: Blackstone Press, 1986), 86–87, summarizes the arguments on youth wages. LPN, *Save Wages Councils*, 3–5,

reports a decline in young people's earnings, as a proportion of average earnings of those over twenty-one, for example from 60.8 percent in 1979 to 53.9 percent in 1988 for the eighteen-to-twenty age group.

12. *Parliamentary Debates* (Lords), 5th ser., 544 (30 March 1993): col. 759, Lord Gilmour; col. 762, Viscount Ullswater; col. 770, Lord Skidelsky; and col. 754, Baroness Seear. The Scottish Low Pay Unit, in "Pay below Par," *Payline*, no. 12 (March 1993): 4, notes that the Department of Employment itself had to correct its unduly optimistic misinterpretation of its own figures.

13. See Princeton professor Alan Krueger, reporting research on the labor market as a social institution: "There are lots of concerns about fairness. The conventional economic model ignores those concerns. It assumes that people make decisions . . . on purely economic grounds." "Two Economists Catch Clinton's Eye by Bucking the Common Wisdom," *New York Times* (22 August 1993): sec. 4, 7.

14. W. G. Runciman, *Relative Deprivation and Social Justice: A Study of Attitudes to Social Inequality in Twentieth-Century England* (Berkeley and Los Angeles: University of California Press, 1966), 194.

15. William W. Fisher III, "The Development of Modern American Legal Theory and the Judicial Interpretation of the Bill of Rights," in Michael J. Lacey and Knud Haakonssen, eds., *A Culture of Rights: The Bill of Rights in Philosophy, Politics, and Law, 1791 and 1991* (Cambridge: Cambridge University Press, 1991), 292. See also Judith A. Baer, *Equality under the Constitution: Reclaiming the Fourteenth Amendment* (Ithaca: Cornell University Press, 1983); and the symposium on "Rights Consciousness in American History," in *Journal of American History* 74 (December 1987): 795–1034.

16. Fisher, "Modern American Legal Theory," 317. See also Stuart Scheingold, *The Politics of Rights: Lawyers, Public Policy, and Political Change* (New Haven: Yale University Press, 1974), on the potency of "the myth of rights" in American politics.

17. Audrey Wise, M.P., *Parliamentary Debates* (Commons), 5th ser., 219 (16 February 1993): col. 190, responding to Gillian Shephard, secretary of state for employment.

18. T. H. Marshall, *Citizenship and Social Class* (Cambridge: Cambridge University Press, 1950). Social rights are written into some European constitutions and into the European Community Social Charter; whether such social provisions, including a minimum wage, should be placed in constitutions is the subject of papers by David P. Currie, Christopher McCrudden, and Cheryl B. Welch, in Vivien Hart and Shannon C. Stimson, eds., *Writing a National Identity: Political, Economic, and Cultural Perspectives on the Written Constitution* (Manchester: Manchester University Press, 1993); on the European right to a minimum wage, see Vivien Hart, "The Right to a Fair Wage: American Experience and the European Social Charter," ibid., 106–24. See also debates about East European constitution making—for example, an exchange in the *East European Constitutional Review*: Cass R. Sunstein, "Something Old, Something New," vol. 1 (Spring 1992): 18–21; Herman Schwartz, "In Defense of Aiming High," vol. 1 (Fall 1992): 25–28; and Cass R. Sunstein, "Against Positive Rights," vol. 2 (Winter 1993): 35–38.

19. Sidney Webb, preface to B. L. Hutchins and A. Harrison, *A History of Factory Legislation*, 2d ed. (London: P. S. King, 1911), ix; Sir Charles Dilke, quoted in Stephen Gwynn and Gertrude Tuckwell, *The Life of the Rt. Hon. Sir Charles W. Dilke, Bart., M.P.* (London: John Murray, 1918), vol. 2, 354.

20. See Davidson, *The Wages Act 1986*, 44–45; LPN, *Save Wages Councils*, 5–6; Anne E. Morris and Susan M. Nott, *Working Women and the Law: Equality and Discrimination in Theory and Practice* (London: Routledge, 1991), 135.

21. Davidson, *Wages Act 1986*, 45–72. At the same time, oversight of the Wages Councils was being cut back; for example, in 1979, 177 inspectors monitored implementation; in 1992, 71. See LPN, *Save Wages Councils*, 15–18.

22. See the summary of these events in LPN, *Save Wages Councils*, 6–8; Department of Employment, *Wages Councils: 1988 Consultation Document* (London: DOE, 1988); Equal Opportunities Commission, "Formal Response of the Equal Opportunities Commission to the Department of Employment's Consultation Document on Wages Councils" (Manchester: Equal Opportunities Commission, [1988]).

23. "Employment Bill Proposes New Rights," *Employment Gazette* 100 (December 1992): 596.

24. On the history since the 1970s of claims of discrimination and rights for British women, see Jane Lewis and Celia Davies, "Protective Legislation in Britain, 1870–1990: Equality, Difference, and Their Implications for Women," *Policy and Politics* 19 (January 1991): 13–25; Sally J. Kenney, *For Whose Protection? Reproductive Hazards and Exclusionary Policies in the United States and Britain* (Ann Arbor: University of Michigan Press, 1992); and Elizabeth Meehan, *Women's Rights at Work: Campaigns and Policy in Britain and the United States* (London: Macmillan, 1985). On the legal status of women workers, see Colin Burn and John Whitmore, *Race and Sex Discrimination*, 2d ed. (London: Sweet and Maxwell, 1993); Morris and Nott, *Working Women and the Law*; and Katherine O'Donovan and Erika Szyszczak, *Equality and Sex Discrimination Law* (Oxford: Blackwell, 1988).

25. See Low Pay Unit, "Minimum Wages for Women"; "Women and the Labour Market: Results from the 1991 Labour Force Survey," *Employment Gazette* 100 (September 1992): 433–42; and Equal Opportunities Commission, "Wages Councils and Low Pay," typescript, November 1992, annex C, "Women and Low Pay: Key Facts."

26. Baroness Lockwood, *Parliamentary Debates* (Lords), 5th ser., 545 (6 May 1993): col. 890.

27. Angela Eagle, ibid. (Commons), 219 (16 February 1993): col. 203. See "Ethnic Origins and the Labour Market," *Employment Gazette* 101 (February 1993): 25–33.

28. "Wages Councils—History," *Outworkers News*, no. 10 (January 1993): 10–11, translations, 12–19 (I am grateful to Eileen Boris for this source); Equal Opportunities Commission, "Wages Councils and Low Pay," August 1992, annex C; and Baroness Turner, *Parliamentary Debates* (Lords), 5th ser., 544 (30 March 1993): col. 753. *LPN, Save Wages Councils*, 1, notes that 28.9 percent of male ethnic minority workers were located in distribution, hotels, catering, and repairs, compared with 16.3 percent of white males. On the separate legal status and provision for enforcement of discrimination law for ethnic groups, see Bourn and Whitmore, *Race and Sex Discrimination*; Jeanne Gregory, *Sex, Race and the Law: Legislating for Equality* (London: Sage, 1987); and Michael Rubinstein, *Discrimination: A Guide to Relevant Case Law on Race and Sex Discrimination and Equal Pay*, 3d ed. (London: Eclipse, 1990).

29. Baroness Lockwood, *Parliamentary Debates* (Lords), 5th ser., 544 (30 March 1993): col. 766.

30. The key provisions for minimum wage policy are article 119 of the Treaty of Rome; and directive 75/117, article 6. For a summary of EC law, see Erika Szyszczak, "The Future of Women's Rights: The Role of European Community Law," in Maria Brenton and Clare Ungerson, eds., *The Yearbook of Social Policy, 1986–1987* (Harlow: Longman, 1987), 49–65. Kenney, *For Whose Protection?* chap. 3, provides a detailed account of the machinery and provisions of discrimination law in Britain and the early impact of the EC. See also Sonia Mazey, "European Community Action on Behalf of

Women: The Limits of Legislation," *Journal of Common Market Studies* 27 (September 1988): 63–84; Christopher McCrudden, ed., *Women, Employment and European Equality Law* (London: Eclipse, 1987), including the text of the relevant directives, 217–34; and Harriet Warner, "EC Social Policy in Practice: Community Action on Behalf of Women and Its Impact in the Member States," *Journal of Common Market Studies* 23 (December 1984): 141–67.

31. Michael Rubinstein, "Wages Council Abolition and EC Law," *Equal Opportunities Review*, no. 48 (March–April 1993): 48; and Baroness Lockwood, *Parliamentary Debates* (Lords), 5th ser., 545 (6 May 1993): col. 890.

32. Equal Opportunities Commission, "Wages Councils and Low Pay," November 1992, annex B.

33. Simon Deakin, "Equality under a Market Order: The Employment Act 1989," *Industrial Law Journal* 19 (March 1990): 1–19.

34. Baroness Lockwood, *Parliamentary Debates* (Lords), 5th ser., 545 (6 May 1993): col. 890.

35. Kenney, *For Whose Protection?* is a detailed account of recent British discrimination law and politics, and the impact of the EC; based on her comparison of reproductive protection, she suggests that the British have a long way to go before they reach the sophistication of Americans on many of the issues involved. See also Joyce Gelb, *Feminism and Politics: A Comparative Perspective* (Berkeley and Los Angeles: University of California Press, 1989); and Elizabeth Meehan, *Women's Rights at Work: Campaigns and Policy in Britain and the United States* (London: Macmillan, 1985).

36. See a hint of this in the discussion of "the treaty base game," in Lord Wedderburn, *The Social Charter, European Company and Employment Rights* (London: Institute of Employment Rights, 1990), 51–54. Given the hostility of successive Conservative governments since 1979 to all social policy, such a development may be awaiting a change of government. See also a piece of American advice to European women, Frances Olsen, "Employment Discrimination in the New Europe: A Litigation Project for Women," *Journal of Law and Society* 20 (Spring 1993): 131–44; and comparisons by Samuel H. Beer, "Reform of the British Constitution: An American View," *Political Quarterly* 64 (April–June 1993): 198–209; and Alan Ryan, "The British, the Americans, and Rights," in Lacey, *Culture of Rights*, 366–439.

37. See Hart, "The Right to a Fair Wage," and Elizabeth Meehan, "Social Rights, Social Facts, and the Written Constitution: European Reflections," in Hart and Stimson, eds., *Writing a National Identity*, 106–24, 135–41.

38. E. P. Thompson, *Whigs and Hunters: The Origin of the Black Act* (London: Allen Lane, 1975), 266.